NATIONAL GEOGRAPHIC

TRAVELER

cambodia

NATIONAL GEOGRAPHIC

TRAVELER

cambodia

by Trevor Ranges
photography by Kris LeBoutillier

National Geographic
Washington, D.C.

CONTENTS

Pages 2–3: Sunrise over the Angkor temple and reflecting pool
Opposite: A young Cham boy at a Phnom Penh mosque after Friday prayers

TRAVELING WITH EYES OPEN

Alert travelers go with a purpose and leave with a benefit. If you travel responsibly, you can help support wildlife conservation, historic preservation, and cultural enrichment in the places you visit. You can enrich your own travel experience as well.

To be a geo-savvy traveler:

- Recognize that your presence has an impact on the places you visit.

- Spend your time and money in ways that sustain local character. (Besides, it's more interesting that way.)

- Value the destination's natural and cultural heritage.

- Respect the local customs and traditions.

- Express appreciation to local people about things you find interesting and unique to the place: its nature and scenery, music and food, historic villages and buildings.

- Vote with your wallet: Support the people who support the place, patronizing businesses that make an effort to celebrate and protect what's special there. Seek out shops, local restaurants, inns, and tour operators who love their home—who love taking care of it and showing it off. Avoid businesses that detract from the character of the place.

- Enrich yourself, taking home memories and stories to tell, knowing that you have contributed to the preservation and enhancement of the destination.

That is the type of travel now called geotourism, defined as "tourism that sustains or enhances the geographical character of a place—its environment, culture, aesthetics, heritage, and the well-being of its residents." To learn more about geotourism, visit National Geographic's Center for Sustainable Destinations at *www.nationalgeographic.com/travel/sustainable.*

cambodia

ABOUT THE AUTHORS & THE PHOTOGRAPHER

Trevor Ranges is a Bangkok-based travel writer whose work includes contributions to the *National Geographic Traveler: Thailand* guidebook and serving as principal writer for *www.tourismthailand.org,* the official website of the Tourism Authority of Thailand. Ranges's love of travel and immersion in different cultures drives him to promote the preservation of the region's cultural heritage and natural resources by featuring culturally sensitive and environmentally friendly tourism operators and attractions.

Kris LeBoutillier produced the images for the *National Geographic Traveler: Vietnam* guidebook, as well as for several *National Geographic Traveler* magazine features around Asia and Australia, including Tasmania, Australia; Rajasthan, India; Singapore; Halong Bay and Hue, Vietnam; and for a piece on the best Asian beaches. LeBoutillier has additionally worked with a wide selection of other newspapers and magazines around the world.

Lis Meyers wrote the Phnom Penh chapter as well as the sections on the coastal regions of Kampot and Kep, and various sidebars. Meyers worked in Cambodia for a year and a half, during which time she immersed herself in Cambodian culture, working with various NGOs and freelancing for local magazines. She hopes that all National Geographic travelers will find Cambodia just as vibrant, charming, and downright impossible to leave as she did.

Nina-Noelle Hall and **Geoffrey Cain** made additional contributions. Hall can fit everything she owns into one suitcase—appropriate for her nomadic lifestyle as a budding travel journalist. For National Geographic, she also authored the Personal Explorer tours for Bangkok and Mexico City. Currently she freelances for *Time Out Singapore* magazine. Cain is a freelance writer based in Phnom Penh. He has written for the *Economist, Far Eastern Economic Review,* and the United Nations.

Charting Your Trip

Many visitors, undoubtedly, are drawn to Cambodia by the great ancient temples of Angkor, the dazzling remains of a once flourishing Khmer capital in the country's northwest. But beyond, you'll discover an agrarian kingdom boasting beautiful countryside, untold architectural delights, and the considerable charm of the Cambodian people, whose carefree, cheerful demeanor is all the more surprising in light of the horrific events of their recent past.

How to Get Around

Cambodia's roads are far better than they were a decade ago, meaning transportation by car or bus is a relatively comfortable means of journeying cross country. Many buses run from the capital city of Phnom Penh, in southern Cambodia, to the city of Siem Reap, gateway to Angkor Wat; the beach resort of Sihanoukville, a three- to four-hour drive southwest of Phnom Penh on the Gulf of Thailand; and most provincial capitals. There are many sights in between these destinations that are interesting to see, however, and buses only stop for food.

Hiring a private car is a great way to see more of Cambodia. You can hire a Toyota Camry with a Khmer driver—whose English ability and knowledge of the sights may vary—for a day trip, a one-way journey, or an entire week, allowing you to stop at attractions on the way. If you don't have the budget for your own car, you can travel via "share-taxi," which is either a Camry or a 4WD pickup truck shared by as many people as can squeeze aboard. Make arrangements for private cars or share-taxis through hotels and travel agents.

Along the coast, it's possible to rent motorbikes. These are equally inexpensive (and unsafe), though you really can't beat beach hopping or seeing the colonial ruins of Kampot from the back of a motorbike.

Tuk-tuks—motorbikes pulling a small carriage—are the best mode of transportation for visiting sights in and around town. They're inexpensive (fares must be negotiated with the driver), fun, and convenient. Note that tuk-tuks

An elephant ride is a must-do on any trip to Ratanakiri Province.

are not always the most comfortable of rides, however, especially in the heat and dust. Tuk-tuk drivers generally don't make good guides.

Outside the major urban areas, most small roads are alternatively muddy morasses or scarred with dry ruts and mud pits, depending on how recently it has rained. To see remote rural Cambodia, a 4WD truck, or off-road motorcycle is mandatory.

If You Have One Week

The distances between destinations and the lack of domestic airline service make it difficult to see many different parts of Cambodia on a short trip. Given this, an ideal one-week itinerary takes in the primary attraction of Angkor Wat, as well as neighboring Siem Reap, the amazing lake and river system of Tonle Sap, and Phnom Penh. International airlines currently fly to both Phnom Penh and Siem Reap, so the suggested itinerary can be followed in either direction. The information given here is for a trip beginning in Phnom Penh." (There are plans to reopen Sihanoukville airport in 2010, perhaps allowing travelers to fly between Siem Reap and Sihanoukville, thereby allowing a circuit by land through Phnom Penh.)

Depending on time of arrival in Phnom Penh, **Day 1** could be spent visiting various attractions in a tuk-tuk and should conclude with a sunset river cruise. **Day 2** can include such attractions as the National Museum, Wat Phnom, the Royal Palace, or the Tuol Sleng Genocide Museum and the killing fields. If you visited those on Day 1, then Day 2 could include a day trip to the Stung Meanchey dump (see sidebar p. 89), or the pre-Angkorian ruins near the town of Angkor Borei and the Phnom Tamao Wildlife Rescue Center.

On **Day 3,** if you are planning a one-way trip to Siem Reap, travel by car may be preferable to a boat trip on the Tonle Sap (see p. 122), since National Highway 5 offers

---

NOT TO BE MISSED:

A moving visit to Tuol Sleng Genocide Museum and killing fields, Phnom Penh **83, 86**

Experiencing floating village life on the Tonle Sap **119–121**

Sunrise at Angkor Wat **135**

Watching the Phare Ponleu Selpak circus perform **145**

Seeing authentic *apsara* dance **154**

A day trip to Banteay Srei temple, Kbal Spean, and surrounding attractions **160–163**

Touring French colonial ruins and relaxing by the river in Kampot **256**

Staying Safe

- Wear purses slung across the body, not draped over one shoulder where they may be snatched more easily.
- Beware of child pickpockets at crowded events like boxing matches.
- Carry a separate, small sum of cash to pay tuk-tuk drivers; avoid flashing a large wad of cash in any circumstance.
- Look four times before crossing the street and stay alert while crossing.

- In land-mine zones, never wander off the beaten path.
- Avoid walking around alone late at night (particularly if you are female).
- Use a safety box in hotel rooms, or put your own padlock on a guesthouse door.
- Avoid arguments with locals in bars or with the police.
- Wear mosquito spray with DEET if traveling outside major tourist zones.

Weather

Cambodia's dry season lasts from November to June; the coolest months of November, December, and January have the lowest humidity and least rainfall. In late January, temperatures begin to steadily climb until April, the hottest month, when temperatures can exceed 100°F (38°C). Intolerable heat and humidity are often exacerbated by power outages that shut down fans and air-conditioning.

The rainy season occurs June through October, with intense daily monsoons bringing relief from the heat. The countryside becomes lush and green, and rivers are replete with fresh water. Roads away from the tourist centers become increasingly difficult, though.

interesting stops along the way. If you are returning to Phnom Penh, travel one way by land and the other by boat, depending on the direction the river is flowing–it's quicker to travel downstream, a direction that changes seasonally! By land, a privately hired one-way taxi will give you the most flexibility.

If you're driving, with an early start, you can stop at the former capital of Oudong, a pottery village, and a floating village at Kompong Chhnang, cross a thousand-year-old bridge, and see other temples along the way (see Central Cambodia, pp. 197–199). Though the temples at Sambor Prei Kuk are only 7 miles (11 km) off the main road, an overnight stop in Kompong Thom is necessary to appreciate them fully. To see the sun set at Angkor, ask your driver to arrive at your hotel in Siem Reap by 4 p.m. Then you can check in, procure a tuk-tuk, and make it to Phnom Bakheng by sunset; a three-day park pass purchased at 5 p.m. will be valid for the next three days.

On **Days 4, 5,** and **6,** explore the temples of Angkor by hiring a tuk-tuk or a car and guide, which will provide more comfort and information on the sights. One day should include a guided trip to Banteay Srei (see pp. 161–162), a 10th-century temple famous for its carvings. Also try to visit Artisans d'Angkor and its affiliated silk-weaving collective. If you missed the National Museum in Phnom Penh, spend a few hours at the Angkor National Museum. In the evenings, catch an *apsara* dance, puppet show, or attractions at the night market.

After several days at temples, you will be ready for a day trip on the nearby Tonle Sap, Southeast Asia's largest freshwater lake that's the lifeblood of millions of Cambodians. The floating and stilted villages of Chong Kneas and Kompong Pleuk provide fascinating insights about life upon and above the water. Serious bird-watchers should journey to Prek Toal Bird Sanctuary, one of the greatest such preserves on Earth. The best way to see the birds is either to get a very early start on the final day or to head out to the reserve

Keeping in Touch While You're Away...

Cambodia's telephone system is quite advanced: A 3G network was installed in 2008 and standard cell phone coverage extends to the most remote provinces. While GSM compatible foreign phones will work in the kingdom, roaming rates are far higher than alternatives. Tourist SIM cards are sold at the international airports, as well as some hotels and stores.

These cards are good for 12 days and the price includes credit that can be used for local and international calls. Once your minutes are up, however, the card will no longer receive calls and cannot be refilled. Internet cafés with headsets are prevalent in major cities. Though connection speeds are slow, Skype (www.skype.com) remains the easiest, cheapest way to stay in touch.

Tuk-tuk travelers get a lift the Cambodian way.

on the sixth night, sleep there, see the birds on the morning of **Day 7,** and then head back to Siem Reap in time to catch your flight.

If You Have More Time

Clearly, seven days is barely enough time to see the attractions near major attractions in Cambodia. An additional week would allow you to visit more sights around Phnom Penh and Siem Reap, or include one of the following options:

If flying into or out of Phnom Penh, follow the one-week itinerary. Then, travel from Siem Reap to Battambang, Cambodia's second largest city, by boat, bus, or car; spend one or two days visiting nearby temples and other sites, plus taking a river cruise. From Battambang, travel south to Phnom Penh, stopping in the town of Pursat, the base for exploring Kompong Luong floating village, if you have a car and driver (you could skip the villages near Siem Reap in favor of this less touristy one).

For several days of beach time, from Phnom Penh head southwest to Kampot/Kep or Sihanoukville.

With additional days, it's arguably better to fly into Siem Reap and out of Phnom Penh: Spend four days in Siem Reap as outlined above, visiting Angkor Wat, then hire a private car or share-taxi to Phnom Penh to see the sights on the way, including an overnight stop at Kampong Thom and the ruins of Sambor Prei Kuk. After two or three days in Phnom Penh, head to Kampot/Kep or Sihanoukville for some beach time.

To include the eastern provinces, you would need a month in Cambodia, unless you forgo Angkor or can afford private air travel between the provinces. ■

Clothing & Etiquette

Dress: Dress in Cambodia is very conservative. Keep shoulders and knees covered when visiting temples and official sites. When swimming among locals, add a layer over bikinis.
Shoes and Feet: Remove your shoes before entering a home or temple. Never point the soles of your feet at others, especially when crossing your legs. If visiting a temple or home, sit with your legs to one side rather than crossed. (For more tips, see sidebar p. 21.)

History & Culture

Shadow puppets are frequently used to tell tales from the classic fable *Ramayana*. Small holes allow light to pass through the leather and project shadows upon a screen.

Cambodia Today

The 21st century has served as a new dawn for the Kingdom of Cambodia. With the scourge of war gone and economic investment flooding in, there is a palpable exuberance throughout the country. And as Cambodia grows integrated in the world economy, foreign visitors, ideas, and trends increase in influence.

This is not to suggest that Cambodia today is as the advertisements present it: happy villagers singing traditional songs, white-sand shores touched only by stilted shacks, an idyllic world where people live harmoniously with their Angkor roots. In reality, Cambodians rarely ride on elephants or sing in circles; Cambodia is a society in the middle of great changes from its traditional agrarian past. The "other" Cambodia—the living, breathing one—is facing the challenges of development, and despite the hope, it has a long road yet to travel. It's a society emerging from decades of war and genocide, and it has almost completed its painful search for stability and democracy. Aside from a short-lived renaissance in the 1960s, the country has never really had free markets, independence, or a middle class until now.

> There is a palpable hopefulness radiating from Cambodians. . . . National pride is on the rise with the kingdom's reemergence . . . on the world stage.

Although many Cambodians remain traumatized by the shadows from their individual and collective pasts, now is their chance to look to the future: They can finally travel freely, open businesses, and live peacefully. Many people see at last that an idyllic Cambodia may someday be a reality. There is a palpable hopefulness radiating from Cambodians, whether they are gathering in parks for the weekend to play or showing off their county's resurgent culture to visitors.

Subsequently, national pride is on the rise with the kingdom's reemergence as a relevant player on the world stage. Images of Angkor Wat, a national symbol, decorate streets, flags, and shops around the country. Bring back the glory of Angkor, people say. The temple complex represents the biggest mark Cambodia has made on the world. And it has served as a unifying symbol in times of strife and tragedy, as well as an inspirational reminder of Cambodia's potential to become a prosperous civilization once again.

Thanks to the temples of Angkor, Siem Reap has seen several years of 30 percent growth in both population and tourist arrivals. While the temples are drawing more than a million visitors each year, Cambodians are flocking to Siem Reap eager to get in on what many see as the best opportunity to secure a foothold in the country's growing tourism economy. Enthusiastic children who can scream "I lello!" in eight different languages sell postcards today and will be tomorrow's temple guides. A new generation of artisans is learning traditional dancing and musicmaking, silk weaving and stone carving. All are eager cultural ambassadors, proudly entertaining and educating visitors, while earning a cherished income and making grand plans for the future. Meanwhile, training schools that provide practical hospitality skills are grooming impoverished

Tuk-tuks **and motorcycles are the main modes of transport in many Cambodians cities.**

Monks passing through the grounds of Wat Ounalom Buddhist temple in Phnom Penh

rural youth for opportunities to get jobs in the city and perhaps pull themselves out of desperate poverty.

In Phnom Penh, the kingdom's current cultural renaissance is more complex than simply meeting the increased interest by international visitors—it's rooted in a new generation of Cambodians. After the Khmer Rouge genocide ended, young couples who were resettling triggered a baby boom in the 1980s, especially in Phnom Penh. Those youngsters only recently came of age, and they now compose a small, but growing, middle class of journalists, lawyers, and nongovernmental organization (NGO) employees. Their youthful idealism, which stems in part from having no memory of their country's traumatic past, is fostering great cultural changes, particularly in the national psyche.

> **Cultural growth and optimism could not have occurred . . . without the equally influential resurgence of a functioning economy.**

Youth culture has certainly made its mark during the past decade. Take a stroll through the legendary Royal University of Phnom Penh, or frequent the capital's new Internet cafés and Wi-Fi hot spots, and you'll see these chattering young hipsters huddled around tables, discussing literature and life over coffee or texting and talking on their cell phones. Adding to homegrown cultural movements, foreign influences are pouring into Cambodia as well. Young Cambodians living in America, Australia, and France—many of them refugees from the Khmer Rouge—have been repatriating to the kingdom as they come of age, bringing with them break dancing and hip-hop, both of which are now popular in the capital. This influx of foreign-reared Cambodians is creating a movement similar to Phnom Penh's colorful 1960s era, when French-educated Cambodians imported foreign literature while reviving their country's Angkor-era arts.

This cultural growth and optimism could not have occurred, however, without the equally influential resurgence of a functioning economy, which is in large part the result of a stable, albeit self-interested, government. In spite of—and in part due to—having one of the most corrupt governments in the world, foreign investment has poured into Cambodia. The wholesale concession of the country's forests, rivers, and hills to global powerhouses in logging, hydroelectric power, and mining has filled government coffers. A boom in garment manufacturing and construction, staffed by needy workers, has provided direly needed income to one of the world's poorest populations. While far from ideal, these early steps in development have been a leap toward greater prosperity and have coincided with the boom in the tourism industry.

A large percentage of Cambodia's tourists are from other Asian nations, South Korea in particular. Those countries are also responsible for considerable economic investment that is literally changing the face of Cambodia. The country's colonial heritage is slowly fading away as Phnom Penh has been undergoing a boom in skyscraper construction. That's a first for the city's low-slung, French colonial skyline, which might soon be dotted with metallic high-rises and neon lights. More tastefully redone perhaps, Siem Reap's development features charming boutique hotels and alleyways of chic bars, restaurants, and cafés, all of which exude nouveau colonial charm.

Basic Cambodian

These basic Cambodian phrases are sure to have you getting around like a pro (also see the Language Guide, pp. 312–313).

Juhm ree-uhp sue (formal) or *Soo-ah s'day* (informal)	Hello
Juhm ree-uhp lee-ah	Good-bye
Jaa (used by women) or *Baat* (used by men)	Yes
Dtay	No
Som	Please
Awe coon	Thank you
Nee-ak soak sa-buy chia day?	How are you?
K'nyom soak sa-buy	I am fine
Nee-ak cha-mua away?	What is your name?
K'nyom cha-mua...	My name is
Sohm dtoe	Excuse me/ I'm sorry

With Cambodia's baby boom revolution coinciding with a groundswell of tourists and an insurgence of foreign investment has come a story of change—a rise from a traumatizing past into a new area of stability and hope. The lawlessness, political violence, and grinding poverty that once characterized the streets of Phnom Penh and other cities have been replaced by a new scene that fuses cosmopolitanism with traditional Cambodian arts. Meanwhile, people from rural communities are flocking to urban areas to cash in on this newfound prosperity. Because many Khmers are learning traditional skills in order to be a part of the new Cambodia, and many individuals and organizations are working to preserve these traditions, Cambodian culture today is rediscovering and reviving, growing on its own and mixing with foreign influences.

It is reinventing and inventing itself at the same time, all with a brazen hopefulness that the Cambodian people have been through the worst and therefore things must only get better.

Lifestyle & Behavior

Despite the urban renaissance sweeping Phnom Penh and the influx of tourism to Siem Reap, day-to-day Cambodian life remains quite traditional and largely centered on the family. Family networks are intricate and extensive, with tightly knit family trees including obscure relatives, all of whom often live together under a single roof.

Cambodian culture is hierarchical, which strongly affects how Cambodians interact with each other. Such beliefs are age-old and reinforced by Buddhist tenets. Monks sit in rank order, and it is commonly accepted that parents are superior to children, teachers to students, and managers to employees. Interpersonal communications are highly defined by such notions, and displays of deference can be seen in the most mundane exchanges (for tips on how to behave, see sidebar p. 21).

The land, lakes, and rivers are also held in great reverence by rural Cambodians. The ability to personally grow rice or catch fish often dictates whether individuals will have enough food to eat or will be able to keep a roof over their heads. Cycles of the harvest and the seasonal fish migrations mandate the ebb and flow of rural life, including holidays, as does the worship of spirits who are believed to inhabit the land and waters of Cambodia.

Celebrations play fundamental roles in Khmer life, with even the most financially strapped families sparing no expense in order to appropriately mark important events. All families will throw lavish tented wedding parties, often shutting down entire streets and serving large feasts to hundreds of guests with no regard for the cost. Buddhist holidays and celebrations that honor spirits are also events of great importance and serve as important social gatherings.

Money Matters

While Cambodia's monetary unit is the riel, the U.S. dollar is accepted throughout the country. The official exchange rate hovers around 4,000 riel to one U.S. dollar, and it is possible to exchange dollars for riel throughout the country. Think of riel as an alternative to change; most transactions over 4,000 riel are typically conducted in dollars (though provinces bordering Thailand also accept Thai baht).

ATMs, which dispense dollars, are found in the major tourist destinations. Credit cards are accepted in most mid-range hotels, airline offices, and some restaurants. Credit card cash advances and money wiring are widely available. Banks and major hotels usually accept traveler's checks, but may charge 2 percent. Dollar bills with tears are generally not accepted, so be sure to check for bad bills.

Independence Beach in Sihanoukville on Cambodia's southwest coast

Leisure Time

Cambodians spend much of their leisure time outdoors, flocking to parks and public areas during the post-work twilight hours. Using these spaces to the maximum potential, families and friends picnic and play badminton. Vendors sell colorful balloons to young children, and teenage boys stand in circles kicking around a *sey,* a toy made from a plastic bottle and chicken feathers that must be kept in the air using only the legs, feet, and knees, much like the American Hacky Sack. Parks are also dating venues, where some young Khmer couples even dare to hold hands! The recent construction of two large fountains in central Phnom Penh that shoot constantly changing colored water has made fountain-watching a new evening activity. Exercise is also becoming a more common leisure activity. Many people rise at dawn for early morning tai chi or attend noisy afternoon group aerobics along parks and rivers.

> **Cambodians spend much of their leisure time outdoors. . . . Many people rise at dawn for early morning tai chi.**

As more Cambodians now can afford modern technology, television has been embraced throughout the country. It is not uncommon for even the poorest families to own a small TV, which the entire family will gather around for hours. Cambodians especially like melodramatic soap operas and variety shows featuring karaoke and slapstick comedy acts. Many people who do not own a TV yet will pop over to their neighbors' homes for a television fix or frequent open-air venues to watch and gamble on kickboxing matches, which they also attend in small boxing venues in the larger urban centers.

Radios are still popular, blasting Khmer and Western tunes around the clock. In urban areas, Internet usage is booming, and there is a dearth of printed materials for leisure reading. Many Khmers remain illiterate, since the adult literacy rate is 74 percent. While many people have yielded to the lure of television and movies over books, this trend is slowly reversing as NGOs and government programs make an effort to promote the development of Khmer literature and increase the use of computer technology in rural educational programs.

While Cambodia generally adheres to the credo "early to bed, early to rise," and cities and towns become virtual ghost towns after 10 p.m. and resume the hustle and bustle in the early morning, a nightlife is slowly developing. Khmer men will spend many evening hours at beer gardens and karaoke bars. Urban youth can be found partying until the wee hours of the morning at packed Khmer discos.

Demographics

Cambodia's 2008 census recorded 13,388,910 citizens, with females making up slightly more of the population than males. Population growth has slowed,

Boats gather for races during a water festival on the Tonle Sap River.

Cultural Etiquette

Cambodian culture has many nuanced customs and social practices. Always take care to consider cultural etiquette.

Eating: Wait for the host to sit before doing so and drink when a toast is made. Do not sit or start eating until the oldest person at the table has done so. Always accept food or tea offered to you; a refusal would be considered insulting to your host. Do not leave chopsticks vertically in your rice bowl or in a v-shape, as both have connotations of death.

It is also wise to bring a small gift when invited into someone's home.

Heads: Never touch someone's head. As the highest part of the body, the head is considered highly sacred.

Keeping Your Cool: Regardless of the situation that arises, avoid showing frustration. Khmers will react awkwardly to such displays of emotion, seen as a lack of self-control. If you stay calm, remain patient, and keep smiling, the situation will be resolved more easily.

National Sensitivity: Be sensitive to the strained relations with Thailand and Vietnam and do not compare Cambodia to these countries.

Personal Interactions: When greeting individuals, especially the elderly or monks, press your hands together at chest level in a *sompiah* while bowing your head and making eye contact. In interacting with new people, address Cambodians by Lok (Mr.) or Lok Srey (Mrs.) along with his/her name. As Khmer culture is very hierarchical, when making introductions, start with the highest ranking individual.

When calling someone to you, motion with the hand facing downward; otherwise it is seen as sexually suggestive. Never point directly at individuals, and always use the right hand when handing things to other people. Special care and respect should be taken when interacting with monks. Women should never touch monks or hand things directly to them.

Photos: Refrain from taking pictures of Cambodians without asking permission first. Taking pictures of monks is generally considered in poor taste. If you must do so, try to be discreet.

particularly because the birthrate has declined, yet the projected annual growth rate remains higher than the average among East Asian countries. Urban migration is also increasing. The capital, Phnom Penh, is the largest city by far, though other major population centers, including Battambang, Siem Reap, and Sihanoukville, are also growing. Nonetheless, it is still estimated that the country's rural population is five times bigger than its urban population, and a few smaller provincial capitals, such as Ratanakiri's Ban Lung, are gradually drawing in people from the countryside. Cambodia's most populous province is Kompong Cham, while Pailin is the least populated. Cambodia also has a high percentage of individuals under the age of 15, and a median age of only 22.

Perhaps this trend toward youth is helping to foster the exuberance and optimism that is prevalent in today's Cambodia. Add to that the country's relative political and economic stability, and it becomes easy to see why, for the first time in several generations, Cambodia and its people have a valid and real hope for the future. ■

Cambodia History

It's difficult to overlook—and important not to overlook—Cambodia's recent tragic past. It is, however, just as important to remember the country's proud history. In its golden age, nearly a millennium ago, the Khmer kingdom dominated much of Southeast Asia.

Earliest History

The earliest settlers of modern-day Cambodia were hunter-gatherers who arrived around 50,000 B.C. More clearly dated evidence shows that the area was inhabited in the Neolithic period. Pots recovered from an archaeological dig in a Laang Spean cave in northwestern Cambodia date from as early as the fifth millennium B.C. and as recently as the ninth century A.D., indicating a continuous inhabitation by peoples who are thought to have developed rice cultivation by the late third millennium B.C. By the fourth century B.C. there were communities living throughout Cambodia that had domesticated animals and subsisted on fish and rice. These early societies worshipped ancestral spirits known as *neak ta*—the ancient people— and natural spirits, who resided in the land and water.

Indianization

Written records of the earliest accounts of Cambodian civilization from that society did not survive the ages. The only substantial documentation that historians have been able to draw upon are texts of Chinese origin. Prior to the third century A.D., China had been trading with India via an overland Silk Road that, for various reasons, became unusable. Trade then became increasingly conducted via shipping routes around and across the Malay Peninsula, including present-day Cambodia and Vietnam. Consequently, there was a gradually increasing Indian (and Chinese) presence along the coast.

> **Cambodian society prior to Indianization appears to have consisted of widely spread, inland subsistence villages.**

Cambodian society prior to Indianization appears to have consisted of widely spread, inland subsistence villages, before becoming increasingly congregated along the coastal Mekong delta area, which grew to serve as a midway point for goods passing between India and China. The first of these trading-port communities is believed to be Oc Eo, located in southern Vietnam, with others, particularly Angkor Borei (an early religious and perhaps political center), connected to Oc Eo by way of ancient canals. As the indigenous population moved to these centers, trading goods from the interior, such as kingfisher feathers and rhinoceros horn, their newfound prosperity owed a great deal to the Indian and Chinese traders who sought those goods. Consequently, Indianization was a gradual process over the first millennium whereby the local populations chose to adopt various aspects of Indian cultural practices and beliefs and assimilate them into their existing Cambodian traditions. Changes included agricultural techniques,

The east exterior *gopura* (temple entranceway) of Angkor Wat

Mythical Beginnings of Kambujadesa

In days of yore, the Hindu god Shiva gave a hermit, Kambu, an *apsara* bride, Mera. Their offspring were the Khmer, citizens of the new Country of Kambu, Kambujadesa. Later abbreviated to Kambuja, the name eventually evolved to Cambodia. The story of Kambu is at least as old as the Angkor era, during which Rajendravarman II (r.944–968) honored him in an inscription on Baksei Chamkrong temple's doorframe.

A Chinese report echoing an Indian legend recounts the tale of the first king and dynasty of Cambodia, which symbolically honors the arrival of Indians and their influence. The story tells the tale of Kaundinya, who, inspired by a dream, traveled to Cambodia and betrothed the local princess, Soma (Moon), daughter of the king of the *nagas* (mystical serpents). In one version the naga king drinks up the sea to create land for their kingdom, symbolizing the irrigation projects early kings initiated to reclaim the land for agricultural purposes. The dynasty of the real Kaundinya, established in the first century A.D., ruled the Funan kingdom for around 150 years and lineage to Kaundinya was often invoked by Angkor kings.

clothing styles, and social hierarchies and were likely adopted by the indigenous people based on their merits, rather than being imposed upon them by newcomers. Indian leadership resulted, perhaps, from the perceived value of those changes.

Further, the religions of Brahmanism, Hinduism, and Buddhism were also brought over from India. While the earliest rulers of Cambodia tended to worship Hindu deities, both Hinduism and Buddhism influenced religious art and worship in Cambodia. As with other aspects of Indian culture, aspects of the new religions melded with local religious beliefs, in this case the worship of both natural and ancestral spirits.

Early Kingdoms Era (circa A.D. 100–802)

Funan: The earliest documentation of a kingdom called Funan is from Chinese historians who recorded having diplomatic relations with the early Cambodian realm beginning in the third century A.D. From these records it seems likely that a prosperous society existed from as early as the first century. These Chinese sources suggest that Funan was a unified kingdom, whose capital, Vyadhapura, may have existed at modern-day Angkor Borei. Records indicate that the kingdom's denizens cultivated plants, lived in raised houses, and had domesticated elephants. They were ruled by a series of kings who drew their legitimacy either directly from the legendary Kaundinya (see sidebar above) or through symbolic association of his union with the native lunar princess, Soma.

> The religions of Brahmanism, Hinduism, and Buddhism were . . . brought over from India.

Chinese records recount a number of rulers from this period and document the growing prosperity of Funan. These kings ruled through association with the cult of Shiva and built temples atop *phnom* (hill). Due to its strategic importance along the trade route to and from India and China, the Funan empire grew as trade flourished; the kingdom maintained consistent ties with India and China and even hosted trade from as far away as the Roman Empire.

Chenla (Zhenla): The kingdom of Chenla was described by the Chinese as a unified kingdom, a vassal state of Funan, lying inland and to the north. Chenla also maintained diplomatic relations with China, and Chinese accounts tell of a prosperous, military power, with a number of urban centers, including its capital, Isanapura (Sambor Prei Kuk).

In the late sixth century, Chenla liberated itself from Funan. A century later, its army overpowered the Funanese. Inscriptions in Sanskrit and Khmer recount the kingdom's gradual deterioration during the eighth century, however, resulting in a split, essentially reverting to the original borders of Chenla and Funan. After it was divided into Land Chenla and Water Chenla, internal and external warfare caused the kings of Water Chenla to go into exile in Java, where Jayavarman II (r.802–850), who would later found the Angkor Empire, witnessed the building of the grand Buddhist temple of Borobudur.

One of many compassionate smiles atop Bayon's towers

Angkor Era (802–1431)

Continuously inhabited since the Neolithic period, the area around Siem Reap became the heart of the Angkor Empire, ruled by its kings between the 9th and 15th centuries. It also was home to Buddhist monks from the abandonment of Angkor in 1432 through the "discovery" of the monuments by Western explorers in the mid-19th century. Unlike earlier periods, for which Chinese sources were the primary means for documenting a murky Cambodian history, a great number of inscriptions in Sanskrit and Khmer and thousands of bas-reliefs have helped piece together a fairly cohesive account of this period.

The only existing, semi-comprehensive record of the kings who ruled during this period is an inscription at Sdok Kak Thom, near the Cambodian border in eastern Thailand. Carved in A.D. 1050, the inscription begins with a biography of Jayavarman II and covers nearly 250 years of Angkorian history. Returning from exile in Java, the sovereign leader of Water Chenla traveled the countryside for years, forging alliances and leading a violent campaign to subdue the disparate realms; ultimately, Jayavarman II was crowned *chakravartin*—universal monarch—of a land approximately equal in size to Cambodia today.

The crowning ceremony took place 20 miles (32 km) northeast of Angkor at Phnom Kulen, a site of ancient mystical power known as Mahendraparvata, the Mountain of Indra, symbolic representation of Mount Meru, home of the gods. A religious ceremony coinciding with Jayavarman's ascension to the throne established the mysterious cult of the *devaraja*, or god-king, a form of supreme spirit worship that associated the king with the gods, particularly through the worship of phallic *linga* stones.

The Angkor era began in A.D. 802 and lasted until 1431, though the empire was in decline for about a century before its demise. Jayavarman II ultimately established his capital in the city of Hariharalaya, which was located at modern-day Roluos. Centuries of subsequent kings would build great religious monuments in this area and honor Jayavarman II as the founding father of their kingdom.

The next king of known importance to the empire's development was Indravarman I (r.877–889), who set a number of precedents for subsequent rulers. He first constructed Preah Ko, an ancestral temple that housed statues honoring both his ancestors and Jayavarman II. His state temple was a gigantic step pyramid, Bakong, which symbolized Mount Meru and housed a linga. He also ordered the construction of an immense reservoir, Indratataka, representing the lakes surrounding the mystical Meru.

The Angkor era began in A.D. 802 and lasted until 1431, though the empire was in decline for about a century before its demise.

Indravarman's son, Yasovarman I (r.889–910) had a similarly influential reign. He completed the Indratataka and the ancestral temple of Lolei before relocating the capital to the north, along the sacred Siem Reap River. He built his state temple atop Phnom Bakheng and fostered the development of his capital city Yasodharapura (modern-day Angkor), a name the city retained for nearly 500 years. Yasovarman initiated a massive irrigation program similar to that created by his father, the even grander East Baray, and supported the construction of religious structures throughout his kingdom, including Preah Vihear. He was instrumental in solidifying Kambujadesa as a legitimately unified kingdom, prosperous from war and trade, and spiritually harmonious, honoring not only Shiva and Vishnu but also the Buddha and ancestral spirits.

Shortly after Yasovarman's death, the seat of power moved when a usurper established a capital city at Koh Ker and assumed the title Jayavarman IV (r. ca 928–941). Ruling from Koh Ker, he built Prasat Thom, his temple-mountain that housed a 59-foot-tall (18 m) linga, one of many aspects of the kingdom that reflected the grandiosity of art and architecture in the Koh Ker period.

Jayavarman IV's nephew Rajendravarman II (r.944–968) reestablished the capital at Yasodharapura, reunited the fragmented provinces of the empire, and constructed temples to his ancestors following the traditions of Yasovarman. During the nearly 60 years of his and his son Jayavarman V's reigns (ca 968–1001), the kingdom undertook successful military conquests, expanded trade, and then underwent a lengthy period of peace that allowed for the development of literary prose and the construction of the delicately ornate, pink sandstone Banteay Srei.

Several years of civil war began in 1001, during which rivals vied for the throne of the kingdom. Eventually Suryavarman I (r.1003–ca 1049) negotiated alliances throughout the kingdom and was crowned at Yasodharapura. During his reign the kingdom expanded to its widest borders, including southern Laos and much of Thailand. The empire became more urbanized, and the king fostered the growth of the capital city, building the Royal Palace and Phimeanakas and expanding irrigation works, including the massive West Baray.

Suryavarman II (r. 1113–ca 1150), like his namesake Suryavarman I, with whom he shared no blood ties, was also an influential ruler. Both followed bloody ascents to the throne, after which they reunited, then expanded, fragmented kingdoms. Each also organized masses of followers to build masterpieces of architecture. Suryavarman II waged successful wars against the Chams, reestablished diplomatic relations with China, and constructed what is arguably Angkor's crowning glory: the iconic Angkor Wat. Suryavarman II successfully attacked the Cham capital in 1145, but there were virtually no inscriptions from 1145 to 1180, during which period the king somehow died.

The lack of inscriptions was likely caused by three decades of destructive infighting following the death of Suryavarman II. The nadir of this period came in 1177, when Angkor was sacked by the vengeful Chams. While several lesser rulers battled for the fragmented occupied kingdom, a prince returned from exile in the Cham capital and led a campaign that resulted in a bloody victory over Angkor's occupiers. Later crowned Jayavarman VII (r. ca 1181–1218), he soon led the empire back to its former glory.

Jayavarman VII was perhaps greatest of the kings of Angkor, and the last to wield vast power. After expelling the Chams, who had desecrated the holy temples of his

An aerial view of Angkor Wat, available to visitors via hot air balloon or helicopter.

Zhou Daguan

In the late 13th century, China sent a number of emissaries to Cambodia, including diplomat and scribe Zhou Daguan (Chou Ta-kuan). Zhou arrived at Yasodharapura (Angkor) just after the ascension of Indravarman III (r.1296–1308). After spending almost a year in Cambodia, he wrote *Memoirs on the Customs of Cambodia*, of which only portions have survived. While Zhou arguably regarded Cambodia as relatively savage compared with China, his accounts of the culture at Angkor are the only detailed, eyewitness descriptions of many facets of both common and royal life.

Zhou describes clothing styles, royal procedures, building designs, religious practices, criminal punishment, holidays, hunting techniques, and sexual behavior. Other details he shares include the tale of the king who ascended Phimeanakas to sleep with a *naga*-woman each evening. Though some of his accounts are highly questionable, he was clearly impressed by Angkorian society, particularly the flourishing Buddhist society and the reverence for the king. There is little doubt that late 13th-century Angkor remained a prosperous society, rather than one described by many historians as on the verge of collapse.

predecessors, Jayavarman VII began a massive rebuilding program, in part to ensure the empire's spiritual well-being. During his more than 35 years in power he constructed Angkor Thom, a city within a city, and parlayed his defeat of the Chams in Cambodia into an invasion of Champa, whereby he conquered and annexed the rival kingdom. As many earlier kings did, he built temples to honor both the gods and his ancestors. Perhaps believing himself to be a Bodhisattva king, however, he constructed his state temple, Bayon, in honor of the Buddha, and consecrated his ancestral temples with representations of his ancestors as the Bodhisattvas Prajnaparamita and Lokesvara. According to (albeit likely biased) inscriptions, the compassionate king also built hundreds of temples and hospitals throughout his kingdom, earning him great respect among his people. However, these massive projects, many of which were completed in haste with slipshod technique, drained the quarries and strained the local workforce. The consequences of these pressures, combined with the swelling population that deforested the hillsides and depleted water sources, may have contributed to the beginning of the end of the Angkor era.

The kings who followed Jayavarman VII reigned over a gradually declining empire, with waning influence on its population and vassal states. This period coincided with an inexplicable iconoclasm in which at least one of the next kings, likely Jayavarman VIII (r.1243–1295), ordered the systematic destruction of Buddhist imagery. Nonetheless, Theravada Buddhism gradually spread across the kingdom and inscriptions in Sanskrit (the language used on religious monuments) became increasingly rare.

The reign of Indravarman III (r.1296–1308), the first Theravada chakravartin, is best known for the arrival of Zhou Daguan, a Chinese emissary who spent nearly a year in the capital and took extensive notes describing a still thriving capital city (see sidebar above). Following Indravarman III's abdication, Srindrajayavarman (r.1308–1327) ruled over a waning kingdom surrounded by growing menaces. Inscriptions in Pali, the language of Theravada Buddhism, first appeared in 1309. The last known Sanskrit inscription was recorded in 1327, marking the effective end of the era of universal monarchs. Angkor was captured by a Thai army in 1353. The Khmers retaliated and managed to recapture it, but the wars and looting continued. In 1431, Angkor Thom fell to the Thais. The region eventually lost its place as a royal capital, and the Angkor era came to an end.

Post-Angkor Era (1432–1863)

The Post-Angkor era, or middle period, lasted from 1432 until 1863, when French colonization began. Much of this era is referred to as Cambodia's "dark ages," both because there are a lack of firsthand accounts of most of the period and because modern research has focused on re-creating an account of the Angkor era.

Among the theories as to the cause of the fall of Angkor, a primary contributing factor was the rise of and military incursions by the neighboring Siamese (Thais). After establishing powerful kingdoms in Sukhothai and later at Ayuthaya, Thai tribes overran Angkor in 1353. For years, the Thais repeatedly attacked the kingdom, each time looting the city and deporting the population. After successive efforts to expel the invaders, the Cambodians succumbed to the pressure when King Borommaracha II (r.1405–1467), aka Ponhea Yat, relocated the seat of power in the 1430s to the Chaktomuk (meaning "four faces"), the intersection of the Tonle Sap, Mekong, and Bassac Rivers—near its current location, Phnom Penh.

> **Among the theories as to the cause of the fall of Angkor, a primary contributing factor was the rise of and military incursions by the neighboring Siamese (Thais).**

After a period of relative prosperity following the move to Phnom Penh, the Siamese again conquered the kingdom and annexed large swaths of Cambodia toward the end of the 15th century. Cambodia remained under Siamese subjugation until the early 16th century when Ang Chan I (r.1516–1566) procured Portuguese arms and drove the Thais from the land, naming the site of his great victory in 1525 Siem Reap, meaning "defeat of the Siamese."

Ang Chan then relocated his capital 25 miles (40 km) north of Phnom Penh to Longvek. A refreshing period of prosperity lasted until 1594, when Longvek fell to the Siamese and the city was thoroughly destroyed. Its structures were razed, documents were destroyed, and the emerald Buddha was ferried off to the Thai capital.

Between a Rock and a Hard Place: Siamese & Vietnamese Influence in Cambodia

Having lost Longvek, King Chey Chetta II (r.1618–1628) established the capital of his subjugated kingdom at Oudong. After marrying a Vietnamese princess, the king gave his royal in-laws the rights to set up trading posts in Prey Nokor (modern-day Ho Chi Minh City). Little by little, the Vietnamese expanded their authority over the area, including military supervision. Over the course of the next few centuries, Vietnamese immigrants poured into the region, effectively Vietnamizing the southeastern seaboard of Cambodia.

An internal struggle for a vacant Cambodian throne sent vying parties in opposite directions to gain support for their claim, one to Thailand, the other to Vietnam, setting the stage for years of struggle between powerful nations intent on holding sway over their common neighbor.

The Vietnamese empire gradually expanded, colonizing eastern Cambodia and provoking Siam. Each time the Thais invaded, however, the Cambodians requested Vietnamese military assistance. In return for this aid, the Cambodians conceded more land to the Vietnamese, thus compelling the Thais to invade once again. And so it went, until the late 1770s, when Vietnamese infighting coincided with a Cambodian power struggle, and the Thais were able to overrun western Cambodia once again.

By the early 1800s, Thailand had annexed a number of Cambodian provinces. The Vietnamese responded to this threat by tightening their grip on Oudong: renaming the provinces, appointing Vietnamese governors, and even forcing the royalty to adopt Vietnamese fashion. In 1841, the area of Cambodia under Vietnamese control was annexed. For nearly five years, with its territories divided between Thailand and Vietnam, Cambodia no longer existed as a sovereign country.

French Protectorate (1863–1953)

At long last, the Vietnamese had pushed the Cambodians too far and a general uprising occurred in 1845, abetted by the Siamese army. In the wake of a military stalemate between Cambodia's neighboring rivals, an agreement was made through which Ang Duong (r. 1848–1859) became king. Having made the acquaintance of a French missionary during his early years in Bangkok, the king began making overtures to France concerning its precarious political situation. Following a decade of delicate, covert, and often convoluted communications, the Cambodian king made it clear that he desired French help. Unfortunately, shortly after the French invasion of Vietnam, the king died without having secured the assistance he desired.

For nearly five years [1841–1845], with its territories divided between Thailand and Vietnam, Cambodia no longer existed as a sovereign country.

It was around this time that the French "discovered" Angkor, and in addition to teak, they came to believe that Cambodia had hidden riches. While these riches weren't forthcoming, the French succeeded in translating inscriptions, uncovering hidden temples, and extracting statuary for display in French—and later Cambodian—museums.

Following Ang Duong's death, his son, Norodom (r. 1859–1904) was crowned under agreement by the French and the king of Siam, foreshadowing the transfer of control from the Siamese to the French, who would handpick the next three kings after Norodom. Like his father, Norodom walked a political tightrope, signing agreements with both France and Siam in an attempt to maintain a semblance of Cambodian sovereignty while clinging to his crown. Under threat of arms by the French, he accepted terms for Cambodia to become a French protectorate, but shortly thereafter ceded Siem Reap Province and Battambang Province to the Thais.

The French continued to exercise political control, culminating in the effective rule of Cambodia by the French governor-general and the appointment of Sisowath (r. 1904–1927) as nominal king following Norodom's death. Sisowath, a Buddhist, appeased his citizens with regular ceremonies and drew praise for overseeing the return of Battambang and Siem Reap to Cambodian sovereignty. Through trial and error, the French established a peaceful period of colonization that lasted until World War II.

A French expedition, with the help of Cambodian laborers, loads sculptures stripped from ancient temples onto rafts, circa 1880.

World War II

After the French succumbed to Germany in 1940, the Japanese government informed France's Vichy government of its intent to land its navy at Tonkin, from which the French had been running weapons to anti-Japanese Chinese leader Chiang Kai-shek. To retain control of the remainder of its Indochinese colony, the French permitted the Japanese to use Vietnamese ports and airstrips. That same year Japanese troops moved into Cambodia while Thai forces invaded from the west. The French Navy subsequently defeated the Thai Navy but was forced by the Japanese to cede much of Cambodia to the Siamese, who then officially changed their country's name to Thailand. Ultimately, the Japanese turned on their French allies, subsumed all of Indochina, and liberated Cambodia on March 9, 1945.

In the aftermath of the Japanese surrender later that year, the French reconquered Cambodia, installed King Norodom Sihanouk (r. 1941–1955, 1993–2004) on the throne, and forced Thailand to return Cambodian territory. Democratic elections held in 1946 and 1947 placed power in the hands of a popularly elected National Assembly (a constitution modeled after the French Fourth Republic). In 1952, Sihanouk dismissed his cabinet, suspended the constitution, assumed control of the government as prime minister, and threatened a popular uprising if France did not grant full independence. Cambodia achieved independence on November 9, 1953. Less than a year later, a formal peace agreement was signed; peace reigned in Cambodia for nearly two decades.

King of Cambodia Norodom Sihanouk reviews troops in 1947 at his Phnom Penh palace.

The Kingdom of Cambodia (1954–1970)

King Sihanouk abdicated the throne in 1955, in favor of his father, Suramarit (r.1955–1960), and assumed the title of *samdech* (prince) so that he could play a greater role in the political process. (When his father died in 1960, Sihanouk again became the de facto sovereign.) His political party, Sangkum Reastr Niyum (Popular Socialist Community), dominated Cambodian politics for the next 15 years, during which Sihanouk's Buddhism-inspired Khmer nationalism led to a period of peace and growing prosperity. Sadly, those of Vietnamese descent were treated more harshly than ever during this era. Yet apart from that discrimination, the period marked an unprecedented intellectual and economic renaissance. The country was on the road to greater development with French, American, and Chinese assistance.

Unfortunately, the ensuing development led to both economic stratification and corruption, and the seeds of communism were sown by leftist intellectuals and fertilized by an autocratic government. As both dissent and repression grew, the party of right-wing Marshal Lon Nol (1913–1985) won national elections in 1966. While Sihanouk initially rallied against the new government, ultimately he supported the appointment of pro-American Lon Nol as the prime minister. The amicable relationship was short-lived, however, and Lon Nol, with tacit approval from the United States, staged a successful coup d'état against Sihanouk on March 18, 1970, deposing him as head of state. Enraged by this action, Sihanouk threw his support behind the communist cause and the stage was set for many bloody years to come.

From Civil War to Genocide to Vietnamese "Liberation" to UN-brokered Peace (1970–1997)

Following Lon Nol's successful coup against Prince Sihanouk, most Cambodian peasants remained loyal to the king and refused to support the American-backed Khmer Republic. Meanwhile, a communist revolutionary group called the Communist Party of Kampuchea (CPK), better known as the Khmer Rouge (Red Khmers), had been gaining strength and popular support for over a decade, and it took the opportunity to get involved in efforts against the new government. The Khmer Rouge formed a partnership with Sihanouk, exploiting him to gain recruits for their growing revolution.

During this time, Northern Vietnamese and Viet Cong troops took refuge in Cambodia. In an effort to combat communism in Vietnam, the United States—with support from Lon Nol's Khmer Republic—launched a secret bombing campaign that targeted communist bases across eastern Cambodia. Previously believed to have started in 1969, new data reveals that the bombings began in 1965 and escalated to carpet bombings in 1969 before ending in August 1973. An estimated 2.76 million tons of ordnance (more than all ordnance dropped by Allied forces during World War II) were dropped across Cambodia. Civilian deaths from the bombings are extremely difficult to confirm—the estimated figures prior to the release of this recent data range from 30,000 to 500,000. Thousands more saw their homes and livelihoods destroyed, which ultimately strengthened the Khmer Rouge's grassroots popularity. In collaboration with Vietnamese communist forces, the Khmer Rouge recruited and trained hundreds of thousands of disillusioned soldiers. By 1973, the Khmer Rouge had gained control over most of the country.

EXPERIENCE: Make a Difference with NGOs

Nongovernmental organizations (NGOs)—private groups that run charities, build roads and schools, and encourage reform—have been a staple in everyday Cambodian life since the 1990s. Khmers call them *angkar,* meaning "organization," ironically the same slang term used for the Khmer Rouge regime. Young graduates rigorously seek NGO jobs for their high pay, benefits, and travel opportunities.

Visitors to Cambodia can participate in NGO-operated programs to improve the lives and living conditions of impoverished Cambodian people. While most do not accept short-term volunteers, the following organizations allow you to help:

Bridges Across Borders—Southeast Asia *(144H Street 143, BKK III, Phnom Penh, tel 855(0)23-220-930, www.babsea .org)* assists local communities on a wide variety of hands-on projects.

The **Cambodian Center for Human Rights** *(798 Street 99, Beoung Trabek, Khan Chamkar Mon, Phnom Penh, tel 855(0)23-726-901, www.cchrcambodia.org)* provides volunteer opportunities for legal, communications, and other professionals to help protect human rights in Cambodia.

In association with 12 other organizations, **ConCERT**—Connecting Communities, Environment & Responsible Tourism *(tel 855(0)92-353-211 or 855(0)63-933-511, www.concertcambodia.org)* supports numerous development projects in and around Siem Reap.

Also in Siem Reap, **Voluntary Projects Overseas** *(tel 855(0)92-594-778 or 855(0)63-390-163, www.voluntaryprojects overseas.org or www.madforgood.org)* provides clean water, builds traditional Khmer houses, and teaches farming techniques to needy families.

The Khmer Rouge took full control of Cambodia on April 17, 1975, when troops marched on Phnom Penh. As soon as they seized power, all soldiers and civil servants from the Khmer Republic regime were summarily executed. Phnom Penh and all other cities were evacuated under the false pretense of imminent American bombing. Forced to walk hundreds of miles to the countryside, many people died on the road.

The Khmer Rouge sought to implement a radical Maoist and Marxist-Leninist transformation of the country to create a rural, agrarian utopia. Relations with the outside world were cut off, the calendar was reset to year zero, money and private property were abolished, all religious and educational sites were shut down, and everyone was forced to dress in identical black pajama-like garments. Adults were selected at random and forced to marry; children were often taken from their homes so that they could attend political indoctrination sessions. The Khmer Rouge instituted a grueling four-year plan designed to produce 3 tons (2.7 tonnes) of rice per hectare (about 2.5 acres) throughout the country. To meet these nearly impossible goals, people worked from sunrise to sundown without

Voters in Phnom Penh on a historic election day, May 23, 1993

adequate rest or food, and centuries-old reservoirs and canals were altered, often to the detriment of a previously functional irrigation system.

Despite having full control over Cambodia, the Khmer Rouge leadership kept the Communist Party a secret, leading under the name Angkar Loeu (High Organization) or simply, Angkar (Organization). The Khmer Rouge was mainly led by Cambodian nationals who had joined the party while studying abroad in France or Russia and who also assumed secret monikers. Pol Pot was Brother Number One and Nuon Chea was Brother Number Two. Their ranks included a cadre comprised of So Phim, Ieng Sary, Son Sen, Ta Mok, Khieu Samphan, Nhim Ros, Ke Pauk, Ieng Thirith, and Vorn Vet. Pol Pot did not publicly admit the existence of the Communist Party of Kampuchea/Khmer Rouge until 1977.

> **The Khmer Rouge was mainly led by Cambodian nationals who had joined the party while studying abroad in France or Russia.**

The leaders of the Khmer Rouge believed they had enemies everywhere. Anyone viewed as impure, suspect, or otherwise not representative of the peasant ideal was arrested and detained in prisons known as security centers where they were tortured to draw out confessions. The worst of these security centers was Office S-21, or Tuol Sleng, where nearly 14,000 people were imprisoned (see p. 83). Around the country, thousands of Cambodians deemed traitors were executed en masse in killing fields (see p. 86). Such individuals included intellectuals, former Khmer Republic officials, ethnic minorities, and anyone suspected of serving the CIA or the Vietnamese. An estimated 1.7 million people fell victim to the Khmer Rouge regime, dying from execution, starvation, overwork, or lack of medical care. Others were sent to reeducation centers to perform slave labor as a means of reformation. Thousands of people were widowed or orphaned, and survivors were left with indelible psychological scars. Even members of the CPK and the army were purged after being accused as traitors. During the worst purge, from 1975 to 1978, an estimated 100,000 people were executed.

While the Khmer Rouge regime sometimes maintained an uneasy alliance with Vietnam, the long-standing animosity between the two countries prevailed in the end. Khmer Rouge forces launched cross-border attacks in 1977 to reclaim the Kampuchea Krom area. On December 22, 1978, Vietnamese troops launched a massive counterattack. These Vietnamese liberators/invaders captured Phnom Penh on January 7, 1979, effectively ending the Khmer Rouge's bloody rule, but setting off another round of civil war and a subsequent guerrilla war that would ultimately last another 20 years.

As the Khmer Rouge and Vietnamese troops battled, rice stocks and fields were destroyed to prevent them from falling into enemy hands, leading to a countrywide famine. Several hundred thousand Cambodians fled across the border to Thailand, becoming refugees. In addition, Khmer Rouge and government forces laid millions of land mines, leading to countless deaths and disabilities that continue to this day.

Victorious Vietnamese forces set up a puppet regime named the People's Republic of Kampuchea (PRK). One of the new government's first acts was convening a show trial in which many Khmer Rouge leaders were tried and convicted in absentia. Meanwhile, Khmer Rouge leaders and soldiers fled to the west, along the Thai border, reestablishing their strength with help from China and Thailand. Blinded by Cold War politics, Western nations rejected the new Vietnamese-aligned government and allowed the Khmer Rouge to maintain its seat in the UN General Assembly until 1993, despite knowledge of its crimes and atrocities.

In the years that followed the Vietnamese invasion, Khmer Rouge troops continued to launch attacks around the country. In September 1989, Vietnam announced that it would withdraw its troops from Cambodia the following year. In the meantime, remaining Khmer Rouge leaders joined forces with Prince Sihanouk's royalist faction, the National United Front for an Independent, Neutral, Peaceful, and Cooperative Cambodia (FUNCINPEC) and the noncommunist Khmer People's National Liberation Front (KPNLF), hoping to gain a political upper hand over the People's Republic of Kampuchea. Prolonged negotiations among the various parties eventually resulted in the October 23, 1991, signing of the Paris Agreement—a peace treaty installing the Sihanouk-led Supreme National Council (SNC) as provisional leader of Cambodia until national elections could be organized under the supervision of the United Nations Transitional Authority in Cambodia (UNTAC).

The Monarchy Today

Always putting forward a smiling face, King Norodom Sihamoni (r.2004–present) is holding together a once mighty tradition of royalty by occupying the throne of Cambodia's modern constitutional monarchy, a system similar to Britain's. After an initial career in ballet, his reign commenced in 2004 after the beloved King Norodom Sihanouk (see pp. 31–33) shocked the country with his resignation. Although it is not required that the eldest heir take the throne, Sihamoni is just that, and he also possesses prior political experience as UNESCO's Cambodian ambassador. His father appeased the nation by staying on as the king's advisor—a role that makes him "the politician who has occupied the world's greatest variety of political offices" in the *Guinness Book of World Records*.

Fair and free national elections were held in 1993 with high voter turnout. The Cambodian People's Party (CPP), representing the former communist government, won 51 seats in the National Assembly, but FUNCINPEC won 58 seats and Prince Norodom Ranariddh was appointed prime minister. Not ready to concede, the CPP unsuccessfully threatened secession of seven eastern provinces, but later grudgingly accepted the elections' outcome. CPP leader Hun Sen was eventually appointed second prime minister. The Khmer Rouge boycotted the elections and refused to demobilize their forces, continuing to fight against the newly established government. Hostilities did not wane until August 1996, when Khmer commander Ieng Sary (then deputy prime minister, foreign minister under the Khmer Rouge) defected to the Royal Government of Cambodia with many of his troops.

On July 5, 1997, Hun Sen staged a coup, ousting Prince Ranariddh and taking full control of Cambodia. The CPP then launched an all-out offensive against the remaining Khmer Rouge leaders in the north. A year later, the Khmer Rouge reached its long-

Cambodian youth in Phnom Penh are increasingly fashion conscious.

awaited demise when Pol Pot died and Brother Number Two Nuon Chea and Khieu Samphan—head of state under the Khmer Rouge—defected to the government.

Post-Khmer Rouge

Hun Sen and his CPP party have gradually consolidated their grip on Cambodia since the 1998 coup. Not receiving enough votes in the 1998 elections to govern alone, the CCP and King Sihanouk (see sidebar opposite) negotiated a settlement to form a coalition government with FUNCINPEC. In the 2003 elections, the CPP increased its control, while the Sam Rainsy Party surpassed FUNCINPEC as the party's main political rival. The 2008 national elections were the country's fourth democratic elections since the UN first supervised voting in May 1993. Cambodians participated enthusiastically, especially younger, first-time voters. With economic prospects looking rosy, a border dispute with Thailand stirring up nationalistic fervor, and a media dominated by the CPP, Prime Minister Hun Sen's CPP solidified 15 years of rule with their most impressive victory to date, capturing 73 of 123 parliamentary seats, enough to form a single-party government for the first time.

Opposition parties, who suffered from the royalist FUNCINPEC Party's fractionalization, cried foul, citing a decline in participation as evidence of voter disenfranchisement. Election monitors conceded that they did not have observers at all polling stations and reported some intimidation tactics, including the murder of a pro–Rainsy Party journalist. Yet the election was marred by fewer incidences of intimidation and violence than in years past, and election monitors praised the democratic nature of the process. ∎

Arts

Art is a revered aspect of Cambodian society. Yet it teetered on the brink of extinction during the Khmer Rouge regime, which attempted to obliterate all forms of artistic expression. As the country begins to mend, its arts are reemerging, largely from refugee efforts. From once forgotten dances of the Angkor Empire to the modern innovations of cinematography, Cambodia's emerging art scene leaves lingering impressions.

Dance & Drama

From the days of Cambodia's early kingdoms, dance has been an honored art form. Traditional dance, performed by the Royal Ballet, was staged exclusively within the royal palace. If it was presented elsewhere, such as during religious celebrations, it was attended only by the king. Dance performers were considered the earthly representations of celestial dancers called *apsaras* and hailed from all levels of society, ranging from the common classes all the way to the royal family. Performances are believed to have been held in specifically designed halls within temple compounds, such as Angkor's Preah Khan and Ta Prohm, both of which feature rooms adorned with carvings of apsara dancers.

Trained from early childhood, dancers perform costumed dances that usually incorporate drama, such as Cambodian versions of the Hindu epic, *Ramayana* (called *Reamker* in Khmer), and tales of romance, mythology, and episodes from the life of the Buddha. Dances are performed to live music and typically emphasize slow, meticulous movements of the arms and hands.

From the days of Cambodia's early kingdoms, dance has been an honored art form.

The tradition was kept alive by trained dancers who escaped the Khmer Rouge to live in refugee camps or exile. Today, the Royal University of Fine Arts trains professional dancers, many of whom go on to perform for the Royal Ballet, which was revived in great part by the efforts of Princess Norodom Bopha Devi, who was trained by her grandmother in the classic art of dance and theater and who went on to tour the world as a prima ballerina in the Royal Cambodian Ballet prior to the Khmer Rouge era.

A variety of ethnic, tribal dances and local Khmer folk dances continue to be performed in rural communities for religious and personal celebrations. These dances are typically performed by groups of young men and women and often feature props made of natural products that are incorporated in dances and depict events common to traditional rural life.

Music

Traditional Cambodian music transcends simple artistic expression or lively entertainment and is played frequently in ceremonial rites. In fact, in Khmer or tribal societies musical accompaniment is a hallmark of most events, including weddings, funerals, and even boxing matches (see sidebar p. 82). While traditional Cambodian musical instruments resemble those of Indian origin, the study and practice evolved into a distinctly Cambodian style. Students learned to play from masters within sacred music halls, where offerings were made to Preah Bisnalokar—the deity of the arts—and a number of other spiritual practices

Young girls learn traditional *apsara* dance at an arts school in Phnom Penh.

were integrated in the instruction process. While much of this mysticism likely has dissipated over the centuries, the instruments played today are nearly identical to those played a thousand years or more ago. Instruments such as the *khsae muoy*, fashioned from a gourd with a single brass string, and the *mem*, a single-stringed violin only played by ethnic minorities in Ratanakiri, are depicted on lintels from 7th-century Sambor Prei Kuk temple and bas-reliefs at the 12th-century Bayon temple. Cambodian music also incorporates a number of wind instruments and an amazing diversity of percussion instruments, many akin to gongs, xylophones, and drums.

Today, traditional musical ensembles perform for all kinds of celebrations. They also perform in association with the other Khmer arts, such as dance, theater, and shadow puppet performances (see sidebar p. 66), all of which are great ways to experience the country's time-honored musical practice.

Temple Art & Architecture

The magnificent temples of Cambodia are considered works of art, especially the pyramidal temples capped with lotus flower–inspired towers, adorned with intricate carvings, and housing statues of religious devotion. Mythical creatures, such as the half-bird, half-man Garuda, are featured prominently, as are statues of lions, elephants, and guardian spirits.

Stone carving techniques are mastered at the Artisans d'Angkor workshop in Siem Reap.

Deified representations of royal ancestors and bas-reliefs depicting Hindu epics and historical accounts showcased the great craftsmanship of early Cambodian artisans, who the kings commissioned to beautify their temples.

The increasing grandiosity and complexity of Cambodian architecture included multi-tiered and towered temples surrounded by galleries, courtyards, extensive causeways, and subsidiary temples, all of which were decorated with elaborate religious iconography. Temples such as Jayavarman VII's Neak Pean, a temple surrounded by ponds, built within an enormous man-made reservoir, represent the creativity of Angkorian architects, who often designed their temples as symbolic representations of the mythical world, particularly Mount Meru, home to the gods.

Sculpture

Cambodian society has produced a powerful body of artistic work in the field of sculpture, with pieces of freestanding statuary gracing museums from Angkor Borei to Paris. The oldest existing statuary, dating from the sixth and seventh centuries of the kingdom of Funan, primarily featured representations of Hindu deities. Typical sculpture, carved from sandstone blocks, depicted four- and eight-armed versions of Vishnu, his avatar Krishna, and images of the Buddha, most in naturalistic poses and often showing obvious Indian influences. As the seat of power relocated first to the Chenla capital of Isanapura (Sambor Prei Kuk), then later to Angkor, and briefly to Koh Ker, Cambodian sculpture underwent a variety of stylistic changes, typified by the sensual curves of Durga (Isanapura), the masterpieces of bas-reliefs on the galleries of Angkor Wat, the lintels and pediments of Banteay Srei, and the monolithic statuary of fighting monkey-men from Koh Ker.

Bronze casting was also highly advanced in Angkorian and pre-Angkorian days. Bronze statuary, some as tall as 5 feet (1.5 m), has been discovered in Khmer temples in Cambodia and Thailand. It often depicted far less common religious iconography, such as one of the primary deities of Tantric Buddhism, the multiarmed dancing Hevajra, which was discovered at Banteay Kdei.

The expertise exhibited in bas-relief carvings, such as those around the gallery of Angkor Wat, were likely an extension of highly developed carving techniques first employed upon wood, early examples of which did not survive the ages. The decline of Angkor coincided with the adoption of Theravada Buddhism as the official religion of Cambodia. From the 14th century onward, therefore, most sculpture created in the country represented Buddhist imagery and was carved from hardwoods, which were frequently covered in lacquer, then painted or adorned with gold leaf.

In modern times, sandstone carvings inspired by Angkorian art are carved at workshops around the province of Siem Reap and marble statuary and relief carvings are centered in the province of Pursat. Organizations such as Artisans d'Angkor are training a new generation of artisans in the traditional methods of carving both wood and stone.

Handicrafts

Considered handicrafts in modern parlance, Cambodian crafts—from clay pottery to silk material—make up a valued part of Khmer arts, both culturally and economically.

Phnom Penh's Arts Cooperative

Conceived by German filmmaker Nico Mesterharm, Meta House *(6 Street 264, Sangkat Chaktomuk, Khan Daun Penh, Phnom Penh, tel 855(0)12-607-465, www.meta-house .com, closed Mon.)* was one of the first cultural institutions to nurture Cambodia's fledgling arts movement. Here, young Khmer artists have been encouraged to develop and showcase their talents, receiving guidance throughout the entire creative process.

The cooperative features both exhibition space and residences for artists. Art permeates the compound: in the galleries and garden, and on the ceilings and walls. Much of the artwork is for sale; all profits go directly to the artists. Past projects have included working with street children and artistically depicting the suffering brought by the Khmer Rouge regime.

Visit Meta House for exhibits, workshops, movie screenings, or drinks at its rooftop bar.

More than mere souvenirs, these crafts are helping to reshape and commemorate a culture that teetered on the verge of extinction under the Khmer Rouge's stranglehold. Thankfully, many of these trades are reemerging out of the woodwork, as it were, with the help of various revival efforts, such as the Artisans d'Angkor and the National Center for Khmer Ceramics Revival, both located in Siem Reap.

Khmer handicrafts are, to a large degree, regionalized depending on the raw materials available in the area. Traditional clay pots, for example, have been crafted for generations in the earthy region of Kompong Chhnang, which translates appropriately to the Port of Pots (see sidebar p. 181). Other regions' specialties include marble carving in Pursat Province, silversmithing near Oudong, sandstone carving in Siem Reap, and silk weaving in both Takeo Province and Koh Daich (near Phnom Penh). However, for the tourists just passing through, many of these handiworks are shipped to Phnom Penh's central markets, though prices, of course, will be higher there.

> Literature, as the West knows it, is actually a fairly new concept in Khmer culture . . . though Cambodia's literary boom ignited during its cultural renaissance in the 1960s.

Literature

Literature, as the West knows it, is actually a fairly new concept in Khmer culture. This is not to indicate that the people didn't embrace stories—their folktales generally were dramatic and poetic verses often depicting life lessons. Historically, however, such stories were recounted orally or, rarely, recorded in writing on fragile palm leaf manuscripts. It wasn't until the 1930s that novels first were printed, though Cambodia's literary boom ignited during its cultural renaissance in the 1960s.

Sadly, however, the extreme Khmer Rouge governance of the 1970s systematically destroyed these and all other literary efforts, with the aim of erasing any indications of unique culture. Anthropologists believe that the Khmer Rouge managed to do away with approximately 80 percent of the country's literature, even using the National Library of Cambodia as a pig stall. Of the few remaining texts, most were saved because copies were stored outside the country, especially in ex-colonialist France, or by refugees who fled the country.

Comic Book Culture

Comic books were all the rage in Cambodia from the mid-1960s to the early 1970s. Yet comic book culture met a quick demise when the Khmer Rouge came to power. Many illustrators were killed and few comics survived.

The art form experienced a brief resurgence in the middle of the 1980s. By the early years of the following decade, however, the industry had withered due to a changing economy and the increasing popularity of video.

With a new emphasis on literacy, Cambodians are hungry for books, including comics. Local NGO Our Books preserves historical comics and nurtures the development of new ones, including *Bopha Battambang—The Flower of Battambang*— a graphic novel by Em Satya, which has even been translated into English.

EXPERIENCE: Khmer Karaoke

Karaoke is a mainstay of evening entertainment in Cambodia. Give a microphone to just about any Khmer and they are guaranteed to have a blast. Foreigners looking for a turn at the mike will find themselves out of luck in most parts of the country, as song selections tend to be strictly Khmer. Those intent on showing off their musical talent (or lack thereof) will have more luck in Phnom Penh.

Mekong River Cruise

Many of the boats for rent along the Phnom Penh riverfront have built-in karaoke systems. Groups can rent a boat and sing the night away. Boat rental, including karaoke, will generally cost $10 to $12 an hour. When renting these boats, you may wish to bring your own music, as boats tend to have limited selections of English-language karaoke CDs and many are barely functional after years of misuse.

Le West Club Karaoke

Usually packed with groups of Cambodians or Korean businessmen, Le West Club Karaoke (*230 Street 501, across from Mondiale Center, Phnom Penh, tel 855(0)23-997-800*) features private karaoke rooms perfect for big groups and has a surprisingly large selection of English-language music. Room rentals cost roughly 25 cents per minute ($15 an hour). The place gets busy, so call in advance for reservations.

A literary revival is taking place, though it is unfolding slowly. Libraries are rebuilding, including several of note at the Buddhist Institute and the Center for Khmer Studies. Moreover, literacy is only now reigniting since the genocide, because much of the reading public, born during the post–Khmer Rouge baby boom, is just reaching adulthood. Some of today's best sellers relate personal accounts of surviving the Khmer Rouge, such as Theary Seng's *Daughter of the Killing Fields: Asrei's Story*.

Cinema

Khmer cinema made its debut during the artistic 1960s, considered Cambodia's cinematic golden age. This decade of savvy artistic expression witnessed the local production of approximately 300 films. Several of these films featured the then Prince Norodom Sihanouk, now the King-Father (r.1941–1955, 1993–2004), who directed, produced, wrote, and even starred in several of his features, including *Rose de Bokor* (1969).

As with the other Khmer arts, however, the Khmer Rouge put an abrupt stop to all film production efforts but their own, which streamed its extremist propaganda. The local film industry was abolished and many actors and filmmakers were killed for being involved in the inherently cultural business.

After the Khmer Rouge were overthrown, movies tentatively relit the big screens, though the industry still was considered dangerous. In the 1990s, however, UN negotiations ushered in a safer—though by no means secure—era for artists. The 1994 Cannes Film Festival featured a Cambodian docudrama, *Rice People*, which went on to compete for the Academy Award for Best Foreign Language Film—the first time a Cambodian film contended for an Oscar. Although today local cinematography tends to focus on karaoke music videos and sitcoms, an independent movie resurgence is earning international recognition thanks to an annual film festival, CamboFest, which started in 2007. ■

People & Religion

Cambodians greet Westerners with warm smiles, bursting with Angkor-inspired national pride. They adore their country's beauty and may complain when forced to eat anything but local food. Generous and welcoming, Cambodians frequently invite guests into their homes for tea or a meal, even if it means that their families will eat less that day, as their Buddhist values require that they show compassion, respect, and deference to others.

Ethnic Identity

Cambodia is the most homogeneous country in Southeast Asia: Over 90 percent of its roughly 13.4 million citizens are ethnic Khmers, and the rest are primarily Cham, Chinese, and Vietnamese. Modern Khmer people are descendants of the Mon-Khmer, who are believed to have migrated to Cambodia nearly 3,000 years ago and eventually populated the early kingdom of Funan, the successor state of Chenla, and later, the Angkor Empire. Until recently, the average Khmer's lifestyle had not changed much for generations: The language is similar to that spoken thousands of years ago and roughly 75 percent of Khmers remain engaged in agriculture. Most also practice an amalgamation of the spiritual beliefs their culture has been exposed to over time, incorporating aspects of animism, Hinduism, and spirit worship in their overriding acceptance of Theravada Buddhism.

> **Modern Khmer people are descendants of the Mon-Khmer, who ... migrated to Cambodia nearly 3,000 years ago and eventually populated the early kingdom of Funan.**

According to estimates, a few hundred thousand Cham Muslims reside in Cambodia. The Cham descend from refugees of the kingdom of Champa (in modern-day Vietnam), rivals of Angkor who succeeded in sacking the city of Yasodharapura in 1177. Eventually persecuted by both the Vietnamese and Khmers, the Cham suffered greatly under the Khmer Rouge, in what some scholars say was the most clear-cut case of genocide perpetrated by the regime. Thousands of Cham were killed, mosques were summarily destroyed, and many were forced to betray their religious beliefs.

Today, many Cham live in distinct communities separate from the Khmers, although Cham and Khmers also live harmoniously side by side in some places. With fishing as their main livelihood, Cham communities are typically found along the banks of the Tonle Sap and Mekong Rivers. In the post–Khmer Rouge years, many mosques were rebuilt, often with funding from Middle Eastern countries. Yet the government also has shut down mosques and religious schools under the guise of fighting terrorism, a fresh manifestation of persecution.

The ethnic Chinese in Cambodia have been here for numerous generations, integrating Khmer culture, language, and identity with their own. Despite their small numbers (one percent of the population), the country is greatly influenced by Chinese culture. Chinese restaurants can be found in larger cities and many urban areas pause to celebrate Chinese New Year. Cambodia's Chinese inhabitants also play a major role in the country's economy, especially as China pumps billions of dollars in investment into Cambodia.

Despite living side by side for so many years, relations remain strained between Khmers and Vietnamese (5 percent of the population). This tension stems from propaganda during the Khmer Rouge years, the subsequent occupation of Cambodia by Vietnam, and issues over the Khmer Krom—ethnic Khmers living in the area

Buddhist monks in a doorway of Bayon temple at Angkor Thom

Traditional attire is worn on the annual holiday celebrating independence from France.

Cambodians call Kampuchea Krom, a small enclave in the south of Vietnam that once belonged to Cambodia.

Small minority groups known as Khmer Loeu (Highland Khmer) live in the country's mountainous regions in Ratanakiri, Mondulkiri, Stung Treng, and Kratie. The largest minority group is the Tampuon; other groups include the Mnong, Krung, Kavet, Brao, and Jarai. Unlike in some parts of Southeast Asia, however, these groups do not maintain a public presence and are not viewed as tourist attractions, though they follow fascinating cultural practices far different from their Khmer neighbors.

In addition to these various groups, Phnom Penh and other cities contain many Western and East Asian expatriates, who have flocked to the country to work and volunteer for NGOs or start their own businesses. Phnom Penh alone boasts thousands of Westerners, Koreans, and Japanese, and their numbers are steadily growing.

Dress

Traditional dress in Cambodia is similar to traditional dress in Laos and Thailand. The legendary king Kaundinya was said to have given the first clothes to women and Khmer attire was heavily influenced by Indian attire for several centuries. The *sampot* (similar to a sarong), is worn like a combined pant/skirt by both men and women, and dates back to the Funan era when the Cambodian king ordered that they be worn throughout the kingdom at the request of Chinese envoys.

Sampots varied depending on social class. Men and women of peasant and lower classes wore simple cloth sarongs, with the ends sewn together and then tied and secured at the waist. Women of higher classes wore *sampot chang kben,* in which the sampot is knotted and pulled between the legs to form loose fitting pants. This style was also worn by men, but with different patterning. Traditionally, neither sex wore an upper-body garment with their sampots until the French colonial occupation, when both men and women started wearing them. Cambodians continued to wear traditional clothing until the 20th century, when Western clothes were more widely adopted.

Beginning 300 to 400 years ago, the Cham also wore simple tube-shaped sarongs with batik printing. Natural or white cotton garb was reserved for priests and ceremonial purposes in religious celebrations. Men from northeastern minority groups wore decorated striped loincloths and no upper-body garment, while women wore sarongs. At present, most minority groups only wear traditional dress for special occasions.

Western clothing is now practically universal. Men tend to only wear sarongs at home, wearing short-sleeved shirts and cotton trousers on a day-to-day basis. Women dress modestly, in either modern attire or traditional sarongs. Despite the high temperatures and humidity, women remain quite covered up. This habit also has to do with protecting their skin from the sun; light skin is seen as more beautiful and representative of a higher social class. Women will even wear long, arm-length gloves when driving motorbikes to prevent the slightest bit of exposure. They will also swim in full daily wear partly for modesty's sake and also for sun protection. It is also common to see women out and about in printed pajamas at any time of day.

Still, special occasions warrant traditional garments. For formal events such as religious festivals and weddings, Khmer women wear silk sampots with matching blouses made of *hol*—colorful patterned silk—during the day and dresses made of *phamuong*—solid silk fabric—with intricate decorations along the hem, at night. Men wear light-colored silk shirts and colored trousers. The color of the attire generally depends on the day of the week on which the wedding falls.

> **Modern Cambodians . . . have active religious beliefs; their everyday lives incorporate the tenets of both Buddhism and spirit worship.**

Religion

A general understanding of the history of religion in Cambodia is instrumental in appreciating both the temples of Angkor and the daily lives of modern Cambodians. The Angkorian temples are predominantly religious monuments, built to honor gods and spirits, because the people believed both were active participants in the world. Modern Cambodians also have active religious beliefs; their everyday lives incorporate the tenets of both Buddhism and spirit worship.

Animism & Spirit Worship: Animism, the earliest form of spiritual belief in Cambodia, has also been the most enduring. The lives of early Cambodians, prior to the arrival of Indian religious beliefs, were greatly influenced by their belief in pervasive, incorporeal spirits that resided in the land, water, trees, and even stone. These spirits influenced their daily lives and rituals were performed to appease them. *Neak ta* (ancestral spirits) were also honored, particularly through shamanistic rites that often required blood sacrifice. Shrines to such spirits are located around the countryside and shamans still practice their craft (see sidebar p. 48).

Animism & Spirit Worship

Cambodians incorporated animist beliefs into their new religions, Hinduism and Buddhism. Spirits continued to be both revered and feared. *Neak ta,* ancestral spirits, were thought to participate actively in worldly affairs, such as the great military victory led by the spirit of Oknha Khleang Moeang near Pursat. Cambodians still believe that a spirit resides within Angkor Wat and routinely pay homage to the Vishnu statue located in the Kuk Ta Reach (Sanctuary of the Royal Ancestor). Shrines to lesser neak ta appear throughout Cambodia, typically housing small statues whose commonplace appearance belies the seriousness with which the population believes in their power.

In tribal regions, local populations still practice traditional animism much like the ancient Cambodians did. In the mountainous northern provinces, an ethnic minority called the Tampuon embraces animism absolutely, believing luck is more than mere chance and that spirits can be both benevolently helpful or maliciously wicked. A sect that has remained secluded off the Tonle San River carries out traditional animist customs in elaborate detail. When a villager falls sick, the Tampuon believe the body has been inhabited by a bad spirit. The cure lies in an exorcism relying on sacrifice of a chicken or a buffalo—the exact sacrifice is dictated via dream and performed by the village healer.

Hinduism: Hinduism had the greatest impact on Cambodian history as Brahman and Hindu philosophies were instrumental in the foundation of the earliest dynasties. Kaundinya, the mythical founder of Kambujadesa, was a practitioner of Brahmanism, which derived its beliefs from ancient texts known as the Vedas. Cambodians drew upon some of Brahmanism's cosmological underpinnings, including the concept of Mount Meru as the center of the universe and home of the gods, an important feature of Angkorian temple design. However, Hinduism, similar to Brahmanism in that it drew heavily on the Vedas, became the more influential religion.

Hinduism is centered around the Trimurti of deities, Brahma, Vishnu, and Shiva, respectively the creator, preserver, and destroyer of the universe, all of whom were worshipped throughout the pre-Angkorian and Angkorian periods. In Cambodia, Vishnu and Shiva (as well as their various incarnations) were the predominant gods of worship and were even represented in the pre-Angkorian era as Harihara, a deity who was literally half Shiva–half Vishnu and was depicted as a juxtaposed amalgam in statuary from.

It was common in Cambodian Hinduism to worship *linga,* phallic stones that channeled the power of the gods and ensured fertility and prosperity. While earlier linga represented the Trimurti, the Angkorian Empire's founder, Jayavarman II (r.802–850) established the cult of *devaraja,* or god-king, a term that has caused much academic debate. The cult was likely centered on a sacred linga housing the combined spirits of Shiva and the reigning king. Shiva-linga worship endured through the Angkor era's early centuries. Linga were often named for the king who consecrated them and then installed in state temples inspired by Mount Meru that shared the name of the linga.

By the 11th century, Vishnu supplanted Shiva as the predominant deity. Vishnu, typically represented as his six-armed avatar, was believed to maintain the balance of power between good and evil on Earth, and Suryavarman II (r.1113–ca 1150) built Angkor Wat in his honor. Kings of Angkor derived much authority from their association with the gods, and named cities after them, such as Jayavarman II's original capital Hariharalaya, or assumed names associating themselves with the gods, such as Indravarman (r.877–889/ meaning "protected by Indra"). Angkorian kings followed a tradition of constructing religious monuments that included a temple combining Hinduism and ancestral spirit worship that fused images of their ancestors with those of gods and goddesses.

Buddhism: Buddhism was based on the teachings of Prince Siddhartha Gautama (563–483 B.C.), who, early in life, was prophesied to become either a great military ruler or a spiritual leader. After growing up in isolated luxury near present-day Nepal, the prince requested to leave the palace grounds. Siddhartha was shocked to discover the suffering caused by age, illness, and death. After much contemplation, he left his wife and newborn son to renounce worldly possessions and seek relief from suffering and death. After unsuccessfully searching for an adequate teacher to show him the way, he and five disciples set out on their own, only to discover that their drastic methods of enduring pain and starvation were equally unsuccessful. Siddhartha then went off alone to attempt the Middle Way, during which he practiced meditation and underwent a series of tests, including an assault by the demon Mara. The Earth bore witness to his accomplishment and he attained enlightenment, becoming the Buddha. His discovery of the Great Reality allowed him to escape the cycle of rebirth; the Buddha began teaching the Four Noble Truths, which would allow others to realize enlightenment themselves. His life inspired bas-reliefs on Angkorian monuments built by Buddhist kings and paintings adorning contemporary Buddhist temples.

Phnom Penh is named after Wat Phnom, a Buddhist temple atop a small hill.

Monks collecting alms is an everyday sight in Cambodia.

Many believe Mahayana Buddhism arrived in Cambodia earlier than Theravada Buddhism. Images of the quintessential Mahayana deity, the Bodhisattva—one who has attained enlightenment but chosen to be reborn in order to aid others—and the Buddha date to the early kingdoms. The people of Funan, Champa, and other states embraced Mahayana Buddhism, interwoven with Brahman beliefs.

Mahayana Buddhism espouses the concept of universal enlightenment and allows all practitioners the possibility of improving their stead in subsequent lives. Jayavarman VII devoted himself to its teachings and integrated Buddhist notions with Cambodian ideas of kingship. He commissioned Bayon, renowned for its serene face-towers likely representing the compassionate Bodhisattva Lokesvara, the "lord who looks down," who vowed to assist every being on Earth attain nirvana.

Theravada Buddhism spread through Southeast Asia between the 13th and 15th centuries, promising the possibility of individual enlightenment: Each individual takes responsibility for his actions and omissions, and belief in a supreme being is not required. Theravada Buddhism gradually supplanted Mahayana Buddhism in Cambodia, Thailand, Laos, and Burma. By the early 15th century, Mahayana's Sanskrit language gave way to Theravada Buddhism's Pali. Theravada Buddhism remains the official religion of Cambodia today.

Religion in Cambodia Today: Modern religious practices incorporate elements of all these earlier diverse beliefs. While most Khmers consider themselves Buddhists, spirit worship and lighting incense in front of Buddhist or Hindu imagery are clearly not included in the teachings of Theravada Buddhism—the Way of the Elders. Several national holidays exemplify these overlapping spiritual beliefs, such as Pchum Ben (see pp. 278–279), when millions of Khmers return to their home villages to visit Buddhist temples and provide offerings to the spirits of their ancestors. Furthermore, most Cambodians keep small shrines dedicated to animist spirits, commonly known as spirit houses, in auspicious locations in both their homes and businesses, and regularly make small offerings to them. Even the ancient beliefs in neak ta and the spirits of the land and water are still widely held. These latter beliefs remain particularly prevalent among the hill tribes of the northeast.

Still, as Buddhists, Cambodians invite monks to their homes for blessing ceremonies and frequently mark Buddhist holidays and important events, such as marriages, by visiting wats (temples). Following the disbandment of the Sangha (Buddhist order) by the Khmer Rouge and the expansion of rural education and increased urban migration in more recent years, the number of Cambodians within the monastic order is far lower than in centuries past. Nonetheless, in Cambodia's highly spiritual society, vestiges of the country's Hindu heritage are embraced, particularly in the revival of traditional arts. For instance, the Royal Ballet still performs episodes from the Hindu epic, Ramayana. ■

EXPERIENCE: Meditation/Interacting with Monks

When visiting Cambodian temples for sightseeing or interacting with monks at a more personal level, it is best to follow accepted cultural customs (see sidebar p. 21). However, in addition to appreciating the art and architecture of Buddhist temples, visitors can learn about Buddhism and practicing meditation.

Dhammaduta Association – Wat Lanka
Informal classes on meditation and Buddhism are available at this revered monastery (Main temple, Wat Lanka, 274 Sihanouk Blvd., Phnom Penh, tel 855(0)12-482-215 or 855(0)23-721-001; 6–7 p.m., Mon.–Tues., Thurs., Sat.–Sun.) near Phnom Penh's Independence Monument. Cushions are provided for those wishing to meditate. One of the monks is on hand to provide instruction just outside the temple doors.

Dhamma Latthika Battambang Vipassana Centre
Vipassana meditation is a 2,500-year-old Indian meditation technique that is taught and practiced at centers around the world. At Dhamma Latthika (Kraper Village, Phnom Sampeau Commune, Banan District, tel [Mr. Buoy Kuon] 855(0)12-365-310 or 855(0)16-729-729, www.dhamma.org), ten-day intensive retreats are regularly scheduled for both beginners and experienced students, during which students practice meditation for ten hours a day and strictly follow a code of silence. These retreats, which include vegetarian meals and simple accommodations, are offered in an isolated location near Phnom Sampeau and are funded by student donations.

Singing Tree Café, Siem Reap
A pro–nongovernmental organization (NGO), vegetarian restaurant, Singing Tree Café (Wat Bo Rd. area, Siem Reap, tel 855(0)92-635-500, www.singingtreecafe .com, closed Mon.) offers monk chats with English-speaking monks from nearby temples on Saturday evenings, and holds Buddhist meditation study on Sundays in a casual and inviting atmosphere.

The Land

At the height of the Angkor era, the Khmer Empire controlled territory that reached into modern-day Vietnam, around the Gulf of Thailand, and down the Malay Peninsula. Seven centuries later, the borders of contemporary Cambodia are largely determined by protective natural boundaries forming a kingdom sandwiched between Thailand, Laos, Vietnam, and the sea.

Cambodia is now the smallest Southeast Asian country, at 69,899 square miles (181,035 sq km), yet its terrain is startling in its diversity. The topography embraces three general geographies: looming mountain ranges; an expansive basin of fertile croplands cradled in Cambodia's center; and thriving waterways including the southern coast and numerous rivers that support the people, flora, and fauna.

Cambodia's Mountainous Framework

Essentially, Cambodia's borders are guarded by jagged mountains. The northeastern provinces, along the borders of Laos and Vietnam, are mountainous regions dense with deciduous jungles with intermingling semievergreen and montane forests. Reaching elevations over 5,000 feet (1,500 m), these mountains feature forests so thick that sections remain largely unexplored, particularly portions of Virachey National Park, which stretches across the north of the provinces of Ratanakiri and Stung Treng. Experts believe that several endangered species live here, including the Indian elephant and the sun bear.

> **[Cambodia's] mountains feature forests so thick that sections remain largely unexplored.**

Farther west, along the arching Thai border, abrupt plateaus include portions of the Dangrek mountain range. These escarpments, located mostly in northwestern Preah Vihear Province, crest at over 2,300 feet (701 m), then slope gently into the heartland, where elevations rarely reach over 300 feet (91 m). Along these grasslands is a sanctuary protecting the Sarus Crane.

Completing the country's fortifications, the Cardamom Mountains, whose southern flank intersects with the Domrei (Elephant) Mountains, follow the angling southwest coastal border just inland from the Gulf of Thailand. Within this range stands the country's tallest peak, the 5,938-foot (1,810 m) Phnom Aoral. The flourishing evergreen rain forests here accommodate nearly all the mammals, amphibians, reptiles, and birds species known to exist in the country. Some of them represent the last of their kind in the world, such as the Siamese crocodile and royal turtle. The Cardamoms' inaccessibility has maintained this thriving wildlife, but conservation efforts now are battling encroaching development by sanctioning large sections of the mountains as protected forests and national parks.

Finally, where the Elephant Mountains recede into the coastline, the southern beaches are lined by tropical mangroves—trees aesthetically famed for their roots, which grow above land into tunnel-like tangles.

Hikers enjoy a rest behind Cha Ung Waterfall near Ban Lung, Ratanakiri.

The Basin

On the low-lying plains, which constitute the vast majority of Cambodia's landscape, crops are cultivated to the rhythm of seasonal monsoons. Most of the patchwork of fields is dedicated to rice. Generally, wet rice is farmed biannually in the lowlands' flooded plains, but dry rice is also cultivated at mountainous altitudes, though this more difficult technique produces only one harvest per year. Rice is Cambodia's principal export, but in recent decades rubber tree plantations have created another major export. Other important crops include tropical fruit, tapioca, sugar palm, and areca palm—an ingredient of the famous betel nut chew. The fields are worked by oxen and buffalo. Diminutive Cambodian horses draw carts, but are rarely used to work the land. The other principal working animal is the elephant, used historically for warfare and for transporting heavy loads, like logs and stone, though their dwindling numbers have relegated the few domesticated elephants to providing tourists with joyrides.

The Waters

The majority of the country's people congregate along the fruitful banks of the Mekong River and Tonle Sap Lake. More than a quarter of Cambodia's population depends on the latter for its livelihood, which contains most of the nearly one-billion-dollar freshwater fishing industry. During monsoon season, the lake swells to up to five times its original size, rising several yards with nutrient-rich waters. The flooded surrounding fields and forests are breeding grounds for birds, fish, and mammals, and visitors can canoe under tangled overhanging branches from trees that during dry season stand over 30 feet (9 m) tall. The lake also is renowned for its spectacular array of birds; it is arguably one of the world's greatest bird-watching destinations.

The freshwater Irrawaddy dolphin, one of the most endangered species in Cambodia

Malaria & Dengue

Malaria is a dangerous mosquito-borne disease prevalent in much of Cambodia, with higher rates of infection in the rainy months of June to October. Malarial mosquitoes are most active around dawn and dusk. Travelers risk exposure if they venture out of Phnom Penh and the area surrounding Tonle Sap Lake. Outside these areas, antimalarial drugs are recommended, though some malaria is resistant to mefloquine (trade name: Lariam).

Travelers also risk contracting dengue, a viral disease contracted via mosquitoes for which there is no preventative medication or treatment. Dengue mosquitoes are active during the day and are found mainly in urban areas. While less dangerous than malaria, dengue can still be quite serious. Consult a physician at the onset of severe flu-like symptoms. While there is a higher chance of contracting dengue than malaria, it is still quite rare in travelers.

Using treated mosquito nets and long-lasting insect repellent with DEET can dramatically reduce the risk of contracting these diseases. Malaria can also be combated through the use of prophylactic medication. (Buy antimalarial medications internationally or at registered pharmacies in Cambodia, as there is a high level of substandard and counterfeit drugs within the country.)

Cambodia's other gushing life force is the Mekong River. Originating from the Himalayan runoff, these wide waters cascade over the Khon Phapeng Falls (the largest by volume in Southeast Asia) that constitute the border between Laos and Cambodia, before winding south through Phnom Penh and veering off into Vietnam. The Mekong hosts more than 1,300 fish species and the endangered Irrawaddy dolphin (see sidebar p. 220). Like Tonle Sap Lake, the river expands during wet season, flooding the central plains and distributing rich, fertile sediment which promotes crop growth.

A Changing Environment

Cambodia's rich, diverse wilderness inspires many visits. The establishment of 7 national parks and more than 20 other protected reserves have had mixed results at guarding its pristine beauty, though, which is continually under threat from government-sanctioned, environmentally unsound development.

Prior to the Khmer Rouge era and the subsequent Vietnamese invasion, Cambodia's expansive forests remained almost intact, but warfare took a toll. Tragically, peace negotiations in the 1990s allowed the onset of widespread logging operations, which since have cleared massive expanses of forests, first for timber exportation and then for plantation development. Consequently, only 25 to 35 percent of the country's original forests remain.

As the wilderness shrinks, so do the populations of indigenous species. Cambodia's wildlife, hunted for centuries by remote, sparsely populated human settlements without apparent impact on their numbers, first began to suffer during the 30 Year War, as locals call last century's overlapping conflicts. Many species suffered their own genocide as warfare gave way to rampant hunting. In the 1990s, hunters met a lucrative demand for tiger carcasses, believed to improve sexual performance, by killing between 100 and 200 tigers per year. Though the number of reported killings dropped significantly in the past decade, only about 50 wild tigers remain here. Such destructive acts no longer are going unnoticed, however, and numerous conservation projects are taking hold (see pp. 202–203). ∎

Food & Drink

Traditional Cambodian cuisine centers on rice and fish, staples of both the diet and most people's livelihood. India's historic influence on early Cambodian culture brought spice pastes, which, when combined with fish or meat and plentiful fruits and vegetables, strikes a harmonious balance between salty, sweet, sour, and bitter. As with other Southeast Asian cuisines, the use of fresh ingredients makes it among the world's healthiest fare.

Food

In this landscape of glittering rice paddies, it is not surprising that rice forms the foundation of most meals. So important is rice to the Cambodian way of life that the Khmer term for eating is *nam bai*, literally "eat rice." The second key ingredient in Khmer cuisine is undoubtedly fish; the country's long coastlines provide abundant saltwater fish, and a multitude of lakes and rivers contain a seemingly endless supply of freshwater food. Fish is eaten grilled, fried, dried, as "meatballs," or in *prahok*, a pungent fish paste nicknamed "Cambodian cheese." A favorite delicacy is *amok*, fish wrapped in a banana leaf and steamed with coconut, lemongrass, and chili.

Many traditional Khmer recipes rely on the country's ample fish stocks, which provide 70 percent of the nation's protein. Otherwise, beef, pork, and chicken are generally stir-fried or barbecued, often right beside the street. After enduring years of starvation during decades of civil war, Cambodians are not particularly averse to eating anything; insects, frogs, and snakes are considered perfectly reasonable ingredients for dishes throughout the country. In some rural eateries, diners may encounter their future meals alive and well, ready to be killed and prepared on demand; in every town of substantial size the local market also features a few alleyways where butchers sell fresh meat and live fish or poultry.

> As with other Southeast Asian cuisines, the use of fresh ingredients makes [Cambodian food] among the world's healthiest fare.

On the flip side of the food spectrum, vegetarianism is a fairly new concept in Cambodia, and many Khmers raise their eyebrows at the idea. Still, vegetarian-friendly restaurants have arisen in tourist areas, but meat or fish may still find their way into dishes, as fish sauce and fish paste are common ingredients in Khmer cooking. Vegetarians and animal lovers alike may shudder just witnessing the general treatment of livestock here. It is not uncommon to see a motorbike zipping through rush-hour traffic hauling a pair of supine—and often sedated—pigs or dozens of flapping chickens tightly secured by chicken wire or in a bamboo cage.

Part of Cambodia's exceptional cooking style stems from its overlap with the culinary flavors of neighboring Vietnam, Thailand, and Laos. In addition, because many such immigrant communities have maintained an enduring identity throughout the ebbs and flows of Khmer history, authentic foreign cuisine is found readily. Areas along the Thai border, for example, generally boast spicy curries similar to those of Thailand. A number of restaurants throughout the country cater to Cambodia's long-standing Chinese and Vietnamese communities, serving authentic roast duck or noodley *pho*. The growing Japanese and Korean populations have brought along their own culinary arts—both spicy and raw. Even Western icons like pizza and KFC are now among the dining options in Phnom Penh and Siem Reap.

Unlike in the West, however, meals here are not generally served in courses. Instead, dishes come as they are cooked and are served communal style with several

Street "chefs" fry up pastries outside an old French colonial building in Battambang.

EXPERIENCE: Cooking Khmer

While less renowned than Thai cuisine, Khmer food is both distinctive and delectable. Unfortunately visitors sometimes don't find opportunities to dine on quality Khmer cuisine, as many local restaurants alter recipes to suit foreign palates. However, several Khmer cooking schools teach authentic Khmer cuisine, allowing visitors to prepare a few dishes and dine on the fruits of their effort. (See also Travelwise pp. 307–308.)

Cooking Cambodian

Classes at Cooking Cambodian (77DE2 Sothearos Blvd., Phnom Penh, tel 855(0)17-602-662, www .cookingcambodian.com) begin with a trip to the market, which is followed by classes conducted on an outdoor patio. After receiving information about the ingredients, students learn to prepare Khmer classics, such as pounding curry paste for amok (a dry curry dish steamed in banana leaves), then dine in the shade. Evening classes are also available.

Smokin' Pot

A reasonably priced, no-frills cooking class at the Smokin' Pot (229 Group 8, 20 Ousephea Village, Battambang District, tel 855(0)12-821-400) includes a morning market tour, followed by instruction in the preparation of Khmer/Thai dishes. They provide students with a recipe book to take home.

Sugar Palm

As a result of decades of war, many young Khmers are unfamiliar with their own culinary traditions. Fortunately, Kethana at the Sugar Palm (Taphul Rd., Siem Reap, tel 855(0)63-964-838) has recipes from her mother and grandmothers, some of which even the staff had never tried. Classes are held in a beautiful wood house, so the atmosphere is as impressive as the cuisine.

large dishes set in the middle of the table to share. For example, at most meals, soups are ladled into tiny bowls and then combined with rice. Popular choices include samlor machou banle, a hot-and-sour fish soup, or samlor ktis, fish soup with coconut and pineapple, as well as suki soups, a steaming mixture of vegetables, fish, and meat.

Cambodians enjoy street food served from bicycle-pulled mobile carts or vendors with sidewalk seating. People come in droves to parks and public areas for twilight picnicking. During these evening hours, street carts are out in abundance bearing a range of foods, including roasted corn, fried bananas, fertilized eggs (see sidebar opposite), and sun-roasted snails sprinkled with chili and salt. Also served from fragrant streetside stalls and bakeries are fresh baguettes—a lingering leftover from French colonialism. For a delicious treat, try the sandwiches made of ice cream and baguettes or the sweet-and-salty popcorn.

Signature treats aside, desserts are not common in Cambodia, though fruit is often served to end a meal. In fact, tropical fruits that are rare in the West are found in abundance here. Standard fruits include duong (coconut), menoa (pineapple), and chek (bananas). Fruits such as tourain (durian), known for its pungent smell, and khnau (jackfruit) are an acquired taste, but give them a try. Don't miss juicy svay (mangoes) or delicious mongkut (mangosteen), truly some of the country's best natural delights.

Drink

Cambodia embraces a lively drinking culture. *Tai* (tea) is practically the national drink, as it is served either iced or warm in local restaurants and usually free. *Kaa fey* (coffee) is easily found also, served either black or Vietnamese style: sweetened with condensed milk, often on ice.

Enjoy a bowl of curry at Malis, one of Phnom Penh's new dining and night spots (see Travelwise p. 287).

The true national drink, however, is Angkor beer, produced in Sihanoukville and sold for about $2 a bottle and mere pocket change for draft. Imported beers are common also, but many Cambodians prefer strong, dark beers, such as 8 percent Black Panther stout. While drinking is a popular pastime, Khmer culture looks down on local women consuming alcohol; though, judging by the popularity of "beer girls" who work at local establishments, women promoting beer seems to be an accepted concept. Beer girls are brand promoters who, once you've chosen a beer, will serve you for the duration of the night; they're usually found at beer gardens.

Sugar palm wine and rice wine are also produced locally, and, while enjoyed for the merriment they induce, their uses also venture into the spiritual realm. In some hill-tribe communities, for instance, rice wine is a principal part of the gifts given to appease animistic spirits, particularly during burial ceremonies. But for celebration purposes, the wine can be found in a unique form: fermented in large clay jars. Once the fermented wine is mixed well with water, it turns into a drink that's intended to be shared and sipped through wooden straws. Rice wines also are found bottled, and both these and foreign wines and spirits, particularly whiskey, are available throughout the country.

On the healthier side, *teuk kralohk* (fruit shakes) are common throughout Cambodia. A range of fruit is thrown into the blender with a generous helping of sugar and sometimes an egg. Be wary of the strong-smelling durian that's often thrown in, and, of course, be mindful of the cleanliness of the ice. Many vendors also offer fresh sugar palm and sugarcane juice, squeezed straight from the stalk.

Avoid drinking the tap water in Cambodia, though it is generally okay to use tap water for brushing teeth. On the other hand, bottled water is readily available and cheap. ■

Khmer Delicacies

Dishes like ant larvae soup, fried insects and arachnids (including tarantulas), dog, and turtle can be found throughout the country, but are not exclusively Cambodian. The following Cambodian foods will either turn your stomach or make your taste buds dance in delight. *Pong tea khon* (fertilized eggs): Unlike normal eggs, which have not been fertilized, these duck or chicken eggs contain tiny fetuses. Sip the broth surrounding the embryo before peeling away the shell and eating the yolk and chick inside with a pinch of salt or chili and vinegar. *Prahok*: Commonly made from mudfish, this crushed, salted, and fermented fish paste is used as a seasoning or condiment. Thanks to its distinctive smell, prahok is known as "Cambodian cheese."

Cambodia's capital city—a fascinating, modern mixture of history, culture, and identity

Phnom Penh

Small reclining Buddhas at the Royal Palace

Phnom Penh

Tourists used to fly in and out of Cambodia via Siem Reap with the sole purpose of seeing the stunning temples of Angkor, but the capital city has recently been put back on the map. Phnom Penh is the political, economic, and commercial hub of the country. Thanks to its central location and international airport, it functions as the gateway to attractions throughout the country—including famed Angkor.

Phnom Penh's Independence Monument and some of the city's notoriously congested traffic

The city is situated on the Chaktomuk (meaning "four faces"), the intersection of three rivers—the Bassac, Mekong, and Tonle Sap—that serve as the country's lifeblood, with Phnom Penh as its beating heart.

Today, Phnom Penh is of the few remaining examples of an old Asian city, featuring picturesque *wats* (temples) with spires that pierce a low-slung cityscape consisting primarily of buildings only a few stories tall. In some parts of Phnom Penh merchants still sell their wares from carts pulled by oxen. Juxtaposed with this mix of old Asian and colonial charm is the buzzing excitement of a developing city. One can't help but feel drawn to its unbelievable energy. Monks in crisp orange robes stroll the streets. Motorbikes whiz by with little regard to traffic laws, often stacked with as many occupants as

possible or even with enormous pieces of furniture that shouldn't logically travel by motorbike. Street vendors push carts bearing exotic street snacks and colorful wares.

Although small in size, Phnom Penh can actually be very difficult to navigate. While the city is laid out on a French-style grid system, numbered streets run in confusing order (for example, jumping from Street 334 to Street 252) and there is little sense to the house numbering system (many house numbers are repeated on the same street). For these reasons, it is best navigated via landmark, relying on markets, monuments, museums, and wats as touch points. In getting around, the city is easily divided into several sections: the Royal Palace area, Independence Monument and around, northern Phnom Penh, the French Quarter,

south of Independence Monument, and western Phnom Penh.

One can easily see the essential sights in just two to three days. Except for the killing fields, all of them are a five- to ten-minute motorbike or *tuk-tuk* ride from each other, making the city incredibly accessible to visitors. While it is possible to squeeze nearly all of the major tourist destinations into a single day, Phnom Penh has a great deal to offer those who have some time to spare. In the last several years, the city has experienced a great resurgence, seeing a veritable blossoming of restaurants serving a wide range of delicious cuisine, fine boutiques, cutting-edge art galleries, and indulgent spas. After exploring the wats, museums, and markets, soak up the rich atmosphere in a café or park and then watch life pass by from a tuk-tuk. Visit a gallery exhibiting local artists' works and melt any worries away with a luxurious massage. Phnom Penh is not easily forgotten. ■

Central Phnom Penh

South of Wat Phnom on the Tonle Sap River, central Phnom Penh has broad avenues flanked by national treasures like the Royal Palace, Silver Pagoda, National Museum, and Royal University of Fine Arts. The bustling, rapidly changing area is also home to verdant parks and a few of Cambodia's most important Buddhist sites: Sarawan Pagoda, Wat Ounalom, and Wat Lanka.

The front gate of the Royal Palace, illuminated at night

Phnom Penh's History

According to legend, Phnom Penh was founded in 1372 when Lady Yeay Penh plucked a floating *koki* tree out of the river. She found four Buddha statues nestled inside the tree and built a small shrine for them on a hill. A town soon formed around the site, which later became known as Phnom Penh (Penh's Hill). In 1434, after the abandonment of Angkor, King Ponhea Yat (r. 1405–1467) relocated the capital to the "four faces," the intersection of the Bassac, Mekong, and Tonle Sap Rivers, near the incipient city of Phnom Penh. The capital was eventually relocated to Longvek and then Oudong before finally returning to Phnom Penh in 1866.

French colonialism (1863–1953) had a profound effect on Phnom Penh's development. Under French rule, the city was divided into numerous districts and many of the city's most important landmarks, including the Royal Palace and National Museum, were designed and constructed. The legacy of French colonialism also includes the city's sprawling avenues and boulevards and a plethora of fine architecture. On any given block, beautifully restored villas may stand beside crumbling colonial buildings.

The population swelled in the early 1970s, when an influx of millions of refugees poured into the capital to escape both fighting between Khmer Rouge and Lon Nol forces and bombing along the Vietnamese border. Phnom Penh's two million inhabitants were soon evacuated from the city, however, when the Khmer Rouge seized control of it. Former city dwellers were considered "new people" and, therefore, were enemies of the Khmer revolution. Such individuals were sent to forced labor camps and detention centers, or were summarily executed.

Though the city was slowly repopulated after Vietnamese liberation, a decade passed before it regained its footing and began rebuilding. Much of this development was spurred by the arrival of the UN, which injected a sudden flow of cash into Phnom Penh. As Cambodia became increasingly secure, international businesses began opening branch offices and investing here. Former governor Chea Sophara sought to clean up and beautify the city, making marked improvements to its appearance and infrastructure until 2003, when he was ousted by Prime Minister Hun Sen. Since then, the government has kept up the development campaign, mostly due to the increasing presence of tourists and international business travelers.

Due to the rapidly developing nature of Phnom Penh, a sense of change pervades the local atmosphere. Entire apartment buildings appear to have sprung up overnight and construction sites displaying pictures of glossy high-rises can be found on many streets. Phnom Penh has yet to be inundated with global chains and fast food restaurants. In fact, it was not until 2008 that Cambodia's first international fast food restaurant opened and curious Khmers and homesick expatriates flocked in droves to KFC. Who knows how the cityscape will be changed in another year, however, or even in just a few months?

INSIDER TIP:

Not all Phnom Penh taxi drivers speak English, and some have been known to get lost. Carry a map and ask your hotel to write down your destination in Khmer, just in case.

—SOLANGE HANDO
National Geographic writer

Royal Palace Area

Most of Phnom Penh's main tourist attractions can be found around the area of the Royal Palace and Tonle Sap riverside, all of which are within walking

Phnom Penh
🗺 63 A3
Ministry of Tourism
🗺 Map p. 71
✉ 63 St. 348, Sangkat Toul Svay Prey II, Khan Chamkamorn
☎ 855(0)23-427-130
🕐 Closed Sat.–Sun.
💲 $
www.mot.gov.kh

EXPERIENCE: Shadow Puppets

Researchers may never be able to determine whether the earliest *sbek* (shadow puppets) were pre-Angkorian creations honoring the god of art and eloquence or were inspired by a perforated buffalo-skin rug at Angkor. Regardless, the art was nearly lost to history until Mann Kosal revived the creation and performance of sbek in 1994.

Today, at **Sovanna Phum** (*111 St. 360, corner of St. 105, Phnom Penh, tel 855(0)23-221-932, www.shadow-puppets.org, shows Fri. & Sat., 7:30 p.m., $$*), visitors can create their own shadow puppets: tanning, dyeing, cutting, and decorating their own cowhide with intricate patterns of holes that are the hallmark of the art. Thanks to this revival, heroes of Hindu lore and a cast of animal characters are featured in performances from Sovanna Phum in the capital to La Noria Hotel in Siem Reap.

At **La Noria** (*Riverside Rd., N of National Highway 6, Siem Reap, tel 855(0)63-964-242, www.lanoriaangkor.com*), disadvantaged children give biweekly performances under the guidance of Krousar Thmey (New Family). The nongovernmental organization also runs workshops in which the children learn shadow puppetry and leatherworking.

Those without time to craft their own puppet or catch a show can purchase them from the **House of Peace** (*National Highway 6 toward airport, by the Cambodian Cultural Village, Siem Reap, tel 855(0)12-913-398, www.house-of-peace.de.ms*). Proceeds from puppet sales are used for direct assistance to orphaned children.

Royal Palace & Silver Pagoda

- Map p. 71
- Sothearos Blvd., between St. 240 & St. 184
- 855(0)23-426-801
- $

distance of each other. It is best to begin your sightseeing tour of the city at the stunning home of Cambodia's royal family, the **Royal Palace and Silver Pagoda.** Constructed by the French protectorate in 1866, the palace today houses King Norodom Sihamoni (r.2004–present) and former King Norodom Sihanouk (r.1941–1955, 1993–2004), and serves as an important symbol of pride for the country. Except for the actual royal residence, the Khemarin Palace, most of the palace's grounds and structures are open to the public.

Upon entering the palace gates, one arrives at the impressive **Chan Chaya Pavilion,** where traditional *apsara* dances were once performed for the king and his guests. In front of this hall is a platform where the king still holds audiences.

The palace contains numerous buildings and gardens within its extensive walled grounds. Among the various structures accessible to visitors, the magnificent **Throne Hall** is truly stunning. Designed in Khmer-architectural style, the hall is only used on special occasions, such as coronations and the presentation of gifts by important dignitaries. The attached tower is 193 feet (59 m) high and was inspired by the towers of Bayon, a temple at Angkor.

The **Royal Treasury** and **Villa of Napoleon III** lie just south of the Throne Hall in the main courtyard. While the out-of-place iron villa is now located in Cambodia, it was originally constructed in Egypt where it provided accommodation for French Empress Eugenie during the opening of the Suez Canal.

Napoleon III gave the villa to the King Norodom in 1873.

Silver Pagoda: Along the northern area of the palace grounds is the magnificent and sacred **Silver Pagoda,** aptly named for the floor that is comprised of 5,329 blocks of silver weighing more than 6 tons (5.4 metric tons). The original structure was built in 1892 by King Norodom (r. 1859–1904) and was primarily made out of wood. King Sihanouk expanded and rebuilt the site in 1962. Not housing any monks of its own, the temple welcomes monks from nearby pagodas when the king practices Buddhist ceremonies there.

The Silver Pagoda presents a rare chance for visitors and Cambodians alike to visit a historical and religious site that was not destroyed by the Khmer Rouge. Rather, the pagoda was consciously left intact to demonstrate to the world that the communist movement sought to preserve the country's cultural treasures. Many of the pagoda's sacred relics and riches were still destroyed or looted by Khmer Rouge troops, but the objects that survived are quite spectacular. Today, there are 1,650 art objects housed in this temple, most of them Buddhist statues made of various precious materials. Many of these treasures were gifts from the king, from the royal family, or foreign dignitaries.

The moment you enter the grounds of the Silver Pagoda, you are greeted by impressive sights. The courtyard is filled with a wide range of proud-looking statues, including a large **equestrian monument to King Norodom.** What visitors seldom learn is that this monument originally represented the French Emperor Napoleon III, though its head was later replaced with that of King Norodom. People say that King Sihanouk prayed for Cambodia's independence in front of this statue. The walls that surround the Silver Pagoda area are decorated with intricate and vivid **murals** depicting scenes from the Hindu epic tale, *Ramayana.* The story begins slightly south of the east

The Sovanna Phum theater is dedicated to keeping traditional theater alive, including shadow puppetry.

gate and winds its way around the courtyard. These murals date back to the early 1900s and required 40 Khmer artists to complete. Although the years have taken their toll on these images, they are still quite magnificent. The courtyard also contains **two stupas**—the south stupa containing the cremated remains of King Ang Duong (r.1848–1859), and the northern stupa holding those of King Norodom.

After ascending to the pagoda itself on a staircase made of Italian marble, one enters a veritable treasure trove. The **Emerald Buddha,** a 17th-century statue made from Baccarat crystal, holds court atop a throne. This statue is considered to be of such great importance that the Silver Pagoda is also known as *Wat Preah Keo Morokat,* or Pagoda of the Emerald Buddha. Just in front of the Emerald Buddha

stands the most eye-catching statue—a **life-size Buddha** crafted out of 198 pounds (90 kg) of pure gold and adorned with approximately 9,584 diamonds It was created in 1904 at the request of King Norodom, who instructed that after his cremation his golden casket should be melted down to make a Buddha image. Just adjacent to this statue is a miniature silver-and-gold stupa containing what are believed to be the ashes of the Buddha, brought over from Sri Lanka. Large bronze and silver Buddha statues can be found on either side. On the far right, tiny golden figurines recount episodes from the Buddha's life.

Just behind the throne, one will find the **royal bed** used to transport the king on coronation day—it's so heavy that 12 men are needed to carry it. Flanking the bed is a marble Buddha statue

---

EXPERIENCE: Tailored to Fit

While lacking an international reputation, Phnom Penh's tailors tend to be talented and inexpensive. Many of them prefer that you bring your own material, so head to the Olympic, Orussey, or Russian Markets to pick up some fabrics first. All tailoring requires one or two fittings for adjustments.

Clothes and interior design items can be stitched in about a week by former street youth at **Friends@ 240** (32 St. 240, www .friends-international.org). This upbeat boutique has fabric on hand or can buy materials for you.

Mondiaux Tailor (85A Sihanouk Blvd., tel 855(0)12-867-655) is the place to visit for custom-made

suits. Mondiaux has fabrics available to save you a trip to the market. Suits take ten days and are considerably more expensive than at other tailors.

The seamstresses at **Monika Modern Tailor** (151 Mao Tse Toung Blvd., tel 855(0)12-824-328) can work magic with photographs from catalogues or even a roughly penned

sketch. Since Monika is a favorite among expats, you can expect a two- to three-week wait.

The many tailors at the **Russian Market Stalls** (corner of St. 163 & St. 444) make clothes very quickly at bargain prices. As the tailors here speak minimal English, bring a copy or a photograph of what you want them to make.

from Burma and silver representations of the Silver Pagoda's library and King Norodom's stupa. Toward the rear of the room, you will find a case containing **two Buddha statues** adorned with diamonds weighing up to 16 carats each. In addition to

pagoda during ceremonies; and **stupas** containing the ashes of Princess Norodom Kantha Bopha and King Norodom Suramarit (r.1955–1960).

When visiting the palace and pagoda, you must be appropriately dressed: Knees and shoulders

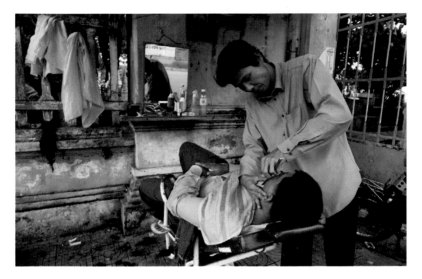

Street barbers, common across Phnom Penh, set up shop in the early mornings and late afternoons.

these treasures, the pagoda walls are lined with numerous Buddha statues, intricate apsara masks, and gifts from foreign heads of state.

Other structures and stupas inside the Silver Pagoda complex include the **Keung Preah Bat,** which has "footprints" of four Buddhas who have reached enlightenment; the **Phnom Mondop,** a man-made hill representing Phnom Kailassa, where Buddha left his footprints in stone; a large **library** filled with sacred texts and discourses of various disciplines; a **belfry** used to signal the opening and closing of the

must be covered and wearing hats is forbidden in the complex. Large shirts are available on loan for those who come unprepared to cover up. Purchase a separate photo pass *($; additional video fee, $)* if you plan on taking pictures or video; be aware that no picture-taking is allowed inside the Silver Pagoda, however. While some who have previously visited the Royal Palace and Emerald Buddha in Bangkok may find this palace a bit less awe-inspiring than its Thai counterpart, it's still well worth a visit.

(continued on p. 72)

Tuk-Tuk Tour of Phnom Penh

The heat, traffic, and lack of clear sidewalks combine to make Phnom Penh a poor place for walking. The city is best toured via tuk-tuk, a motorbike hitched to an open-air cabin. Slow-moving and breezy, the tuk-tuk is the perfect way to see the sights.

Start on the corner of Suramarit Boulevard and Sotheros Boulevard at the **Vietnamese Friendship Monument.** The surrounding park is perfect for evening walks.

Head west on Suramarit, past **Hun Sen Park,** which features two statues of Khmer literary figures: Choun Nath and Krom Nguy. Continue to **Independence Monument ❶** *(corner of Norodom Blvd. & Sihanouk Blvd., tel 855(0)23-216-666, $),* take a lap around it, and then head north on Norodom Boulevard to view some impressive colonial villas and mansions.

Turn right on Street 240, Phnom Penh's posh boutique street. Stop to shop or enjoy a snack at one of its cafés. Then proceed east on 240 to Sotheros and turn left at the **Royal Palace and Silver Pagoda ❷** *(Sotheros Blvd., bet. St. 240 & St. 184, tel 855(0)23-426-801, $)* residence of the royal family.

Continue north to the **National Museum ❸** *(St. 13, Sangkat Chey Chumneas, tel 855(0)23-211-753, $),* the country's leading historical and art museum. Turn left onto art-gallery-lined Street 178 for some quick browsing.

Turn around and head north on Sotheros, passing the ornate **Wat Ounalom ❹** *(Sotheros Blvd., tel 855(0)12-773-361, $)* just as Sotheros Boulevard merges with Sisowath Quay and the **riverfront.** Sisowath offers bars, restaurants,

NOT TO BE MISSED:

Riverfront • National Museum • Wat Phnom • Tuol Sleng Genocide Museum • Russian Market

shops, and great people-watching.

If you bear left on Street 130, you will see many colonial buildings that have yet to be restored. Make a circle around the art deco **Central Market ❺** *(St. 130, N of St. 63, tel 855(0)23-216-666, $),* a Phnom Penh landmark, where you may choose to shop for a while.

Head north on Street 63, right on Street 114, and then left on Norodom Boulevard, which leads to the soaring pagoda of **Wat Phnom ❻** *(St. 96 & Norodom Blvd., tel 855(0)12-934-623, $),* where you may feed mischievous monkeys.

Continue around the *wat* and turn right on Street 92. Pass the enormous American Embassy, the **National Library,** and then the iconic **Raffles Hotel Le Royal** (see p. 81).

Turn left on busy Monivong, which passes the art deco **train station.** Veer right on Charles de Gaulle Boulevard (Street 217), where a yellow-and-green female statue charms a crocodile. Continue straight until Charles de

---

Day in the Life of a *Tuk-Tuk* Driver: Li Heng

Li Heng wakes up every day at 6 a.m., kisses his wife and children good-bye, and mounts his tuk-tuk to ferry people around Phnom Penh. He usually makes about $7.50 a day, but on some days it's as little as $2.50 or as much as $17.50. The days are long, with Li usually working until 9 p.m.

Originally from Kompong Cham Province, Li was forced by the Khmer Rouge to quit school. Though he has been driving a tuk-tuk since 2006, he drove a motorbike for 12 years to save up enough money to buy a tuk-tuk. And he won't stop there: Li aspires to buy his own taxi one day.

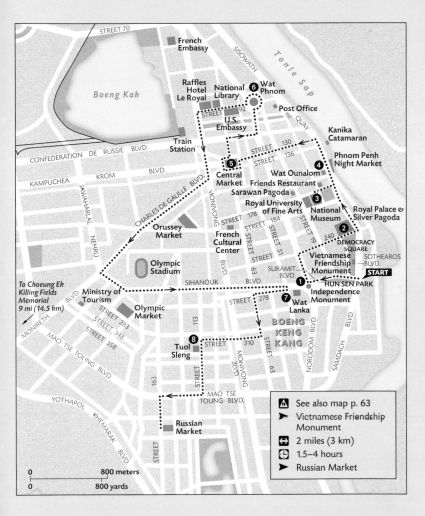

Gaulle becomes Monireth and you'll see the Vann Molyvann–designed **Olympic Stadium.**

At the traffic circle, turn onto the increasingly upscale Sihanouk Boulevard and continue past the site of the Gold Towers: a pair of 42-story towers that will dwarf everything in the city upon completion in 2011. Go right on Street 51 to visit the peaceful **Wat Lanka** 7 *(Sihanouk Blvd., tel 855(0)23-216-666, $)* where Buddhist monks provide meditation instruction on some evenings (see sidebar p. 51).

Turn right onto Street 278 and then left on Street 63, the heart of the Boeng Keng Kang

area—home to numerous NGOs, expatriate residences, and ubiquitous SUVs. Go right on Street 310 and pass over a small canal. Then turn left on Street 113, which leads to the **Tuol Sleng Genocide Museum** 8 *(corner of St. 113 & St. 350, tel 855(0)23-300-698, $)*, once the notorious S-21 Khmer Rouge detention center.

Head south on Street 113 until it hits Mao Tse Toung Boulevard, where you turn right. Your next left is onto Street 163, where the tuk-tuk tour ends at the famous **Russian Market** *(corner of St. 450 & St. 163, tel 855(0)23-723-949, $)* and you can shop until you drop!

National Museum

 Map p. 71

✉ St. 13, Sangkat Chey Chumneas

☎ 855(0)23-211-753

$ $

National Museum

Just a few minutes north of the palace is the distinctive National Museum. It is widely considered one of the finest examples of architecture in the city, fusing Asian and colonial influences in an eye-catching terra-cotta red structure with an ornate tiled roof topped with *nagas* (mystical serpents). The museum, which was designed by famous French architect George Groslier and scholars from the École des Arts

Bronze Vishnu from East Mebon at the National Museum

photography exhibitions; the museum even hosted a unique Rodin exhibition featuring apsara-inspired works created while the artist was in Cambodia. The building's roof is also home to a number of bats.

For those hoping to delve deeper into Cambodia's rich history of art and sculpture, multi-lingual guides are on hand. Additionally, a number of books can be purchased on-site for self-guided tours. Photography is forbidden inside the museum.

Street 178 & Around

Those inspired by the fine art and artifacts at the National Museum should wander Street 178, running just north of the museum. Known as **Artist's Street,** it is lined with local art galleries displaying traditional and modern artwork. While some of what is sold in the area may seem a bit generic and mass-produced, it is possible to find some stunning works here.

Just off Street 178 on Street 13 is **Friends Restaurant** and the **Mith Samlanh Center,** run by the nongovernmental organiza-tion (NGO) Friends-International (FI). The center and the charming restaurant both are Phnom Penh institutions. Friends, one of the city's most popular restaurants, is run by former street children as part of a two-year, three-tiered training program. It serves tasty East-meets-West tapas in a bright, cheerful setting. The Mith Sam-lanh Center *(closed to the public)* is located just behind the restaurant; one can support it in a number of ways so it may continue to protect

Friends Restaurant and Mith Samlanh Center

 Map p. 71

✉ 215 St. 13

☎ 855(0)23-426-748

🕐 Closed Khmer holidays

$ $$

www.friends-inter national.org

Cambodgiens, was dedicated by King Sisowath in 1920.

The museum houses the world's foremost collection of **pre-Angkorian and Angkorian artifacts,** with more than 5,000 objects spanning the 4th to the 13th centuries on display in the four courtyards. Thousands of additional artifacts are stored in the vaults. Modern art is not completely absent, as the art space features constantly changing and assist Cambodia's most disadvantaged children.

Just west of the museum off Street 178 is the original campus of the **Royal University of Fine Arts,** housed in a lovely complex of rust-red buildings. The academic arts center dates back to 1918, when the school was established under the name École des Arts Cambodgiens. Today, it seeks to train a new generation of young Khmers in traditional and modern arts, allowing students the chance to study various art forms from bronze casting to traditional Khmer music and circus arts. Archaeology, architecture and urbanism, and fine arts are taught at the Street 19 campus, while choreographic arts and music are taught at a second site several miles outside of the city. The university welcomes visitors, who can occasionally catch students rehearsing traditional apsara dance in the pavilion toward the back of the compound.

Several blocks north, **Sarawan Pagoda** sits at the corner of Street 19 and Street 178. Unlike other temples in the city, it has yet to be restored, although it is in remarkably good shape. Located off the tourist track, Sarawan Pagoda offers many of the attributes of the more popular pagodas, minus the crowds. It is a wonderfully peaceful place to visit during the late afternoon hours and is a worthy spot for quiet reflection. The temple complex features beautiful buildings in peach, rose, and orange. Numerous Buddha images adorn the main temple.

Restaurants, shops, and bars line Sisowath Quay, the congested road that runs parallel to the Tonle Sap River. A hot spot at nearly anytime of the day, the **riverfront** is home to many of Phnom Penh's tourist-oriented restaurants and late-night bars, though early birds will delight in picturesque sunrises over the river as Khmers

Royal University of Fine Arts

🅰 Map p. 71

✉ 72 St. 19

☎ 855(0)12-444-589

💲 $

Sarawan Pagoda

🅰 Map p. 71

✉ Corner of St. 19 & St. 178

💲 $

EXPERIENCE: Khmer Language Classes

Khmer is not a tonal language like Thai, and is therefore somewhat easier to learn. It's not difficult to pick up a few words quickly, and Cambodians love to help foreigners learn their native tongue.

Royal University of Phnom Penh, Cambodia's oldest and most elite university, offers three-month Khmer classes that span one year for a language certificate. Novice students study under the legendary scholar and language teacher Soeung Phos *(Coordinator, Institute of Foreign Languages, tel 855(0)12-866-826, www.rupp.edu.kh),* who has toured the

world lecturing about Khmer. Short-term tourists may find the content too detailed, however, as the course is geared to expatriates doing business or charity work.

For casual learners, Siem Reap's **Singing Tree Café** *(tel 855(0)92-635-500, www .singingtreecafe.com)* provides a forum for one-hour Khmer classes taught by a Buddhist monk from nearby Wat Bo *(contact Santey, tel 855(0)12-554-812).* Greetings, general conversation, and other useful sentences are included in these reasonably priced *($4/hour),* informal classes, held Tuesday to Sunday at your convenience.

Maxine's

- ✉ 71 Tonle Sap Rd.
- ☎ 855(0)12-200-617
- 💲 $$

Kanika Catamaran

- 🅰 Map p. 71
- ✉ Sisowath Quay, docked opposite St. 136
- ☎ 855(0)12-848-802
- 💲 $$$$

Chenla Luxury Boat

- ✉ Sisowath Quay, passenger port near St. 104
- ☎ 855(0)12-758-992
- 💲 $$$

congregate for morning tai chi (see sidebar below). For night owls, **Maxine's** is a well-known bar among the city's expatriates and is an excellent spot to view the setting sun. Those hoping for a relaxing riverfront stroll may be disappointed, as beggars flock here. A number of NGOs work to assist the poor (see sidebar p.33) and donating directly to beggars will only continue to place them at risk. Say no (*dtay*) with a smile.

To get the most out of the waters here, take a short **boat tour** along the Tonle Sap River and Mekong River. Boats typically follow along the central riverfront area, which features impressive views of the Royal Palace and the Phnom Penh skyline, and then turn up the Mekong River. Along the Mekong, one can view floating villages and local fishermen at work. A nice escape from the city's

EXPERIENCE: Sunrise Tai Chi

Wake up just before daybreak and journey to the banks of the Tonle Sap along Sisowath Quay to witness not only a sublime sunrise, but also a daily Cambodian ritual. With the dawning of each new day, hundreds of Khmers gather riverside to stretch their sleepy limbs and practice tai chi together. Their synchronized, graceful movements set against a vibrant backdrop of oranges and pinks make a spectacular sight, suited for capturing some beautiful photographs.

Visitors are highly encouraged to join in and learn how to do tai chi. A similar exercise ritual can be witnessed each day at the Olympic Stadium (see p. 87).

INSIDER TIP:

After a dusty day on the capital's streets, an evening drink at the lively bar of the restored Foreign Correspondents' Club (FCC) on Sisowath Quay, overlooking the Mekong River, will restore your spirits.

—JOHN SEATON CALLAHAN
National Geographic contributor

intense and stagnant heat, floating along the river is a great way to find a cool breeze. If requested, boats will stop on the other side of the Tonle Sap. Cruises are most popular around sunset, however the best lighting for photographers is in the early morning when the rising sun illuminates the front facade of the Royal Palace.

Boat operators can be found all along the main stretch of the river and will generally offer their boats at $10 to $15 an hour, depending upon the size of the vessel. One- to two-hour cruises can be arranged on the spot, though higher-end boats require reservations; they include the nonprofit **Kanika Catamaran**, which offers high tea and dinner cruises, or the deluxe **Chenla Luxury Boat**.

Near the riverfront, a few streets north of the museum, is **Wat Ounalom**. Widely considered the focal point for Buddhism in Cambodia today, the wat was constructed in 1443 to hold a sacred eyebrow hair of the Buddha. At one point more than 500 monks resided within the temple grounds. Because it is one of the country's most important religious sites, the Khmer Rouge was particularly brutal in their treatment of this wat and its inhabitants. Cadres killed a large number of monks, vandalized the temple, and sacked its relics. Fortunately, the pagoda was restored once the Khmer Rouge was ousted from Phnom Penh.

On the second floor of the wat's main building is a **statue of Huot Tat,** the fourth patriarch of Cambodian Buddhism, who was killed by Khmer Rouge soldiers. The statue was made before his death in 1971 and later cast into the river by the Khmer Rouge to symbolize the end of Buddhism. The statue was fished out of the river and restored at Wat Ounalom. Across from this statue stands a **statue of a former patriarch of the Thummayuth Buddhist sect.** On the main building's third floor, you will find further evidence of the Khmer Rouge's hatred of religion: A marble Burmese Buddha which was smashed to pieces, but later restored, and a cement Buddha statue which was stripped of its silver covering. However, the **eyebrow hair** of the Buddha remained safe and can currently be found beneath a stupa just behind the main building. While it may be easy to become overwhelmed by the sheer number of wats, pagodas, and temples in Cambodia, Wat Ounalom is certainly worth a visit.

Foreign Correspondents' Club (FCC)

See p. 285

Wat Ounalom

- Map p. 71
- Sothearos Blvd.
- 855(0)12-773-361
- $

Few traffic rules are heeded on chaotic Phnom Penh streets.

EXPERIENCE: Phnom Penh's Night Market

Phnom Penh's night market (*across from Wat Ounalom, Fri.–Sun., 5 p.m.–12 a.m.;* see map p. 71) is a maze of overlapping stalls featuring locally made products. Goods for sale include paintings, handicrafts, clothes, silks, and food. The area also holds nightly music and dance performances. The outdoor market is placed strategically along the popular riverfront area in close proximity to many of Phnom Penh's main attractions, as well as a large number of restaurants and bars.

The Ministry of Tourism has high expectations for the market. They hope it will expand to stimulate the local economy like other successful night markets throughout Southeast Asia, such as those in Bangkok or Luang Prabang.

Independence Monument

 Map p. 71

✉ Corner of Norodom Blvd. & Sihanouk Blvd.

💲 $

Vietnamese Friendship Monument/ Democracy Square

 Map p. 71

✉ Sothearos Blvd., near corner of Suramarit St.

☎ 855(0)23-211-593

💲 $

Independence Monument & Around

Built to celebrate Cambodia's independence from foreign rule in 1953, the Independence Monument was completed in 1958, five years after Cambodia gained independence. The 1950s and 1960s were a time of rapid growth and beautification for Phnom Penh as King Norodom Sihanouk sought to demonstrate the success of the country's independence, launching numerous public works projects in Phnom Penh and throughout the country. Renowned Cambodian architect Vann Molyvann (b. 1926) designed the monument, using the Angkor-era Banteay Srei temple (see pp. 161–162) as the main inspiration for the motifs while ensuring that it had a distinctively modern feel. The monument also serves as a memorial to those who died in war and is occasionally referred to as the Victory Monument. In 2007 the Cambodian government launched a large-scale refurbishment of the monument, commissioning the installation of multicolored fountains around the site, which have since become a major attraction for local Khmers.

The austere looking **Vietnamese Friendship Monument** lies a mere half-mile (0.8 km) northeast of the Independence Monument in **Democracy Square.** Dedicated to the Vietnamese soldiers who toppled the Khmer Rouge in 1979, the monument has unsurprisingly failed to rectify decades of testy foreign relations between the two countries. The square received its name in 1998, when Cambodians held a lengthy protest against the victory of the Cambodian People's Party in the national elections. While crowds were ultimately dispersed by government troops, the name stuck around. The square was also the site of a failed bomb plot in 2007. Part of the citywide beautification campaign, the area was converted to a park with yet another large and colorful fountain (this one with musical accompaniment) and topiary in the shape of dragons and other animals.

West of the Independence Monument roundabout is **Wat Lanka.** One of the city's five original wats, Wat Lanka was founded as a library for holy writings in 1422. While the wat was originally situated northeast of Wat Phnom, it was relocated in 1916. The wat has long had a close link to the royal family, with Cambodia's monarchy providing for the temple until 1967. Many members of the royal family attended school in the wat or had their ashes buried within the temple's stupas, which can be viewed in front of the main shrine hall in the middle of the wat. Today, approximately 247 monks from all over Cambodia live in the complex. An additional 300 students study at the secondary school housed inside the temple grounds. Wat Lanka is also the site for a significant religious ceremony held just before the Khmer New Year, during which the ten stories of Buddha are read. For those who hope to delve deeper into Buddhism, Wat Lanka holds open meditation classes at 6 p.m.

Wat Lanka is situated just beside the **Boeng Keng Kang** (BKK) area of Phnom Penh, often affectionately known as "NGO Land" due to the large number of nongovernmental organizations that have their offices here. BKK is also where a number of the city's expatriates have chosen to live, and one can easily spot the recently constructed apartment buildings catering to this Western influx. Due to the large numbers of Westerners who live and work here, there is a large variety of restaurants, bars, cafés, spas, and shops in the surrounding area.

Street 278, just across the street from Wat Lanka, is considered the heart of BKK, cramped with mid-range guesthouses typically with the word "Golden" in the name.

Northern Phnom Penh

Central Market or Psar Thmei is packed to the brim with just about everything you might ever want—and a few things you probably don't! Another of famed architect Vann Moly-vann's creations, the domed, yellow, art deco building is a Phnom Penh landmark, certainly the most architecturally interesting market in town. Psar Thmei actually translates to "new market" in English, but the name "Central Market" caught on due to its central location. The ultimate one-stop-shopping spot in the city, Central Market

Wat Lanka

 Map p. 71

✉ Sihanouk Blvd. (St. 274)

$ $

Central Market

Map p. 71

✉ St. 130, N of St. 63

Phnom Penh's Lonely Elephant

If you spot a 10-foot-tall (3 m) elephant roaming Phnom Penh, don't be alarmed. The resident elephant, Sambo, is often marched to and from her home at Wat Phnom, where visitors can ride or feed her.

While the appearance of a solemn elephant among *tuk-tuks* and SUVs may seem dismal, this elderly pachyderm is actually an emblem of resilience.

Sambo grew up on a farm with her handler, Sin Son. In 1977, Sambo barely escaped an attempt on her life by the Khmer Rouge. In 1979, Sin Son returned from the labor camps to learn that Sambo was alive and being used for hard labor in the Cardamom Mountains. He arranged for Sambo's release and brought her to Phnom Penh, where the pair has remained ever since.

The art deco Central Market, one of Asia's largest classic markets and largest free-standing domes

Wat Phnom

- 🗺 Map p. 71
- ✉ Corner of St. 96 & Norodom Blvd.
- ☎ 855(0)12-934-623
- 💲 $

bears an impressive selection of goods, from food to clothes to electronic appliances. Stalls bearing colorful arrays of flowers and fruits make for great photo ops.

A trip to one of the city's dizzying markets, or *psar,* is a must while in Phnom Penh. One can find anything and everything ranging from faux-designer sunglasses to exotic fruits to a wide variety of shirts displaying Angkor Wat on them. Each market has a distinctive feel and reputation, and all feature great photo opportunities. The markets are generally open every day from 6 a.m. to 5 p.m., though the worst hours to visit are between noon and 2 p.m., when the heat is absolutely stifling.

Farther north, the towering **Wat Phnom** is perhaps the most famous of all the city's pagodas. Crowning the top of Phnom Penh's only hill, Wat Phnom is where Lady Penh installed the four Buddha statues she discovered

on the banks of the Mekong. The main entrance to the pagoda features a grand staircase adorned with guardian lions and nagas. Upon climbing the steps of this hilltop pagoda, one finds a *vihara* (temple sanctuary), numerous **small shrines,** and an immense **stupa.** The temple is a local favorite, with many Khmers visiting daily to pray for luck and prosperity. Those who see their wishes granted return with flowers and small offerings of thanks. Wat Phnom is also known for its Chinese New Year celebrations. At the southern base of the hill there is a huge clock that is illuminated at night. The surrounding park area is always populated with an assortment of Phnom Penh characters, including vendors hawking edible and nonedible goods, beggars, and even the odd prostitute. However, the most notable residents of the wat's surroundings are the local monkeys, who are well-known mischief-makers; their habits include stealing purses and throwing their contents from the trees and one amusing newspaper article even referred to these curious critters as "gangster monkeys," describing how the government had put out a price on their head due to their disruptive nature. Vendors at Wat Phnom sell lotus blossoms, the monkeys' favorite snack. One can also feed or ride Phnom Penh's one and only elephant, Sambo (see sidebar p. 77).

History lovers will be disappointed to learn that the original temple is no longer intact, the current sanctuary having been restored or rebuilt numerous times in 1434, 1890, 1894, and 1926. A large stupa toward the back of the complex holds the remains of King Ponhea Yat (r. 1405–1467) and his royal family; he is known for his decision to move the capital of Cambodia from Angkor to Phnom Penh in 1434. Paying homage to the city and wat's founder, a **statue of Lady Penh** can be found between this stupa and the vihara. The altar is known for bringing particularly good luck to women. If you are all templed-out after Angkor, this is perhaps the one temple to see in Phnom Penh.

INSIDER TIP:

Head up the winding staircase to reach towering Wat Phnom for a taste of local life and fine hilltop views over Phnom Penh.

—SIMON WILLIAMS
The Nature Conservancy

French Quarter

Just east of Wat Phnom, this quarter of the city displays the grandeur of Cambodia's colonial past. Many of the buildings have undergone lengthy restorations; others remain in desperate need of repairs, but are beautiful nonetheless. The heart of the former French Quarter is the square beside the **Post Office,** where belle epoque banks, offices, and hotels once dominated the

French Cultural Center

Aside from stunning mansions evoking the belle epoque and delicious baguettes, the greatest legacy of the French colonial presence in Cambodia is perhaps the French Cultural Center *(218 St. 184, Phnom Penh, tel 855(0)23-213-124)*. With branches in Siem Reap *(Bldg. 418, Wat Bo St.)* and Battambang *(Prek Mohatep Village, Svay Por Commune)*, the Centre Culturel Français (CCF) is a bastion for all things French. Though the CCF caters more to homesick French expats and Francophiles from all over than to locals, it is renowned for its cultural events: art exhibitions, special events, and guest speakers. Le Cinema, one of Phnom Penh's few movie theaters, shows international documentary and art-house films. CCF's bookstores and libraries feature French books, magazines, and newspapers.

EXPERIENCE: Shopping for a Cause

These NGOs produce and sell high-quality silks, handicrafts, and other goods. You can feel good buying from them, as proceeds go to worthy causes and help provide training to vulnerable individuals. Look for their products in markets or at their own boutiques.

The **Cambodian Craft Cooperation,** *(22C St. 371, Phnom Penh, tel 855(0)11-984-879, www.cambodian-craft.com),* or CCC, helps support small and family-run local textile and craft producers by teaching them improved management skills and marketing techniques.

Friends 'n' Stuff is a cheerful shop *(215 St. 13, Phnom Penh, tel 855(0)12-426-748, www.friends-international.org)* beside Friends Restaurant (see p. 72) that features unique bags, clothing, and jewelry designed by former street children and their parents.

Previously unskilled and unemployed women receive training to produce silks, handicrafts, toys, and more at **Nyemo** *(Phnom Penh & Siem Reap, tel 855(0)23-213-160, www.nyemo.com).* This NGO also provides numerous social services to Cambodia's disadvantaged women.

Rajana Association is an income-generating and skill-training project for young Cambodians countrywide. Rajana boutiques *(Phnom Penh, Siem Reap, & Sihanoukville, www.rajanacrafts.org)* offer fair-trade handicrafts, natural spices, jewelry, and textiles.

The funky stall at **Tooit Tooit** *(Stall 312, Russian Market, Phnom Penh, www.friends-international.org)* stands out amid the market hubbub. Parents of former street children help send them to school by making products from recycled materials.

Directed by acclaimed weaver Carol Cassidy, **Weaves of Cambodia** *(Preah Vihear or 24 St. 29, Phnom Penh, tel 855(0)12-737-116, www.villagefocus.org)* trains land-mine survivors and other disabled people in traditional silk weaving, creating breathtaking textiles.

Post Office

- Map p. 71
- ✉ St. 13, corner of St. 102
- ☎ 855(0)23-725-400

Van's Restaurant

- ✉ 5 St. 102, corner of St. 13
- ☎ 855(0)23-722-067
- 💲 $$$–$$$$

landscape. The lemon-colored Post Office is viewed as one of the finest architectural examples of French colonial architecture in the city. Built in 1894 and restored at the turn of the 21st century, it is still the city's primary post office.

Beside the Post Office on Street 102 is **Van's Restaurant,** a fine-dining establishment steeped in the rich history of Phnom Penh and Cambodia. This elegant ocher-yellow mansion was built by Indochine Bank in 1898 and later purchased by the Van family in the 1960s, who converted it into a private home and offices. When the family was

forced to flee the Khmer Rouge, the CPK government used the estate to store ammunition; it also stashed diamonds and gold in the old bank vault. The house was restored in 2003 to its rightful owners, who renovated the building and transformed a section of the house into a high-end French restaurant, homage to the house's French colonial roots.

Beside Van's, another beautifully restored colonial building is now the **Asia Insurance headquarters** *(5 St. 13, tel 855(0)23-427-981).* At the north entrance of the square on the left, the old police station is a fine example of an unrestored colonial building.

Backtracking west past Wat Phnom, you can't miss the gargantuan **U.S. Embassy,** built in 2006. If you happen to be in Phnom Penh near Christmas, the Christmas lights around the embassy complex are over the top. Taking a Khmer twist on the holiday, watch for Santa on a motorbike or *tuk-tuk.*

Farther west on Street 92, the **National Library** is another example of the French influence on the city. A fierce hatred toward education and intelligence caused

and the Queen of Spain. During the 1970s, it was renamed Le Phnom and hosted journalists covering the country's civil war. On April 17, 1975, the hotel was declared a neutral zone by the Red Cross, but it was forcibly emptied by Khmer Rouge cadres by evening as they took over the city.

The hotel sunk into slow decay under the Khmer Rouge, who used the hotel as offices and residences for its cadres

U.S. Embassy

- Map p. 71
- 1 St. 96, Sangkat Wat Phnom
- 855(0)23-728-000
- Closed Sat.–Sun.

National Library

- Map p. 71
- Daun Penh (St. 92)
- 855(0)12-951-582
- Closed Sat.–Sun.
- $

Raffles Hotel Le Royal

- Map p. 71
- 92 Rukhak Vithei Daun Penh, corner of Monivong Blvd. & St. 92
- 855(0)23-981-888
- $$$$–$$$$$

Raffles Hotel Le Royal, Phnom Penh

the Khmer Rouge to destroy many of the library's books and convert the building into pig stalls. Some of the surviving books were returned to the library after the bloody regime was ousted from the city.

Farther down Street 92, **Raffles Hotel Le Royal** has long served as a symbol of Phnom Penh's colonial luxury. Built in 1929, the hotel was expanded between 1957 and 1958. From its beginning, the hotel has attracted celebrities and royalty, including Charlie Chaplin, Jacqueline Kennedy, Bill Clinton,

and Chinese advisors. After the Vietnamese came to power, the hotel was reopened under the name Hotel Samakki. It remained in a sorry state for years, even though UNTAC workers stayed in the hotel through the early 1990s. Le Royal did not see a return to its former grandeur until 1997, after the Raffles hotel group purchased and renovated the property. Today, Raffles Le Royal is again the city's emblem of former colonial splendor. The hotel's **Elephant Bar** is a Phnom Penh institution:

Train Station

⚠ Map p. 71

✉ St. 107, corner of Confederation De La Russie

French Embassy

⚠ Map p. 71

✉ 1 Monivong Blvd.

☎ 855(0)23-430-026

🕐 Closed Fri.–Sun.

the perfect place to sit back and relax with a drink and take in the sumptuous surroundings.

Just to the left, along busy Monivong Boulevard, the **train station** has a slightly more art deco feel. While some trains do pass through from time to time, you'll have better odds getting to your intended destination in a tuk-tuk than on a train until renovations of the rail line are completed in upcoming years (see sidebar p. 173).

The historic **French Embassy** is at the northernmost part of Monivong. As Phnom Penh fell to Khmer Rouge troops in 1975, some 800 foreigners and 600 Cambodians sought refuge in the embassy compound. Eager to arrest the Cambodians within the complex, the Khmer Rouge

threatened to kill everyone at the embassy if they were not turned over. Although Cambodian women who were married to foreign men were allowed to remain inside the embassy, Cambodian men who were married to foreign women were handed over. The dramatic scene of friends, colleagues, and families being torn apart and sent to uncertain fates can be seen in 1984 film *The Killing Fields*. Most of the Khmers expelled from the embassy were deemed enemies of the Angkar and most certainly killed. Foreigners were allowed to remain within the embassy for several weeks before being expelled and evacuated from the country. While the embassy briefly served as a local orphanage, it is now the diplomatic locus of all things *français*.

EXPERIENCE: Khmer Boxing

While *muay Thai*, or Thai boxing, is world renowned, before Thailand existed there was *Bokator*, an ancient Khmer martial art. *Pradal Serey* (Khmer freestyle boxing) was derived from Bokator, and Pradal Serey, in turn, begat muay Thai.

The Cambodians may have a ways to go before outmuscling their neighbors in boxing, but Bokator, which means "attack the lion," takes combat to the next level. Bas-reliefs on the temples of Angkor Wat depict Khmers employing combat techniques and an 11th-century manual was recently discovered that catalogs fighting maneuvers from the days of Jayavarman VII. The art was nearly wiped out by the Khmer Rouge, who distrusted the masters of the martial art and their powerful skills, but it has since been revived by a handful of elderly masters.

Cambodian Bokator Academy

Krama are traditional colored scarves, each of which corresponds to a different level of mastery and represents an animal (e.g., monkey, lion, elephant, or crocodile). Foreigners who wish to earn their krama can study at the academy (*169E St. 161, Sangkat Orussey II, Phnom Penh, tel 855(0)12-651-845, $5/hr. or $120/mo. Classes Mon.–Fri., 5:30–6:30 p.m. & Sat.–Sun. all day*) with Grand Master San Kim Sean. He is working to catalog and standardize the more than 10,000 techniques of the art that cover both weaponry and hand-to-hand combat.

Paddy's Fitness Centre

To study Pradal Serey (freestyle boxing) at this gym (*635 National Highway 5, Phnom Penh, tel 855(0)12-217-877, www.paddysgym. com*) visitors can attend one-hour classes (*$$*) on Mondays and Wednesdays.

Choeung Ek is one of the most infamous killing fields from the Khmer Rouge days.

South of Independence Monument

With the exception of two not-to-be-missed sites, the area just south of Boeng Keng Kang is less popular among visitors to the capital city. It is, however, a good place to get an authentic slice of Phnom Penh life.

The **Tuol Sleng Genocide Museum** is perhaps the most important site in all of Phnom Penh. Formerly the Tuol Svay Prey high school, the Khmer Rouge converted the site into the country's largest and most notorious prison and interrogation facility, known as S-21. Inmates here were unlawfully detained, subjected to inhumane living conditions, and systematically tortured over the course of several days or months in order to extract confessions of traitorous activities and names of additional criminals. After prisoners made confessions, they were transported to the killing fields of Choeung Ek and brutally executed. Of the estimated 16,000 people who were detained at S-21, fewer than a dozen people are believed to have survived.

The site was converted into a poignant museum and memorial in 1979. The prison has been maintained in the state it was found in when the Khmer Rouge were forced to flee the city. Walking through dimly lit and emptied halls, one can imagine the laughter of happy schoolchildren converted into screams of pain and terror. Signs throughout the site describe what happened in each room, pointing out cells for high-level prisoners and informing all visitors that barbed wire was installed upon the balconies so that no prisoner was able to escape interrogation and torture by leaping to his or her death. A series of rooms on the left side of the compound displays images of the bodies that were found tortured to death in those rooms.

The Khmer Rouge kept meticulous records, so all prisoners were photographed upon arrival at S-21. These black-and-white images are now the subject of a particularly moving exhibit. One cannot help but feel haunted by the pleading and abandoned eyes of the dead. A wide range of torture instruments are also on display, many of which are shockingly primitive. The museum also

(continued on p. 86)

Tuol Sleng Genocide Museum

🔺 Map p. 71

✉ Corner of St. 113 & St. 350

☎ 855(0)23-300-698 or 855(0)23-210-358

💲 $

Khmer Rouge Tribunal

The first attempt to bring the leadership of the Khmer Rouge to justice was the People's Revolutionary Tribunal, held shortly after the Vietnamese toppled the Khmer Rouge in 1979. Lasting just five days, it was largely deemed a show trial, lacking standards of international criminal law or consequences for those found guilty.

The Tuol Sleng Genocide Museum displays images of genocide victims in the former S-21 prison.

Since the Khmer Rouge continued its armed resistance into the 1990s, the co-prime ministers of the Royal Government of Cambodia, Hun Sen and Prince Ranariddh, issued a letter formally requesting that the UN help bring Khmer Rouge leaders to trial. Nonetheless, as Khmer Rouge defectors and repatriated so-called prisoners from Thailand gradually returned to Phnom Penh, they were met with mixed receptions. Complicated political alliances and strategic realities sent a number of high-ranking leaders into retirement in Pailin, a longtime Khmer Rouge stronghold. Only a few were actually imprisoned and a number of top Khmer Rouge leaders passed away without having to face any reprisal, including General Secretary and Brother Number One Pol Pot, Defense Minister Son Sen, and the notoriously cruel military leader Ta Mok. As the years passed, it seemed that nothing

would be done to hold those responsible accountable for their crimes.

In January 2001, the Cambodian National Assembly approved the ECCC law, which established the Extraordinary Chambers in the Courts of Cambodia (ECCC). A couple years of negotiations between the Cambodian government and the UN followed, during which the two sides debated how to coordinate such a tribunal. Contentious issues included the appointment process for judges and prosecutors, as well as the power the court would have over retribution and punishment. The UN was particularly concerned with maintaining fair standards of justice and due process. Terms were finally agreed upon in June 2003.

The Cambodian government had insisted that the trial be held in Cambodia with Cambodian judges and lawyers. Because of the country's poor legal system and the international nature of the crimes, international assistance was ultimately deemed necessary. Called a "hybrid tribunal," the ECCC was established as a mixed judicial body that blended national and international laws, features, and participation. Divided into national and international sides, the ECCC was to be funded by both international donors and the Cambodian government, and staffed by both local and international lawyers, judges, investigators, and administrators.

The court's limited mandate only enables it to try senior leaders for crimes committed in Cambodia between April 17, 1975, and January 6, 1979. Suspects can be tried for international crimes such as genocide, crimes against humanity, and war crimes, as well as crimes under Cambodian law such as murder, torture, or religious persecution. The maximum sentence is life in prison, as the death penalty is unconstitutional in Cambodia.

The ECCC has arrested and indicted five Khmer Rouge leaders—Kaing Guek Eav (aka Duch), the former chief of the notorious Tuol Sleng Prison; Nuon Chea, former deputy secretary; Khieu Samphan, chairman of Democratic Kampuchea State Presidium; Ieng Sary, Pol Pot's deputy prime minister and minister of foreign affairs; and Ieng Thirith, the former minister of social affairs.

The court began its pre-trial stages in November 2007. The Duch trial began in

March 2009 and was still under way in June 2009. The developments of the ECCC trials will certainly be interesting to watch over the coming years as the natures of the crimes are diverse, including a transgender Cambodian who was forced to marry a woman and consummate his relationship. The court also has been rocked by numerous corruption allegations. Assuming the court can overcome its fiscal troubles and find donors to provide the millions of dollars needed to keep the trials up and running, Cambodia is finally on the road toward justice. Further information about the trials can be found at *www.cambodiatribunal.org*.

Most proceedings are open to the public. You also can arrange for a tour of the court (*Extraordinary Chambers in the Courts of Cambodia, National Highway 4, Phnom Penh, tel 855(0)23-219-814, www.eccc.gov.kh*) on days when hearings are not in progress.

Documenting Khmer Rouge Atrocities

Since its inception in 1995, the Documentation Center of Cambodia (DC-Cam; *66 Sihanouk Blvd., tel 855(0)23-211-875, www.dccam.org*) has been the world's foremost research center and repository of documents and other sources regarding the Khmer Rouge. As an independent NGO, DC-Cam strives to record and preserve the history of the Khmer Rouge regime for future generations. It has also compiled and organized a great deal of information used as evidence in the Khmer Rouge tribunal.

For those interested in learning more about the Khmer Rouge, DC-Cam has an on-site public information room with archives and various media on the brutal regime. The organization also publishes a magazine, *Searching for the Truth,* which is written in both Khmer and English. It can be found online, at DC-Cam, and at other locations throughout Cambodia.

Choeung Ek Killing Field Memorial

🅰 63 A2

✉ Sangkat Choeung Ek, Khan Dangkor

☎ 855(0)-12-646-574

💲 $

features Tuol Sleng survivor Vann Nath's (b. 1946) paintings, which depict torture and other mistreatment experienced by prisoners. Now a renowned Khmer artist, Vann Nath used his artistic ability to survive in the prison by painting for many high-ranking officers.

While some might hope to avoid confronting such harrowing images on a vacation, a visit to Tuol Sleng is a must. One cannot experience or properly understand Cambodia and its people today without facing the most formative

event in the country's recent history. While it may seem possible to shut out thoughts of the Khmer Rouge for a more carefree vacation, the trauma and destruction they wrought cannot be ignored.

While not geographically close to the museum, many choose to go directly from Tuol Sleng to the **Choeung Ek Killing Field Memorial,** located 9 miles (14 km) southwest of Phnom Penh. This itinerary follows the thousands of Tuol Sleng prisoners who were commonly taken directly from the prison to this remote field, where they were killed and dumped in mass graves. Disoriented prisoners arrived in the night, blindfolded and bound, and were often bludgeoned to death in order to save bullets. The site that was once an orchard and Chinese cemetery is now one of the bloodiest symbols of Cambodia's past. Other such killing fields can be found throughout the country, but Choeung Ek is the most noteworthy. The pockmarked land around the memorial makes it clear just how many bodies were buried in the site's 129 mass graves. Various signs in Khmer and English describe the events that took place at each location. Piles of bones and decaying clothing can be found in small piles throughout the memorial. A large **memorial stupa** at the center of the site contains thousands of skulls found in the killing fields. It is estimated that 8,895 corpses were found on site. Local guides can be found at the site and nearby vendors sell books on the Khmer Rouge for those wanting to do further reading. The dusty 20- to 40-minute drive from the city is

The crowded stalls at Phnom Penh's Russian Market sell everything from pottery and clothes to meat and produce.

INSIDER TIP:

Pailin Jewelry, near the Russian Market at 124 Street 135 (behind the Diamond Hotel), is an excellent jewelry store with an impressive ruby selection.

—BRIAN MCNAMARA
National Geographic contributor

certainly worth making to pay your respects to the millions who lost their lives under the brutal regime.

Those in desperate need of an activity to lighten the mood after experiencing the tragic Tuol Sleng museum and the killing fields should head south from S-21 to the famous **Russian Market,** or Psar Toul Tom Pong. The market got its name from the heavy Russian presence at the market in the 1980s. While less architecturally interesting than other markets in the city, the Russian Market certainly has the best range of goods for tourists. Stalls upon stalls bear silks, carvings, paintings, handicrafts, and other curios. While the goods sold here might not be of the best quality, they make excellent, affordable souvenirs. A number of tailors can be found in the middle of the market. Stalls near the main entrance of the market sell Western clothes made in garment shops around Phnom Penh, sold here for a mere fraction of what they might cost back home. As the market caters mainly to tourists, vendors will generally double their prices. Learn how

to say *t'lai naa* (too expensive) in Khmer and bargain your heart out. Morning is the ideal time to visit, because the market really heats up under the afternoon sun.

Western Phnom Penh

Even though there certainly has never been an Olympic Games held within Cambodia, Khmers take great pride in their very own 1960s-era **Phnom Penh National Olympic Stadium,** located within the National Sports Complex. Sports fans should inquire if anything noteworthy is occurring, as the large arena often holds Khmer boxing and volleyball matches (Cambodia has one of the best disabled volleyball teams in the world). The grounds of the National Sports Complex also feature tennis courts, a large outdoor track, and fields for pickup games.

Just a short way from the stadium is **Olympic Market.** While less interesting to shop in than the Central and Russian Markets, it is the most bearable market with minimal crowds and better air circulation, making it less stifling than the others. The market has a great selection of fabrics on the second floor, divided into two sections: Cottons and synthetic fabrics are in one and traditional materials commonly used by Khmers for special occasions are in the other.

Those who can't get enough of exploring markets should also check out **Orussey Market.** Housed in a modern building, this market is known for its costume jewelry, brightly colored clothing, and toiletries. ∎

Russian Market
- Map p. 71
- Corner of St. 450 & St. 163

Phnom Penh National Olympic Stadium
- Map p. 71
- Corner of Sihanouk Blvd. & Monireth Blvd.
- 855(0)12-930-177
- $

Olympic Market
- Map p. 71
- Corner of St. 286 & St. 193

Orussey Market
- Map p. 71
- Corner of St. 182 & St. 141

Around Phnom Penh

The area surrounding Phnom Penh is quite diverse, incorporating attractions from three or even four different provinces. A day trip can combine, history, culture, wildlife, and even a little adventure, including either bicycle or motorcycle tours.

The temples at the Angkor Empire's former capital of Oudong

**Koh Daich &
Koh Okhna Tey**
🅼 63 A3

Nearby temples include the Funan-era temple of Phnom Da, the Angkor-era Phnom Chisor and Ta Phrom of Tonle Bati, the post-Ang-korian capital cities Longvek and Oudong, as well as a few modern marvels of religious devotion. Wildlife enthusiasts may enjoy visiting the Phnom Tamao Zoological Garden and Wildlife Rescue Center or bird-watching along the myriad of lakes and rice fields. Those interested in handicrafts may wish to visit Koh Daich, among other destinations. Khmer resorts and picnic sites offer respite between the sights a chance to meet the locals.

Mekong Island

For an easy, pleasant day trip from Phnom Penh, visit **Koh Daich** and **Koh Okhna Tey,** neighboring islands about 6 miles (10 km) to the northeast of the city, across the Tonle Sap and Mekong Rivers. Both are home to villagers involved in tra-ditional weaving. The charming, unhurried pace of these commu-nities is a refreshing change from the chaotic capital. Confusingly, both islands are referred to as Mekong Island, depending on whom you ask.

While both islands are covered with mazes of narrow dirt trails that pass wooden houses on stilts, Koh Daich is perhaps the nicer of the two. A lively picnic site lies on the northern tip of the 7.5-mile-long (12 km) island. During the dry season, **Kbal Koh**—a sandy beach—is exposed by the receding river. Islanders, Phnom Penh residents, and international travelers all come here to dine on barbecued chicken and fruits and vegetables, particularly bananas and corn, crops that supplement the islanders' other means of income—weaving.

Beginning your visit at the beach, you will invariably be shown a number of silk and cotton cloths and scarves by enthusiastic vendors. Many of them are young girls who will happily escort you back to their homes, almost every one of which contains at least one traditional wooden loom, to show you how the weaving process works. The village specializes in traditional weaving of silk and cotton cloth, including *phamuong*, silk fabric that you may use for tailoring clothes, or finished products, such as *krama* (traditional checkered scarves). If you arrive on the island in November you may be on hand to watch the local boat races that

INSIDER TIP:

Visitors who are interested in responsible travel should look for businesses displaying the Heritage Friendly Tourism logo: They have been selected as outstanding examples of corporate citizenship and they support local art, culture, and development.

—DOUGALD O'REILLY
Director, Heritage Watch

commence from two of the three pagodas on the island.

The islands are accessible only by boat, which you may hire from Phnom Penh near Street 136 (*$$$*). You also can drive a motorbike along National Highway 6 to the west bank of the Mekong and then take a ferry (*$*) across with your vehicle. The latter option allows you to explore the islands more freely. If you drive, begin by

Dump Dwellers

More than 500 of Cambodia's most impoverished citizens wait until garbage is picked through several times before they get to scavenge for food and recyclable materials. The residents of Stung Meanchey dump just southwest of the city literally live in a toxic-waste field. While a new medical incinerator is scheduled for construction, as recently as 2008 biomedical waste deposited at Stung Meanchey included blood and human remains. The efforts of a few dedicated individuals, however, offer occasional relief. Members of the Cambodia Charity Development Foundation (*www.ccdfkh.org*) take visitors and volunteers to a market to buy bread and fresh fruits and vegetables. Then they personally distribute food to exuberantly appreciative people—a truly heart-wrenching experience.

crossing the Japanese Friendship Bridge to Chrouy Chang Va Island. As you cross the bridge, take note of the corrugated rooftops along the riverside—a number of Muslim Cham people live a traditional fishing lifestyle here despite the development that is going on around them. After driving some distance past a number of large restaurants, keep your eyes open for small blue

Friday prayers at one of Phnom Penh's small mosques located along the Tonle Sap River.

signs indicating ferry crossings. If you feel you may have missed the first one, turn right toward the riverfront road and continue north until you reach the International School. You will see a ferry landing for cars and motorbikes there.

Phnom Oudong & Along National Highway 5

Traveling north from Phnom Penh, National Highway 5 quickly becomes a narrow isthmus flanked by water on both sides. To the east sit houses on stilts and the Tonle Sap, which

encroaches on the road in the rainy season. To the west, you'll see fish farms beside the road, and expansive rice fields meld into the ponds and lakes on the horizon, beyond which the peaks and stupas of Phnom Oudong become visible after almost half an hour of driving. Note several Cham mosques along the western, lake side of the road.

Twenty-three miles (37 km) from Phnom Penh, near the roadside village of Preak G'dam are several traditional silversmith villages. The easiest to access, **Kompong Luong,** is situated just past Preak G'dam, on a small road to your right, marked by a fading Cambodian Craft Corporation sign immediately before a soccer field—if you've reached the statue of the general on horseback, you've traveled too far. The manual techniques for casting, molding, and designing the silverworks are mostly traditional. The workers, who are typically families, spend their days working in the shade beside their houses. The cost of silver has forced increased use of copper alloy and silver plating, but the jewelry, cutlery, boxes, and bowls remain unique in design.

Phnom Oudong: Soon after leaving Kompong Luong, you will near Phnom Oudong ($). Oudong, which means "the victorious," functioned as the capital of post-Angkor Cambodia for nearly 250 years, from 1618—after the abandonment of Longvek—until 1866, when King Norodom (r.1859–1904) relocated the capital to Phnom

Penh. Longvek (aka Longva) is 3 miles (5 km) farther north of Phnom Oudong along National Highway 5, though no sights remain there.

More than 20 monarchs ruled from Oudong, including King Norodom and his father, Ang Duong (r. 1848–1859), who presided over the most prosperous period of post-Angkor Cambodia. Several interesting sights endure in and around the old capital of Oudong, which covered several mountains, particularly those atop the largest hill, also called Phnom Oudong (or Phnom Preah Reach Throap). Sadly, though, most historic structures, which once

numbered in the hundreds, were first ravaged by American bombs during the Vietnam War, and later by both the Vietnamese and Khmer Rouge, the latter of whom entrenched themselves atop the mountain for a number of bloody years.

As you approach Phnom Oudong, the road forks: The main entrance and the majority of both concessions and mendicants are to the left, while a quieter back entrance is to the right. Before arriving at the road to the rear entrance, you will see an imposing, gilded, modern *wat.* Just beyond and across from the temple, a short, steep road leads to the north entrance. If you've hired a

Kompong Luong
▲ 63 A3

Phnom Oudong
▲ 63 A3

EXPERIENCE: Bicycle Tours

Cambodia's topography, which features both expansive plains and rugged mountains, is ideal for both beginner and experienced bike riders. Leisurely cross-country tours are a great way to see the beauty of the countryside and hard-core mountain-bike adventures explore regions of the country that are only beginning to open up to tourists.

Grasshopper Adventures
Leading bike tours through 13 Asian nations, Grasshopper *(Thailand: 66(0)87 929 5208, USA: (818) 912-7101, www.grass hopperadventures.com)* features Cambodian journeys that range from quiet day rides around Phnom Penh to multiday Angkorian temple tours and weeks-long multi-country adventures. Some tours include trekking, boating, and photography in addition to biking to provide a well-rounded and entertaining historical and cultural experience

Pepy Ride
While this NGO's primary focus is education, Pepy *(No. 188, Salakanseng Village [National Highway 6 to the airport, near the ACLEDA/Western Union], Siem Reap, tel 855(0)12-474-150, www.pepyride.org)* combines sightseeing and fund-raising to create fun, beneficial rural bicycle tours. Riders pay for their tours, which include food and accommodations, as well as contribute $500 a week through a personal tax-free donation or via sponsorships that can be coordinated on the organization's website. One- and three-week rides visit the projects funded by the contributions. Visitors can see how their money is spent (and appreciated) and participate in volunteer activities, such as taking local kids to historical temples. Month-long rides—from Siem Reap through Phnom Penh to the coast across mostly flat, dirt roads—are conducted at the riders' own pace. Bikes are available from Pepy.

A smiling girl wears a *krama*, a traditional headscarf.

car, have your driver drop you here and pick you up later at the main entrance on the other side. If you came by motorbike or on a tour, the stairs from the main entrance lead directly to the Buddha Stupa, from which you may then follow the circuit along the ridge.

The *chedeys* (the Khmer word for "stupa") from the rear parking lot, as well as those along the 500-plus steps to the top of Phnom Preah Reach Throap (Hill of Royal Fortune), house the remains of royal family members. Here, the **Buddha Stupa** commands spectacular views of the countryside. Though its base lies lower than the neighboring stupas, its silver spire rises above them all. The stupa, which was commissioned in 2002 by King and Queen Norodom Sihanouk, contains Buddha relics, purportedly a tooth and bones.

The stupas continuing up and across the ridge house the remains of King Srei Soryapor (r.1603–1618) and either his queen or King Ang Duong, depending

on whom you ask. From here you can also see the stupas on the smaller ridge ahead of you and to the left. Continuing down an aging stone stairway, you will come to the Angkorian inspired stupa for King Monivong (r.1927–1941), decorated with intricate bas-relief and capped with four faces.

The remainder of the structures along the path down the hill sustained heavy damage or total destruction from years of war. Today, they honor various entities, including the *neak ta* (ancestral spirits) of a five-star general, Preah Ko (the sacred bull), and the Buddha. Toward the far end of the hill, on the site of a grand temple, **Vihear Preah Ath Roes,** a reconstructed Buddha and temple replace those that were blown up by the Khmer Rouge in 1977.

INSIDER TIP:

Buy yourself a *krama*, the traditional multi-purpose checkered scarf. It will keep you warm on chilly winter evenings, protect you from dust storms, and give you a fashionably local look.

—TREVOR RANGES
National Geographic author

Continuing down the stairs, you will soon arrive at the base of the hill. From here, a dirt road leads to the main entrance, where you will probably be accosted by people soliciting for the hammock-strewn restaurants located there. After your climb, it's a treat to swing in the shade while sipping from a fresh coconut, just as local families do. If you plan to picnic at the temples further down the road, order some take out here. Before departing, pay your respects at the **memorial tower** honoring victims of the Khmer Rouge.

Leaving Oudong, you can go back the way you came to spend a few hours exploring Koh Daich (see pp. 88–90) or continue north to see the floating villages around **Kompong Chhnang** (see pp. 180–181). Yet if you are interested in seeing a selection of distinctive temples, instead turn south on Route 51 for a two-hour detour (including a temple visit) that will reconnect to National Highway 5, from where you may head back toward Koh Daich if you have time.

Phnom Braset and Phnom Reap are on Route 130, a bumpy dirt road that leads east from Route 51, approximately 6 miles (10 km) from Oudong. Nearly 30 minutes down this road are the **Phnom Braset Mountains,** two small hills that feature several different styles of temple. The top of the first—and smaller—hill features Neang Kong Siim, a modern, Chinese-style temple, and Baksei Chaim Krong, purported to be an ancient stupa restored from ruins in the 1990s. The larger, northern hill features a fairly commonplace modern wat at its summit.

Visitors can park in the dirt lot (before the steep road flanked by *nagas* ascends to the modern temple). From here, follow the trail that leads to a reclining Buddha and

then down toward **Prasat Neang Krub Leakh** (Temple of the Ideal Girl). This 16th-century temple, though partially collapsed and carelessly patched with bricks, retains many of its original flowery reliefs and rests in a peaceful, shady clearing. Local legend describes a secret tunnel leading from the temple to distant Phnom Oudong, once accessible by the Oudong kings who possessed magic to complete the underground journey. A peek inside the cramped temple interior reveals several female statues and a tunnel beyond.

Several minutes from Phnom Braset lies **Phnom Reap,** a series of extravagant functioning

Phnom Braset & Prasat Neang Krub Leakh

🗺 63 A3

💲 $

Phnom Reap

🗺 63 A3

💲 $

Krama

The most distinctive aspect of Khmer dress may be the krama, a checkered scarf with striped ends made from colored cloth. The krama has been a focal point of Khmer attire since the first-century reign of Preah Bath Hun Tean. With a multitude of uses, it is worn as a sarong or scarf, or for protection from the elements (to protect the skin from the sun or the face from dust and wind). The krama can be worn around the head and even around the feet. Women tie them across their shoulders to carry their babies and they can also be used as makeshift sacks. The most famous krama are made in Takeo and Kompong Cham Provinces.

EXPERIENCE: Photography Tours

With 20 years of experience as a professional photographer, British-born Nathan Horton ought to be able to share a thing or two about how to snap a quality photo. Horton's photography tours, however, go much further than providing simple technical advice. They incorporate aesthetics, including visiting sights under optimal lighting conditions, and ethics, particularly how to respectfully approach human subjects to make them comfortable and elicit authentic poses. His tours attempt to avoid the tourist hordes and lead visitors beyond mere sightseeing or photo shooting. Instead, he aims to help his students gain an appreciation of Cambodian culture and history.

Based in Phnom Penh at So Shoot Me Studio (*1st Floor, 126 St. 136, tel 855(0)92-526-706, www.nathanhortonphotography .com*), Horton offers day trips to nearby destinations, such as Kompong Chhnang (see pp. 180–181) and Oudong (see pp. 190–191). He also offers personally designed private tours throughout the entire country.

Buddhist temples in an unusual rural location. They are built in the classic Angkor style and their ornate exterior bas-reliefs of red concrete depict scenes of the Buddha's life and Hindu mythology.

The two entrances to the temple grounds are several hundred yards apart and the compounds are not connected from the interior. Each entry is framed by a gate topped with Bayon faces and covered in bas-reliefs. The first entrance leads to an impressive reproduction of Angkor Wat, though its interior is nearly empty and undecorated, save a small shrine on one end and statues lining one wall. Slightly more interesting is the neighboring wat, where a fading kaleidoscope of colorful statues and bas-reliefs includes a pair of dancing Hanuman images that flank the entrance. A smiling Buddha sits beneath a bas-relief bodhi tree, whose green leaves spread up and across the ceiling, painted to resemble blue sky.

Phnom Reap's second entrance includes an Angkor Thom–style causeway. It leads to the larger, newer compound that contains four completed Angkor-style temples and a rather large *baray* (an artificial body of water). Several temples are under construction.

South of Phnom Penh: Takeo Province

Takeo city is about 50 miles (80 km) south of Phnom Penh on National Highway 2. Along the way you will pass through bustling Phnom Penh suburbs that quickly give way to expansive rice fields and rural roadside communities where children, cows, and chickens skirt the shoulder of the dusty road. Along the road to Takeo, there are a number of sites, specifically of historical and archaeological interest. They can all be visited in a day, provided that one gets an early start; however, depending on their interests, visitors can be selective and experience a more leisurely day.

The most remote sites, the town of **Angkor Borei** and nearby **Phnom Da** are best visited in the morning; consequently, beginning there and working one's way back toward Phnom Penh is the most reasonable way to visit the attractions. Both Angkor Borei and the temples around Phnom Da are sites of the earliest Khmer civilization in Cambodia. Human remains excavated in the area indicate that the area was inhabited as early as the second century B.C. and evidence points to the area as having been the center of the Funan empire. What little is known of the kingdom of Funan has been extrapolated from Chinese records written during the era (ca first to seventh centuries A.D.). While debate continues as to whether Funan was a unified kingdom or a federation of smaller, allied rulers, it appears that ancient Angkor Borei was an important area, perhaps the capital, but certainly an area of great religious significance.

The bulk of existing artistic and archaeological evidence found in the region comes from the sixth and seventh centuries, around the estimated time of the "conquest" of Funan by neighboring Chenla. Included in these treasures are a number of Buddhist and Hindu statuary that indicate a prosperous society with well-developed artistic talent, and stone inscriptions, including the earliest known use of the Khmer language.

The style of art developed during this era is named for the small hill known as Phnom Da, where several important temples are located. The finest examples of Phnom Da–style sculpture are on display at the National Museum in Phnom Penh (see p. 72), though a larger number of beautiful pieces in excellent condition are located at a small **museum** (*$*) in Angkor Borei. These works are prized as some of the most impressive ever created in Cambodia.

The **temple** atop Phnom Da is an 11th-century *prasat* (tower) of sandstone and brick, built in all likelihood on the site of an earlier Funan-era temple constructed by King Rudravarman (*r.*514–550), the last of the Funanese kings. The temple honored Shiva and its *yonis*—pedestals representing the female component of the fertility symbol—once housed *lingas* (see p. 48). One of these lingas is at the

Takeo

🗺 63 A2

Phnom Da

🗺 63 B2

💲 $

Excellent examples of pre-Angkorian Phnom Da sculpture are on display in Phnom Penh's National Musuem (see p. 72).

A Cambodian female tiger, Kmi, takes a rest in the Phnom Tamao Wildlife Rescue Center.

Angkor Borei museum. Little else of interest remains, as the majority of bas-reliefs fell from the prasat and are displayed at the museum.

Roughly 500 yards (457 m) southwest lies the **Ashram Maha Rosei,** which predates the existing one atop Phnom Da, built in the seventh or eighth centuries. The design of the tiny temple, which is surprisingly intact, is strikingly different from those of the Angkorian-era, as are the statues discovered there. This is both indicative of the non-Khmer influence of the region's early rulers as well as the continuity of art and architecture that followed the relocation of power from Funanese Angkor Borei to Chenla's Sambor Prei Kuk.

Phnom Da lies about 3 miles (5 km) southeast of Angkor Borei and 3 miles (5 km) northwest of the Vietnamese border. The entire area is connected via both ancient and modern canals that crisscross the area's rice fields and extend into Vietnam, where Oc Eo—the primary port of Funan—was once located. Visitors to both sights must first drive to the city of **Takeo,** where small speedboats can be hired (*$$$$$*) for the 30-minute trip along the canals. The ride is more enjoyable in the rainy season, when the waters surpass the banks of the canal and submerge the surrounding rice fields, effectively making Phnom Da an island. An unmarked dirt road off National Highway 2 leads to Angkor Borei and passes Prasat Neang Khmau and Phnom Chisor along the way, but it should only be traveled by those who are driving sturdy 4WD vehicles or off-road motorcycles and have a guide with them.

While Phnom Da temple itself isn't much of an attraction other than for its historical significance, Ashram Maha Rosei is unique. Combined with the boat ride, which passes through beautiful scenery, and a visit to charming Angkor Borei, where the museum is located, it makes a pleasant two-hour excursion from Takeo.

About 15 miles (24 km) from Takeo, north toward Phnom Penh, is the turnoff to the bumpy dirt road that heads back toward Angkor Borei. A short, easy ride down this road will lead to **Phnom Chisor** *($)*. Though two stairways lead up to the temple, the most accessible entrance is from the south staircase. It commences beside a local school, where friendly children will eagerly show off their rudimentary English skills, particularly in regard to the 400-plus steps you must climb to reach the temple grounds.

At the top of the stairs there are a number of newer temple structures before you reach the ancient temple itself. From a small wat, a Buddha image gazes to the east, toward the temple's main entrance gate in the distance. The large linga to the west is visible from the bottom of the staircase beside the Buddha's Bath. Beyond the reclining Buddha lies the remains of Suryaparvata (Mountain of the Sun God), built in the late 10th to early 11th century. It was probably completed around 1015, a date mentioned in Sanskrit inscriptions found at the temple, which was just after the crowning of the Buddhist king Suryavarman I (r. 1003–ca 1049).

Phnom Chisor

🗺 63 A2

Lions, Tigers, & Bears

The Phnom Tamao Zoological Garden and Wildlife Rescue Center (see p. 98) is far from your average zoo. Situated inside more than 5,000 acres (2,025 ha) of protected forest, it provides refuge for indigenous animals that have been victims of the illegal wildlife trade. The center prepares animals for release into the wild or provides lifelong care for those that cannot be released. More than 1,200 species currently reside at Phnom Tamao, including elephants, gibbons, lions, sun bears, and Indochinese tigers.

Visiting the animal rehabilitation center is surprisingly enjoyable and upbeat. Several NGOs provide funding and support for the center, helping to ensure that high standards of care are met.

Located 25 miles (40 km) from Phnom Penh, the wildlife center is best visited via *tuk-tuk*. For those making the journey on their own, head south on Norodom Boulevard until it becomes National Highway 2 and stay on it through Takmao, heading in the direction of the city of Takeo. Turn right onto a dirt road marked with a sign for the park and continue several miles down this road to the center *(7:30 a.m.–5 p.m.)*.

Foreign visitors are asked to pay an admission fee *($$)* to help provide care for the park's fauna. Local guides show visitors around the large park, helpfully searching out the best animals. Be sure to give them a few dollars in return for their assistance.

Phnom Tamao Zoological Garden and Wildlife Rescue Center

🅰 63 A2

As with most Hindu-style temples of the day, the temple's entrance faces the east. Down the precipitous 405-step eastern staircase lie the ancillary temples of Sen Chhmo and Sen Ro Vang, the distant entrance gate to the grounds, and Tonle Oum—a square baray—just beyond. The temple is in major disrepair, having been ravaged by years of 20th-century warfare. The bodhi tree just north of the entrance has fared better: It's reportedly 143 years old. Nonetheless, both the temple and the spectacular view are impressive.

INSIDER TIP:

In Takeo Province, visit Phnom Chisor— an 11th-century hilltop temple that offers splendid views of the Mekong Delta—and the fine 12th-century ruins of Ta Prohm at Tonle Bati.

—MIRIAM STARK
National Geographic field researcher

As you climb the stairs to the temple, note the relief of Hanuman riding an elephant and the curling naga above the door. Within the temple grounds, two libraries flank a small shrine to Vishnu and the large central sanctuary tower. One set of Sanskrit etchings survives in the western doorway of the library to the right; a bas-relief adorns the eastern facing side of the library to the left.

The main shrine is home to a pair of attendants who have surprisingly comfortable and colorful beds set up beneath the corrugated roof. They will assist you with paying your respects to the Buddha, Vishnu, and Shiva, all of whom are represented in the main chamber. Shiva is shown by a stone linga rubbed glossy by devotees' hands.

A short drive back from the junction with National Highway 2 is the quiet tenth-century **Prasat Neang Khmau**, or Temple of the Black Lady—or Virgin ($). As it sits just beside the road, it's worth a short stop. The temple is named after a "black lady" said to have founded the site after being banished from her kingdom for promiscuity—or conversely a virgin imprisoned here to prevent such behavior. Two of at least three original brick prasats survive beside a sandy courtyard, flanked by a school and an active pagoda. A statue of the black lady stands within a small pagoda beside the prasats but is often locked. Some surviving lintels and inscriptions remain in good condition.

Heading back toward Phnom Penh, animal enthusiasts may enjoy the **Phnom Tamao Zoological Garden and Wildlife Rescue Center** (see sidebar p. 97), home to more than 1,200 indigenous species. Those looking for something more relaxing can continue on to **Tonle Bati** ($), a popular weekend hangout for lovers and families who rent thatched-roof platforms along the lake's edge and dine on local delicacies. A restaurant with proper tables allows visitors to have a drink in the shade, enjoy the breeze from the water, and take in the view of the modern wat on the far shore.

Included in the admission to the lake is access to the late 12th- to early 13th-century temples of **Ta Prohm** and **Yeay Peau.** Commissioned by Jayavarman VII of Angkor Thom and Bayon fame, this pair of well maintained temples has male and female orientations. The temples were originally dedicated to honor both Buddha and Hindu gods, and Ta Prohm today houses a number of headless Buddha images from the 13th century as well as several lingas. Ta Phrom, the larger of the two, is still quite charming, with wildflowers growing in the west courtyard beyond the inner enclosure, which houses a large central tower flanked by laterite libraries and galleries, typical of the style of the day. The area itself has been continuously inhabited since the pre-Angkorian days of the Funan era—an ancient inscription recovered here indicated that there may have even been a Funan-era temple at this site. The temples themselves are well maintained; signs of development and renovation date to the 16th century. A number of children roam the grounds, hoping to sell incense and flowers to visitors. Elderly Khmer also reside within the temple grounds. They all request handouts from tourists.

Prey Veng, Svay Rieng, & the Vietnamese Border

Other than people with a particular interest in history or those heading overland to Vietnam, tourists rarely visit the provinces to the southeast of Phnom Penh, which contain far fewer attractions than most parts of rural Cambodia. Most visitors simply pass through both Prey Veng and Svay Rieng on their way to Ho Chi Minh City, while some make the trip to see historic Ba Phnom, of which little of interest remains to be visited.

Prey Veng, which borders Phnom Penh to the east, is a predominantly agrarian province, with beautiful countryside and

Prey Veng
🅼 63 B2

Millions of rural Cambodians work the rice fields such as these wet-rice harvesters.

People from Prey Veng Province prepare fish to be made as *prahok* **(fermented fish paste) at Chrang Chambres village.**

often a bit of a wait to cross, it can also be a charming experience, as you get to appreciate a bit of life along the Mekong, rather than speeding over it.

Other than off-the-beaten-path weaving villages and remote temple sites, all of which can be quite challenging to locate, the primary destinations in Prey Veng Province are the town of Prey Veng and Ba Phnom. **Prey Veng town** lies roughly 20 miles (32 km) north of National Highway 1 along Route 11. Prey Veng may be Cambodia's least developed provincial capital, a string of dirt roads around a town center with a mini–Independence Monument. But the town is known for its regular festivals and gatherings, a testament to its tight-knit community. Enjoy a serene walk along the riverside, which resembles a smaller version of Phnom Penh's riverside and offers a breezy dock sporting Khmer art, a popular student hangout.

Ba Phnom *($)* was one of the earliest and most important religious sites in Cambodia. Referred to as the "cradle of Khmer civilization," it was recognized as such by Jayavarman II (*r.*802–850), founder of Angkor, who conducted a religious ceremony at the site as part of his claim to the throne of all Cambodia. Such a ceremony indicates both the importance of the site as a spiritual center and the necessity of Cambodian kings to link their authority to that of previous rulers of the land. Indeed, kings of Chenla as well as the rulers of Angkor following Jayavarman II

welcoming Khmer and Vietnamese populations. One interesting aspect of the trip through Prey Veng is the ferry crossing at Neak Luong. Despite the popularity—and economic necessity—of National Highway 1 for travel between Cambodia and Vietnam, there is still no bridge across the Mekong here. While this lack can be seen as an inconvenience since there is

INSIDER TIP:

Taking a bus into Vietnam is a common, economical mode of transport, though schedules (and border regulations) change whimsically. For updates, check *www .canbypublications.com/ cambodia/buses.htm.*

—TREVOR RANGES
National Geographic author

made the journey to Ba Phnom to participate in the rituals.

Ceremonies held at Ba Phnom often included both animal and human blood sacrifice, the latter of which was conducted until the second half of the 19th century (see sidebar this page). Today the hill contains a number of colorful concrete temples and the ruins of Preah Vihear Chann, an 11th-century temple that rests at the base of the hill. It may hold little of particular interest to average visitors, though, particularly those who have already been to the grand temples around Angkor or even to Phnom Chisor.

East of Ba Phnom is the province and its capital city of the same name, Svay Rieng, one of the poorest areas in all Cambodia. There is little reason to stop along the way, though the countryside, rife with farms of all sorts, offers beautiful, albeit repetitious scenery. The town itself is quite populous, having benefited from growing trade between Cambodia and

Vietnam, whose border is a mere 25 miles (40 km) away. Still, it's a far cry from Phnom Penh, and many travelers enjoy visiting the tranquil **town of Svay Rieng,** where they are greeted more often with smiles than with goods for sale or *tuk-tuk* rides.

Few man-made attractions dot the border, which boasts a panorama of lush green mountains. Cultivating an identity separate from Cambodian culture, the local Khmer Krom population—a minority group in Vietnam—speak in Vietnamese-Cambodian dialects and warmly offer cheap, quality Vietnamese food to visitors passing through. The area remains somewhat inaccessible, however. Guards will request that visitors who want a Cambodian visa at this checkpoint bring photocopies of their passports with them from town *(15 min. away).* ■

Svay Rieng
 63 C2

Blood Sacrifice

The temples at Ba Phnom date from the earliest pre-Angkorian kingdom of Funan and were long after considered places of great spiritual significance. Ceremonies continued to be conducted at the temples by the most powerful Angkorian kings. Ritual blood sacrifices of buffalo were made in honor of the goddess Durga, an incarnation of the wife of Shiva, who slew the buffalo-demon Mahisa.

As recently as the late 19th century, however, human sacrifices were still practiced in religious ceremonies at Ba Phnom. Firsthand accounts detail the decapitation of a slave or criminal, after which devotees would examine the resulting gush of blood, which was thought to foretell the rainfall pattern for the upcoming season.

Boutiques, cafés, and neocolonial luxury in the shadow of magnificent ancient temples

Siem Reap & Tonle Sap

Street vendor selling bananas at Chong Khneas village, Tonle Sap Lake

Siem Reap & Tonle Sap

Siem Reap town lies roughly at the center of the greater Angkor area, 4 miles (6 km) south of Angkor Wat, and 8 miles (13 km) west of the area's first capital at Roluos. The city has grown from a small village in the late 19th century, when European explorers "discovered" the temples, to a rapidly developing tourist hot spot.

Since the turn of the 21st century, the city has exploded with new hotels and guesthouses, restaurants and bars, shops and massage parlors. Yet it retains a lot of charm, from the Royal Crusade for Independence Garden (or Royal Independence Garden) and the Siem Reap River to French colonial architecture and Buddhist monasteries. Most visitors stay about three days to explore the temples of Angkor, visit a floating village on Tonle Sap Lake, and perhaps check out such cultural attractions as a traditional *apsara* dance performance or silk-weaving village.

A number of NGOs and nonprofit organizations are working with disadvantaged Cambodians in the area. Through them, visitors can educate themselves, purchase goods, contribute to a worthy cause, or participate as volunteers. Finally, shoppers will enjoy the local markets, boutiques, and night market, which sells handicrafts, silks, and all sorts of other curios.

Most of Siem Reap's attractions can be discovered easily by touring on foot or bicycle (bikes are available at many guesthouses and hotels). Don't forget a map if you choose to tour on your own. As most of the town's streets don't have names, however, remember that local *tuk-tuk* drivers generally know where everything in and around town is located and charge fairly standard rates. In central Siem Reap, tuk-tuk trips cost a flat $1 fee.

Outside of town, along National Highway 6, attractions include a weapons graveyard that was converted into a war museum; a ceramics workshop and silk-weaving village that are helping preserve traditional Khmer arts; a stable where you can ride horses; and two 18-hole golf courses.

North of Siem Reap, several sites can be combined into a very full day of sightseeing if you get an early start. The mountaintop temple of Phnom Bok, the exquisitely beautiful temple of Banteay Srei, and the nearby river carvings of Kbal Spean all are technically part of the Angkor Archaeological Park. Yet these sights can be visited along with the Angkor Centre for Conservation of Biodiversity (see p. 163), and Cambodia Landmine Museum and Relief Facility (see p. 163). Although the more remote ruins of Beng Mealea temple

NOT TO BE MISSED:

Relaxing on Pub Street   **107**

A "foot massage" at Dr. Fish in the Angkor Night Market   **107**

Taking in Cambodia's history and culture at the Angkor National Museum   **108–109**

Visiting the Preah Ang Chek–Preah Ang Chorm Shrine   **108, 110**

A "Dr. Beatocello" performance   **109**

A day trip to nearby Buddhist monasteries, such as Wat Bo and Wat Preah An Kau Sai   **109, 112**

Attending a Buddhist chat at Singing Tree Café   **112**

Learning about traditional handicrafts at Artisans d'Angkor   **116–117**

Exploring a floating village or flooded forest, or both   **122**

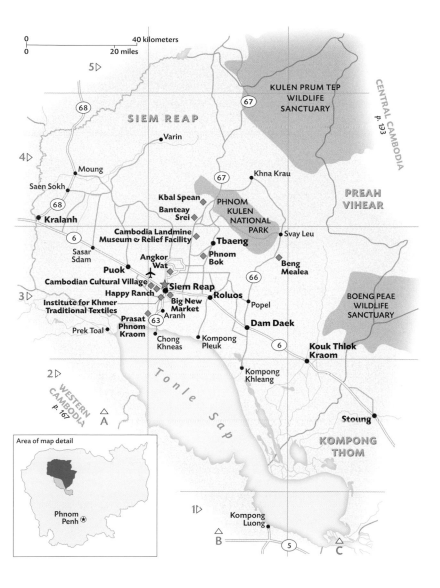

CENTRAL CAMBODIA p. 193

WESTERN CAMBODIA p. 167

(and Koh Ker) require their own day trip, a new road has made access to them easier than ever (see Around Angkor Drive, pp. 160–163).

The city is also a great base for exploring Tonle Sap Lake, which features villages on stilts and floating villages. It's also home to one of the nation's most important bird sanctuaries, Prek Toal (see p. 123). These activities can be arranged through most guesthouses and hotels, though it's best to find a tour that visits less touristed sites or travels at nonpeak hours.

Ongoing road development and the deregulation of the airport will allow greater access to Siem Reap. Considering all the attractions found here, it seems quite likely that the average visit to the city will grow longer. ∎

Siem Reap Town

Most Cambodian cities are centered around a market. While Siem Reap is slowly turning into an urban sprawl, the triangular downtown endures between the Old Market (Psar Chas) located on Pokambor Avenue along the Siem Reap River, and the Central Market (Psar Kandal), situated a number of blocks north. The Old Market has gradually diversified from its original village market function and has increased its stock of tourist-oriented goods during recent decades.

A narrow alley lined with boutiques and restaurants in downtown Siem Reap

Siem Reap

🅰 105 B3

Tourism Offices

✉ Across from Raffles Grand Hotel d'Angkor; and

✉ Near Old Market on St. No. 10

☎ 855-(0)92-631-600

Though the **Old Market** (Psar Chas) still contains a great variety of handicrafts and souvenirs of Cambodian origin, such as silk products, silver betel nut containers, and stone and wood carvings, it also sells a large volume of imported products from China, Laos, Myanmar, Thailand, and Vietnam. While there are some bargains to be found here, for quality authentic Cambodian handicrafts, it's best to try smaller boutiques or the Artisans d'Angkor (see pp. 116–117).

Running northwest from the Old Market to the Central Market, Hospital Street and Sivatha Boulevard frame the busiest portion of the downtown area for about four blocks. Nearly all of the businesses in this area cater to tourists: open-air restaurants, boutiques, massage parlors, and Internet cafés are the most popular establishments, the majority of which are housed in colorfully renovated French colonial buildings. Most banks, currency changers, and pharmacies also are located here.

Pub Street lies in the center of this tourist district. The 100-yard-long (91 m) street has a crowded collection of restaurants and boutiques. It also contains a handful of late-night party venues, several of which date back to the late 1990s, which marked the beginning of the town's tourist development. Two small alleys just south and north of Pub Street have respectively developed into **"Restaurant Alley,"** with some of the best eateries in town, and **"Lounge Avenue,"** with chilled-out expat venues.

Less than 100 yards (91 m) northeast of the Old Market, along the banks of the Siem Reap River, is one of the town's many Buddhist monasteries, **Wat Preah Prohm Rath.** While the temple was founded in 1915 and the primary pagoda constructed in 1945, a 2008 renovation literally changed the face of the principal *vihara.* Now surrounded by a tall laterite wall, the interior enclosure around the temple features 44 colorfully painted panels depicting the life of the Buddha, a large seated image of whom is positioned "calling the Earth to witness" within the temple itself.

The western side of the downtown area, beyond Sivatha Boulevard, has a pair of interesting markets: the **Noon-Night Market** and the **Angkor Night Market.** Both are located down the same east-west oriented alleyway: the newer Noon-Night Market is situated just east of its counterpart

and sells virtually the same souvenirs, though, as you might guess, it opens at noon. There is a fine restaurant in the back of the market if you need to grab a bite.

INSIDER TIP:

Looking for inexpensive and light art? The Old Market sells parchments bearing the impressions of Angkor statues. They cost about $20 but look like they belong in an antiquity museum.

—ALAINA APPLEMAN
National Geographic contributor

Beyond this smaller market, the Angkor Night Market is a thatch-roofed "village" selling handmade toys, rice-paper products, lamps, paintings, jewelry, wood and stone carvings, bags, clothes, and other curios. In addition to shops, the charming market features handicrafts workshops, a jungle-garden Island Bar, and a curious massage parlor called **Dr. Fish,** where small fish will nibble the dead skin off your feet. Music at the market entrance is performed by a band of land-mine victims. To learn more about their plight, watch the documentary about land mines shown at the market's **movie theater** toward the back. Here, you'll also find regular screenings of films about the Khmer Rouge and a 3-D film about commercial snake hunting.

Old Market
- Map p. 111
- Downtown intersection of Hospital St. & Pokambor Ave. along Siem Reap River

Wat Preah Prohm Rath
- Map p. 111
- Less than 100 yards (91 m) N of Old Market, along Pokambor Ave. (road that parallels Siem Reap River)
- $

Noon-Night Market
- Map p. 111
- 2 blocks SW of Pub St. & 1 block W of Sivatha Blvd. on E-W alleyway before Night Market

Angkor Night Market
- Map p. 111
- 2 blocks SW of Pub St. & 1 block W of Sivatha Blvd. on E-W alleyway immediately after Noon-Night Market

Central Market

⬛ Map p. 111

✉ Corner of Achamean St. & Sivatha Blvd.

Royal Independence Gardens

⬛ Map p. 111

✉ Corner of Pokambor Ave. & National Highway 6

💲 $

Angkor National Museum

⬛ Map p. 111

✉ 968 Charles de Gaulle St.

☎ 855(0)63-966-601

💲 $$$

www.angkornational museum.com

The **Central Market,** Psar Kandal, is at the corner of Achamean Street and Sivatha Boulevard, toward Siem Reap's geographic center. The domed, corrugated roof houses stalls selling clothes, jewelry, handicrafts, books, and watches, but it may be the least interesting of the town's markets.

The northern half of town is centered around the **Royal Independence Gardens,** located on the corners of Pokambor Avenue and National Highway 6, just west of the Stone Bridge. The gardens, given their name because the king's Royal Residence lies just south of the park, are actually owned and maintained by the Raffles Grand Hotel d'Angkor, located just to the north. Many of the city's finest hotels are situated around or near the gardens.

On the park's south side are two important local shrines. At the **Preah Ang Chek–Preah Ang Chorm Shrine,** devotees line up to rub enchanted waters on the outstretched palms of a pair of Buddha images (Ang Chorm is the smaller of the two). Outside the shrine, monks chant and offer blessings while a traditional Khmer band plays exceptionally melodious music. The atmosphere is more festive than reverent, however, particularly when a wedding party is present. Just west, on an island in the center of National Highway 6, is the **Ya-Tep Shrine,** which contains the relic of a powerful *neak ta* (ancestral spirit) thought to provide protection to Siem Reap.

Northeast of the Royal Gardens along Pokambor Avenue, which eventually leads to the main entrance to the temples of Angkor, the somewhat helpful **Siem Reap Tourism Office** is located catty-corner from the park's northeast. About 100 yards (91 m) farther northeast is the **Angkor National Museum.** The museum provides descriptions of the country's historical eras and the artistic styles that developed

---

EXPERIENCE: Creating Traditional Khmer Ceramics & Bronzes

The National Center for Khmer Ceramics Revival *(National Highway 6, toward the airport, 3.5 miles (2 km) past the Cambodian Cultural Village, tel 855(0)63-761-519, www. khmerceramics.com)* is an auspicious project with humble origins. The small center outside Siem Reap is attempting to re-create these classical Angkorian arts using traditional techniques. Clay from nearby Banteay Srei is thrown using a kick wheel, fired in a reproduction of an Khmer antique kiln, and then glazed using a combination of wood ash, laterite,

sandstone, and clay. In addition to working with archaeologists who have unearthed artifacts related to the craft, the center offers ceramics workshops lasting from one hour to three weeks; visitors can create their own handcrafted pieces, the proceeds from which go to providing young Khmers from rural areas with the skills to earn greater income.

In an incipient bronze-casting project elderly artisans will train low-education Khmers in their skills to prevent this traditional art from dying out.

over time, and then presents quality examples from various temples in a thoughtful and well-organized manner. The Angkor Wat–inspired Gallery of a Thousand Buddhas is impressive, and while the signage here contains occasional lapses in historical accuracy, the information will greatly enhance an appreciation of the nearby temples.

Northeast of the Angkor museum, on the road to Angkor Park, is **Jayavarman VII Children's Hospital.** This is one of several successful efforts organized by Dr. Beat Richner, who has been ameliorating the suffering of impoverished Cambodian children since 1975. These hospitals are funded primarily by private donation via the doctor's classical "Beatocello" (Beat + cello) concerts *(tel 855(0)63-964-803, www.beatocello.com).*

Around ten bridges cross the Siem Reap River from the generally more commercial west side of town to the quieter, less developed east side. Once home to backpacker-oriented guesthouses, the side streets between the Siem Reap River and Wat Bo Road have seen the gradual development of several boutique hotels and restaurants, particularly those with a charity focus. Reasonably priced rooms remain available in the area, however. Eastern Siem Reap is still greatly populated by local residents, particularly along the riverbanks to the north of town, where a number of Buddhist monasteries are located.

From the Old Market Bridge, located beside the Old Market at the southeastern tip of town,

Locals having breakfast at the Vietnamese Market, also known as the Old Market

it's a short walk or drive to **Wat Damnak.** The *wat* is an active site of Buddhist scholarship and home to the **Center for Khmer Studies,** which has a research library of more than 5,000 scholarly materials related to Khmer and Southeast Asian studies. The temple is also the headquarters of the Life & Hope Association, an NGO that assists orphans, vulnerable children, and disadvantaged people.

Farther northeast, where Wat Bo Road intersects with Achamean Street, cross Wat Bo Bridge to find **Wat Bo,** one of the city's oldest, most venerated temples. The main *vihara* was constructed in the 18th century and features elaborate 19th-century murals. Regularly scheduled meditation lessons

(continued on p. 112)

Wat Damnak

Map p. 111
Salakamreuk Commune by Old Market Bridge
855(0)63 761 810
$

www.watdamnak.org

Wat Bo
Map p. 111
Over Wat Bo Bridge to E

$

Siem Reap Bike Ride

Experiencing temple fatigue? Perhaps a leisurely day exploring the sights in Siem Reap will adequately change the pace. The town is small enough to explore on foot, though some guesthouses and hotels offer bicycles that will make exploring a bit more enjoyable. Just be aware of one-way roads and careless Cambodian drivers!

Start at the **Old Market (Psar Chas) ❶** (see pp. 106–107; *corner of Hospital St. & Pokambor Ave.*), where you can browse for handicrafts while practicing your haggling skills. Note the architecture of the buildings surrounding the market in the riverfront district; many date back a century to the French colonial period.

Follow the Siem Reap River northeast to Wat Bo Bridge, the third one you will pass, including the Old Market Bridge across from the market. *(On a bike you may feel safer crossing the road at the second bridge, to avoid riding the wrong way down a one-way street.)* Follow the road across the bridge to **Wat Bo ❷** (see pp. 109 & 112; *2 blocks E of Wat Bo Bridge, 1 block beyond Wat Bo Rd., $*) and step into the main *vihara* to look at the beautiful murals painted within. If it's locked, ask one of the friendly, helpful monks to let you in.

Return to the river and turn right along the east bank—a grassy park. Continue north about a mile (1.6 km) and take the first right after the second bridge; about two blocks east you will find **Angkor Wat in Miniature ❸** (see p. 112; *2 blocks S & about 1 block E of Wat Po Lanka, $*).

Back at the riverside, head northeast on the east bank through the villages that are some of the few vestiges of authentic Cambodian life left here. The road heading east from the next bridge north leads to **Wat Preah An Kau Sai ❹** (see p. 112; *E bank of Siem Reap River, NE Siem Reap, $*). Beyond the early 20th-century Buddhist monastery are the remains of two Angkor-era towers. Behind them is the **House of Peace,** which aids orphaned children.

Directly across the river from the temple is the **Banteay Srei Fine Arts stone and wood carving workshop** that makes custom

NOT TO BE MISSED:

Old Market (Psar Chas) • Wat Bo • Wat Preah An Kau Sai • Angkor National Museum

sculptures for clients. Continue northwest to the main road, where almost immediately to your left you will see the **Angkor National Museum ❺** (see pp. 108–109; *968 Charles de Gaulle St., 855(0)63-966-601, $$$*). The museum houses an impressive display of artifacts from nearby temples and its air-conditioning provides a respite from the midday heat.

Heading south from the museum on Charles de Gaulle Street leads you to the Siem Reap Tourism Office and the Royal Independence Gardens. If you are so inclined, indulge in lunch or a drink at the **Raffles Grand Hotel d'Angkor ❻** (*1 Charles de Gaulle St., tel 855(0)63-963-888, $*), the oldest hotel in town. Crossing in front of the hotel, take a stroll through the **Royal Independence Gardens,** (see p. 108) which lie between the Grand Hotel and the Royal Residence of the Cambodian King. On the south side of the park, alongside National Highway 6, you will find a pair of religious shrines. The one on the park side is the **Preah Ang Chek–Preah Ang Chorm Shrine ❼** (see p. 108; *National Highway 6 & Royal Independence Gardens, $*), where devotees pay homage to a pair of Buddha images. On an island in the middle of the road, the smaller **Ya-Tep Shrine** honors a *neak ta*, or ancestral spirit, which is believed to provide protection for the town.

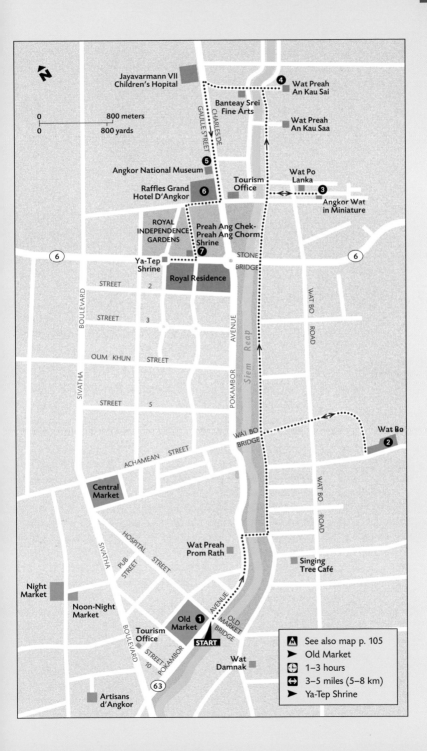

Jayavarmann VII Children's Hopital

Banteay Srei Fine Arts

4 Wat Preah An Kau Sai

Wat Preah An Kau Saa

GAULLE STREET
CHARLES DE

800 meters
800 yards

Angkor National Museum **5**

Wat Po Lanka

Raffles Grand Hotel D'Angkor **6**

Tourism Office

3 ↔

Angkor Wat in Miniature

ROYAL INDEPENDENCE GARDENS

Preah Ang Chek-Preah Ang Chorm Shrine **7**

Ya-Tep Shrine

STONE BRIDGE

6

Royal Residence

STREET 2

STREET 3

WAT BO ROAD

BOULEVARD

OUM KHUN STREET

AVENUE POKAMBOR

Siem Reap

STREET 5

SIVATHA

WAT BO BRIDGE

↔

Wat Bo **2**

ACHAMEAN STREET

WAT BO ROAD

Central Market

HOSPITAL STREET

Wat Preah Prom Rath

Singing Tree Café

Night Market

SIVATHA

PUB STREET

Noon-Night Market

Tourism Office

Old Market **1**

START

AVENUE
OLD MARKET BRIDGE

POKAMBOR

STREET 10

Wat Damnak

BOULEVARD

63

Artisans d'Angkor

See also map p. 105
Old Market
1–3 hours
3–5 miles (5–8 km)
Ya-Tep Shrine

Wat Po Lanka, Wat Preah An Kau Saa, and Wat Preah An Kau Sai

🗺 Map p. 111

✉ Northeast Siem Reap

💲 $

Big New Market

🗺 105 B3

✉ National Highway 6, E of town center (beside Angkor Grand Guesthouse)

Cambodian Cultural Village

🗺 105 B3

✉ On National Highway 6 (Airport Rd.), Svay Dangkum Commune, Krous Village

☎ 855(0)63-963-836 (also fax)

💲 $$

www.cambodian culturalvillage.com

Cambodian Living Arts

✉ 37 St. 105 (corner of St. 242), Sangkat Boeng Prolit, Khan 7 Makara

☎ 855(0)12-797-578 (Siem Reap)

💲 $

www.cambodian livingarts.org

and conversations on Buddhism take place each afternoon on the temple grounds. Similar events are held each weekend at the nearby **Singing Tree Café** (see sidebar p. 51; *2nd lane bet. Wat Bo Rd. & Siem Reap River, tel 855(0)92-635-500, www.singingtreecafe.com*).

The next bridge, just one block north of the stone bridge, leads to a curious attraction: **Angkor Wat in Miniature** (*$*). Scale models of Angkor Wat, Bayon, and Banteay Srei are among the finely detailed hand-carved and molded works of art displayed in this small, if somewhat run-down, gallery.

The northeasternmost stretch of the Siem Reap River before the town gives way to the less populated fringe of the **Angkor Archaeological Park,** is Siem Reap's most densely populated Cambodian community. The village, which consists of riverside houses on stilts and roadside shop houses—town houses with ground-floor businesses—is worth visiting, particularly for its contrast to the more touristy part of town.

Three of Siem Reap's most charming temples, **Wat Po Lanka, Wat Preah An Kau Saa,** and **Wat Preah An Kau Sai,** are located close together, near the river road. Wat Preah An Kau Sai is the most interesting of the trio, built in 1911 atop the ruined laterite blocks of an Angkor-era temple. The two brick towers that remain standing behind the Buddhist vihara date from the Angkor era. The **House of Peace,** which sells traditional shadow puppets to benefit orphaned children (see sidebar p. 66), is also on the wat's grounds.

On National Highway 6

National Highway 6 passes through the middle of town and there are a number of attractions along it. To the east of town, near the bus terminal, is the **Big New Market** (Psar Leu Thom Thmei) an apt name for what could easily be called Siem Reap's answer to Wal-Mart. This sprawling market sells under one roof everything one could ever need, including fresh produce, bulk tobacco, clothing, gold jewelry, stereo systems, and barbecue equipment.

INSIDER TIP:

Mystères d'Angkor [see p. 289] is a boutique hotel located behind Wat Po Lanka. It's built around an old Khmer house and features a beautiful tiled pool and a fine restaurant.

—BRIAN MCNAMARA
National Geographic contributor

Northwest of town, on the airport road, you'll find a number of attractions and activities. The **Cambodian Cultural Village** is an immense tribute to the diversity and history of Cambodian culture. Examples include full-scale models of hill-tribe houses (including their inhabitants) and reenactments of Khmer weddings. Performances, including traditional dances, run throughout the day, and visitors may come and go.

For the past decade, **Cambodian Living Arts** has been working to revive the traditional arts of Cambodia, after an estimated 90 percent of the country's performance artists were killed during the civil war. By recording surviving masters' knowledge and training a new generation of artists, they aim to make their mark on the international scene by 2020.

Farther west, behind the Angkor Reach Hotel, the **War Museum** is little more than a depot for rusting Soviet and American artillery and tanks. The small arms and land mines displays have some signage, however. The guides, some of whom are survivors of the war that employed these very weapons, provide moving and knowledgeable talks about these weapons and their impact.

Activities along or near National Highway 6 include a pair of golf courses: the **Sofitel Angkor Phokeethra Golf & Spa Resort** *(Charles de Gaulle St., Khum Svay Dang, Kum Angkor, tel 855(0)63-964-600, www.sofitel.com, $$$$$)* which features an 11th-century bridge beside the first tee, and the Nick Faldo–designed **Angkor Golf Resort** *(tel 855(0)23-212-887, www.angkor-golf.com, $$$$$).*

The countryside around Siem Reap is a spectacular attraction of its own. The **Happy Ranch** *(off Airport Rd., tel 855(0)12-920-002, www.thehappyranch.com, $$$$–$$$$$)* provides riding lessons and trail rides. You can explore local villages and rice fields via 4WD, off-road quad bikes with **Quad Adventure Cambodia,** which specializes in getting off the beaten path. ∎

War Museum

 Kasekam Village, Sra Nge Commune

 $

Quad Adventure Cambodia

Near Wat Damnak (watch for signs)

855(0)17-784-727

$$$$$

www.quad-adventure-cambodia.com

EXPERIENCE: Khmer Massage

Forget the terry cloth slippers, organic face masks, and even massage tables—traditional Khmer massage is different, to say the least. Foremost, Cambodian massage isn't necessarily a relaxing luxury.

Depending on the style of massage—and there are many—some are considered fundamental necessities. When sick with a fever, for example, locals believe that a *gos khjol,* or coining, massage excises the fever and rebalances the person's energies back to health. Using a more vigorous approach than, say, chicken soup (the Western folk treatment for a cold), a practitioner uses the edge of a coin or can lid to scrape symmetrical lines into the back or chest. A good massage leaves raised, red bruises.

Cupping embraces a similar healing notion, but a different technique: suction. Tiny, lit candles are placed on the skin, usually over the back or forehead, then covered by small glass teacups. As the glass heats and the flame extinguishes, the cup suctions the skin, leaving large, red welts.

Cupping and coining are also revered locally for relieving headaches. They are thought to work by opening the surface blood vessels, which in turn cools the blood. Some Cambodians swear by them.

If you're healthy, however, try one of the massage parlors found in cities and towns. The ladies there generally offer variations on more relaxing massages, such as oil, hot stone, or even a four-handed pressure massage inspired by elephants. The trick to finding a good massage is choosing the right practitioner—the more experienced, and thus older, the better.

In Siem Reap, try **Frangipani** *(tel 855(0) 63-964-391, www.frangipanisiemreap.com).*

Around Siem Reap

Route 63 from Siem Reap toward Tonle Sap is best visited via *tuk-tuk,* which allows you to explore more than a tour bus would. While most people flock in droves to the Chong Khneas floating village, the sights on land are equally interesting. The floating villages (see pp. 119-123) farther afield are less touristy, and therefore more authentic.

The village of Chong Khneas on Tonle Sap Lake south of Siem Reap

Institute for Khmer Traditional Textiles

🗺 105 B3

✉ No. 472, Viheachen Village, Svaydongkum Commune (road to Tonle Sap Lake, near crocodile farm)

☎ 855(0)63-964-437

💲 $

http://iktt.esprit-libre.org/en

Toward Tonle Sap Lake

Just as Route 63 heads south from Siem Reap toward Tonle Sap Lake, watch for the **Institute for Khmer Traditional Textiles,** located just around a bend on the right. A small workshop and sales room, located in an old wooden house, feature traditional tools of the trade.

A few miles farther south on the road to Tonle Sap is another interesting detour: the village of **Aranh.** Keep your eyes peeled for a faded blue sign advertising the riverside village just beside one of many small bridges crossing the Siem Reap River. The road across the bridge leads to Wat Pu, but the real attraction is Aranh itself. Turn right along the riverside, where a dirt road leads through the village. Locals dry fish and rice in front of their homes, which are separated by banana gardens. Houses on stilts along the river often have small paddleboats docked outside and friendly children flash pearly smiles and enthusiastically shout "Hello!" Turn back onto Route 63 at the second bridge, about 2 miles (3 km) south, and continue toward the lake.

Phnom Kraom

Route 63 connects Siem Reap and the hilltop temple of Phnom Kraom, which overlooks Tonle Sap. Just prior to the hill, you may be stopped at the checkpoint for boat trips on Tonle Sap (see p. 122); simply inform the staff that you are headed to the temple. Situated 10 miles (16 km) south of Siem Reap, Phnom Kraom was one of three sites where Yasovarman I (r.889–900) chose to build temples. While he located his state temple at Phnom Bakheng, the temples atop Phnom Kraom and Phnom Bok were smaller complexes, similar in design, with three sandstone towers built in honor of the gods Brahma, Shiva, and Vishnu (see p. 48).

While the temple, **Prasat Phnom Kraom,** has suffered from exposure to the elements, the view it commands is the prime attraction here. Although it's a long, hot climb to the summit, there are resting places along the way, each of which reveals a more stunning view than the last one. This is particularly true during the wet season, when the elevated roads leading out to the lake appear as long tendrils stretching across the water from the base of the hill.

Beng Mealea

If you have more than a few days to spend exploring temples, take a day trip to the isolated ruins of Beng Mealea. "Discovered" by Westerners in the 1920s, the expansive temple complex— one of the largest built during the Angkor era—was part of the building frenzy initiated by Suryavarman II (r.1113–ca 1150). Constructed along one of the ancient highways that spanned the kingdom, it was once again lost to the jungle during the 20th-century civil war.

INSIDER TIP:

Village shops along the road north of Siem Reap make and sell palm sugar, a grassy-tasting sap from the date palm that's boiled into a sweet and soft confection.

—PAT HENLEY
National Geographic contributor

Beng Mealea was rediscovered in the late 1990s, though land mines, banditry, and horrific road conditions kept all but the most intrepid explorers at bay. Though it still receives few visitors, a new road ensures an enjoyable car or tuk-tuk trip—the red dirt and green jungle offer a beautiful ride. A boardwalk makes exploring the temple complex safer, though scampering over the scattered stones is part of its allure. In much of Beng Mealea, nature is winning the war with the man-made structures. Visiting this secluded ruin is a magical experience well worth the half day it takes. Other good day trips from Siem Reap include Koh Ker (see pp. 208–209) and Preah Khan (see pp. 158–159). ■

Prasat Phnom Kraom

🄰 105 A3

✉ On top of Phnom Kraom hill, 7.5 miles (12 km) S of Siem Reap; stairway entrance is just before turnoff to main Siem Reap Port, Phnom Kraom, Chong Khneas Commune

💲 $

Beng Mealea

🄰 105 B3

✉ 37 miles (60 km) E of Siem Reap off Rte. 67

💲 $

Training a New Generation of Artisans

A perusal of the intricate bas-relief carvings of Banteay Srei or a tour of the National Museum in Phnom Penh will testify to the unparalleled skills of Angkorian and Early Kingdom's artists and artisans. For example, the museum includes such treasures as the lithe torso of the goddess Durga, discovered at Sambor Prei Kuk.

Artisans d'Angkor: Women painting Cambodian scenes on silk

The techniques to produce such stunning beauty were passed down through generations of Khmers for centuries until the rise of the Khmer Rouge regime. With no need for such skills in their nightmarish utopia, the Khmer Rouge executed many who might have passed on their knowledge. Nonetheless, in the decades following the demise of the Pol Pot regime, a handful of dedicated individuals and organizations began reviving the traditional arts of the Khmer civilization.

In 1992, the Chantiers-Écoles de Formation Professionnelle (CEFP) was established in Siem Reap to help young Cambodians earn a living through handicraft production. With the assistance of master artisans from Europe, CEFP created a professional training program for motivated, low-education Cambodians who had artistic ability. These apprenticeships proved to be so successful that in 1998 the European Union supported the establishment of an offshoot, Artisans d'Angkor (Stung Thmey St., Siem Reap, tel 855(0)63-963-330), which serves as a school-to-work transition for a new generation of artisans dedicated to preserving Khmer cultural heritage.

Qualified apprentices spend six months at the Chantiers-Écoles program in Siem Reap.

INSIDER TIP:

Artisans d'Angkor runs a retail shop at Phnom Penh airport where young artisans sell their works at reasonable prices.

—BRIDGET A. ENGLISH
National Geographic contributor

They are given a daily allowance and are trained in one of four departments: silk painting, stone carving, wood carving, and polychromy—lacquering and gilding on sandstone or wood.

Using the nearby monuments as inspiration, apprentices at the training center learn to wield their handmade tools on introductory projects, such as carving small busts of Jayavarman VII. As they progress from apprentices to interns, students spend an additional three to six months honing their skills. Students in the polychromy department slowly master the art of making stone and wood sculptures appear to be ancient artifacts. Apprentice silk painters, the majority of whom are deaf or mute women, draw upon Wat Bo's beautiful murals to create inspirational works of art. These students also learn international sign language.

Now training roughly 75 apprentices a year, Artisans d'Angkor has established 12 workshops around Siem Reap Province, providing work for more than 1,000 people. Approximately 750 certified artisans from the program have established their own association of craftspeople; they now own a 20 percent stake in the organization.

Artisans d'Angkor: A reproduction of a Khmer sandstone carvings from nearby temples

These modern artisans are not simply reviving their trade based on the artistic inspiration of their ancestors, they are active participants in preserving this heritage. Under supervision of archaeologists, graduates of Artisans d'Angkor have reproduced missing portions of the bas-relief carvings at Kbal Spean (see pp. 160–163) and will soon begin a project at the South Gate of Angkor Thom (see p. 140). Further, they are leaving their own legacy by creating their own masterpieces, including the Pavilion of Honor at the Phnom Penh airport.

National Silk Center

Essentially a natural resource, silk seemed an ideal product for a project to improve the economic prospects of impoverished rural Cambodians. In 1993 the National Silk Center (CNS) founded the Angkor Silk Farm in Puok District, Siem Reap. Today, the facility serves as an active sericulture operation, producing quality silk fabrics with traditional weaves and designs, such as *hol* and *phamuong*—once reserved for religious or official ceremonies. The working silk farm offers guided tours, including an exhibit of traditional tools and clothing, plus information on philanthropic work by their sponsor, the Chantiers-Écoles de Formation Professionnelle.

Tonle Sap

If water is the lifeblood of Cambodia, then Tonle Sap Lake represents its beating heart. The dynamic ebb and flow of Cambodia's great lake is the centerpiece of a nation of rivers, reservoirs, and irrigated rice fields.

Even children must learn to navigate boats within Tonle Sap's floating villages.

The lake is connected to the **Tonle Sap River,** an unusual body of water that flows in opposite directions at different times of the year. The commencement of the rainy season coincides with the snowmelt in the Himalaya, the source of the Mekong River. The increased flow of the Mekong, which crosses the Tonle Sap River near Phnom Penh, forces the water in the Tonle Sap River to flow upstream, thereby causing Tonle Sap Lake to swell nearly fivefold, raising its waters from 3 to 6 feet (1–2 m) deep to nearly 35 feet (11 m) deep.

When the rainy season concludes in November, the Mekong loses its advantage and the great lake's mass of water pushes back, reversing the flow of the Tonle Sap River toward the southeast, past Phnom Penh, and into the sea. To commemorate this unusual aquatic event, Phnom Penh hosts **Bonn Om Tuk**—a raucous water festival replete with boat races— during November's full moon.

The fertile waters from the Mekong help support a diverse Tonle Sap ecosystem, including more than 200 species of fish, a majority of which migrate upstream during floods. The migratory patterns of many exotic waterfowl (see sidebar p. 121) are also guided by the rise and fall of the lake, as are those of a number of mammals, including otters.

If you take Route 63 south from Siem Reap and continue past the turnoff for Aranh (see p. 114), you will eventually reach the checkpoint for boat trips on Tonle Sap Lake, near Phnom Kraom (see p. 115). Options include day trips to Chong Khneas and Prek Toal, as well as longer voyages to Battambang and Phnom Penh (see sidebar p. 122). It is better, however, to arrange such trips through a tour operator rather than attempting to set them up here on your own.

Floating Villages

In addition to wildlife, Tonle Sap Lake supports millions of Cambodians living in villages on stilts and floating villages, such as **Prek Toal, Chong Khneas,** and **Kompong Pleuk,** the three nearest to Siem Reap. In fact, while the lake at its fullest only occupies 7 percent of the country's total area, its waters and banks are home to more than 25 percent of Cambodia's population, including Khmer,

Vietnamese, Chinese, and Cham ethnic groups.

Chong Khneas: Tourists flock to Chong Khneas due to its proximity to Siem Reap, but a truer glimpse of everyday life in the floating villages is found farther afield (namely in Kompong Pleuk and Prek Toal). That said, Chong Khneas has cleaned up its act (quite literally) in recent years. These changes may result from the programs of the **GECKO Environment Center,** a government-affiliated organization that promotes environmental education and trains members of the local community in wetlands management. Ask your boat driver to stop at their floating headquarters to learn more about their work.

Like most floating villages, Chong Khneas is organized like your typical land village. Structures abut each other, including buildings not specifically designed for commerce, such as floating gas stations that double as shop houses with small waterfront markets. Within the village confines, tight corridors

Chong Khneas

🔼 105 B3

GECKO Environment Center

✉ Main Siem Reap Port, Phnom Kraom, Chong Khneas Commune

💲 $

http://jinja.apsara .org/gecko

Tonle Sap's Fragile Ecosystem

Sadly, the lake's ecosystem is under pressure from a growing human population. Overfishing and deforestation of both upland and coastal flooded forests are stressing the lake. The flooded forests, which serve as the primary fish- and wildlife-breeding grounds, were reduced by nearly 40 percent during the second half of the 20th century. For these reasons, Tonle Sap Lake has become a protected biosphere reserve, with core

areas located at Prek Toal, Boeng Tonle Chhmar, and Stung Sen. The goals are to promote conservation; environmentally and socially harmonious development activities; and research, education, and information exchange. An informative exhibit, "Tonle Sap, Source of Lives," on the lake's fragile ecosystem has been set up by NGO Krousar Thmey at the school for blind children on the road from Siem Reap to the Angkor Archaeological Park.

A lesser adjutant stork on Tonle Sap Lake

husbands fish, wives may spend their days stitching fishing nets while infants swing in nearby hammocks. Young girls and elderly ladies paddle small boats around the village selling everything from fresh produce and rice to shampoo and laundry detergent. In fact, up to 30 percent of floating village residents are employed in trades other than fishing, including merchants and boatbuilders.

Villagers of Chong Khneas, for example, are involved in farming crocodiles. Both captured and bred crocodiles are retained in man-made pits connected to Chong Khneas' principal floating docks. While the deep piles of toothy crocs have become a tourist attraction, the scaly animals are farmed for meat and crocodile-skin merchandise.

Village children attend floating schools, which in certain villages include private institutions teaching Vietnamese. Some villages even have floating churches. Kompong Luong in Pursat Province has a Christian church founded by Japanese and French missionaries. Weddings are even performed on floating banquet boats!

Fishing is a seasonal occupation, because fishing for trade is restricted to the dry months, when the villages are moved farther from the shore. During the wet season, however, villagers must only fish to feed themselves. These restrictions on fishing allow enough time for the fish stocks to be replenished.

Kompong Pleuk: Many tours to Chong Khneas also feature a

of canals bustle with boats scraping past each other on their way into or out of the "suburbs." As with the houseboats moored farther out, the villagers take pride in their homes—many are painted blue with a kaleidoscope of lintels, shutters, and awnings, and decorated with flowering plants.

Entering the wider "boulevards" of the village, the canals that pass through flooded treetops feature both houses that are actually boats and boats that are used as houses. (Boats have inboard motors so their owners can relocate them easily from season to season.) The standard house design appears to be the more common of the two, with a front porch for socializing that opens to living quarters and kitchens where woodburning stoves are just out of sight. Incongruously, the amenities at many of these homes also include televisions— the antennas are a giveaway.

Life on the lake seems to move to a pleasant rhythm. While

visit to the incredible stilted village of Kompong Pleuk. Boasting a population of nearly 2,500 people, predominately of Khmer decent, most of the community is engaged in the fishing trade. Despite the fact that their towering homes are built in fixed locations, the villagers move with the ebb and flow of the lake. Each dry season, when Tonle Sap Lake shrinks, the residents of Kompong Pleuk relocate closer to the water, where they build temporary houses. As the waters rise, they disassemble their huts to move first to the lower levels of their houses on stilts and then to the uppermost floors as the level of the lake deepens. Among these bamboo "skyscrapers" are a pagoda and a lofty primary school, which was undergoing renovations during 2008 to install taller stilts.

Kompong Pleuk is located just south of the Roluos temple group, southeast of Siem Reap along National Highway 6. With your own transportation (tuk-tuk) you can drive to the edge of the lake in the dry season and rent a boat. Boatmen here generally charge by the hour, not per person, so trips

EXPERIENCE: Bird-watching

The Cambodian Department of Forestry and Wildlife, along with international conservation organizations, has identified 40 important bird areas across the country. As Cambodia features one of the largest freshwater lakes in Asia, plus numerous wetlands and rivers, it is one of the most important breeding grounds for many critically threatened and endangered bird species, including the sarus crane, Bengal florican, greater adjutant stork, milky stork, spot-billed pelican, white-rumped vulture, slender-billed vulture, white-shouldered ibis, and giant ibis—Cambodia's national bird.

A number of organizations, such as the Wildlife Conservation Society and the **Sam Veasna Center for Wildlife Conservation** (No. 0552, Group 12, Wat Bo Rd., Siem Reap, tel 855(0)63-963-710, www.samveasna.org), have been working with local communities to incorporate bird-watching tours. Supporting this new activity for visitors is part of a wider effort that includes integrated community development, nature conservation, and sustainable tourism. Exotic birds can be found throughout the country, including at Angkor's Preah Khan, whose ruins shelter hundreds of different species of birds. The top destinations for bird-watchers, however, are Prek Toal (see p. 123), Seima Biodiversity Conservation Area (see p. 203), Ang Trapaeng Thmor (see pp. 185–186), and Tmatboey Ibis Project (see below and pp. 202–203).

Kulen Prum Tep Wildlife Sanctuary's Tmatboey Ibis Project, a 2007 Responsible Tourism Award winner (www.responsibletourismawards.com), includes habitats ranging from open waters and flooded forests to grasslands and upland forests. All of these habitats are home to a number of endangered and threatened bird species. Some areas are remote and therefore best visited over the course of several days; packages are available through the Sam Veasna Center for Wildlife Conservation, which offers numerous birding-oriented tours throughout Cambodia, including Prek Toal, a convenient day trip from Siem Reap.

EXPERIENCE: Boat Trips on the Tonle Sap

With thriving fishing communities and pulsating waters, both Tonle Sap Lake and River offer unparalleled glimpses into authentic Khmer culture and enchanting wilderness. Whether you take a day trip or a multiday cruise that visits more remote attractions, boating the peaceful lake is sure to be a highlight of your visit.

Sightseeing Day Trips

Embarking from Siem Reap, rows of multicolored longtail boats service several day-trip destinations. It is best to organize these trips through your guesthouse or a tour operator, such as **Terre-Cambodge** (tel 855(0)92-476-682, www.terrecambodge.com). The most worthwhile sites are located an hour or more off the mainland, so bring a

seasonal flooded forest that's truly a scenic wilderness.

While you are here, tour the Prek Toal bird sanctuary with a preservation organization, such as the **Sam Veasna Center for Wildlife Conservation** (No. 0552, Group 12, Wat Bo Rd., Siem Reap, tel 855(0)63-963-710, www.samveasna.org) or **Osmose** (www.osmosetonlesap.net). Both groups' tour fees include the

Compagnie Fluviale du Mekong (tel 855(0)12-240-859, www.CFMekong.com) offers three-day/two-night cruises from Phnom Penh to Siem Reap. Arrange the voyage well in advance, as the trip actually departs from Ho Chi Minh City (Saigon) and stops briefly in Phnom Penh, where you can hop aboard. The cruise anchors daily for guided tours of silversmith villages, a rare 19th-century temple, a floating village, and even an oxcart ride. Berths are comfortable by Western standards and the food is superb.

Boating as Transportation

Speedboats offer a viable way to travel from Siem Reap to Phnom Penh or Battambang. This option is as fast, if not faster, than going by road.

Budget ferry options include one that travels the Siem Reap–to–Phnom Penh route and another that navigates Siem Reap to Battambang (and vice versa). Ferries will reach the capital in about six hours or Battambang in four, depending on water depths and the river's direction. Check with your hotel or guesthouse before boarding as ferries often get stuck in shallows, especially during the dry season, which can easily double the journey time and increases risk.

A Tonle Sap tourist boat trip continues to be a popular Siem Reap day trip.

picnic and start early, when waters are at their calmest.

An hour's journey from the Siem Reap pier leads to Kompong Pleuk (see pp. 120–121), the towering village on stilts. Built to accommodate the monsoons, these lofty structures line muddy roads in the dry season that then give way to deep waterways during the wet season. Nearby you will find a

entrance fee ($$$$$) into the reserve. The best times for bird-watching are early in the morning or in the late afternoon. If you arrive here in the afternoon, you could segue into an overnight homestay.

Multiday Trips

Combining luxury and culture at a lulling pace, overnight cruises are catching on. The French company are considerably cheaper if there are several people in your group.

A visit to Tonle Sap can be combined with the amazing lakeside view from the historic temples atop Phnom Kraom (see p. 115). Although a tuk-tuk is the easiest way to visit Phnom Kraom, do-it-yourself visits to Chong Khneas, including private boat rental, are considerably more expensive than a tour package, which often won't allow you to venture off to the temple. Your best bet is to check out the lake's floating villages with the services of a small tour operator, then visit the temple on your own via tuk-tuk to see an amazing sunset.

Prek Toal

Situated at the northwestern tip of Tonle Sap Lake, Prek Toal is one of the Tonle Sap Biosphere Reserve's three core areas. (The other two core areas are Boeng Tonle Chhmar and Stung Sen.) The reserve's almost 104,000 acres (over 42,000 ha) contain an important bird sanctuary and thriving floating villages. The primary attraction of Prek Toal is the biodiversity of waterbirds, including storks, pelicans, ibises, cormorants, and darters, all of whom return to the area for annual breeding. Other species inhabiting the region include flying foxes, otters, and slow lorises—the world's smallest primate.

Visits to Prek Toal must be approved by the Wildlife Conservation Society (WCS), which strictly monitors the bird sanctuary and collects an admission fee

($$$$$) for the maintenance of the reserve. Several bird-watching and ecotourism outfits, particularly the Sam Veasna Center for Wildlife Conservation and Osmose (see sidebar opposite), are involved with the WCS or local villagers. Both groups provide early morning bird-watching with an experienced guide, along with a visit to a floating village, where guests may sleep over and experience authentic village life.

INSIDER TIP:

When Tonle Sap's waters are running high, don't miss a boat trip to Prek Toal, a floating village on the edge of a seasonally flooded forest. It's the most prolific waterbird habitat in mainland Southeast Asia; rare species abound.

—KAREN COATES
National Geographic writer

Many smaller operators attempt to visit Prek Toal without permission or payment of the fees and occasionally run afoul of armed fishermen protecting their exclusive fishing zones. Prek Toal is best visited from Siem Reap as a day trip. The ferries to and from Siem Reap and Battambang skirt the village, allowing for some amazing sneak peaks and photo opportunities along the way. ∎

Mysterious stone-faced towers, elaborately adorned monuments, and centuries of artistic and religious accomplishment

Angkor

Smiling faces appear out of every doorway and window at Bayon temple.

Angkor

The Angkor era (A.D. 802–1431) began when a king, after subjugating an area of land similar in size to modern-day Cambodia, was crowned *chakravartin*, universal monarch, and assumed the name Jayavarman II (*r.*802–850), Protected By Victory. The founding father of the Khmer Empire settled on the city of Hariharalaya, 8 miles (13 km) southeast of Siem Reap at Roluos, for the location of the empire's first capital.

At Hariharalaya, Indravarman I (*r.*877–889), the successor to Jayavarman's son, began a tradition for the great kings who followed. He built the ancestral temples of Preah Ko and the state temple Bakong, as well as commissioning the massive Indratataka reservoir.

The Roluos temple group, which includes Lolei, the ancestral temple of Indravarman's successor, Yasovarman I (*r.*889–910), is a great place to kick off a trip to Angkor. It is a particularly good starting point if one wishes to appreciate the history of Angkorian kings and the development of Angkorian architectural styles, including the increasing use of religious symbolism.

Though Hariharalaya was the Khmer Empire's first capital, it was not Angkor. Many people confuse Angkor with a specific temple or an individual city, as this is somewhat true in both instances. Over time, however, many cities were built within the present-day Angkor Archaeological Park, which includes the temples at Roluos. "Angkor," a modern variant of the Sanskrit word *nagara*, simply means "city." The word is used in modern Khmer names for expansive temple complexes that once were supported by populous religious and political communities.

The place we generally refer to today as Angkor began to develop after Yasovarman I chose to move his empire's capital to the northeast, closer to the sacred waters of the Siem Reap River. Atop the hill called Phnom Bakheng, Yasovarman established the first state temple of the great city of Yasodharapura, essentially, "city of Yasovarman." The king was so revered that the capital of the Khmer Empire was called Yasodharapura by its inhabitants for roughly 500 years. Yasovarman's temple atop Phnom Bakheng is both a logical and convenient place to begin a visit to Angkor, as multiday passes begin the evening before the first day. Bakheng is a spectacular, if crowded, location from which to watch the sunset.

Over the centuries that followed Yasovarman's reign, the original walls of Yasodharapura were abandoned as subsequent kings built their own temples, fortified cities, and massive public waterworks. Of these, the grandest and most well known are Angkor Wat and Angkor Thom. Angkor Wat, literally "city temple" is arguably the world's largest religious structure. Angkor Thom, literally "big city," is a fortified city

NOT TO BE MISSED:

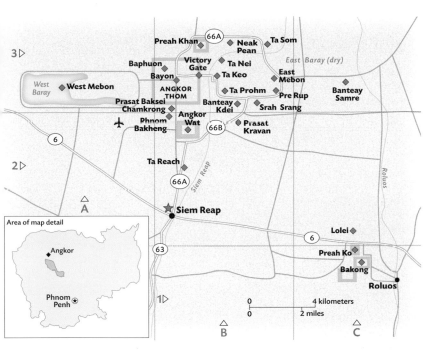

whose magnificent gates open to a forested 500 acres (203 ha) containing dozens of impressive religious and royal stone structures.

Angkor Wat, the 12th-century state temple of Suryavarman II (r. 1113–ca 1150) that derives its name from its conversion to a Buddhist temple in the 14th century, is justifiably a top attraction. It is famed not only for its grandiosity but also for its ornate decoration, most of which cannot be seen in less than three to four hours. Those staying in the area longer than a day typically visit Angkor Wat more than once. Since most of Angkor Wat's attractions are in enclosed chambers and galleries, it draws crowds from sunrise to sunset, rain or shine.

Although Angkor Wat is the most famous Angkor, Jayavarman VII's (r. ca 1181–1218) Angkor Thom was the centerpiece of the capital for the last several hundred years of the empire. The mythologically inspired causeways and elaborately adorned fortified gates that lead into the city are attractions of their own, and Jayavarman VII's state temple, Bayon, with its multitude of face towers, is arguably as breathtaking as

Angkor Wat. The grounds of Angkor Thom also feature the 11th-century state temple, Baphuon; the Royal Palace Enclosure, featuring the Phimeanakas; and the ornately decorated Terrace of the Leper King and Terrace of the Elephants, from which kings held court and witnessed events upon the massive royal plaza.

While both Angkor Wat and Angkor Thom are fascinating enough to fill a week's vacation (or a couple of centuries' worth of archaeological research), they still represent only part of the attractions here. Other temples and cities within the Angkor Archaeological Park include Jayavarman VII's other temple complexes, Ta Phrom and Preah Khan, Rajendravarman II's East Mebon and Pre Rup, and the exquisite pink sandstone temple of Banteay Srei—near the sacred river carvings at Kbal Spean.

Visiting temples from so many different time periods can be overwhelming, so some tourists organize their trips chronologically. Since short-term visitors may find it more practical to organize their trips in a more spatial manner, however, this chapter follows that model. ■

Angkor Wat & Nearby

Angkor began to develop as the Khmer Empire's center at modern-day Roluos, where Jaya-varman II established his capital at Hariharalaya and Indravarman I built Bakong, Preah Ko, and the Indratataka Baray. Shortly thereafter, Yasovarman I established the city of Yasodharapura, centered around Phnom Bakheng, near which Suryavarman II later built Angkor Wat.

The temple of Angkor Wat at sunset

Roluos Group

After Jayavarman II (r.802–850) was crowned universal monarch of Cambodia in 802 he began construction at three sites, one of which, Hariharalaya (near present-day Roluos), ultimately became his capital. Although Jayavarman II was recognized by later kings of Angkor as the empire's founder, it was actually Indravarman I (r.877–889) who established a tradition that would be followed for centuries—his ancestral temple (Preah Ko), state temple (Bakong), and waterworks (Indratataka Baray) inspired many later kings.

One of the oldest temples in the Angkor area is **Preah Ko**. An inscription from the temple commemorating its founding in 879 recounts the dedication of three statues of Shiva and three statues of female goddesses, each in honor of former kings and their wives, one for each of the temple's six towers. Thus, Indravarman fostered the association between the kings and the gods, paid homage to the spirits of his ancestors, and established a precedent for the royal commission of ancestral temples.

The modern temple name is based on the tale of the brothers Preah Ko and Preah Keo—one bull and one man. The former was associated with Nandi, the mount of Shiva. The remains of three carved images of Nandi kneel on the ground facing the temples.

In addition to the Nandi sculptures, the attraction at Preah Ko is the decorations adorning the towers. Once covered with intricately carved stucco, portions of the towers have surprisingly intact stucco, some of which has revealed traces of paint. While most of the stucco has deteriorated, the sandstone lintels above the towers' doorways and false doorways retain some spectacular adornment. Although the carvings on each tower are unique, all feature garlands and mythical creatures, particularly *garudas*—bird-man hybrids.

Completed in 881, just two years after Preah Ko, **Bakong,** located at the heart of Hariharalaya, was the first Khmer temple-mountain at Angkor—a five-tiered pyramid representing Mount Meru. Shiva was honored at the summit of Bakong through the *linga* Sri Indreshvara. Bakong is surrounded by three enclosure walls and two moats, the outermost of which is now dry. Four causeways lead into the temple, each of which features seven-headed *nagas*, whose snaky bodies form low balustrades, the first known instance of such causeway embellishment.

From the eastern entry tower of the interior enclosure the causeway passes several small structures. The small square building immediately to the north once housed the stela that profusely honored Indravarman as "a lion among kings."

INSIDER TIP:

Visiting Angkor at sunrise? Across from the main entrance, friendly ladies in tent restaurants sell French coffee and baguettes for breakfast.

—JOHN SEATON CALLAHAN
National Geographic contributor

Continuing east, the two long halls flanking the causeway were later additions from the 12th or 13th century. Wat Bakong, a Buddhist monastery, occupies the northeast corner of the grounds.

Before ascending the pyramid, walk around the inner enclosure and examine five of the eight remaining sanctuary towers. Like those at Preah Ko, these towers were constructed of brick and covered in stucco.

At the end of each causeway, pavilions located at the base of the main temple house statues of Nandi—mostly unrecognizable except for the one to the west. Looking up one of the stairways,

Angkor Wat

 105 B3, 127 B2, & 161

✉ 3 miles (5 km) N of Siem Reap on Rte. 66A

$ $$$$–$$$$$

you will notice that the temple has a false sense of scale; each of the four levels above the first decreases slightly in size to increase the perception of height. Along the stairways leading to the top of the temple are lions and the corners of each of the three lower levels feature elephants, all of these also diminish in size at each level. Surrounding the temple's fourth level are 10 of 12 remaining towers that once housed lingas, and portions of the bas-reliefs that once encircled the entire level. The best evidence of the bas-reliefs depicts *asuras* (demons) on the south side of the temple.

An apsara adorned "library" at Angkor Wat

The temple's uppermost tier features a 49-foot (15 m) central sanctuary: a lotus-shaped *prasat* that is indicative of 12th-century architecture. Only the base of the original tower remains. Some believe that the tower met its fate during the struggle for power following Indravarman's death.

North of Bakong and Preah Ko, the temple of **Lolei** rests on an island in Indravarman II's artificial lake, the **Indratataka Baray,** which is presently dry. Although construction on the *baray* began only five days into his reign, Indravarman I died prior to its completion. He had already laid the foundation for a temple at its center, however. His son, Yasovarman I (*r.*889–910) completed the northern dike that enclosed the baray and built Lolei as his ancestral temple.

Lolei consists of four brick towers, though their alignment suggests that the original plan called for six. As at Preah Ko, the easternmost towers feature *dvarapalas*, guardians carved of sandstone, though the false doors at Lolei consist of single sandstone slabs. The carvings on these doors and the lintels above them remain considerably intact. In the towers' center rests a small platform, where a linga was likely placed; the four sandstone channels leading away from the platform appear to be *snanadronis* (spouts), from which libations poured over the linga would have flowed.

Today the temple is adjacent to a Buddhist monastery, Wat Lolei, which has a few charming wooden buildings that serve as quarters for monks and their apprentices.

How to Visit Angkor Wat

One-, three-, and seven-day passes are available to Angkor Archaeological Park for $20, $40, and $60, respectively. Though multiday passes are only available at the park's south entrance, one-day passes can be bought at Banteay Srei. Passes must be shown at all temple entrances and used on consecutive days. Passes purchased after 5 p.m. are valid for the sunset on the evening prior to your first day. Passes allow access to all the monuments except for three requiring separate fees: Beng Mealea ($5), Koh Ker ($10), and Phnom Kulen ($20).

You can explore the temples by bicycle, tuk-tuk, car, or van. Motorbike rentals are prohibited in Siem Reap. A bicycle rental will run you $2 or $3, tuk-tuks can be hired for $15 to $20, and cars for $25 to $30. Visits to attractions farther afield, such as Banteay Srei, Kbal Spean, and Beng Mealea will cost between $20 and $75, depending on the type of transportation you hire. Your hotel or guesthouse can arrange for a certified guide to the park (about $20/day). If you go without a guide, ask your tuk-tuk driver to help you plan based on the temples you wish to visit.

Phnom Bakheng & Prasat Baksei Chamkrong

Following the death of his father, Indravarman II, Yasovarman I began constructing his state temple atop Phnom Bakheng, in the center of his new kingdom, Yasodharapura. Larger than the later city of Angkor Thom, Yasodharapura was enclosed by four 2.5-mile-long (4 km) earthen walls; the westernmost one was later used as a retaining wall for the West Baray.

Though the temple once could be approached from stairways on the east, north, and west, visitors now have only two options: the elephant walkway and the safety path. The **Elephant Walkway,** unsurprisingly, is the path taken by elephants upon which visitors may ride through lush tropical foliage on the south side of the hill. The **safety path** wraps around the hill's north and west sides, crossing over those respective stairways. Both paths terminate near the south side of the temple.

Whichever path is chosen, the best approach to the temple once atop the hill is from the east, toward which the temple was originally oriented. Turn your back to the temple and face the lower eastern stairway to see a small structure at the top of the stairs containing a **Buddha's footprint** (a carved image revered as an actual footprint of the Buddha), which dates later than the temple.

The step pyramid of Bakheng is similar in design to Bakong (see pp. 129–130), the state temple of Yasovarman's father. Phnom Bakheng is also a representation of the heavenly peaks of Mount Meru. The main body of the temple was cut directly into the summit of the hill and encased in terraced, sandstone platforms. At the base of each stairways leading up to the summit of the temple there were four statues of the sacred bull, Nandi. The Nandi statue at the base of the southern stairway was restored by monks and nuns from Battambang.

ANGKOR WAT NIGHT TOURS: Visiting the temples at night is a magical experience once reserved for only monks performing religious ceremonies on full moon nights and during occasional special events staged at Angkor Wat. Nowadays, anyone can enjoy a traditional Khmer dinner and then witness a reenactment of festivals once held at Angkor Wat, featuring sword fighting and apsara dancers. (Phum Thnal Village, Khum Sror Nge, Siem Reap, tel 855-(0)13-656-600, www.angkorwat nighttours.com)

Before ascending the pyramid, note that the temple, like Bakong, was designed to give a distorted impression of height, with each terrace and each lion alongside the stairs having been built slightly smaller than the ones below it.

Atop Bakheng once stood a quincunx (five towers arranged in a square with one at each corner and one in the middle), though the four towers that once surrounded the **central sanctuary** were disassembled in the 16th century for the construction of a seated Buddha, itself no longer "standing." Within each of the five towers was a linga; the central sanctuary contained the Shiva-linga Yasodharesvara. In 907, the temple was consecrated to and named after him, "the lord who bears glory." While this linga is gone, one stone linga endures, where the northeast tower once stood. The corners of the central sanctuary are adorned with *devatas* (female deities) and the faces of the 33 Hindu deities appear above the four doorways. Note the inscription on the upper left side of the doorway that faces north.

Just below the peak of Phnom Bakheng lies Prasat Baksei Chamkrong, "the bird with sheltering wings." Originally constructed to honor the parents of Harshavarman I (r. ca 910–ca 923), the temple once contained statues of Shiva and his consort. Rajendravarman II (r.944–968) rebuilt and rededicated the temple in 947, again to Shiva, who was then represented by a golden statue according to the inscription on the eastern doorway, which also pays homage to the lineage of kings dating back to Jayavarman II, founder of the Khmer Empire, and even Kambu, the mythical namesake of Kambudjaesa—eventually Cambodia (see sidebar p. 24).

Angkor Wat

The "temple which is a city," or literally, "city temple," is the largest religious monument in the world.

How to Avoid the Crowds

Roughly a million tourists visited Angkor in 2008. The number of visitors increases every year; it's getting difficult to take a photo of a temple without 25 other people in the shot. On those special occasions when you are the first or only one at a temple, however, the experience is ineffably enhanced. Here are some tips to help you avoid the hordes:

Get up early and go somewhere different: Hundreds visit Angkor Wat for sunrise (which you can't actually see from the temple), then head off to other temples. Watch the sunrise from Srah Srang instead, then be the first at Ta Prohm or East Mebon.

Get up even earlier: Arrive at Angkor Wat before dawn to see the sun's first light from the south library. Then, head for Neak Pean just as everyone else is getting to Angkor Wat.

Explore less popular temples: Everyone visits Angkor Wat and Bayon. Exploring smaller temples like Ta Nei and Prasat Phnom Bok is also wonderful, with a fraction of the visitors.

Visit Angkor in the rainy season: Even the rainiest months, September and October, are still mostly sunny. The lake and reservoirs are full, the countryside is green, and touring enclosed temples like Angkor Wat in the rain is pleasant and peaceful.

Pack a lunch: It's undeniably hotter at midday, but it's also much quieter. Visit a shady temple or one that's primarily indoors, like Angkor Wat or Preah Khan.

Including its moat and interior grounds, Angkor Wat covers almost 500 acres (203 ha). Though Suryavarman II (r. 1113–ca 1150) commissioned the temple at the beginning of his reign, it was not completed until after his death, in the second half of the Angkor era. Since Suryavarman was a devotee of Vishnu, the temple likely was originally consecrated to him. Yet Angkor Wat derived its name from its conversion to a Buddhist sanctuary several hundred years later, after Theravada Buddhism became the established state religion. After the fall of Angkor in 1431, the city was abandoned as a capital, but Angkor Wat's grounds were continuously inhabited by Buddhist monks until the Khmer Rouge era.

Although it is grand in scale, the temple's layout is quite simple. This generally straightforward design allows for greater appreciation of the monumental bas-reliefs that grace its walls, as well as the majestic beauty of the temple itself. Nonetheless, considering its size, the experience is greatly enhanced by visiting Angkor Wat with a competent guide. That said, it is one of the few temples with signs that explain most of its features and can be pleasurable to tour on your own.

The temple only occupies a tenth of the area enclosed by the moat; the remaining land probably was occupied by the royal palace and other impermanent structures for the inhabitants of the capital city. Others believe Angkor Wat was more than just a temple to

Local tourists explore the Angkor Wat temple complex.

honor Vishnu and may have been built as a mausoleum or even a cosmic observatory. However, as with most Hindu temples at Angkor, particularly those that served as state temples, the temple is a representation of Mount Meru, abode of the gods (see Interpretations of Design, pp. 150–151).

Angkor Wat is oriented westward, somewhat unusual for a Cambodian temple. It is from this direction that the **primary causeway** passes over the 623-foot-wide (190 m) moat and leads toward the west *gopura* (entrance gate or pavilion) and into the grounds containing the temple proper. The **west gopura** consists of a series of doorways with lotus-shaped towers above the center-most three. The smaller central doors were likely reserved for the king or high officials, while the two to the north and south were built large enough that elephants could pass through them.

INSIDER TIP:

Most temples at Angkor face east, so morning provides the best direct lighting for photographers. The one exception: Angkor Wat, which faces west.

—DAVID LAMB
National Geographic contributor

The southernmost of the three central entrances leads to the chambers known as **Kuk Ta Reach,** the Sanctuary of the Royal Ancestor, where a tall, eight-armed statue of Vishnu resides. This may be the statue that once stood in the temple's central sanctuary. While several *neak ta* (ancestral spirits) are believed to inhabit Angkor Wat, the most revered of these is Ta Reach, a royal spirit of immense power who inhabits this Vishnu statue. Each January or February, depending on lunar cycles, locals participate in the Leang Ta Reach ceremony: Musicians perform while a sha-man chants and dances before becoming possessed by the spirit of Ta Reach. Just prior to entering the Kuk Ta Reach, you may also notice a number of bullet holes in

the exterior doorframe, reminders that even these temples were not unscathed by Cambodia's civil war.

Beyond this outermost gopura, the towers of Angkor Wat rise up at the end of the second causeway. As you walk toward this causeway, look back toward the gopura through which you just passed to see the first of almost 3,000 apsara figures carved on the temple walls. Although arguably devatas (female deities), the carvings at Angkor are generally referred to as apsaras (celestial dancers), who were created during the Churning of the Sea of Milk (see sidebar p. 151), which is depicted on one of the temple's most impressive gallery walls. The apsaras at Angkor are nearly all unique, featuring a variety of hairstyles, clothing, jewelry, and poses. On the west gopura's interior, one even shows a toothy smile.

The 1,150-foot-long (350 m) interior causeway leading toward the temple proper is flanked by naga balustrades and is interrupted by six sets of stairways leading north and south. These probably once led out toward city streets. The fourth series of stairs leads to two large **stone libraries,** which make fine, peaceful places to await the sunrise or read about the temple before entering.

Just beyond the libraries is a pair of ponds. The **northern pond** contains water nearly year-round and is a popular place to take pho-tos of the temples, particularly at sunrise and sunset. Standing at the northwest corner of this pool will allow you to capture all five towers of the temple in its reflection.

The interior causeway ends at a stairway leading up to a large, **cruciform terrace,** where it is believed ceremonies were once conducted. Apsara dances were—and occasionally still are—performed here.

The doorway of the next gopura enters the temple proper and leads to the bas-relief gallery carvings that encircle the temple. Heading toward the central sanctuary, the entrance leads to the cruciform cloister, so named for the cross-shaped, interconnected, corbel roof corridors that surround four large, roofless pools that were likely once filled with water.

This chamber's northern and southern sides are designated the **Hall of Echoes** and the **Hall of a Thousand Buddhas.** The echo is a curious acoustic effect caused by the construction of the tall doorway exiting the north of the chamber—try standing with your back against the wall and thumping your chest soundly. The Hall of a Thousand Buddhas (Preah Poan) was added in the post-Angkor era (or Middle Period), as inscriptions on the columns dating from the 16th to the 18th centuries mention pilgrims who brought images of the Buddha here and took vows to dedicate themselves to Buddhist values. Most of the Buddha images were removed or destroyed around the time of the 20th-century civil war.

Another set of stairs passes through a dark gallery, then continues to the **innermost enclosure,** where the central sanctuary's five towers ascend almost vertically before you. While no longer accessible to visitors, they were once only open to the king and his high priests. These towers, collectively known as **Bakan,** are surrounded

---

EXPERIENCE: Sunrise & Sunset at Angkor

Given the large number of soaring temple pyramids with spectacular views, great opportunities to enjoy a sunrise or sunset abound. Reflections against the waters of an Angkorian *baray* (reservoir), a temple moat, or even a royal bath are as magical as the fading hues of a temple tower against dwindling sunlight.

The sun must have been shining on Yasovarman I (r.889–910), when he built three hilltop temples, one of which became the first state temple of Yasodharapura, now known as Angkor. Watching a sunset atop Phnom Bakheng (see pp. 131–132), where Yasovarman's ninth-century state temple overlooks the West Baray, Tonle Sap, and Angkor Wat, is immensely popular. While the crowds jockeying for photos dampen the atmosphere somewhat, Bakheng is the most convenient place to catch a sunset on your first day in the area. A multiday pass for Angkor (see sidebar p. 131) begins the evening before.

The always stunning view atop Phnom Kraom (see p. 115), on the banks of Tonle Sap, is particularly spectacular at sunset. Yasovarman's towers to the Hindu Trimurti here are weathered from the elements. It's a moderate walk to reach them; you can rest at overlooks along the way.

For sunrise, visit Prasat Phnom Bok (see pp. 160–161). A steep climb leads to three temples that are the more charming sisters of Phnom Kraom's temples. Prasat Phnom Bok lies about 15 miles (24 km) northeast of Siem Reap and is the perfect place to get an early start on a day trip to Banteay Srei (see pp. 161–162).

A crowd gathers to watch the sunrise at Angkor Wat.

by stairways. The western stairs are set at a 50-degree angle (the others are at 70 degrees) and are cut purposefully narrow—a technique used at many temples to ensure that devotees could not turn their backs as they descended.

Visitors are barred from the uppermost chambers, but a walk around the enclosure instills admiration for the towers—the center one rises 180 feet (55 m) above the ground. Excavations revealed a well beneath the central sanctuary as deep as the tower is tall that contained a sarcophagus (lending credence to the mausoleum theory). They also uncovered a small seated Buddha, now in the eastern gallery behind the Bakan.

Note the row of 16 apsaras in the southeast corner of the courtyard to your left before making a circuit around the Bakan. Then, return to the main entrance to tour the bas-relief galleries.

Angkor Bas-reliefs

At Angkor Wat, each bas-relief consists of an uninterrupted wall of carvings, two on each side of the temple. Bas-reliefs generally recount episodes from the Hindu epics *Ramayana* and *Mahabharata,* though they also depict a procession for Suryavarman II. They were not all carved during or shortly after his reign, however. Two northeastern panels, originally left bare, were added in the 16th century.

Unlike at most temples, the bas-reliefs were meant to be visited in a counterclockwise direction, beginning with the south section of the western gallery. This practice is associated with Hindu death rituals (see Interpretations of Design, pp. 150–151).

West Gallery, South Wing— Battle of Kurukshetra: This scene depicts the final battle in

the feud between the Pandava family (on the left) and the Kaurava family (on the right), the last episode of the epic *Mahabharata*. As you progress along the 160-foot (49 m) bas-relief, the soldiers engage in more viciously pitched battle, culminating at the center of the carving.

Southwest Pavilion: The interior walls of the south-west corner are decorated with low-relief carvings that depict episodes from the epic *Ramayana*, accounts of the gods Vishnu and Shiva, and even the Churning of the Sea of Milk.

South Gallery, West Wing— Historic Procession: This gallery commemorates the reign of Suryavarman II, who is mentioned in an inscription by his posthumous name, Parama-vishnuloka, suggesting it was carved following his death. The king appears twice on the relief carvings and is easily identifiable as he is larger than any other figure surrounding him. In the first instance he is seated in a sedan chair beneath parasols,

Temples & Their Functions

TEMPLE	KING	BUILT	FUNCTION	DEDICATED TO
Preah Ko	Indravarman I	879	Ancestral Temple	Shiva
Bakong	Indravarman I	881	State Temple (Hariharalaya)	Shiva
Indratataka	Indravarman I	889	Baray (reservoir)	
Lolei	Yasovarman I	893	Ancestral Temple	Shiva
Bakheng	Yasovarman I	ca 900	State Temple (Yasodharapura)	Shiva
Yasodharatataka	Yasovarman I	ca 900	East Baray (reservoir)	
Prasat Kravan	Harshavarman I	ca 921	Hindu Temple	Vishnu/Lakshmi
Prasat Thom	Jayavarman IV	ca 920	State Temple (Koh Ker)	Shiva
East Mebon	Rajendravarman II	952	Ancestral Temple	Shiva
Pre Rup	Rajendravarman II	961	State Temple (Yasodharapura)	Shiva
Banteay Srei	Guru of Jayavarman II	967	Hindu Temple	Shiva
Ta Keo	Jayavarman V	1000	State Temple (Yasodharapura)	Shiva
Royal Palace & Phimeanakas	Suryavarman I	end 10th–11th	Palace in Yasodharapura	Shiva
Preah Vihear	Suryavarman I	ca 11th–12th	Hindu Temple	Shiva
West Baray	Suryavarman I	early 11th	Baray (reservoir)	
Baphuon	Udayadityavarman II	ca 1055–1066	State Temple (Yasodharapura)	Shiva
Angkor Wat	Suryavarman II	early 12th	State/Funerary Temple	Vishnu
Angkor Thom	Jayavarman VII	late 12th	Capital City of Yasodharapura	
Terrace of Elephants	Jayavarman VII	ca 1200	Ceremonial Platform	
Preah Khan	Jayavarman VII	1191	Ancestral Temple (father)	Buddha/Lokesvara
Ta Prohm	Jayavarman VII	1186	Ancestral Temple (mother)	Buddha/Pranjnaparamita
Terrace of Leper King	Jayavarman VII	ca 1200	Unknown	
Bayon	Jayavarman VII	late 12th–13th	State Temple (Yasodharapura)	Buddha
Banteay Chhmar	Jayavarman VII	late 12th–13th	Ancestral Temple (son)	Lokesvara

while attendants fan him. In the other carving, he is shown standing atop the 12th elephant in a procession led by attendants carrying an ark containing the sacred flame.

INSIDER TIP:

Wear sturdy shoes to Angkor. The ground is often rough, with steep, uneven steps— and keep an eye out for snakes in the undergrowth.

—SOLANGE HANDO
National Geographic author

South Gallery, East Wing— Heavens and Hells: One of the most deteriorated bas-reliefs at Angkor Wat, this gallery depicts the 37 heavens and 32 hells of Buddhist mythology. Inscriptions explain which heaven (on the uppermost portion of the gallery), and which hell (on the lower portion) are being showcased. Yama, the god of death, is shown with 18 arms, judging who should go where.

East Gallery, South Wing— Churning of the Sea of Milk: The Churning of the Sea of Milk is a creation myth in which the asuras (demons) and *devas* (gods) collaborated to extract *amrita,* the elixir of immortality, by using the naga Vasuki to rotate Mount Mandara. The process created

a number of mythical creatures, including the apsaras, celestial dancers seen erupting from the mountain's center. Vishnu appears several times, particularly as his turtle avatar, Kurma, who aided in the churning (see sidebar p. 151).

Eastern Gopura, Causeway, Inscription & Stupa: From the eastern gopura, an earthen causeway crosses the moat but holds little interest for visitors. However, beyond the gopura, in the corridor before the north wing of the east gallery, a large inscription on the interior wall corresponds to the brick stupa (funerary spire) to the east. The 18th-century inscription commemorates the death of the wife and son of a provincial governor.

East Gallery, North Wing— Vishnu's Victory over the Asuras: These bas-reliefs were carved in the 16th century, several hundred years after the temple was built. While commissioned at a time when Angkor Wat had already been converted for the worship of Theravada Buddhism, they are a testament to the religious tolerance of Buddhism and the respect later Khmers had for their history. The scenes depicted here, which are of inferior quality to the earlier carvings, feature the god Vishnu in battle with the asuras.

North Gallery, East Wing: Krishna's Victory over Bana: These bas-reliefs were also sculpted in the 16th century and also pay homage to Vishnu, shown as his avatar Krishna defeating Bana, a demon god. The battle proceeds as you walk west, with Vishnu gradually severing the hands of the multiarmed Bana before finally sparing his life at the behest of Shiva. Shown toward the end of the relief as an ascetic, Shiva is identifiable by his trident and his son Ganesha seated beside him.

North Gallery, West Wing—Battle of the Devas & Asuras:

Perhaps depicting the battle over amrita that followed the Churning of the Sea of Milk, gods and demons are at war here. Shiva rides the sacred bull, Nandi, and Brahma is atop his mount, Hamsa the goose. Indra is fighting from the back of Airavata, the three-headed elephant. In the gallery's center, Vishnu rides the half-man, half-bird Garuda. In all, this 308-foot (94 m) finely carved gallery wall depicts 21 gods accompanied by their respective mounts.

Northwest Pavilion:

The relief carvings of the northwest corner depict scenes from *Ramayana* in particularly impressive, if eroded, designs.

West Gallery, North Wing— Battle of Lanka:

Also one of the most impressive bas-relief carvings at Angkor, this chapter from *Ramayana* depicts Rama and the monkey general Hanuman. They lead the monkey army against the demon king Ravana, who kidnapped Sita, Rama's wife, and imprisoned her on the island of Lanka. ∎

A monkey explores the lush grounds of Angkor Wat.

Angkor Thom

Yasodharapura (Angkor) was decimated by the invading Chams in 1177. Four years later, Jaya-varman VII (r. ca. 1181–1218) defeated the Cham king and began rebuilding both the capital and the empire. At the heart of the capital, he built Angkor Thom, "big city." Surrounded by a moat approximately 8 miles (13 km) in circumference, the city was accessible by five causeways and gates, one in each of the four cardinal directions and one leading directly to the Royal Palace.

The South Gate of Angkor Thom

Angkor Thom

 127 B3, 161

✉ 5 miles (8 km) N of Siem Reap on Rte. 66A off Hwy. 6

💲 Admission included in Angkor pass (see sidebar p. 131)

Each causeway is flanked by nine-headed *naga* balustrades supported by 54 *asuras* (demons) on the right and 54 *devas* (gods) on the left (see Interpretations of Design, pp. 150–151). The gates, each capped by four smiling faces, feature three-headed elephants pulling up lotus flowers beside entranceways clearly built to allow real elephants to pass through. The southern causeway and gate are the most

intact. Though you may get the best photos of the causeway at the **South Gate,** they will likely include many fellow visitors.

The other gates are quieter and nicer to visit. The **Victory Gate** leads not to the city center, but to the Terrace of the Elephants and the Royal Palace Enclosure. Though similar to the South Gate, this gate is in a greater state of disrepair. A pleasant walk on top of the enclosure wall leads from the gate south to the **East Gate,** or Gate of the Dead, thought by some to have been used for funerary processions. The lack of an elaborate causeway here suggests the gate was not regularly used, however. Your driver can drop you at the Victory Gate and pick you up at the rarely visited East Gate some 15 minutes later.

Bayon

Jayavarman VII built his state temple at the center of Angkor Thom. As the first state temple dedicated to the Buddha, Bayon differed greatly in design from earlier state temples, which were typically square, pyramid-shaped representations of Mount Meru. Bayon was originally constructed at ground level, though it was eventually modified with three terraces. Since Angkor Thom was so well fortified, subsequent kings adopted the city as their capital. Rather than building new state temples, they altered and added to Bayon. Centuries of such changes resulted in the temple's current state of crowded, confusing corridors and chambers.

Face Towers: The face towers are Bayon's distinguishing feature. Of the 49 original towers, 37 remain; most are graced by four faces looking in the cardinal directions. The **main terrace** offers countless photo opportunities, with smiling faces nearly everywhere one looks. Note that some of the faces had a third eye carved into their foreheads as part of the anti-Buddhist backlash after Jayavarman VII's death.

Bas-Reliefs: The carvings adorning the galleries represent Bayon's other great attraction. The **outer bas-reliefs** were part of Jayavarman VII's original construction and primarily commemorate his victory over the Chams, though they also offer insights into everyday Angkorian life. The **inner gallery** was carved later and depicts episodes from Hindu mythology. The walls feature three levels of densely decorated, elaborate scenes, so it's well worth hiring a knowledgeable guide to explain them.

INSIDER TIP:

Get to Bayon pre-dawn and watch the morning sun slowly light up the smiling faces carved into the temple's towers.

—SIMON WILLIAMS
The Nature Conservancy

Tours generally lead along the **south section of the east gallery** and the **east side of the south gallery,** which are the most interesting. This part of the east gallery depicts the Khmer army marching to war and it also features commoners, including people who appear to be Chinese, engaged in activities such as preparing food and sacrificing a buffalo. The first section of the south gallery depicts the ferocious naval battle in which Jayavarman VII conquered the Cham, as well as daily life along the waterfront. The unfinished

Bayon

 127 B3, 161

✉ 6 miles (10 km) N of Siem Reap on Rte. 66A off Hwy. 6

$ Admission included in Angkor pass (see sidebar p. 131)

Baphuon

🗺 127 B3

✉ 6 miles (10 km) N of Siem Reap on Rte. 66A off Hwy. 6

💲 Admission included in Angkor pass (see sidebar p. 131)

bas-reliefs around the temple's west and north sides feature several interesting carvings. These include a monk climbing a tree to escape a tiger (south side of the west outer gallery) and circus performers (west side of the north outer gallery).

INSIDER TIP:

Ask your guide or *tuk-tuk* driver to take you to off-the-beaten-path temples. Angkor is at its best at its quietest, most solitary moments.

—KAREN COATES
National Geographic writer

Beyond those highlights, Bayon is pleasurable to explore at random. Portions of the upper level are undergoing restoration and certain chambers are off-limits, but the **central sanctuary,** which houses a small seated Buddha, is accessible. A larger Buddha discovered beneath the sanctuary in 1933 currently resides at nearby Vihear Prampil Loveng (see p. 147).

When exiting the temple from the north, the path is graced by the seated image of a meditating Jayavarman VII, one of the most iconic images in Cambodian art.

Baphuon

Directly north of Bayon, on the road to the North Gate, is the entrance to Baphuon. This impressive temple pyramid, built prior to Angkor Thom during the reign of Udayadityavarman II (r. 1050–1068), served as his state

temple and represented Mount Meru. The five tiers upon which a single tower once rested rise approximately 80 feet (24 m) above the ground. The missing central sanctuary is thought to have been constructed of light materials, perhaps rising to an ultimate height of 140 feet (43 m), and may have been covered in bronze. The second largest structure built at Angkor was the victim of its own grandiosity—it collapsed on itself from its massive weight.

From the eastern *gopura* (entrance gate) the temple is approached via a 650-foot-long (198 m) elevated walkway flanked by ponds. Halfway along the path is a cruciform pavilion that once featured bas-relief carvings unique to Angkorian art: finely detailed images in small panels, oriented vertically, and generally read from bottom to top. The temple is undergoing a major reconstruction, so most of these carvings have been temporarily removed. In fact, in the 1960s the entire temple was undergoing anastylosis—it was disassembled into 300,000 numbered loose stones, then was going to be pieced back together with the broken or missing stones replaced. The plans for the reassembly, however, were destroyed by the Khmer Rouge during the civil war. Participants in the original project have since reunited to complete the world's largest "jigsaw puzzle."

Baphuon is closed while it is under reconstruction. You may be able to walk around to the rear of the temple, where the **western gopura** has been repaired, and see examples of the aforementioned **bas-reliefs** on the far side. From the rear, looking eastward, you can make out the rough form of an enormous reclining Buddha on the second tier of the pyramid. The head lies to your left and the nose is somewhat discernible.

From the temple's north side, you may pass through a small doorway in the enclosure wall to your left, which leads directly to Phimeanakas and the Royal Palace grounds. Alternatively, you may go back the way you came, exit the temple, and follow the southern portion of the Terrace of the Elephants, which leads to the main entrance to the palace grounds.

Royal Palace

At some point during his reign, Rajendravarman II (r.944–968)

built a royal palace in Yasodhara-pura, just north and west of what is now the center of Angkor Thom. The Royal Palace grounds were thereafter occupied by the kings of Angkor for several hundred years, in part because Jayavarman VII later built the city of Angkor Thom around it. As other kings occupied the palace grounds, a number of changes and additions were made.

Considering that the palace grounds cover nearly 37 acres (15 ha), the area seems surprisingly devoid of ruins. In fact, the palace and most of the original buildings were built of wood and have long since deteriorated to dust. Essentially all that remains are Phimeanakas, several ponds, and a few smaller stone structures of uncertain purpose.

The Almighty *Linga*

Lingas are phallic fertility symbols that were an integral part of religious worship in pre-Angkorian and Angkorian kingdoms. Linga worship derived from Indian Hinduism; it was likely embraced by ancient Khmers because of their animist belief that spirits could be embodied in stone. While lingas were typically stone, some were made of precious metals, including silver and gold. A linga was installed in a symbolic vulva, known as a *yoni*, with a *snanadroni* (spout) from which libations poured over the linga could flow.

While lingas eventually came to be strictly associated with Shiva, they originally represented the Hindu Trimurti: a square base represented Vishnu, an octagonal middle represented Brahma, and a rounded tip symbolized Shiva. As the cult of Shiva became predominant, lingas

were worshiped as conduits for Shiva's spirit and may have been instrumental in the cult of *devaraja* (god-king) through which the king drew divine association. The most sacred Shiva-lingas, as well as the state temples that housed them, were named after the kings who ordered their consecration. For example, Yasovarman's state temple contained a linga called Yaso-dharesvara, "the lord who bears glory," and the temple, now known as Phnom Bakheng (see pp. 131–132), also was originally referred to as Yasodharesvara.

Upon his death, the king's spirit was believed to merge with that of the Shiva, and the king assumed a posthumous name synonymous with the linga and temple. Only high priests and the king were allowed access to these mystical temple mountains, which literally were abodes of the gods.

A statue of the Hindu god Vishnu, clad in silk, at Angkor Wat's entrance

Phimeanakas: Who built the first structure at Phimeanakas is unknown. The existing pyramid was built by Suryavarman I, but evidence indicates that other structures predated it, and later kings clearly added to it. Regardless, the uppermost levels of the pyramid were thought to have been built of wood and Zhou Daguan described it as crowned by a "golden tower" (see sidebar p. 28). While Phimeanakas means "celestial palace," it was *not* the royal palace where the king resided; it may have housed a golden *linga*. The kings of Angkor were told to ascend here each night in order to make love to a powerful nine-headed naga in the guise of a woman to safeguard the kingdom (or so Zhou Daguan said). Visitors may ascend via a wooden staircase on the western side of the pyramid.

The grounds around Phimeanakas are shady and quiet; two ponds sit just north of the temple. These pools may have been designated for male and female users (as they are currently named Srah Srei and Srah Bros). The **larger pool,** to the west, is surrounded by three tiers of bas-relief carvings—*apsaras,* nagas, crocodiles, and fish—on its west and south banks. The **smaller pool** is unadorned. To the north of the smaller pool, a gopura passes through the enclosure wall where a dirt path leads toward the terraces and the Royal Plaza.

Terrace of the Leper King:

This terrace is situated toward the northern end of the Royal Plaza—just north of the Terrace of the Elephants—up a flight of stairs at the back. The small platform is surrounded by two retaining walls, between which there is a deep, narrow corridor. Atop the terrace sits a naked, androgynous figure with bared fangs, hitherto unknown in Angkorian art. This **statue** is a reproduction; the original is housed at the National Museum in Phnom Penh (see p. 72). The current consensus is that it represents Yama, the god of death or judgment in the underworld, rather than a real or mythical king afflicted with leprosy.

The terrace is surrounded by two 20-foot-high (6 m) retaining walls with multiple levels of **bas-reliefs** featuring smiling *devatas* (female deities), apsaras, grimacing figures holding swords and clubs, and multiheaded nagas. The second wall seems to have been built to expand the original terrace or to buttress it as the original wall began to crumble. After perusing both walls, you may access the Terrace of the Elephants just to the south.

Terrace of the Elephants:

The upper platform is the most interesting section of the nearly 1,000-foot-long (305 m) terrace overlooking the Royal Plaza. Similar to the Terrace of the Leper King, the lower, exterior retaining wall has an excavated, **interior series of relief carvings.** This wall's front features the three-headed elephant Airavata pulling up lotus flowers with each trunk. In the chamber behind this wall, accessible from the main platform, several **deep bas-reliefs** depict a five-headed horse, thought perhaps to be Balaha, an incarnation of the Bodhisattva Lokesvara. The upper

Circus

Evidence of *seak boran* (traditional circus) dates back to pre-Angkorian Cambodia; it seems to have been practiced through the height of the civilization. Bas-reliefs depicting jugglers, acrobats, illusionists, and sword swallowers have been found at Bayon, Terrace of the Elephants, and Angkor Wat.

While professional circus techniques were lost over the centuries, *pahi*—traveling medicine men—still roam the countryside. Pahi sell medicinal elixirs and perform magic tricks, such as snake charming, occasionally with the assistance of trained monkeys.

Today, *seak samai* (modern circus) is performed in both Battambang and Phnom Penh. Beneath a big-top tent, disadvantaged Khmer children are trained as professional circus performers at **Phare Ponleu Selpak Center** *(Anh Chanh Village, Ochar Commune, Battambang, tel 855(0)53-952-424, www .phareps.org; see p. 305),* which fuses circus with traditional and modern dance.

In Phnom Penh, **Sovanna Phum** *(111 St. 360, corner of St. 105, tel 855(0)23-987-564, www.shadow-puppets.org)* combines circus with shadow puppetry and traditional dance, and provides workshops upon request (see sidebar p. 66).

platform also features two life-size Airavatas flanking the demon Kala surrounded by apsaras, above which is an empty lotus-blossom shaped pedestal.

The terrace's main platform lies south at the end of the **Victory Road.** The king led his troops into battle along this route and through the Victory Gate. The terrace's grand central platform sits at the entrance to the Royal Palace Enclosure and is ornamented with bas-relief *garudas* (bird-man hybrids) naga balustrades, and statues of lions. Carvings along the platform also include circus performers and other features of the public events that occurred on the Royal Plaza.

Royal Plaza: A procession of bas-relief elephants adorns the Terrace of the Elephants as it leads southward, along the Royal Plaza, a field several hundred yards long and 40 to 50 yards (37–46 m) wide. Grand processions, public gatherings, and other ceremonies were held on the plaza. Chinese envoy Zhou Daguan (see sidebar p. 28) described monthly festivals for which bleachers were built to hold thousands; entertainment included impressive fireworks.

Prasats Suor Prat & the Kleangs: Across the plaza to the east of the Terrace of the Elephants are a series of identical towers called **Prasats Suor Prat,** "towers of the tight-rope dancers." A legend claims that acrobats performed high-wire routines between the towers. Despite its fantastical name, the towers' real purpose has yet to be determined. Zhou Daguan said that they were used to settle disputes: Two men would enter one and after several days the guilty party would assume some affliction. The dozen towers

EXPERIENCE: Bird's-eye View of Angkor

Many believe a powerful spirit resides in Angkor Wat and prevents birds from flying over it. The Cambodian government does likewise for commercial aircraft. You, however, can get high enough and near enough in a balloon or a helicopter to get a bird's-eye view of these majestic temples:

From almost 650 feet (198 m) up, the view of Angkor Wat with **Angkor Balloon** (.5 mile [1 km] west of Angkor Wat, tel 855(0)11-886-789, $15) is spectacular. Looking down on Prasat Phnom Bakheng to the northwest is the perfect perspective for appreciating the step pyramid carved out of the hill's summit. Sunsets over the West Baray are stunning. The

smooth-riding balloon is enclosed by a net, so even the most acrophobic rider should feel secure. The balloon goes up every ten minutes during the high season; get there early for sunrise and sunset flights.

Flights with **Sokha Helicopters** (sales office: 24 Sivatha Rd., Siem Reap, tel 855(0)63-966-072, www.sokhahelicopters .com, $110 for 12 min., $250 for 30 min.) last 12 to 30 minutes and depart from the domestic terminal of Siem Reap airport, near the temples. Longer flights combine temples, including the Roluos Group, with floating villages and Siem Reap. Extended tours and charter flights focus on photography or more remote attractions.

Hindu devas and asuras flank the South causeway of Angkor Thom.

are nearly evenly spaced, with six on either side of the Victory Road. The laterite-and-sandstone towers have very little adornment and are best appreciated from the Terrace of the Elephants.

Just beyond the Prasats Suor Prat is a pair of sandstone structures called the **Kleangs,** which face the Royal Plaza. While their original purpose is unknown, inscriptions recounting the oath of allegiance to the king suggest that they were used by visiting provincial leaders. The northern Kleang predates the southern one, which was probably built to make the view from the terrace symmetrical.

Vihear Prampil Loveng: As you go east along the Victory Road toward the Victory Gate,

watch for a small turnoff to the right (south), just past the Prasats Suor Prat. A low wall encloses a gradually ascending terraced shrine. Rarely visited Vihear Prampil Loveng has a 12-foot (4 m) **statue of the Buddha** sheltered by the naga Muchalinda, discovered in a pit beneath the Bayon's central sanctuary in 1933. The statue was found in fragments, perhaps destroyed during the iconoclasm that followed Jayavarman VII's death. It may be the Buddharaja image that once graced Bayon's innermost sanctum. Completely reconstructed, the Buddha was presented to King Sisowath Monivong (r.1927–1941) in 1935, who directed that it be placed at Vihear Prampil Loveng.

Srah Srang & Banteay Kdei

⚠ 127 B3

✉ 8 miles (13 km) N of Siem Reap on Rte. 66A off Hwy. 6

💲 Admission included in Angkor pass (see sidebar p. 131)

Preah Pithu: If you have time and are heading through Angkor Thom's northern gate, several small temples in the northern part of the city are worth a quick visit. In the northeast corner is a group of five temples known as Preah Pithu. Though these generally unrelated temples are relatively uninteresting to the common visitor, their shady, quiet grounds hold a few attractions. While most of the temples honor Vishnu, the easternmost temple

East of the Victory Gate

Srah Srang & Banteay Kdei: A beautiful setting to enjoy a sunrise or unwind near day's end, Srah Srang is known as the Royal Bath, but inscriptions indicate that the "water has been stored for the benefit of all creatures." Srah Srang has remained a popular picnic destination and swimming hole for local residents since its construction by Rajendravarman II in the tenth century. Jayavarman VII, who built the

Sacred Sword

The Preah Khan, or "sacred sword of Cambodia," was the palladium of the kingdom for over a thousand years, though exactly when the tradition first began remains a mystery. Jayavarman VII (r. ca. 1181–1218) is depicted in a bas-relief at Bayon holding the sacred sword. He also consecrated a Buddhist temple complex named the Preah Khan (see pp. 158–159, 164), which features an unusually designed building that may have housed the sacred weapon responsible for the protection of the kingdom. Zhou Daguan (see sidebar p. 28) visited Angkor in the 13th century

and recounted having seen the king "standing on an elephant . . . holding a sacred sword in his hand."

Even during the early 20th century, descendants of Brahman guardians continued to keep a 24-hour vigil over the 43-inch (108 cm) steel sword with bejeweled hilt and gold-and-silver scabbard that featured scenes from the Hindu epic *Ramayana*. Following the rise to power of the Khmer Rouge, the sacred sword disappeared from the Royal Palace in Phnom Penh, and its whereabouts are unknown to this day.

was dedicated to Buddha—the innermost sanctuary features bas-relief Buddha images. The temple to the west of this sole Buddhist sanctuary features a west-facing lintel decorated with a ten-armed dancing Shiva flanked by Brahma and Vishnu.

Just opposite Preah Pithu are **Tep Pranam** and **Preah Palilay.** Again, neither holds much of interest to the average visitor, but there is an active Buddhist monastery on the grounds of Tep Pranam.

neighboring temple of Banteay Kdei, constructed the **landing** on the western bank that features naga balustrades and images of garudas and lions. This landing, directly opposite Banteay Kdei, offers the best view of the pond.

Combine sunrise at Srah Srang with a walk from east to west through Banteay Kdei. Since the temple's layout is similar to those of Ta Prohm and Preah Khan—Buddhist temples dedicated to Jayavarman VII's parents—it is probable that Banteay Kdei served a similar function as a Buddhist monastery and ancestral shrine during the reign of Jayavarman VII.

Banteay Kdei is oriented eastward, facing the west platform of Srah Srang. Before passing beneath the gopura capped with face towers, note the 6-foot-tall (2 m) garuda sculptures on each side of the entryway. A short distance west is a rectangular terrace and then the original outer gopura. Within this **entry chamber** is a seated Buddha. This was not part of the original temple, as most Buddha imagery in the kingdom was systematically destroyed after the death of Jayavarman VII.

Perhaps related to this iconoclasm, Banteay Kdei was the site of an astonishing discovery. In 2001, researchers found a pit containing a large cache of fragmentary and intact Buddhist images. Portions of 274 statues were unearthed from this pit, which was covered with large sandstone blocks, suggesting they may have been buried to consecrate a temple that was intended to be built there.

Beyond the entry, a naga-lined causeway leads to a large, roofless, rectangular room. It is called the **Hall of Dancers** for the apsaras carved on its pillars. Ritual dances probably occurred here.

The **central sanctuary** seems to have been heavily defaced. The westward facing front just prior to the western interior gopura does feature a bas-relief of the Buddha. This image was likely spared because it was hidden behind a wooden ceiling, part of a later addition to the original temple.

Ta Prohm: Ask your *tuk-tuk* driver to pick you up Banteay Kdei's western end and drive you to Ta Prohm's east entrance. Set immediately northwest of Banteay Kdei, Ta Phrom remains in a natural state. Towering silk-cotton trees and strangler figs perch on the temple, their tentacle-like roots crawling along the crumbling stone walls. The trees, which sprout from between the stones, eventually die and cause towers and chambers to collapse.

INSIDER TIP:

The jungle-encased ruins at Ta Prohm contrast dramatically with Angkor Wat's massive expanse. Set aside a few hours to walk its root-strewn corridors.

—CHRISTY RIZZO
Adventure travel expert

Ta Prohm was built by Jayavarman VII to honor his mother, represented as the Bodhisattva Pranjnaparamita, the "perfection of wisdom." It functioned as a Buddhist monastery. Preah Khan (see pp. 158–159, 164) honored his father and served a similar purpose. As with Preah Khan, the ground-level temple was built within an immense walled enclosure that contained a large city and was surrounded by an additional 3,000-plus villages whose population of nearly 80,000 was devoted to the maintenance of the monastery.

(continued on p. 152)

Ta Prohm

 127 B3

✉ 1.8 miles (3 km) W on Rte. 66A from Banteay Kdei

$ Admission included in Angkor pass (see sidebar p. 131)

Interpretations of Design

As early as the first-century kingdom of Funan, Cambodian kings built temples as earthly representations of Mount Meru, the mythical home of the gods. Early kings built atop actual mountains; later kings commissioned increasingly complex versions of Mount Meru, including step pyramids with towers representing its five peaks.

The face towers at Bayon are full of ancient symbolism.

These pyramids were surrounded by enclosures and moats representing the continents and seas around Mount Meru. The central sanctuary atop the temple enshrined a sacred item, typically a Shiva-*linga* (see sidebar p. 143) which simultaneously sanctified the spirit of the king and served as the conduit for the spirit of the god.

Phnom Bakheng

By the Angkor era, kings were increasing the symbolic complexity of their temples. When founding the city of Yasodharapura, Yasovarman I (r.889–910) established Bakheng, one of the first state pyramids inspired by Mount Meru. Bakheng's (see pp. 131–132) seven levels corresponded to the seven heavens of the god Indra. The 12 towers on each

ascending level corresponded to the animals of the zodiac. In all, there were 108 towers, a number with both Hindu and Buddhist cosmological significance (the sum of the moon's four 27-day cycles representing earth, fire, water, and air). A maximum of 33 towers were visible at one time, correlating with the number of Hindu deities.

Angkor Thom & Bayon

By the time Angkor Thom was built in the 12th century, religious symbolism was incorporated at increasingly complex levels. The coy smiles of the face towers adorning Bayon temple (see p. 141) and the city gates of Angkor Thom are an enduring mystery. Jayavarman VII (r. ca.1181–1218), a devout Buddhist, may have believed himself to be a Bodhisattva, an enlightened being who forsook nirvana to be reborn and help others. If so, the faces may be amalgamations of the Buddha or Lokesvara (the Bodhisattva of compassion) and Jayavarman VII, who sent 23 small images of the Buddha in his likeness—Jayabuddhamahanatha—to his kingdom's far reaches. Yet as spires of a Mahayana Buddhist temple, the faces atop Bayon may simply represent Lokesvara, or, as 13th-century Chinese envoy Zhou Daguan stated flatly, the Buddha.

Bayon's symbolism begins outside the city, at the causeways of Angkor Thom, flanked by rows of massive statues of demons and gods holding the bodies of *nagas*. Since naga embellished causeways as early as Bakong (see pp. 129–130), causeways were associated with their role in the Hindu myth of the rainbow bridge linking the world of men to that of the gods. The demons and gods at Angkor Thom, however, appear to be engaged in a tug of war, drawing obvious allusions to the Churning of the Sea of Milk (see below). The demons flank the right side of each gate, effectively pulling against gods on the opposite side of the city. This suggests that Bayon temple, at the center of Angkor Thom,

represents Mount Mandara, the focus of the churning. The 54 demons and 54 gods on each causeway again total the mystical number, 108.

Angkor Wat

Angkor Wat was consigned by Suryavarman II (r. 1113–ca 1150), who broke from tradition by promoting Vishnu—not Shiva—as the supreme god. Angkor Wat's greatest mystery lies in its atypical westward orientation; it was the only major Angkorian temple that did not face east. Equally unusual was the layout of the bas-reliefs, designed to be followed in a counterclockwise direction. As Hindu custom was to walk funerary temples in a counter-clockwise direction and west was the direction often associated with death, some believe Angkor Wat was built as a mausoleum for Suryavarman II. Others believe that a westward orientation was more appropriate for a temple honoring Vishnu. It likely was a place of worship to a deified king in spiritual union with his patron god. Further speculation suggests Angkor Wat could have been a massive cosmological representation of the "calendar" of Hindu gods.

Churning of the Sea of Milk

The popular Hindu creation myth, the Churning of the Sea of Milk—the cosmic ocean—is often represented at Khmer temples, notably the East Gallery of Angkor Wat (see p. 138). The tale begins when the *asuras* (demons) and *devas* (gods) were weakened by the absence of *amrita*, the divine elixir of immortality, which was lost during the re-creation of the universe.

As both sides struggled to extract the amrita, the god Vishnu resolved the turmoil by getting them to work together—churning the Sea of Milk. The gods and demons took turns pulling on opposing ends of an enormous serpent, the *naga* Vasuki. Coiled around Mount Mandara, which served as the churning rod, the naga

suffered this tug-of-war for a thousand seasons, during which he nearly poisoned the cosmic sea by vomiting. Shiva saved the precious elixir by drinking Vasuki's vomit, which poisoned the god, turning him blue.

At one point Mount Mandara began to sink, and Vishnu transformed himself into the turtle Kurma and swam beneath the mountain to keep it afloat. As the years went on, the naga's breath grew labored and hot, nearly suffocating the demons. Just in time, however, the amrita was produced, along with other deities, including the seductive *apsaras* (celestial dancers).

While the demons got their hands on the amrita first, the gods ultimately proved victorious with Vishnu's help.

Ta Nei & Ta Keo

🗺 127 B3

✉ 0.6 mile (1 km)
W of Ta Prohm
on Rte. 66A

💲 Admission
included in
Angkor pass
(see sidebar
p. 131)

Entry to Ta Prohm is best from the east. Exit the large, complex temple from the west, where your driver can retrieve you perhaps an hour later. After passing through the outermost enclosure wall, a causeway leads past the first of two moats to the first of four primary gopuras. You'll begin to see the towering trees that are majestically, gradually destroying the temple.

INSIDER TIP:

Ascend Ta Keo from the east, even if you arrive from the conventional west side of the temple—the east side is far less steep and therefore safer.

—TREVOR RANGES
National Geographic author

Next is the rectangular **Hall of Dancers,** named for the apsara carvings on its pillars and likely once used for ritual dance. From here, a series of wooden walkways leads visitors through the least collapsed corridors, beneath the massive roots of trees, and toward the **central enclosure and sanctuary.**

Due to its complexity and surprising number of hidden carvings, Ta Prohm is best appreciated with a guide. However, the temple guards provide excellent information. They appreciate a tip for pointing out the most interesting attractions, including the **pediment** featuring the "Grand Departure" of the Buddha and a **small relief carving** of what appears to be a stegosaurus.

Ta Nei: Just north of Ta Prohm's west gopura, Ta Nei is tucked away in the jungle, accessible only by foot or bicycle. The primary access to it is a gate beside the public toilets between Ta Prohm and Ta Keo. You can be dropped here and picked up on the west side of Ta Keo. The sandy road to Ta Nei passes through several miles of shady forest.

The temple, likely commissioned by Jayavarman VII, has undergone some restoration, but remains in great disrepair. Towering trees perch atop its almost entirely destroyed enclosure walls. Only the eastern gopura allows access into the temple. The paths to Ta Nei, which you must follow almost due north to arrive without getting lost, end at the temple's west side. Walk around to the east to begin exploring the ruined temple. After visiting Ta Nei, return back along the same path, veering right toward the road's end to approach Ta Keo.

Ta Keo: If you follow the correct path, you will arrive at Ta Keo from the east, the direction to which the step pyramid is oriented. A clearing in the forest reveals the towering state temple of Jayavarman V (r. ca. 968–1001). The temple was left incomplete, likely because the king died during construction. According to an inscription, lightning also struck the temple and this bad omen may have convinced the builders to abandon the project.

Ta Keo stands 72 feet (22 m) high, capped by **five towers,** each sitting on its own raised platform.

Stairways lead up the platforms to the summit from each of the cardinal directions. Once atop the summit, visit the **shrine to Buddha** in the central sanctuary. The towers themselves are unadorned, though a few pedestals and a linga (beside the western stairway) indicate they were consecrated to Shiva.

Chapel of the Hospital & Spean Thma:

Across from Ta Keo, the Chapel of the Hospital was constructed next to one of 102 hospitals built by Jayavarman VII. The inscription here mentions the *dharmasalas* (rest areas) the king had built along roads that connected far-flung provinces to his capital. These roads included stone bridges, such as Spean Thma, on the road from Ta Keo to Thommanom. Spean Thma offers a glimpse of these bridges' former magnificence, though it's not the best example of one.

Chau Say Tevoda & Thommanon:

Just west of Spean Thma lie two small, single-tower temples built during the reign of Suryavarman II. Their similarity and location, opposite each other outside the Victory Gate, have led to speculation they are a pair. However, the association is convenient at best.

Approaching Chau Say Tevoda from the east (your left if facing the temple from the parking area), square boundary markers and a cruciform terrace precede a raised causeway. Go through the entry tower and toward the **central sanctuary;** its exterior features both original and reconstructed devatas. The **southern library** has a nearly intact bas-relief pediment. Exiting by the north entrance, you will see Thommanon directly ahead. This temple was reconstructed in the 1960s, so it's difficult to tell where renovations have taken place. Left incomplete at the end of Suryavarman II's reign, Thommanon has well-preserved carvings, particularly the elaborate devatas and scenes on lintels and pediments. Note the carved pediments in the antechamber of the **central sanctuary** and the lintels above the doorways to the inner chamber, the second of which features Vishnu riding garuda. The road from Thommanon leads to the Victory Gate. ■

Renowned devatas adorn Thommanon Temple.

Apsaras

Several ancient Hindu texts recount the story of the Churning of the Sea of Milk (see sidebar p. 151). As depicted on the East Gallery of Angkor Wat, *asuras* (demons) and *devas* (gods) churned the Sea of Milk to extract *amrita*, the elixir of immortality. The process released a number of creatures, including the *apsaras*, celestial dancers who can be seen flying along the top of the bas-relief of the Churning at Angkor Wat.

In Hindu lore, apsaras could seduce the gods, as their beauty knew no rival. They also possessed great dancing ability, and it is in these two regards that Angkorian artists chose to represent them in carvings on their temples. Angkor Wat alone features more than 3,000 bas-relief apsaras, renowned not only for their intricacy, but also for their unique designs. Each one seems to have her own pose, hairstyle, clothing, and jewelry.

INSIDER TIP:

Of all the *apsaras* at Angkor Wat, only one is smiling enough to show her teeth. She's just to the right of the main entrance to the complex. Don't miss her!

—TERRESSA DAVIS
Heritage Watch

While the temples of Angkor are frequently graced with their serene beauty, Angkorian apsaras went beyond simple carvings and were emulated in real life. The temples of Preah Khan, Banteay Kdei, and Ta Prohm were reputed to have thousands of dancers residing within their grounds and devoted halls to ceremonial dancing, the pillars and lintels of which feature exquisite carvings of dancing apsaras. The tradition of apsara dancers dates at least as far back as the earliest Cambodian kingdom of Funan, which sent an emissary to China in A.D. 243 with an offering of court dancers. When the Siamese invaded Cambodia a number of times beginning in the 14th century, they often made off with thousands of dancers, spawning or at least greatly influencing the art of Thai classical dance.

Other than the above exceptions, for more than a thousand years apsara dancing was only performed at the Royal Court or on temple grounds in order to pay homage to the king, ancestral spirits, or the gods. After the fall of Angkor, apsara dancing was becoming a lost art until King Ang Duong (r. 1848–1859) began a revival. In the 20th century, apsara dancing was championed by Queen Sisowath Kossamak Nearireach, who re-created the costumes and choreography based on 12th-century carvings. During the attempt by the Khmer Rouge to destroy all remnants of Cambodian traditional arts, apsara dancing was kept alive by masters living both in refugee camps and in exile. Fortunately, Queen Kossamak had also trained her granddaughter, Princess Norodom Bopha Devi, who became an accomplished prima ballerina and furthered her grandmother's efforts to introduce the Royal Ballet to the rest of Cambodia as well as the world.

Today's apsara dancers typically study at the Royal University of Fine Arts. From an early age, they learn over 1,500 intricate positions, many of which employ precise finger and wrist movements that require subtlety and grace. Performances on special occasions by the Royal Ballet feature dancers in elaborate silk costumes and golden tiaras or masks, accompanied by sacred music by a live band. A choir contributes dialogue from epic tales, such as the Cambodian version of the Hindu *Ramayana*, the *Reamker*.

Many hotels and restaurants, particularly in Siem Reap, organize apsara performances of varying quality, typically including set dinners.

Around the East Baray

The area around the East Baray, a massive artificial reservoir, contains temples from the reigns of various kings. You can visit these temples in a half day, at most, then take a sunset climb up Phnom Bok or visit another group of temples. Those north of Angkor Thom are a bit quieter than most and feature their own impressive and unique characteristics.

A boy plays in waters near the East Baray.

Near the southwest corner of the East Baray lies **Prasat Kravan,** the Cardamom Sanctuary, perhaps the finest Angkor-era brick monument. Dedicated to Vishnu in 921, probably by Harshavarman I (*r.* ca 910–ca 923), the temple is extraordinary for a number of reasons. First, the **five towers** feature nearly perfectly square bricks that are almost seamlessly stacked, held together by a thin adherent of vegetable sap. In addition, the interior walls of both the central and northernmost towers feature **bas-reliefs** that are carved directly into the brick.

The images feature Vishnu and his consort Lakshmi in various incarnations. Those in the central tower are almost perfectly restored and depict Vishnu as his ultimate avatar on the east-facing wall. The south- and north-facing walls depict Vishnu as the dwarf Vamana and Vishnu with four arms, upon the half-man, half-bird *garuda,* respectively. The northernmost tower features Lakshmi in various incarnations. The partial relief on the northern wall is

Pre Rup

🏛 127 B3, 161

✉ 1.25 miles (2 km) E of Rte. 66B Rte. on 66A

💲 Admission included in Angkor pass (see sidebar p. 131)

Banteay Samre

🏛 127 C3

✉ 3 miles (5 km) E of Pre Rup via Rte. 66A and Rte. 204

💲 Admission included in Angkor pass (see sidebar p. 131)

incomplete, however, as a result of the restoration during the 1960s that replaced the temple's missing or damaged original bricks.

Pre Rup

Beyond the Srah Srang, turning east away from Angkor Thom, lies Pre Rup. Consecrated in 961, Pre Rup was the state temple of Rajendravarman II (r.944–968), after he relocated the capital back to Yasodharapura (Angkor) following several decades at Koh Ker.

INSIDER TIP:

Bring a compass; guides usually explain temple features based on their cardinal directions. A compass is essential for the serious exploration of Khmer temples and their ornamentations.

—TREVOR RANGES
National Geographic author

Pre Rup is a step pyramid, temple mountain, as was the tradition for state temples. The three-tiered temple was capped with a quincunx of towers, the central one dedicated to the *linga* Rajendrabhadresvara. The other four towers honored Shiva, Vishnu, and Uma as representations of Rajendravarman II, his half-brother King Hashavarman, one of his maternal ancestors, and his maternal aunt. His gesture honoring the Hindu gods

was one of several aimed at establishing his new kingdom's legitimacy at the seat of traditional power.

Just before the eastern stairway, flanked by libraries, rests a small **rectangular basin** thought by some to have served as a crematorium, though it may have originally been a pedestal for a statue of the sacred bull, Nandi. It was common practice to "turn the body" (the literal meaning of *pre rup*) of the deceased as they were cremated. However, there is no evidence that such rites were conducted there.

The second platform is surrounded by 12 brick towers that once housed lingas. On the uppermost level, **four ancillary towers** are guarded by male and female deities. These *dvarapalas* were lightly carved into the brick, then covered with stucco, some of which remains in fair condition.

The other distinguishing features of Pre Rup, which spawned its own artistic style, are the elaborate **sandstone carvings** on the lintels, colonnettes, and false doors. Intact lintels here include several elephant motifs, including Indra on his three-headed mount, Airavata; Ganesha; and an elephant being consumed by Kala.

East Baray

To the north of Pre Rup, the road passes through a tree-topped berm and expansive rice fields open up on either side. You have just entered the Yasodharatataka, Yasovarman I's massive reservoir, known today as the East Baray. The enormous public waterworks required the Siem Reap River to be diverted from its original course.

At the *baray*'s center is **East Mebon.** Similar in style and design to Pre Rup, Rajendra-varman II's East Mebon is capped by five towers and the central one once housed a linga. The temple appears to be pyramidal, though this design would have been less obvious when it was surrounded, as it originally was, by water that was 10 feet (3 m) or more deep.

At each of the cardinal directions, East Mebon has stairways—once generally submerged—leading to platforms that were formerly boat landings. From the east landing it is a pleasant stroll around the **first terrace,** where elephant statues are posted on each corner. The southwestern statue is the finest of the bunch.

A narrow walkway on the **second terrace** also has four elephants, with the southwestern figure again the most elaborately detailed. Note that these elephants are smaller than the ones below, a technique to amplify the perception of the temple's height. Near the southwestern elephant, a conduit on the ground ends in a lion's-head spout.

Atop the **highest platform** are five towers. While the central tower housed a Shiva-linga, the four surrounding towers featured representations of the king's ancestors as deities. The lintels and false doors of each tower are fine examples of the Pre Rup style of art—the main tower's eastern lintel depicts Indra atop Airavata. Just to the east of the central tower is a small platform where it is likely a statue of Nandi once stood.

Banteay Samre

Just southeast of the East Baray, on the road running east from East Mebon, sits Banteay Samre, the "citadel of the samre." The name is derived from the legend of a cucumber farmer of Samre ethnicity. Though the king had instructed the gardener to kill anyone who stole the cucumbers, he foolishly entered the garden plot one night. In the

---

East Mebon's Courtyard Masterpieces

The inner courtyard of East Mebon's second terrace features five rectangular libraries and eight brick towers, which once housed *linga*. All boast elaborately carved sandstone lintels, colonnettes, and false doors of exquisite beauty. The towers were covered in small holes to help stucco adhere to them. Walk around the courtyard and examine the finely carved decorations on the structures, as the designs vary greatly.

---

darkness, the loyal gardener did not recognize the king and killed him. As the king had left no heir, the royal elephant was consigned to select the new sovereign. The pachyderm knelt before the gardener, who subsequently became the king. Lacking the support of the aristocracy, the Samre king withdrew to a walled citadel. Eventually he disposed of those who were disloyal to him and reigned over a peaceful land.

Preah Khan

▲ 127 B3, 161

✉ 2.5 miles (4 km) N of Angkor Thom on Rte. 66A

$ Admission included in Angkor pass (see sidebar p. 131)

Although the origin of Banteay Samre's name may be questionable, the designation of citadel is certainly valid. Consigned by Suryavarman II (r. 1113–ca 1150), the temple is surrounded by an imposing 20-foot-high (6 m) enclosure, with primary entries from elevated causeways to the east and west.

The **central sanctuary** lies within two enclosures, both of which contain concentric galleries. Before entering the sanctuary, note the *naga* balustrades framing the walkway around the interior enclosure. These nagas, symbolically associated with water, signify that this enclosure functioned as a unique interior moat.

Wander the walkways around the moat and examine the lintels above the doorways. The pediment above the lintel on the **northeast library** features Vishnu reclining on a naga as a lotus, from which Brahma arises, grows out of his navel.

North of Angkor Thom

The North Gate of Angkor Thom is the quietest gate, but then it also has the fewest remaining statuary. Beyond the North Gate lie three other spectacular religious monuments commissioned by Jayavarman VII (r. ca. 1181–1218), as well as the unnoticeable remains of his once enormous—now dry—baray. These temples are best visited in the early morning.

Preah Khan: The Sacred Sword Temple is in Nagara Jayasri, the "city of victorious royal fortune," the last great accomplishment of Jayavarman VII. In addition to honoring Jayavarman VII's father,

Preah Khan, a royal city of Jayavarman VII

Preah Khan also housed shrines to 515 individuals deified by the consecration of Hindu and Buddhist images in their honor.

The foundation stela recounts a population of 97,840 in service of the city, including a thousand scholars and a thousand dancers. Preah Khan is believed to have been a Buddhist university, where Jayavarman VII's second wife was chief scholar. The temple may also, as the name suggests, have been the location for the palladium of the kingdom, the sacred sword (see sidebar p. 148).

Considering its size, enter Preah Khan from the east and exit to the west. Your *tuk-tuk* driver can pick you up perhaps an hour after dropping you off. The temple is laid out horizontally, with the central sanctuary lying along the east-west axis.

Pass through the city's exterior wall and follow the first stretch of causeway. Then you will arrive at an imposing **sandstone barrier** featuring 72 garudas, each 16 feet tall (5 m) and protruding from the wall every 165 feet (50 m).

Then the trail leads to an elevated platform and the center-most of three cruciform *gopuras* (entrance gates or pavilions) that pass through to the temple proper. Within this third enclosure, the first building is the impressive **Hall of Dancers.** Low-relief *apsaras* grace the pillars; bas-relief chains of the celestial dancers line the interior facing lintels.

Before passing into the central compound, take a short detour to the north (the right), where a walkway leads east to an unusual **two-story structure** built on large, round pillars. It may have once housed the sacred sword.

Returning to the gopura that leads into the central compound, enter a labyrinth of interconnected chambers, corridors, and courtyards. Shortly thereafter, the hallway is missing a roof entirely and the **central sanctuary** rises

INSIDER TIP:

Seek out secluded Preah Khan. This quiet complex is a bit off the beaten path and stands in the midst of overgrown jungle.

—SIMON WILLIAMS
The Nature Conservancy

up before you. Notice the holes punctuating the pillars leading up to the central tower. The primary function of the holes, which also adorn the interior and exterior of the tower, was to anchor brass panels. Though inscriptions do mention jewels adorning the walls, they also indicate that 1,500 tons (1,361 tonnes) of brass adorned the central sanctuary.

The image of Lokesvara in the likeness of Jayavarman VII's father once stood in the central tower. Today a stupa (funerary spire) graces the innermost sanctum. Modern Buddhists hold the stupa in great reverence, believing it has the power to grant wishes.

From the central sanctuary, the shrines to Shiva, Vishnu, and
(continued on p. 164)

Around Angkor Drive

The civilization at Angkor wasn't confined to that area; north of the city, Phnom Kulen was an important religious site and the carvings in the Siem Reap River that flowed through Kbal Spean consecrated the water of Angkor. Banteay Srei and Phnom Bok were also important temples. They can be visited along with centers that aid victims of Cambodia's tragic war and protect endangered animals.

A *tuk-tuk* carries passengers through the gates of Angkor Thom.

Many people make the 20-mile (32 km) drive north of Siem Reap to see the exquisite tenth-century temple Banteay Srei. The river carvings at Kbal Spean are often visited following Banteay Srei. However, there are other attractions along the way that can make up an incredibly diverse day trip. Plan your trip at your hotel or guesthouse with a *tuk-tuk* driver the night before, so he knows that you are interested in visiting a variety of sights, rather than the two or three normally included in such outings. Considering the sheer volume and variety of carvings, visiting Banteay Srei is significantly more interesting with a guide; ask your hotel or guesthouse to recommend one. Finally, as your tour will start early in the morning and both Banteay Srei and Kbal Spean require visitors to have

NOT TO BE MISSED:

Prasat Phnom Bok • Banteay Srei • Kbal Spean • Angkor Centre for Conservation of Biodiversity • Cambodian Landmine Museum and Relief Facility

valid passes to Angkor Archaeological Park, it is essential you get a ticket to the park the previous evening at the latest.

Start your day around 5 a.m., toting a picnic breakfast to eat along the way. **Prasat Phnom Bok ❶** sits atop a nearly 700-foot-tall (212 m) mountain 15 miles (24 km) northeast of Siem Reap. The temple atop Phnom Bok was one of the three hilltop temples built by Yasovarman I (r.889–910) founder of Yasodharapura (Angkor). While the temple is essentially the same design as the one atop Phnom Kraom (see p. 115), the condition of Prasat Phnom Bok's bas-reliefs is far superior. The ruined state of the towers makes clambering around the rubble quite fun. The temple, which is accessible up a long and fairly steep stairway, is an excellent place to watch the sunrise before heading up to Banteay Srei.

Taking advantage of your early start, next visit **Banteay Srei** ❷, a masterpiece of Angkorian art and architecture. Despite its remote location, Banteay Srei, "citadel of the women," is one of the most popular temples at Angkor and is best appreciated early in the

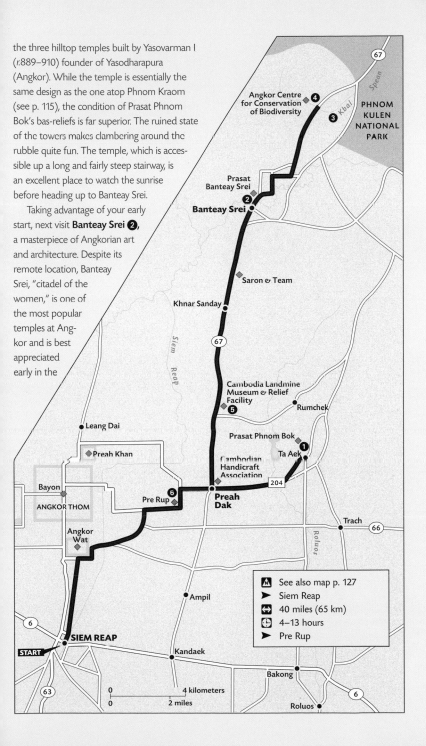

See also map p. 127
Siem Reap
40 miles (65 km)
4–13 hours
Pre Rup

morning. Its curiously miniature dimensions, construction of pink sandstone, and elaborate, delicate, and well-preserved bas-reliefs combine to establish it as one of the greatest artistic accomplishments of the Angkor era.

One of the few temples not built for one of the Angkorian kings, Banteay Srei was commissioned by a counselor of Rajendravarman II (r.944–968) and guru of his son, the child-king Jayavarman V (r. ca. 968–1001). Known in its day as Tribhuvanamahesvara after the Shiva-*linga* enshrined in its central sanctuary, it was completed around the time of Rajendravarman's death. Many residents of the small city of Ishvarapura, in the center of which the temple was set, were likely employed in its service.

INSIDER TIP:

Don't miss Banteay Srei, a beautiful little tenth-century Hindu temple elaborately carved from red sandstone. It appears miniature, and is more human-scaled than Angkor Wat or Angkor Thom. Bring a tripod to steady your camera for the best pictures.

—PAT HENLEY
National Geographic contributor

Like the exquisite carvings at other temples built during the reign of Rajendravarman II, notably the East Mebon, the deep relief carvings at Banteay Srei are particularly refined. The temple's dense, pink sandstone allowed the artisans to showcase carving techniques they had mastered on wood. Nearly the entire surface of the temple is ornately decorated, with episodes from the epics *Ramayana* and *Mahabharata* gracing many lintels and pediments; other notable artistic elements include *devas* (male deities) and *devatas* (female deities) guarding

the doorways. Freestanding half-human, half-monkey (or half-demon, half-lion, or half-bird) sculptures surround the central sanctuary.

Just 11 miles (18 km) north of Banteay Srei, the **Kbal Spean River** ❸ is a small tributary of the Siem Reap River, which is the source of the water that flows from the Kulen Mountains to the temples and *barays* of Angkor. The Khmers of Angkor associated the mountains and rivers with their mythological counterparts in Hindu lore, and believed their water to be sacred. Consequently, they commissioned the carving of religious imagery in the stones over which the river flowed. Near the carvings, 11th-century inscriptions aptly describe the Kbal Spean as the "river of a thousand lingas" for the rows upon rows of phallic linga, representations of fertility, that consecrated the water as it passed over these sacred carvings.

The carvings also include bas-reliefs of Shiva, Uma, Vishnu, and a few aquatic animals. The carvings are located nearly a mile (1.6 km) along a shady, moderately difficult trail that is part of the Phnom Kulen National Park, home to 145 species of birds. Listen for the echoing hoots of pileated gibbons as you make your way first to a waterfall, then to the lingas, and finally to the natural stone bridge for which Kbal Spean is named, where two reclining Vishnu scenes are carved into opposing rock faces. A number of the carvings are more or less visible depending on the level and clarity of the river—the tail end of the rainy season is the optimal time to visit.

Your day of touring could include a side trip to see more of **Phnom Kulen National Park** *(9 miles/14 km E of Banteay Srei, $$$$$)*. Kulen Mountain was a place of great religious significance even before the establishment of Angkor, as Jayavarman II (r.802–850), founder of the Khmer Empire was crowned *chakravartin*—universal monarch—at a temple atop the mountain. While most of the temples are generally inaccessible and in ruins, the prime attraction at Kulen Mountain is the impressive waterfall. Although this cascade is an immensely popular weekend destination for the local population, it may not be not spectacular enough to justify the $20 entrance fee charged to foreigners. However, a large reclining Buddha carved into the top of an enormous rock and a portion of the river carved with lingas make the bumpy trip worthwhile if you have time.

The **Angkor Centre for Conservation of Biodiversity** ❹ (ACCB; *Rte. 67, 26 miles/42 km NE of Siem Reap, tel 855(0)99-604-017, $*) is a wildlife rescue center and nature conservation area located beside the entrance to Kbal Spean. Monday through Friday at 1 p.m., the ACCB provides free guided tours of its facility, which includes wildlife such as pangolins, eagles, and porcupines. In addition to its conservation and environmental education efforts, the ACCB also runs an active beekeeping program.

Farther south along Route 67, the small sculpture workshop of **Saron and Team** *(Kor Koh Jrum Village, Rte. 67, tel 855(0)92-991-002, $)* employs several disabled Cambodians who craft religious figures from the Buddhist, Hindu, and Christian faiths. The difficult-to-spot shop is located about 2 miles (3 km) south of Banteay Srei. Watch for a sign on the east side of the road.

Nearly 4 miles (6 km) south of Banteay Srei, the **Cambodia Landmine Museum and Relief Facility** ❺ *(Mondul 3 Village, Slorkram Commune, Rte. 67, 15 miles/24 km NE of Siem Reap, tel 855(0)12-598-951, $)* provides an excellent opportunity to learn about the horrific impact of land mines on the Cambodian people. The museum features a video documentary and displays deactivated mines and other weapons. It also has profiles of children whose lives have been adversely affected by these awful instruments of war who have been helped by a project conducted by the museum and an associated nongovernmental organization. Together they also are offering assistance through education and land-mine clearance.

Another project that aids Cambodians with disabilities is the **Cambodian Handicraft Association for Landmine and Polio**

The intricately decorated Hindu temple of Banteay Srei

Disabled *(N of jct. of Rte. 67 & Rte. 204, tel 855(0)12-913-861, www.bigpond.com.kh/users/wthanchashop)*. They provide skills training, and their small workshop produces many of the silk products for sale in their showroom.

Turning west, back toward Siem Reap, Route 204 passes through the village of **Preah Dak.** Villagers sell a number of handicrafts here, as well as fresh palm sugar cooked in large, open wok-like pans. Free samples are available from friendly vendors.

Finally, if you are returning late in the day, ask your driver to stop at **Pre Rup** ❻ (see p. 156), a popular place to catch the sun's last rays. The state temple of Rajendravarman II is spectacular at any time of day, but it makes an excellent place to view the sunset at the end of your trip.

Neak Pean & Ta Som

▲ 127 B3

✉ Neak Pean: 1.5 miles (2.5 km) E of Preah Khan on Rte. 66A; Ta Som: 1.25 miles (2 km) E of Preah Khan on 66A

$ Admission included in Angkor pass (see sidebar p. 131)

former kings of Angkor lie directly north, west, and south. The south path leads past crumbling towers to a generally unadorned and uninteresting shrine. Turn north (right) instead, and pass through a series of diminishing doorways, the smallest of which is the entrance to the **shrine of Shiva.** Exiting east (right) from this shrine, the finest of the temple's **relief carvings** features Vishnu reclining on a naga. A lotus flower grows above him, symbolizing the beginning of a new cosmic cycle of the universe.

Backtracking to the central sanctuary, turn west (right) toward the shrine of Vishnu and arrive at a **small courtyard.** The wall to your right is elaborately decorated with hermits meditating beneath jack-fruit trees. Beyond this courtyard, you will soon enter the rear of the west-facing **shrine to Vishnu** where a pedestal now features a headless, seated Buddha.

Neak Pean: Due east of Preah Khan, Neak Pean was referred to in an inscription as "a lotus rising that carries the image of the supreme god." This image alludes to the legend of Brahma, who was born out of Vishnu's navel as a lotus flower, and may symbolically represent the rebirth of Angkor following Jayavarman VII's redemptive defeat of the Cham. The lotus-shaped **central sanctuary** indeed rises up from within a central pond that is surrounded by four ancillary ponds, essentially an aquatic quincunx.

The **central pond** may even represent the mythical lake Anavatapa, whose waters were believed to have restorative powers. The lake also was the home of the nagas Nanda and Upananda. Such symbolism is supported by other inscriptions, which describe Neak Pean as "a sacred island, drawing its charm from its ponds and clearing away the sins of those who approach it." In addition, the temple's central sanctuary is surrounded by a **pair of serpent statues:** Their hooded heads are raised at the eastern entrance and their tails are entwined at the back of the structure. The temple draws its modern name, Neak Pean (the

West Baray & West Mebon

The West Baray, a 5-by-1.4-mile (13 x 2.3 km) artificial lake commissioned by Suryavarman I (r.1003– ca 1049), was the largest of the hydraulic projects constructed at Angkor. It is the only one of the *barays* that still retains water.

West Mebon was located on an island (*accessible only by boat*) at the baray's center. The island, which remains a popular weekend picnic destination for locals, once housed a massive, bronze, reclining Vishnu (now in the National Museum in Phnom Penh; see p. 72). Little of the temple remains here. The combined *tuk-tuk* and boat ride to the island (*available at pier at midway point of baray's S coast, $$*) is probably worth the trip only if you are spending more than a week in the area and want a relaxing way to take a few hours off from visiting temples.

The atmospheric ruins at Ta Som

entwined serpents), from these two statues.

A road leads across the Jayatataka Baray to the northern pond. Descend this empty pool's stairs and walk into the small, **arched alcove.** Four of these alcoves each contain a spout in the form of an animal head from which water once flowed and devotees received ablutions. The northern spout is in the form of an elephant, the east is a man, the south is a lion, and the west is a horse.

The **carvings** above Neak Pean's four sanctuaries and adorning its central *prasat* depict episodes from the life of the Buddha. Jayavarman VII also honored the Bodhisattva Lokesvara in the central sanctum. The statue facing the island (just to its east) is an avatar of Lokesvara, Balaha, a horse who saved a group of shipwrecked sailors.

Ta Som: This Buddhist temple also was commissioned by Jayavarman VII. You approach the temple from the west, near the eastern edge of the now dry Jayatataka Baray. Pass through the **outermost gopura,** capped with smiling faces of Lokesvara. Once inside the interior enclosure, walk around the central temple complex, past the reconstructed, freestanding pediments with relief carvings, toward the eastern gopuras. The final one is draped with the roots of a strangler fig, offering a great photo opportunity amid the smiling faces and bas-relief *devatas*.

Back at the temple, be aware that several passages within the interior of the temple are partially or completely collapsed. Navigating the maze of interconnecting corridors and clearings can be difficult, but the challenge makes the temple enjoyable to explore. ■

Magnificent temples and exotic wildlife in remote border provinces, once the garrison of Thai invaders, and Pol Pot's final resting place

Western Cambodia

Funerary stupas surrounding Wat Tahm Rai Saw in Battambang

Western Cambodia

Western Cambodia incorporates most of the provinces along the border with Thailand and those located in the plains south of Tonle Sap and north of the Cardamom Mountains. Begin at Battambang, western Cambodia's popular hub, and explore the day-trip destinations surrounding it. As many travelers make the journey between Battambang and Phnom Penh, the attractions along National Highway 5 follow.

The French colonial former Governor's Residence in Battambang town

Conclude with the less explored northwestern provinces of Banteay Meanchey and Oddar Meanchey, which are accessible from Thailand, Battambang, and Siem Reap.

Geographically central to the western provinces is Battambang Province; the capital city of the same name is Cambodia's second largest city. Despite its relative size and strategic location, few tourists visit Battambang as a destination in itself. Instead, it is a sort of nexus through which one must pass en route to or from other destinations, including Thailand, Phnom Penh, or Siem Reap. Nonetheless, the town's laid-back style and surrounding natural and historical attractions have fostered a number of tourist-oriented businesses, including a cooking class, restaurants, bars, and boutique hotels.

National Highway 5 connects Phnom Penh and Battambang by passing through Oudong, Kompong Chhnang, and Pursat. Oudong functioned as the capital of Cambodia for 248 years following the abandonment of Angkor

(see p. 29). Kompong Chhnang and Pursat each feature a few interesting sights worth quick stops. Kompong Chhnang is renowned as a port for fish caught in the Tonle Sap River and for the nearby traditional pottery villages. Pursat is home to the intriguing Kompong Luong floating village and a shrine to an ancestral spirit believed to have helped the Khmer defeat the Siamese in a legendary battle. Pursat is also the town from which the adventurous set off into the southern Cardamom Mountains.

From Siem Reap, visitors often arrive in Battambang via ferry by way of the majestic Tonle Sap. Along the way, few realize that they are passing by the bird sanctuary at Prek Toal,

NOT TO BE MISSED:

The circus show at Phare Ponleu Selpak, Battambang **172–173**

A day trip from Battambang to Wat Ek Phnom, or from Battambang to Phnom Banon, Phnom Sampeu, and Kamping Puoy **173–174, 176–179**

Meditating at Dhamma Latthika Battambang Vipassana Center **178**

The floating village of Kompong Luong **181**

Learning about silk weaving in Phnom Srok and spotting a sarus crane **185**

Exploring the remote temple complex of Banteay Chhmar in Banteay Meanchey Province **186–187**

4▷

THAILAND

O Smach

Dangrek Range

BANTEAY Ampil
CHHMAR
PROTECTED
LANDSCAPE

ODDAR MEANCHEY

Anlong Veng

Prasat Ta Prohm ◆ Banteay Chhmar
Thmor Pouk ◆ Banteay Top

Samraong (56)

KULEN PRUM TEP
WILDLIFE SANCTUARY

BANTEAY
MEANCHEY

*Ang Trapaeng
Thmar Baray* (68)

Srah
Chik

SIEM REAP &
TONLE SAP
p. 103

Area of map detail

3▷

Poipet (56)

Sisophon (5)

Phnom
Srok

Choob

Kralanh (6)

Phnom ⊛
Penh

RONEAM
DOUN
SAM
WILDLIFE
SANCTUARY

Lvea (5)

Bavel

Prey
Chas

Siem Reap

0   40 kilometers
0   20 miles

Wat Ek
Phnom

Wat Somraoung
Knong & Killing Field

Battambang ◆ Prasat Basseat

Kamping
Puoy

Wat Kor

Phnom Sampeu ◆ Kompong Seyma

Phnom Banon ◆ Amatak Prasat
Phnom Banorn
Winery

Pailin (57)

Sangker

Doun
Tri

- - - Unpaved road

Tonle Sap

CENTRAL
CAMBODIA
p. 193

2▷

PAILIN

Samlot

BATTAMBANG

Moung Russei (5)

Neak Ta Khleang
Muong

Kompong
Luong

Pursat

Krakor

Ponley

PHNUM
SAMKOK
WILDLIFE
SANCTUARY

Thma
Da

PURSAT

Kompong
Chhnang

Cardamom Mountains

AORAL
WILDLIFE
SANCTUARY

Romeas (5)

KOMPONG
CHHNANG

1▷

SIHANOUKVILLE
& SOUTHERN
COASTAL
PROVINCES
p. 235

△   △
A   B

Oudong

To Phnom
Penh

C

which lies within Battambang Province though it's more accessible as a day trip from Siem Reap (see p. 123).

Leaving Battambang, many travelers continue west to Thailand, passing through Sisophon on the way to Poipet, a border town notorious for ramshackle casinos and scam artists. The more adventurous journey from Battambang to Pailin, a small remote province whose forests and gemstones harbored and financed the Khmer Rouge for three decades. Other travelers choose to go into southern Pursat, the northern border of the

Cardamom Mountains, where some of the last remaining exotic wildlife in Southeast Asia have survived amid forests that are still strewn with land mines.

With more time (and reliable transportation), visitors can make a border province circuit. Travel north to Banteay Meanchey Province, which contains a number of less frequented Angkor-era temples, such as Banteay Chhmar. Then, skirt the Thai border toward Anlong Veng, Pol Pot's final resting place, before finally continuing on to Siem Reap. ■

Battambang & Vicinity

Battambang was established under Thai occupation in 1795. Over a century later, the Thai withdrew, taking the city's inhabitants with them. Cambodians repopulated Battambang, largely in the current location on the Sangker River's banks. Occupied by the Japanese during World War II, Battambang (which included Banteay Meanchey) was again ceded to the Thai. They established a prisoner of war camp and built National Highway 5 using forced labor.

The early morning sun illuminates Battambang's wide boulevards and historic storefronts as motorbikes make their way through town.

Battambang was returned to Cambodia after the war, but it continued to suffer. The Khmer Rouge evacuated the city in 1975 and forced thousands to build the "Killing Dam" of Kamping Puoy. The area was then caught in the crossfire among Khmer Rouge, Vietnamese, and Cambodian government soldiers, which continued until 1996.

Today, Battambang town is referred to as Cambodia's "second city," but its wide, uncrowded boulevards and sleepy nightlife make it feel more like another provincial capital. The town features a few markets, a number of older *wats* (temples), a lovely riverside park, and some well-preserved buildings from the French colonial period. It's worth spending a few days here to unwind; many visitors take in the surrounding sights via day trips from the city. Historical attractions include the 11th-century temples of Ek Phnom and Phnom Banon, and sites of Khmer Rouge atrocities. The beautiful countryside features century-old wooden houses, villages engaged in traditional agriculture, and even a winery. Finally, a man-made reservoir serves as a popular weekend destination.

Battambang City

In lore, the founding of Battambang occurred when Ta Dambong Kranhoung, whose power was derived from a magic black stick, overthrew the local king. The king's youngest son, who had nearly been burned alive during a skirmish, escaped to a nearby monastery. After seven years, seven months, and seven days, the prince was returning to the kingdom when he met a Brahman, who asked him to watch his horse. The miraculous horse cured the prince of his burns, made him strong, and ferried him through the air. Ta Dambong Kranhoung threw his stick at the prince, but missed. The magic stick fell to the earth and was swallowed by a stream. Ta Dambong Kranhoung fled and the prince founded his new kingdom at Bat Dambang, meaning "lost stick." The city features both a statue of Ta Dambong Kranhoung *(in traffic circle where National Highway 5 from Phnom Penh enters Battambang)* and one of the prince on horseback *(N end of St. 3).*

Battambang itself isn't chock-full of sights; you can see the city's highlights in a day. A walking tour is the most enjoyable way to get a feel for the town. During the hotter summer months, however, a bicycle or moto-taxi *(motodop)* might be more advisable—inquire at the tourist information office or your guesthouse for bike rentals and moto-taxi or *tuk-tuk* tours.

A good place to begin exploring is the **Meeting Market** (Psar Nat), which is the physical and social center of the town. Like many Khmer markets, it's geared less toward tourists than toward locals buying their groceries, particularly in the cooler morning hours. In the center of the market, jewelers sell gems from both Cambodia and abroad. Emeralds and rubies from nearby Pailin are harder to come by, however; the mines have long since been tapped out (see sidebar p. 176).

INSIDER TIP:

With 800 historic buildings still standing, Battambang has some of the best preserved architecture of any city in Southeast Asia.

—TERRESSA DAVIS
Heritage Watch

Wat Phiphetaram (aka Wat Phephittam) is located directly north of the market. Each morning, the wat's monks can be seen collecting alms around the colonial-style shop houses nearby. The temple is one of the oldest in the city, and its shady, peaceful grounds make for a pleasant visit. Wat Phiphetaram is a short walk from the Sangker River, where

Battambang
🅰 169 A3
Tourism Information Office
✉ 2 blocks W of New Iron Bridge, then half block N
☎ 855(0)12-969-542
Fax: 855(0)53-730-217
💲 $
www.tourist-office .org/cambodia/ tourist-office-battambang.htm

Meeting Market
✉ Between St. 1 & St. 3 on W bank of Stung Sangker, 3 blocks N of Old Iron Bridge

Wat Phiphetaram
✉ Less than 100 yards (91 m) N of the Meeting Market
💲 $

Battambang Provincial Museum

✉ St. 1, Kamakor Village, Svay Por Commune, Battambang District (near post office)

🕐 Closed Sat.–Mon.

💲 $

Wat Tahm Rai Saw

✉ Bet. St. 2 & St. 3, 1 block W behind Battambang Provincial Museum

💲 $

Governor's Residence

✉ 4 blocks W of New Iron Bridge

🕐 Closed Sun.

💲 $

Wat Sangker, Wat Pachhaa, Wat Kandal, Wat Borvil, & Wat Bo Knong

✉ N of park on riverside road

💲 $

boats can be hired by the hour (*a few blocks N at bus/boat station*) to explore the sights along the river. Prices are negotiable and may vary on the size of your party and the boat. Generally, boat drivers speak English well.

Toward the southern end of town, **Battambang Provincial Museum** houses a number of artifacts from all over Cambodia, some dating back to as early as the seventh century. The museum is closed more often than not, particularly in the afternoon. The gallery of informative displays that provides insight on regional attractions, culture, and history is generally open, though.

One block behind the museum to the west is **Wat Tahm Rai Saw** (White Elephant Pagoda). Built in 1840, the wat (aka Wat Damrey Sar) features, unsurprisingly, statuary of white elephants. One of them is ridden by the Buddha, who is witnessing the world's suffering. In addition to these somewhat graphic depictions of the world's ills and the grandeur of the temple itself, the diverse styles and designs of the surrounding stupas are a curious attraction.

Toward the southern end of the riverfront Road No. 1, a right fork leads to the government buildings, magnificently maintained colonial-era structures. The **Governor's Residence** was designed by Italian architects for the last Siamese governor of Battambang. It's hard to imagine that within this quiet grassy compound once stood the *kamphaeng*, a fort built by the Siamese in the late 1830s which housed stables, elephants, and an

arsenal of over a hundred cannon. The neighboring **Tourism Information Office** is an indispensable source of information for visitors to the province. In addition to offering maps and friendly advice, the office also organizes day trips to the surrounding attractions.

INSIDER TIP:

The Battambang tourism office is the best in Cambodia. The staff is friendly and provides a multitude of services. Most important, it's open most of the time.

—TREVOR RANGES
National Geographic author

The east side of the river is more of a residential neighborhood, with colonial houses and temples facing the river. Battambang's H. E. Sar Kheng park also lies along the Sangker's east bank. Sunset is the best time for a walk through the park, when children play badminton, teenagers flirt, and women do group aerobics.

Along the riverside road north of the park are a number of Battambang's other principal temples, **Wat Sangker, Wat Pachhaa, Wat Kandal, Wat Borvil,** and **Wat Bo Knong,** each of which has interesting features.

Evenings in Battambang are very subdued, though one surprising treat not to be missed is the circus performance at **Phare Ponleu Selpak.** It was founded by artists who returned from the

Cambodian Railroad

The rail line between Phnom Penh and Battambang was completed in 1942 and has rarely been upgraded, making most tracks more than 60 years old. Decades of war—including land mines laid along the tracks—and major erosion caused by annual monsoons have damaged many of the bridges, which were simply patched together rather than replaced. Trains make the painfully slow voyage only twice a week, going to Phnom Penh on Saturday and back to Battambang on Sunday. In the intervening days, the tracks bustle with bamboo railway cars, so called for the bamboo frames of the small motorized carriages that seat several passengers, along with a few goats, a motorbike, and whatever else can be crammed aboard. These frighteningly fast, loud vehicles are both an essential source of transportation for villagers along the rail lines and an exhilarating tourist attraction.

However, it seems that development is slowly on its way. For most, it's a welcome change as the standard trains are loud, slow, and sometimes dangerous. (In 2008, armed bandits boarded a train, targeting foreigners.) The anticipated train improvements will upgrade the train and track systems, and will connect Singapore to Kunming, China, with a railroad that snakes through the Southeast Asian nations. As Cambodia is the missing link on this Southeast Asian track, the country's old rail lines are scheduled to eventually be ripped up soon and a newer, larger gauge track will be laid. This may make travel tricky for the bamboo train operators and tourists who want to ride with them, so inquire at the Battambang Tourism office (see p. 171).

refugee camps in Thailand following the Khmer Rouge years to foster artistic expression and build cultural pride among disadvantaged children. The location is a bit tricky to find and the performance schedule is irregular, but it's a unique, touching experience (see sidebar p. 145).

North of Battambang

The enjoyable ride to the north of Battambang, either by car or moto-taxi hired at the Tourist Information Office, is quite different from the bumpier one leading south. North of Battambang, the nearly perfect river road skirts the Sangker River, snaking through leafy banana trees and tranquil "middle-class" villages that flank the road. The vibe here is that of a surprisingly refreshing tropical paradise. Stop along the way to chat with local villagers, many of whom are employed producing rice paper for wrapping spring rolls.

Ten miles (16 km) along this well-marked road lies **Wat Ek Phnom.** The wooden Buddhist temple in the parking area was rebuilt in 2000 to replace an older structure, which presumably had replaced another, and so on dating back around 700 years. The older stone temple behind it dates to the 11th century, possibly 1027, and thus was built during the reign of Suryavarman I (r. 1003– ca. 1049). The temple suffered considerable damage at the hands of both Siamese invaders and the Khmer Rouge, and the sections that remain standing look like a precarious house of cards.

Wat Ek Phnom

🅰 169 A3

✉ Phum Tkov, Khum Peam Ek, Srok Steung Sangke, Khet Battambang

💲 $

Wat Samraoung Knong & Killing Field

🗺 169 B3

✉ About 6 miles (10 km) N of Battambang in Ek Phnom District, cross the Sangker River & turn R

💲 $

Prasat Basseat

🗺 169 B3

✉ Khum Tapoan, Srok Steung Sangke, Khet Battambang; near Ek Phnom, about 5 miles (8 km) from Norea

💲 $

Although the Hindu temple is thought to honor Shiva, it is oddly oriented westward. Although no remnant survives of either a *yoni* (pedestal representing the female component of the fertility symbol) or a Shiva-*linga*, the wat has some well-preserved Sanskrit inscriptions and a few beautiful bas-reliefs. Depictions on the lintels include the Churning of the Sea of Milk (see sidebar p. 151) and Vishnu riding an elephant—"magic water" drains from his forehead, though it's unclear whether this was part of the original design.

Head south, back toward Battambang. Veer off toward Daun Teaw village, where many locals are employed at a dried-fish processing facility that manufactures Khmer "cheese," a pungent type of fish paste called *prahok*. If you cross the Sangker River and turn right, **Wat Samraoung Knong** is a short distance along this alternate route back to Battambang. Built in 1907, the temple is a fascinating fusion of colonial and Khmer architecture.

Sadly, the temple also has a dark history. It functioned as a prison and interrogation facility during the Pol Pot regime. A memorial behind the small pond where the monks reside houses the remains of the 10,008 victims murdered at this **Killing Field,** one of many discovered throughout the country. The memorial has bas-reliefs around the base recounting atrocities that occurred in Battambang.

A day trip to Ek Phnom can include a visit to **Prasat Bassaet**—the ruin of another 11th-century temple built by Suryavarman I—located east of Battambang. Traveling south from Wat Samraoung Knong, turn left at the village of Norea. This riverside community is populated by a large number of Muslim Cham, who have built several mosques in the area. Prasat Basseat lies amid beautiful countryside. The temple is in great disrepair and can be explored in a short time. What has survived did so miraculously—the Khmer Rouge were in the process of dismantling the *prasats* (towers) here to construct a dam, but rumors say the magic endowed in the temple roused protective ghosts. Ensuing misfortune apparently convinced the Khmer Rouge to abandon their destruction of the temple.

South of Battambang

Another day trip lies about ten miles (16 km) south of Battambang. The main attractions are a pair of hilltops, with an ancient temple situated atop one, Phnom Banon, and modern temples and a tragic Khmer Rouge site on the other,

Early evening aerobics in a riverside park in Battambang draws an enthusiastic crowd.

EXPERIENCE: Responsible Tourism

Tourists to Cambodia are hardly passive visitors; their presence makes an impact, both on the temples, where hands and feet are gradually wearing away the stone, and on the people, many of whom are increasingly reliant on tourist revenue.

Responsible tourists acknowledge their influence on Cambodia's historic monuments, culture, and people. Visitors should always follow appropriate cultural etiquette (see sidebar p. 21) and patronize businesses and organizations that actively encourage beneficial development.

Protecting Cambodia's Vulnerable Children

One of the most disconcerting sights in Cambodia is children begging and working on the streets. The country's approximately 24,000 street children face a wide range of risks, including poor health, hygiene, and nutrition, as well as physical and sexual abuse. While these pleading, wide-eyed children will certainly tug at your heart, for numerous reasons it is best not to give them money directly.

The **ChildSafe Network** (www.childsafe-cambodia .org) works to protect vulnerable youth from all forms of abuse. ChildSafe has created a network of businesses, *tuk-tuk* drivers, and guesthouses, and compiled a list of tips for travelers to help protect at-risk youth. Every traveler can make a difference by picking up the handy pocket-size *ChildSafe Travelers Tips* at participating businesses, such as Friends-International (www.friends-international.org) in Phnom Penh and/or by following these guidelines:

- Support organizations that are members of ChildSafe.
- Refrain from purchasing anything from children on the streets or in temples and avoid giving money to begging parents or children.
- Purchase products certified by ChildSafe.
- Be aware of the dangers of orphanage tourism.
- Never take a child to your hotel room.
- Do not patronize businesses that tolerate or encourage prostitution.
- If you see a child in danger, immediately inform the local authorities (*police hotline tel 855(0)23-997-919*) or ChildSafe (*hotline tel 855(0)12-311-112*).

Protecting Cambodia's Culture & Heritage

Heritage Watch (www.her ltagewatchInternational.org) began its work to prevent looting from cemeteries and temples around Cambodia. It has since branched out to try to protect various aspects of Cambodian culture. The organization provides visitors with heritage friendly advice, offers a directory of heritage friendly businesses, and produces educational campaigns encouraging Cambodians to preserve their culture.

The epitome of culturally beneficial businesses are featured in a free publication, *Stay Another Day Cambodia* (www.stay-another-day.org). Affiliated organizations promote commercially viable tourism that benefits society and "supports conservation of the natural, historic, and cultural resources on which tourism depend." These shops and restaurants either train, employ, or benefit disadvantaged Cambodians (see sidebar p. 80). Cultural immersion destinations include members of the **Cambodian Community-Based Ecotourism Network** (www.CCBEN.org; see Eco-tourism, pp. 222–223) .

Visiting Temples

Though your individual touch of a bas-relief or temple inscription is unlikely to cause damage, millions of visitors doing likewise will certainly contribute to the accelerated destruction of centuries-old works of art and invaluable remnants of Cambodia's history. Millions of feet tramping over the temples may be gradually causing instability; try to walk on established paths and avoid clambering over the temple walls whenever possible. Furthermore, while visiting Siem Reap, attempt to conserve water, as the area's dropping water table may also contribute to the future collapse of these majestic temples.

Finding Gems

The 1970s and 1980s were the heyday of Cambodian mining. Although Cambodian rubies once were considered of inferior quality due to excess iron that made the stones dark, treatments to improve the stones' appearance catapulted the country to the top ruby exporter. Sadly, these mines primarily benefited the Khmer Rouge, who controlled Pailin Province, source of the best rubies and sapphires. Mines—once rudimentary pits dug by individual prospectors—were dug by massive numbers of hired prospectors. Today, the government has restricted mining operations in Pailin, though both rough and cut stones from the region can be procured in Pailin and Battambang.

Nowadays, Ratanakiri remains popular among individual prospectors digging for high-quality zircons and garnets. Though rubies and sapphires may still exist here, most miners eke out livings from the few quality stones that they unearth. International business interests have procured concessions for major mining operations in both Mondulkiri and Ratanakiri, including gold and bauxite quarries.

Stones from prospectors are sold in the Ban Lung market (see p. 225). While the market has loose stones, including onyx and amethyst at reasonable prices, buyers without some knowledge of gem quality should beware of "special price" emeralds and other precious stones.

Ancient House

- ⊠ Over 1 mile (2 km) S of Battambang en route to Phnom Banon
- 🗺 $

Amatak Prasat Phnom Banorn Grape Wine Company

- 🅰 169 B2
- ⊠ No. 72, Group 6, Botsala Village, Chheu Teal Commune, Banan District; about 2 miles (3 km) S of Battambang
- ☎ 855(0)12-665-238

Phnom Banon

- 🅰 169 A2
- ⊠ 18 miles (30 km) S of Battambang
- 🗺 $

Phnom Sampeu. While the trip can begin with either mountain, it is more enjoyable to go down a long, bumpy dirt road in the direction of Wat Banon, and to return to Battambang along the relatively smoother ride from Phnom Sampeu.

Just over a mile (2 km) down the river road south of town, just beyond Wat Kor, watch for a sign for an **Ancient House** (Khor Song) one of many along the road through Wat Kor Village. These houses are built of the hardwood *pchek* tree, and are topped by the period's trademark two-tiered rooftops. This first Khor Song, built in 1907, contains a beautiful interior ceiling and a number of antique pieces of furniture. A history of the home is displayed in English on the wall beside the front door.

If the road south of Wat Kor Village is in good condition (i.e., monsoon season ruts have been repaired), take the opportunity to experience rural agrarian life. **Kompong Seyma,** whose wat contains sacred stones *(seyma)* believed to provide magical protection for Battambang, offers oxcart rides through the rice fields. **Ksach Puoy Village** contains a number of fruit orchards. Farther down the road, watch for the large sign for **Amatak Prasat Phnom Banorn Grape Wine Company,** which produces Cambodia's only red wine with grapes from the Chan Thay Chhoeung Winery. The proprietress often sets up a wine-tasting stand beside the road.

Farther south, you will find **Phnom Banon.** Atop this 250-foot (76 m) hill, the 11th-century, easterly facing Wat Banon is thought to have been sponsored by the Shiva-worshipping Udayadityavarman II (*r.*1050–1068). It may have been rebuilt, however, by Jayavarman VII (*r.* ca. 1181–1218),

who is thought to have rededicated the temple to the Buddha,
even flipping one lintel to feature
Buddhist, rather than Hindu,
iconography.

A 352-step staircase leads to
five prasats that are in generally
good condition, despite the hill
having been occupied alternately
by Khmer Rouge and Vietnamese
soldiers, who actively dismantled
sections of the temple. All five of
the towers are made of sandstone

prasat are more indicative of the
fate of the original art, most of
which was looted over the centuries. Before leaving, look to the
northwest, where Phnom Sampeu
is clearly visible.

Turning back toward Phnom
Penh, stay left to head to **Phnom
Sampeu** (Boat Mountain). After
a 15- to 30-minute drive, you
will see the modern, colorful
Wat Phnom Sampeu. The main
attraction here, however, is not this

Phnom Sampeu & the Killing Caves

  169 A2

✉ 5 miles
(9 km) SW of
Battambang

$ $

Jewelry makers working in the Battambang Central Market

and laterite. Along with the *nagas*
at the base of the stairs and the
lions stationed near the top, some
artwork remains from the original
structure, including bas-reliefs
and lintels on the hilltop prasats.
Several yonis, which used to house
Shiva-lingas, also survive. The Buddha's feet in the northern prasat
and the faceless *devatas* (female
deities) on the rear of the central

temple at the base of the cliff, but
the spectacular mountaintop view.
Sadly, it also overlooks the Khmer
Rouge **Killing Caves.** If you aren't
interested in an arduous hike, you
can drive up the steep side road
immediately after the temple to
reach the caves and the summit.

In the unassuming rectangular
building halfway up the hill—once
a Buddhist pagoda—the Khmer

A street restaurant in the casino area of Bavet

Dhamma Latthika Battambang Vipassana Center

✉ Kraper Village, Phnom Sampeu Commune, Banan District; 5 miles (8 km) S of Phnom Sampeu

☎ 855(0)12-365-310 or 855(0)16-729-729 (Mr. Buoy Kuon)

💲 $

www.latthika.dhamma.org

Kamping Puoy

✉ 15 miles (24 km) from Phnom Sampeu on side road off Rte. 57

💲 $

Pailin & Samlot

▲ 169 A2

Rouge interrogated thousands of people before killing them and dumping their bodies into the nearby chasms, nicknamed the Killing Caves. The stairs lead down from the interrogation room to the largest chamber, where a small shrine houses bones from a number of victims. Before the genocide, this cave once featured theater performances by local people.

Driving farther up the hill, a stairway leads to a number of pagodas at its pinnacle. As you climb, note the pair of antiaircraft guns, remnants of the Khmer Rouge occupation. Despite the conflict that raged around the hill, the stupa and temples on Phnom Sampeu, built primarily in the 1960s, remain amazingly intact. Particularly surprising is the near-perfect condition of the intricate concrete funerary tower dedicated to the wife of Khmer Rouge adversary Marshal Lon Nol (1913–1985). Beyond this stupa is a temple honoring Rumsay

Sok (see below) and a hilltop Buddhist prasat with a panoramic view of the countryside.

For another spectacular view, continue driving along the road past Phnom Sampeu. Turn right at the sign for the **Dhamma Latthika Battambang Vipassana Center,** where ten-day meditation retreats are held (see sidebar p. 51). From the center's entrance, you can see the mountains related to the local legend of Phnom Sampeu, which involves a crocodile, King Reachkol, and his fiancée, Rumsay Sok. The king was on his way to meet his betrothed when the jealous crocodile attacked his boat. To appease the crocodile, the king threw overboard cages containing both chickens and ducks. Then, as depicted at local temples, Rumsay Sok let down her long hair and released a magic hairpin, which soaked up the water and saved her beloved from the toothy beast. Looking back toward

Phnom Sampeu (representing the sunken boat), the crocodile-shaped Phnom Krapeu (Crocodile Hill) lies to the right ahead of you. Wat Giribunyaram rests atop Drung Muon (Chicken House Temple) to your left; Drung Dtia (Duck House) is just behind you.

Kamping Puoy (Morning Glory Lake) is about 15 miles (24 km) north of Phnom Sampeu, on a side road that meets Route 57 about a half mile (0.8 km) from the mountain. The lake is actually a reservoir, built during the Khmer Rouge years by thousands of forced laborers, more than 10,000 of whom died during its construction. Despite the reservoir's tragic inception, villagers and residents of Battambang flock to its shores each weekend, particularly in the wetter months when it is full. The lake is a bit of a detour, but is worth a visit if you have a few spare hours.

Pailin, Samlot, & the Thai Border

Tiny Pailin Province is one of the most remote places in Cambodia. The province plays an intriguing role in Khmer folklore, as Ta Dambong Kranhoung (see p. 171) hailed from Pailin. In more recent history, it was instrumental as an enclave of the Khmer Rouge, who began their offensive from the town of Samlot in 1968 and held out there until 1998. During that time, the region's renowned forests and ruby and sapphire mines supplied them with tens of millions of dollars to fund their military operations. Eager to wrest control of those resources from the Khmer Rouge, the government staged massive offensives in the area, which became one of the most heavily land-mined places in the country.

The area has been heavily deforested and the gem mines have been exhausted, for the most part. The province is difficult to access,

Gambling

Gambling in Cambodia once included horse racing and turtle fighting, an ingenious—albeit cruel—game whereby turtles with candles on their backs struggled to escape through a doorway. Today, this wagering spirit is alive with rain gambling, betting on whether or how much it will rain.

To try your luck, join the Thai and Vietnamese who hit the behemoth casinos at the border towns, from Bavet to Poipet. Room prices begin at $30 and often include $15 of free chips for playing both Chinese games of chance and roulette or blackjack.

Phnom Penh's Nagaworld Hotel and Casino (see p. 284) may be more convenient, however. The clientele is predominantly Khmer and Korean. Nagaworld's prom theme, including a corny cover band, is perfect for low-limit table action.

but that is part of the attraction for those looking to really get away from it all. From here, travelers can visit remote hill tribes, and attempt to spot rare species of animals, such as tigers, Siamese crocodiles, and exotic birds. In Pailin town, you can shop for low-grade souvenir gemstones and fine wooden furniture or even cross into Thailand to sightsee in the nearby provinces or continue on to Bangkok. ∎

Between Phnom Penh & Battambang

Since National Highway 5 is one of the better roads in the country, the journey between Phnom Penh and Battambang can be made in five to six hours. Take a few hours to play along the way by including some sightseeing. The stops are approximately one or two hours apart, breaking up your ride through the countryside into shorter, more comfortable legs.

The fertile Cambodian basin along National Road No. 5 features spectacular skies.

Oudong

▲ 169 C1

Kompong Chhnang

▲ 169 C1

Starting out from Phnom Penh, the first sight along National Highway 5 is the former capital of **Oudong,** which lies 23 miles (37 km) to the northwest. Oudong's proximity to Phnom Penh makes it a popular day trip. The walk around the stupas (see p. 92) takes about an hour; you can add it to your itinerary if you get an early start.

About two hours from Phnom Penh, 41 miles (66 km) beyond Oudong is **Kompong Chhnang,**

the capital of the province of the same name. Kompong Chhnang means "the port of pots," referring to its location along the Tonle Sap and the clay pottery for which the province is best known.

Driving into the town, you may notice parks overgrown with weeds and dilapidated French colonial buildings. While the town has seen better days, it remains the largest port for fish caught in the Tonle Sap River. On the way to the riverside, National

Highway 5 passes a market and a smaller version of Phnom Penh's Independence Monument. Veering right from the market, stop at **Wat Yeah Tep** to take in the view of the riverfront. Farther down the river road, an information desk doubles as the boat launch for trips to a nearby floating village *($$)*, though you may wish to save that experience for Pursat (see below). Beyond that, you'll see the morning fish market and a few smaller boats that can paddle you around the closer alleyways of the floating village *($)*.

Although a bit tricky to locate, the pottery village of **Ondong Rossay,** not five minutes outside of Kompong Chhnang town, is worth a quick side trip. Follow the southern spoke of the road leading away from Independence Monument, which soon forks left onto a dirt road leading to the sparsely populated village (see sidebar this page).

After crossing into Pursat Province, 40 miles (64 km) from Kompong Chhnang, take the turnoff beside Sukimex gas station outside of Krakor. Follow the road to the end to reach the boat launch for **Kompong Luong** floating village. Note that the floating villages are best appreciated in the morning or late afternoon, so plan the timing of your visit accordingly.

Seventeen miles (28 km) beyond Krakor is the provincial capital of **Pursat.** Though Pursat Province is the fourth largest in Cambodia, stretching from the shores of Tonle Sap Lake to the Cardamom Mountains, it has one of the smallest populations. It is best known for its oranges and beautiful countryside. Pursat town, which lies on the Pursat River, is surprisingly charming and worth a stroll if you have a few hours to spare. The marble-carving village of **Banteay Del** and its lovely riverside are especially pleasant (see Pursat Bike Tour, pp. 188–189).

Just beyond Pursat town, the shrine to **Neak Ta Khleang Muong** is down a red dirt road, demarcated by a statue topped by a bird. The fountains, gardens, and statues surrounding the shrine honor Khleang Muong, a Cambodian general who took his life prior to a major battle with Siamese invaders. The general's spirit then contributed to a decisive victory, immortalizing him and his wife, who also took her life. They sacrificed themselves in an open pit that now stands in front of the shrine housing their statues. ∎

Wat Yeah Tep

 Kompong Chhnang, 64 miles (103 km) from Phnom Penh

$ $

Kompong Luong

🗺 169 C1

Chhnang Clay Pots

At the end of the 13th century, Chinese emissary Zhou Daguan (see sidebar p. 28), renowned for his recordings of life at Angkor, visited a village along the banks of the Tonle Sap. Impressed by the clay pots produced there, he referred to the area as the port of pots and the name stuck. Today a number of villages in Kompong Chhnang, literally "port" and "pots," continue to produce the iconic terra-cotta pots. Villagers employ the same techniques they have used for centuries, passing the knowledge down through the generations, though many use modern throwing wheels to aid in their labor. These pots and jars of various sizes are sold throughout Cambodia, often by itinerant vendors, some of whom still use oxcarts to transport their wares.

Physical & Psychological Impact of War

Like an anthill crushed underfoot, Cambodia was brought to near ruins during the war and turmoil of the 20th century. One conflict gave way to another. For more than 30 years, it seemed as if steel-toed boots were grinding out unforgettable destruction on a helpless population.

Political unrest exploded in 1969 when the United States began carpet bombing northeastern Cambodia, a fatal by-product of the war between the United States and Vietnam. Mere months later, Cambodia erupted into civil war that transformed for a time into

Demining operations continue across the Cambodian countryside.

a "revolution" led by the genocidal Khmer Rouge regime (1975–1979), responsible for millions of deaths.

Cambodian society was thus splintered by destruction and extermination. Both the initial violence and its lingering physical and psychological impacts have been devastating.

Sadly, these are not unfamiliar stories, even today. While working in the fields, a boy inadvertently detonates a land mine. Unable to get his son to a hospital in time for treatment, his father uses a handsaw to amputate the boy's leg. In another province, a child discovers a shiny metal object—her newfound toy. The girl and her friends play catch with it for days, until it unexpectedly detonates when she drops what is actually a cluster bomb.

Such scenarios have been occurring in Cambodia for more than 30 years. "America's Secret War" alone dropped more tonnage of explosives than was dropped in all of World War II. This total included an estimated 285 million cluster bombs in Cambodia, Laos, and Vietnam, up to 30 percent of which remain hidden and intact.

During the subsequent 30 Years War more than eight million land mines were laid. Small and devastatingly destructive, both physically and mentally, land mines were nicknamed the "perfect soldiers" by Khmer Rouge Brother Number One, Pol Pot. Land mines still affect a fearful society; the UN estimates that between four and six million unexploded mines remain undiscovered in Cambodia.

While the number of people who have sustained physical disabilities can be tallied (nearly 50,000 from land mines alone), those suffering psychological disorders have yet to be counted.

Mental health problems are so prevalent, and resources so rare, that the number is impossible to count with any reliability—itself a disheartening reality (see sidebar below.)

During the Khmer Rouge era, families were torn apart. Children witnessed their parents being murdered and even babies and toddlers were imprisoned, tortured, and killed. These stories are typical to all Cambodians who were "lucky" enough to survive, such as Theary C. Seng, author of *Daughter of the Killing Fields: Asrei's Story*. Regarding psychological disorders, Seng says, "The symptoms of trauma in Cambodian society are many, diverse, and deep."

Cambodia's sole psychiatric hospital estimated in 2008 that 28.4 percent of the population has been diagnosed with post-traumatic stress disorder (PTSD). However, Seng disagrees: "I would put the figure at over 80 percent, which means all Cambodians who lived under the Khmer Rouge years have a certain degree of trauma to this day, most of us with PTSD."

Though the outlook seems bleak, survivors are banding together to create various methods for coping with and recovering from trauma. Seng encourages writing as a therapeutic outlet that bestows power and control through the safe distance of words. As the executive director for the **Center for Social Development,** Seng provides safe environments where victims can

INSIDER TIP:

You'll notice a lot of young Cambodians and many old ones—but not a lot in middle age. Many were killed in the genocide or died in the ensuing years of desperate poverty.

—KRIS LEBOUTILLIER
National Geographic photographer

relate their stories, whether in court or on paper. "Every Cambodian has a story," she says.

Taking another approach, sports clubs are helping empower the nation's amputees through team spirit and competition. Since 1 out of every 290 people in Cambodia has undergone a mine-related amputation, sources of hope are much needed. Comprised mostly of players living with the aftermath of mine injuries, the Cambodian National Volleyball League (Disabled) (CNVLD) proudly presents its success story: The team ranked third in the 2007 Standing Volleyball World Cup, the first team medal ever brought home to Cambodia.

The CNVLD organizes regional teams in nearly every province. A game schedule can be found at *www.StandUpCambodia.net.*

The Dark Legacy of War

Decades of war left many Cambodians with severe post-traumatic stress disorder (PTSD) and other psychological problems. Yet the country lacks the resources to treat these disorders—many of which go undiagnosed 30 years after the atrocities ended—making postwar life unduly hard for Cambodians.

Today, only 32 Khmer psychiatrists and 8 psychiatric specialists work in Cambodia. This is only a slight step up from when the country opened its first psychiatric outpatient clinic in 1994,

when it had no psychiatrists. Ku Sunbaunat, head of the government's mental health department, told the *Phnom Penh Post* that Cambodia needs "hundreds of psychiatrists" to deal with such patients, but that the negative perception of psychiatrists as "mad doctors" keeps young people from entering the profession.

When dealing with local people, don't forget that many have suffered beyond anything imaginable. A good attitude and a warm demeanor can really make a difference in how they respond to you.

Northern Border Provinces

The northern border provinces are Banteay Meanchey and Oddar Meanchey, both relatively new provinces that once were parts of Battambang and Siem Reap, respectively. Over the past half millennium, both provinces were annexed by Thailand from time to time. Therefore, the local culture reflects that of neighboring Thai provinces, which were part of the Khmer Empire in earlier times. Both sides of the border once contained many Angkor-era towns and temples.

These towns were located along highways that connected Angkor with its outposts in Thailand and included the massive walled city of Banteay Chhmar. Today, for the average traveler, the area's proximity to Thailand means that Thai baht are more useful than dollars, Thai food is more readily available than elsewhere in Cambodia, and the Thai language is frequently used.

Few tourists venture into the northern provinces, other than those who are traveling to Thailand from Siem Reap or Battambang via Poipet. However, smaller attractions along the road between Siem Reap and Battambang include villages known for stone carving and silk weaving. Nature lovers can visit a sanctuary for threatened bird species at Ang Trapaeng Thmor, an Angkor-era *baray* (reservoir). Pushing farther north to the Khmer Rouge holdout of Anlong Veng, where Pol Pot passed his final days, a border province circuit includes spectacular sights that few tourists make the effort to visit.

Poipet

Poipet is a bustling border town that almost perfectly epitomizes the differences between Cambodia and Thailand. Poipet town, dusty in the dry season, muddy in the wet, is a place of both conspicuous poverty and garish wealth. Driving closer to the border, the low-rise shop houses and barefoot children suddenly

Heads of garlic are separated and the cloves set to dry in a village between Poipet and Sisophon.

give way to high-rise hotels with casinos and their well-dressed patrons. The landscaping around the casinos alone more closely resembles Bangkok's shopping malls than even the finest neighborhood in Phnom Penh. For visitors not interested in gambling, there is no reason to stay in Poipet other than to

INSIDER TIP:

No one visits Poipet for its ambience, but a stop in this grotty border town is fascinating nonetheless, as it gives you a quick and pointed view of Cambodian poverty and its fallout.

—KAREN COATES
National Geographic writer

get your passport stamped on the way across the Thai border. Those looking to try their luck, however, can choose from a number of **casinos** (see sidebar p. 179). Those crossing the border may do so between 7 a.m. and 8 p.m.

Poipet is connected to Siem Reap via National Highway 5, which eventually works its way into National Highway 6. The latter route includes a number of attractions and the excellent road between the two cities makes the trip a breeze. Uninterrupted, the route between Poipet and Siem Reap can be completed in as little

as three hours. The simplest stop along the way is the stone-carving village of **Choob,** approximately 7 miles (11 km) east of the provincial capital of Sisophon, itself a rather uninteresting town. Choob is impossible to miss, as both sides of the highway are lined with workshops and sandstone statuary of various sizes. The larger pieces of the hand-chiseled statues are consigned by hotels and other businesses, though displays of smaller pieces, including likenesses of Jayavarman VII, *apsaras,* elephants, and *lingas* are for sale at reasonable prices. Otherwise it's intriguing to simply watch them transform the sandstone blocks into works of art.

Just a mile (1.6 km) or so west of Choob, a turnoff leads to the silk village of **Phnom Srok** and the **Sarus Crane Reserve** at Ang Trapaeng Thmor. About 30 minutes down a well-maintained, red dirt road, Phnom Sruk and several other communities have benefited from an effort initiated by an NGO to train villagers in the business of sericulture. (The program is now sponsored by the European Union and Royal Cambodian government.) In their homes, villagers raise mulberry moths, pluck the cocoons, extract and dye the silk, and weave silk scarves and skirts. If someone is at the **Khmer Silk Village** office, he or she may offer to show you around. Otherwise, flash a friendly smile and the villagers will likely demonstrate the process for you themselves.

Although it's only a few miles from the silk village, it's helpful to ask directions to the nearby

Poipet
◭ 169 A3

Choob
◭ 169 A3

Phnom Srok
◭ 169 A3

Sarus Crane Reserve at Ang Trapaeng Thmor
✉ Sam Veasna No. 552, Group 12, Wat Bo Rd
☎ 855(0)63-963-710
$ $$$$$
www.samveasna.org

Khmer Silk Village
✉ 20 miles (32 km) from Choob on side road off National Highway 6
$ $

Ang Trapaeng Thmor baray. The reservoir is believed to have been built in the days of Angkor, a theory supported by the ancient highway that runs directly past it and the remnants of an Angkor-era stone bridge just before it. The reservoir was redeveloped through slave labor during the Khmer Rouge regime, but today it serves as a sanctuary for sarus cranes, who flock to its waters in

Even remote, forgotten ruins help embellish an otherwise subtle sunrise.

Banteay Chhmar

- 169 A4
- 60 miles (97 km) N of Sisophon on Rte. 56
- $–$$

the dry season months, particularly February to May. To organize a birdwatching tour, contact the Sam Vaesna Center for Wildlife Conservation in Siem Reap (see p. 122).

From Ang Trapaeng Thmor, if you are heading toward Siem Reap, take the road straight through the village circle (rather than the one to the right, which leads back to the Khmer Silk Village office) to Kralanh. This is an alternative route to **Kralanh,** which is located at the intersection

of Route 68 North to Oddar Meanchey or National Highway 6 East to Siem Reap. Although this road is slightly trickier to navigate, it follows a short leg of the ancient highway and passes an intact, functioning **Angkor-era bridge.** While there are a number of these old bridges around the northern border provinces, this is one of the most accessible and beautiful.

North of Poipet

The wondrous, remote Angkorian temples of Banteay Chhmar, Prasat Ta Prohm, and Banteay Top (or Banteay Toup) are still in relatively natural, somewhat ruined states. All of them are well off the tourist tracks—in the low season, visitors arrive perhaps once every week or two. The cluster of temples can be visited along the northern border route from Anlong Veng through Samraong or, with an early start, as a day trip from Battambang or even Poipet.

Route 56 is the worst of the major roadways in all Cambodia, passing through one of the least developed areas of the country. This was not always the case, however. **Banteay Chhmar** was one of the great cities of Angkor, and lay near the ancient highway that connected the Khmer capital with Phimai, the major Angkorian urban center now located in modern-day Thailand. Mysteriously named the "citadel of the cat," Banteay Chhmar rivaled both Angkor Thom and Angkor Wat in size and splendor. Today, the moat surrounding the city makes clear the scope of its size, though inside the tree-covered, collapsing walls of the city, only the imagination can recall what once was here.

With the entire compound to yourself, climbing over piles of rubble and sneaking through dark doorways to discover the remaining **bas-reliefs** (some of the artistically most impressive of the era) is quite an amazing experience. Many of Banteay Chhmar's reliefs have been relocated to museums, however, including those in Phnom Penh and Battambang.

Bas-reliefs are found here and there throughout the complex, particularly around the outside gallery. They include multiarmed Avalokiteshvara (Lokesvara, the Bodhisattva of compassion) and numerous battle scenes. You also get glimpses of Jayavarman VII's personal life, such as the king spending time with his wife and his concubines. These depictions have been instrumental to historians piecing together a picture of everyday life in the kingdom.

Nonetheless, the temple remains an enigma. The central

INSIDER TIP:

When walking the perimeter of Banteay Chhmar, you'll notice that a 40-foot (12 m) section of the outer wall is missing. Stolen by looters in the late 1990s, it's a reminder of why you should never buy ancient artifacts as souvenirs.

—TERRESSA DAVIS
Heritage Watch

stupa is surrounded by towers capped with Bayon-style four faces (only a few are intact). Though it is believed to be a funerary temple, likely for Jayavarman VII's son, Prince Sri Indrakumara, surrounding bas-reliefs indicate an original construction several kings earlier.

Just south of the collapsed southern causeway to Banteay Chhmar, a small dirt road leads to the bright, airy **Prasat Ta Prohm.** Like the Ta Prohm of Angkor, the *prasat* (tower) is capped by the four faces of Lokesvara. This version consists of a small, fairly intact prasat, surrounded by a moat in which children swim and around which residents of the nearby village walk their cows. Benches allow visitors to relax and enjoy the atmosphere.

The strategic location of Banteay Chhmar, near a gap in the Dangrek Range leading to Thailand, is evidenced by the nearby

(continued on p. 190)

Don't Forget the DEET

Be aware that while the area around Banteay Chhmar is marked as de-mined, it certainly is not de-mosquitoed. The forested temple compound is teeming with insects, and, as this area is within the malarial hot zone, it's important to protect yourself accordingly.

Pursat Bike Tour

Situated along the Pursat River, the town of Pursat features natural beauty, colonial architecture, and friendly, rural inhabitants. The town is small enough to explore on foot; however, if your guesthouse rents bicycles, a leisurely bicycle tour is a pleasurable way to sightsee.

Bicycles are a popular countryside mode of transportation.

Begin at the former **Pursat Museum,** at the corner of National Highway 5 and Street 1. While the building now houses a school, the museum, which was built in the 1960s, remains a Pursat landmark.

Several blocks north, the **Pursat New Market** ❶ *(St. 1)* is the hub of activity in the town and worth a gander if you haven't spent much time in Khmer markets. Within the market, locals shop for groceries, household goods, and clothing. Vendors selling the province's renowned *kroch po sat* (Pursat oranges) are typically set up on the side of the market that faces the river.

Four blocks past the market, the street transforms from shop houses to ministerial offices. Although many of these colonial-style buildings are fairly recent constructions, others, such as the Governor's Residence, date back to the 1940s. One of the first ones you will come

NOT TO BE MISSED:

Wat Banteay Dei • Wat Po • Koh Sompeau Meah • Banteay Dei Village • Magic Fish restaurant

across is the **Tourism Office** *(St. 1),* where maps of the town and province of Pursat are available from a helpful tourism official. The buildings are best appreciated from the riverside park known as **7 January Park** ❷ *(St. 1).* The date commemorates the end of the Pol Pot regime, which had destroyed the original park while in power.

Half a mile (0.8 km) north of the park, you will see **Koh Sompeau Meah** (Golden Boat Island) ❸ *(across from hospital, St. 1, $)* in the middle of the river. The island's name is derived from a local legend regarding a boat that ran aground here. After unsuccessful attempts to dislodge it, the villagers left the boat to the river, where it gradually became overgrown and turned into an island. Prime Minister Hun Sen sponsored the construction of a 55-yard-long (19 m) concrete "boat" in 2008 and 2009, the resulting park offers green space with a *sala* (gazebo) at each end.

Following Street 1 north, the riverside restaurant **Magic Fish** is a pleasant site to stop for a drink. The spillway beside the restaurant is a popular place for children to swim and adults to fish. **Wat Po ❹** (*$*) is located farther downstream, across an old wooden bridge that leads directly to the road that offers access to the temple. After visiting the *wat*, return down

the east bank of the river, following a dirt road that passes through a shady rural village.

Once back on the paved road, beyond Golden Boat Island, **Wat Banteay Dei ❺** (*$*) sits directly opposite the new bridge. The main pagoda is more than 100 years old; the wat that once stood here and the Buddha that remains from it are more than 200 years old. Heading east through the back of the temple grounds brings you to **Banteay Dei Village ❻**, whose inhabitants are marble carvers. If you make right turns at each of the intersections in the village, you can watch the villagers creating their sculptures and then return to the main road beside a small wooden bridge. A large shop here sells marble statuary, and you can complete your circuit of the town across the bridge.

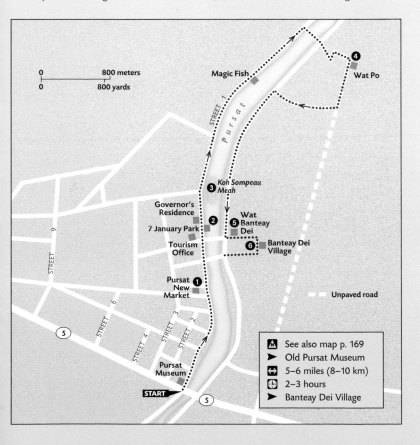

Prasat Ta Prohm
- 🅜 169 A4
- ✉ S of Banteay Chhmar southern causeway; 60 miles (97 km) N of Sisophon
- 💲 $–$$

Banteay Top
- 🅜 169 A4
- ✉ On side road 5 miles (8 km) S of Banteay Chhmar
- 💲 $

Anlong Veng
- 🅜 169 C4

Banteay Top (Army Fortress). The turnoff to Banteay Top (or Banteay Toup) is located 5 miles (8 km) south of Banteay Chhmar. While less aesthetically pleasing than the other sights in the area, the teetering **towers** of massive stones here are an impressive sight either from afar or underneath.

As the ride out to Banteay Chhmar and environs may take several hours at best, you may consider a homestay in a neighboring village. One homestay also features silk weaving (see Ecotourism, pp. 222–223).

Oddar Meanchey Province

Anlong Veng is a small border town, roughly 90 miles (145 km) north of Siem Reap and just 7 miles (11 km) from Thailand in Oddar Meanchey Province. The sleepy provincial town of Anlong Veng holds the distinction of being the last refuge of the Khmer Rouge, where Pol Pot spent his last days. As the town is quite remote and most attractions are related to this facet

of its history, only those deeply interested in Khmer Rouge history are likely to make the long journey to reach it.

North of Anlong Veng, on the paved road leading away from the **Dove of Peace monument,** lies the last holdout of several Khmer Rouge leaders, including Brother Number One, Pol Pot. Just before the Thai border, a trail leads to his **final resting place.** Following Pol Pot's somewhat mysterious death in 1998, he was cremated atop a pile of tires and furniture. The "grave" is framed by an unadorned shack of sorts, though pilgrims still come here to pay their respects, or perhaps simply to receive winning lottery numbers as recompense for his legacy of destruction. Beyond the grave an easterly gravel road leads up toward the cliffs of the Dangkrek Range where Pol Pot and his cohorts Ta Mok and Son Sen lived.

While Pol Pot's suitably pathetic grave is far from Anlong Veng, the **lakeside home** of an equally notorious Khmer Rouge leader, Ta Mok ("The Butcher"), is located in town.

Ins & Outs of Borders

There are six border crossings between Cambodia and Thailand at Anlong Veng, Duang Lem, Koh Kong, O Smach, Pailin, and Poipet. Most foreigners can enter Thailand for 15 days without a Thai visa, though proof of onward travel is occasionally required.

Entry points to Laos at Dom Kralor and Vietnam at Bavet, Kaam Samnor, Phnom Den, Preak Chak, and Trapeang Phlong have no visa services for foreigners, who must arrive at the border with

valid visas for the respective countries.

Cambodian visas are generally available at the border crossings with Thailand and Laos, but are available only at Bavet and Kaam Samnor for arrivals from Vietnam. Always bring dollars and extra passport-size photos for Cambodian visa applications. Cambodian visas are also now available on the internet via e-visa with a credit card and jpeg photo at *evisa. mfaic.gov.kh.* (See also Travelwise pp. 269–271.)

Traditional means of fishing are employed in a channel at Anlong Veng in Oddar Meanchey.

Ta Mok, Brother Number Five, ultimately became commander in chief of the Khmer Rouge. He withdrew to Anlong Veng with Pol Pot in 1979, where he consigned his former leader to house arrest. Eventually Ta Mok was captured, though he died in custody awaiting trial for crimes against humanity. His Anlong Veng residence has some interesting murals, which are worth seeing simply as there are few other sights in the town. Also, the nearby lake is relatively pleasant and is a popular weekend swimming hole. Note the brick outhouse in the middle of the lake; it is the remains of **Pol Pot's home.**

Despite its location within Oddar Meanchey, Anlong Veng is really only accessible from Siem Reap. In the dry season, the roads are better, though far from good. If you have a number of days to spare, you can travel a loop from Siem Reap through Anlong Veng, over to Preah Vihear (pp. 204–207), and then back through Koh Ker (pp. 208–209) and Beng Mealea (p. 115). Talk to a tour operator in Siem Reap for this multiday and challenging expedition.

The provincial capital of Oddar Meanchey, **Samraong,** has little for visitors to stop and see. However, it is the gateway one must pass through on the way north to the border town of **O Smach** or south to the temples along Route 56. The O Smach border has a casino on the Cambodian side and is only advisable for those looking for a shortcut for overland travel through eastern Thailand and up to Vientiane, Laos. ∎

Samraong

⚑ 169 B4

O Smach

⚑ 169 B4

Sambor Prei Kuk's seventh-century artistic splendor, vertigo-inducing Preah Vihear, and other remote temples

Central Cambodia

Exploring the ruins of Beng Mealea temple

Central Cambodia

Central Cambodia consists of two provinces: Kompong Thom, which lies just east of Tonle Sap Lake—roughly the geographic center of Cambodia—and Preah Vihear, situated between Kompong Thom and Thailand. The area includes wildlife reserves where you can search for exotic flora and fauna. You can also explore a number of remote temple complexes, such as Sambor Prei Kuk, which dates to the seventh century.

Kompong Thom—the capital of the province of the same name—is located along National Highway 6 about halfway between Phnom Penh and Siem Reap. This unassuming town is the closest one to the historical ruins of Sambor Prei Kuk, originally known as Isanapura, which likely functioned as the Chenla Empire's capital in the seventh century. Other temples around Kompong Thom date from the 7th to 11th centuries. The temples that are most convenient to stop at on this stretch of National Highway 6 are the small ruins of Prasat Kuh Nokor (aka Prasat Kuha Nokor) and the mountaintop temple complex of Wat Phnom Santuk. Also located within the province are two of the three core areas designated for the protection of wildlife around Tonle Sap Lake: Boeng Tonle Chhmar and Stung Sen Biosphere Reserves. The town of Kompong Thom is at the intersection of National Highway 6 and Route 64, which heads north into Preah Vihear Province.

Most of the historical and archaeological attractions in Preah Vihear Province are far less visited than their counterparts in Siem Reap. In part, this is due to the relative inaccessibility of its temples—the former Angkorian capital of Koh Ker, Preah Khan of Kompong Svay, and Prasat Preah Vihear. While road construction continues throughout Cambodia, reaching the temples of Preah Vihear Province can still be a challenge. This is particularly true during the rainy season, when many roads are only navigable on a dirt bike or in a 4WD vehicle.

Koh Ker functioned as the capital of Angkor for almost 20 years during the tenth century,

when Jayavarman IV seized the throne and built monumental structures to validate his reign. The local prevalence of sandstone lent itself to a period of temple construction and artistic development renowned for its grandiosity.

Preah Khan of Kompong Svay is a massive temple enclosure that dates back to the ninth century reign of Jayavarman II. It also clearly bears the 12th- and 13th-century architectural trademarks of the Buddhist kingship of Jayavarman VII. Though Preah Kahn lies along the ancient highway connecting Angkor to its more distant provinces, today it is one of the most isolated temple complexes in Cambodia. However, while the temples here can be difficult to reach, this challenge simply adds to their charm. These majestic ruins are mostly surrounded by lush tropical forest and they are

NOT TO BE MISSED:

A day trip to Isanborei Craft Hut, Sambor Prei Kuk 197–198

Roaming the shady Sambor Prei Kuk ruins 197–199

Discovering Preah Khan by dirt bike 199

A walk across the Ancient Bridge at Kompong K'day 201

Touring the expansive Prasat Preah Vihear 204–205

The ruins of Beng Mealea 206

Exploring dozens of temples at Koh Ker 208–209

far less frequented by tourists than their more easily accessed counterparts.

Farther north, the spectacular ruins of Prasat Preah Vihear perch on the cliffs of the Dangrek Range overlooking Thailand. In 2008, the listing of Prasat Preah Vihear as a UNESCO World Heritage site set off an intense border dispute between Cambodia and Thailand, during which lives were lost in outbursts of military conflict

(see sidebar p. 205). Generally accessible year-round via Anlong Veng or Koh Ker, Prasat Preah Vihear is one of the most awe-inspiring temples in the entire country. ■

Area of map detail

Phnom Penh

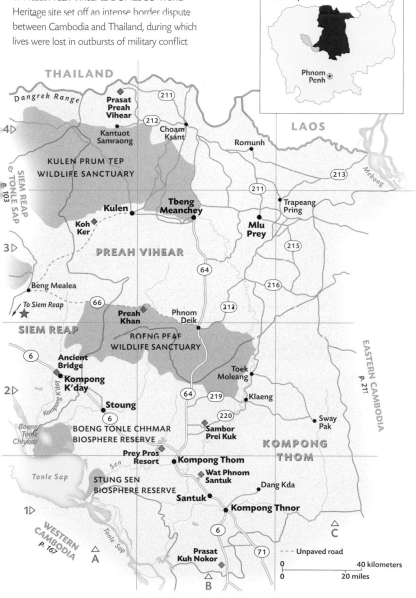

THAILAND

Dangrek Range

Prasat Preah Vihear

211

212

LAOS

Kantuot Samraong

Choam Ksant

Romunh

213

Mekong

KULEN PRUM TEP WILDLIFE SANCTUARY

211

Kulen

Tbeng Meanchey

Trapeang Pring

SIEM REAP
@ TONLE SAP
p. 103

Koh Ker

Mlu Prey

PREAH VIHEAR

215

64

Beng Mealea

66

216

To Siem Reap

Preah Khan

Phnom Deik

213

SIEM REAP

BOENG PEAF WILDLIFE SANCTUARY

6

Ancient Bridge

Kompong K'day

Toek Moleang

EASTERN CAMBODIA
p. 211

Stoung

64

219

Klaeng

Boeng
Tonle
Chhmar

6

220

Sway Pak

BOENG TONLE CHHMAR BIOSPHERE RESERVE

Sambor Prei Kuk

KOMPONG THOM

Prey Pros Resort

Kompong Thom

Tonle Sap

STUNG SEN BIOSPHERE RESERVE

Wat Phnom Santuk

Dang Kda

Santuk

Kompong Thnor

WESTERN CAMBODIA
p. 167

6

C

A

Tonle Sap

Prasat Kuh Nokor

71

Unpaved road

0   40 kilometers
0   20 miles

B

Kompong Thom Province

Kompong Thom Province, which lies just east of Tonle Sap Lake, is home to a variety of interesting ancient temples. The star of the show is the wonderful pre-Angkorian temple complex at Sambor Prei Kuk. The province also contains the Boeng Tonle Chhmar and Stung Sen Biosphere Reserves, both created to protect the fragile ecosystem around the Tonle Sap.

In Kompong Thom farmers and their children catch crickets in a rice field at night.

Kompong Thom
🅰 195 B1, 207

Wat Kompong Thom
✉ 100 yards (91 m) W of Stung Sen River Bridge on National Highway 6

It's understandable to be confused by the name of Kompong Thom ("big port"), as there isn't a particularly large port there. The town was originally called Kompong Pos Thom, or "big snakes port," a name drawn from a legend concerning a pair of extraordinarily large snakes that appeared in the Stung Sen (Sen River) during Buddhist holidays. For simplicity's sake, the name was shortened during the French colonial period. The town of **Kompong Thom** is located on the Sen River, 110 miles (177 km) north of Phnom Penh—roughly the midpoint along the road to Siem Reap. It has a moderately interesting modern Buddhist temple, **Wat Kompong Thom,** and a small, run-down museum under the auspices of the Department of Arts and Culture (jct. National Highway 6 & Procheatepatay

Rd., $). As of 2008, the town's tourism office appeared to have shut its doors, perhaps testifying to the relative lack of attractions around town. However, an office of the **Sambor Prei Kuk Conservation Project** provides information and offers tours of the temples and surrounding countryside.

Sambor Prei Kuk

The history of pre-Angkorian Cambodia is still somewhat shrouded in mystery. Debate continues as to whether Chenla was a unified kingdom when it overpowered neighboring Funan in the early seventh century. Less than a century later, Chenla fragmented into two kingdoms— Land Chenla and Water Chenla— which may have coincided with the boundaries of the original two realms. The temples of Sambor Prei Kuk may (or may not) represent evidence of the capital of Water Chenla. In any case, these temples were part of a major Hindu religious center that likely served the seventh-century city of Isanapura, which is now believed to have existed just west of the primary ruins.

The ruins of Sambor Prei Kuk are spread over an area of roughly 6,000 acres (2,428 ha). They include Isanapura, which was once bounded on three sides by a moat and an earthen wall, and three primary temple complexes. Two causeways, each several miles long, lead from the temples toward the village of Kompong Cheauteal and the Sen River. Although more than a hundred temples have

been discovered here, only a fraction remain intact or have been restored. These include the structures within the three enclosed temple complexes referred to either by name or location: Prasat Sambor or North (N) Group; Prasat Tor or Center (C) Group;

INSIDER TIP:

An unsung wonder in Kompong Thom is the pre-Angkorian ruins collectively known as Sambor Prei Kuk. The site has the largest collection of well-preserved brick architecture in the country but gets relatively little visitation.

—MIRIAM STARK
National Geographic field researcher

and Prasat Yeay Puon or South (S) Group. All are accessible via foot or bicycle *(available on-site, $).* The turnoff to the historical park lies approximately 7 miles (11 km) north of the town of Kompong Thom on Route 64. The Sambor Prei Kuk Conservation Project in Kompong Thom can arrange a tour of the area that includes an oxcart ride, a picnic lunch, and a guided bicycle tour.

The parking area and **Isanborei Craft Hut** are alongside the **N Group,** which is accessible from the north. At the craft hut, you can learn about the temples

Sambor Prei Kuk Conservation Project

- ✉ 16 Procheate-patay Rd., Kompong Thom
- ☎ 855(0)92-254-829 or 855(0)12-637-693
- 💲 $

Sambor Prei Kuk Temple Site

- 🗺 195 B2, 207
- ✉ 7 miles (11 km) N of Kompong Thom on Rte. 64 to turnoff, then 10 miles (16 km) on side road (Rte. 220)
- 💲 $$

Isanborei Craft Hut

- ✉ Sambor Village, Sambor Commune, Prasat Sambor District, Kompong Thom Commune
- 💲 $

and local villages and purchase traditional handicrafts. Inscriptions indicate this complex was originally constructed in the seventh century, though they also mention tenth-century king Rajendravarman II (r.944–968), who likely made renovations here. **Statuary** found in the N Group is considered to be among the most outstanding art in Cambodian history. In particular, the shapely torso of the goddess Durga, a reproduction of which is located within **shrine N9,** is the epitome of the Sambor style of art.

INSIDER TIP:

If you don't have your own transportation to the temples at Sambor Prei Kuk, a *tuk-tuk* or tour operator in Kompong Thom can arrange a visit.

—TREVOR RANGES
National Geographic author

Just to the south, **N10** contains a reproduction of the image of Harihara (half Shiva, half Vishnu). Excavation just beside this tower led to the discovery of a statue of Ganesha in July 2008. The south-western corner of **N7** contained a tenth-century statue of Vajimukha. A reproduction of this incarnation of Vishnu, with a human body and a horse's head, is scheduled to be installed in its original shrine. N7 is one of a number of remarkable octagonal towers featuring relief carvings known as **flying palaces** on each exterior facade. In these

reliefs—thought to house the temples' guardian spirits—figures gaze out the windows. The palaces are multilevel, idealized representations of the towers, inhabited by royalty and gods. The **central sanctuary of Prasat Sambor** (N1) features a *yoni* pedestal that once contained a massive *linga,* indicating the temple complex was likely consecrated in honor of Shiva.

A path through the woods leads to the **C Group,** the largest group of buildings at Sambor Prei Kuk. In addition to being called the Prasat Tor Group, it is known as the Lion Temple Group for the **lion statues** that flank the staircase of the central sanctuary. Elements of the temple's decoration, including the two remaining lions, suggest a ninth-century influence from the reign of Jayavarman II (r.802–850), the first king of the Angkorian era. The sandstone lintels and octagonal colonettes of the temple's **false doors,** more indicative of pre-Angkorian art, deserve inspection for their remarkable intactness and elaborate detail.

Through the forest to the southeast, the **S Group** has a number of interesting elements. The **exterior entrance** features inscriptions within its doorway, which leads to a second **enclosure wall** that is decorated with a series of circular carvings on its interior. The scenes depicted on two of these four carvings appear to represent a monkey making an offering to Vishnu (second from door) and a figure, perhaps Durga, battling a lion (fourth from door). According to an inscription here, the eastern-facing central sanctuary, **S1,** once housed a golden linga called Prohateysesvara (the Smiling Shiva). Directly east of S1, **S2** reputedly housed a silver image of Nandi. The small sandstone shrine where the bull once knelt features small faces, the likes of which are otherwise unknown in Angkorian or pre-Angkorian art, and which suggest a surprising Hellenistic influence. The Prasat Yeay Puon Group also features the aforementioned **flying palaces** on five octagonal brick towers. Each flying palace is slightly different from the others, and the towers feature them on seven of their eight exterior walls. Exit to the east, where the roots of a tree hold together the eastern doorway of the otherwise collapsed exterior enclosure wall.

National Highway 6 to Kompong Thom

If you are traveling to Kompong Thom from Phnom Penh on National Highway 6, an interesting detour is the temple complex of **Prasat Kuh Nokor.** It's located 50 miles (80 km)

Prasat Kuh Nokor

⚐ 195 B1

EXPERIENCE: Adventure by Off-road Motorcycle

Cambodia is an off-road motorcyclist's dream come true: Nearly 75 percent of Cambodia's roads are unsealed and many spectacular sights are in remote locations. While some operators simply will rent you a 250cc bike and send you on your way, be aware of what you're getting into. Many roads are little more than oxcart trails that sometimes terminate at rivers, where makeshift bridges are often washed away by torrential rains. Mountain trails can be steep, slick, and dangerous, some requiring riders to drive across fallen trees over precipitous crevasses. These experienced operators listed below are familiar with the terrain and know where to sling a hammock if you need to spend a night in the bush.

Dancing Roads
A small, personal outfit, Dancing Roads (*66C St. 368, W of St. 163, Phnom Penh, tel 855(0)12-822-803 or 855(0)12-753-008, www.dancingroads.com*) is more suitable for experienced motorbike riders who are looking for longer adventures, as there are few fun trails near Phnom Penh. Still,

beginners are well looked after by owner/guide Paeng, who has years of experience exploring the country's back roads.

Norden House
Ratanakiri has some of Cambodia's most remote backcountry roads and fascinating sights including hill-tribe villages, volcanic lakes, and ruins from 20th-century warfare. The proprietor of Norden House (*Yak Lom Rd., Ban Lung, Ratanakiri, tel 855(0)12-488-950, www.nordenhouseyaklom.com*), Nisse, has a few bikes and a lot of experience traveling through this gorgeous province.

Siem Reap Dirt Bikes
With easy-to-ride motorbikes and outstanding guides, Siem Reap Dirt Bikes (*tel 855(0)99-823-216, www.siemreapdirtbikes.com*) is the ideal company for beginners to learn some off-road skills and experienced bikers to challenge themselves. Customized tours around Cambodia, particularly to the temples of Beng Mealea or Preah Vihear, may soon include cross-border excursions into Laos. Specializes in tours throughout Central Cambodia.

Kompong K'day's "Ancient Bridge," largest of the laterite bridges along the Khmer ancient highways

**Wat Phnom
Santuk**

🔺 195 B1

before the town of Kompong Thom, 14 miles (23 km) north of Skuon. The construction of the Prasat Kuh Nokor complex at the turn of the 11th century coincided with a struggle for supremacy during which Suryavarman I (r. 1003–ca 1049) and a rival were vying for the throne. Suryavarman was able to capture the Angkorian capital of Yasodharapura and eventually vanquished his rival. Highlights of Prasat Kuh Nokor include a sandstone throne adorned with carved lotus flowers and several semi-intact sculptures.

Wat Phnom Santuk: About 10 miles (16 km) southeast of the town of Kompong Thom on National Highway 6 is the turnoff to Wat Phnom Santuk. The temple is a place of great

reverence for local people and the focal point of a legend about a king from the northern Dangrek mountains. The monarch was duped by a court official, who conspired with the king's second wife to usurp him, into banishing his first wife and their son. The exiled queen and prince were set adrift on a raft, but were spared a tragic fate by a pair of preternatural white crocodiles who steered them to a small island. The gods then heeded the queen's prayers and transformed the island into a tropical paradise.

Eventually, an officer of the king's army arrived on the island and told the pair that the king had been imprisoned. The young prince returned with the naval officer to defeat the usurper and the treacherous queen, though he spared the life of his innocent half brother. The prince became king and made the island his capital. His half brother later took the throne. The sea eventually receded and the island became a mountain.

Over the years, Phnom Santuk has undergone a series of name changes. Local people have long paid homage to the spirit of the young prince who established his bygone kingdom there. Today, visitors from around Cambodia pay their respects at dozens of **shrines** both along the 809 steps leading up to the summit and at the top the mountain. The shrines vary tremendously, honoring the brothers, ancestral spirits, Bodhisattvas, and the Buddha. At one shrine, visitors can get coins (pennies!) to make offerings, including dropping them down a narrow crack in Chan Re boulder. A Buddha's footprint (a carved image revered as the actual footprint of the Buddha) here is said to have restorative powers. A Chinese temple and other shrines date back to the 16th-century reign of Ang Chan.

Northwest from Kompong Thom

Ten miles (16 km) northwest of Kompong Thom, along National Highway 6 toward Siem Reap, is **Prey Pros Resort.** This waterside rest area is popular for both dining and recreation. While events such as running and bicycle races are held here during national holidays, inner tubes and paddleboats are available year-round. Visitors also may dine on relatively expensive, but delectable, whole fried fish.

Ancient Bridge: Farther northwest, just past Kompong K'day, National Highway 6 bends suddenly before passing over the Kompong K'day River. Prior to this new span's completion in 2006, the span north of it was the river crossing for nearly 800 years. The dry-jointed, laterite block bridge, known as the Ancient Bridge, is the largest Angkor-era bridge in Cambodia, spanning approximately 280 feet (85 m) at a height of 45 feet (14 m). This bridge has 9-foot-tall (3 m) hooded *nagas* at the end of its railings and is still used by motorbikes and bicycles. ∎

Prey Pros Resort
🔼 195 B2

Ancient Bridge
🔼 195 A2

Wildlife Sanctuaries

Boeng Tonle Chhmar and Stung Sen are far less accessible than Prek Toal, the third of the three core areas constituting the protected wildlife sanctuaries around Tonle Sap Lake. Yet the biosphere reserves are outstanding destinations for serious wildlife enthusiasts, particularly those interested in waterfowl. As of 2008, however, there was no infrastructure to support mainstream ecotourism here. The area is home to several floating villages whose residents earn their livelihood fishing amid the flooded forests of Tonle Sap.

Conservation

At the turn of the 21st century, Cambodia had some of Southeast Asia's most pristine forests and wetlands. The land mines that littered the countryside from years of war hampered human encroachment in remote wilderness areas, protecting threatened and endangered species. However, these enclaves are being destroyed by the development of hydroelectric dams and a recent boom in logging, farming, and mining.

A fisherman on the Tonle Sap untangles his catch.

Conservationists are fighting to protect Cambodia's remaining unspoiled native ecosystems. The **Northern Plains** are an expansive landscape of grasslands, decidu-ous and semievergreen forests, and seasonal freshwater wetlands spanning the northern provinces from Preah Vihear to Banteay Meanchey. Endangered species found here include tigers, elephants, and a host of birds, including ibises, cranes, and vultures. Deforestation and hunting are the biggest threats to the country's dwindling wildlife populations. Organizations like the Wildlife Conservation Society (WCS; *21 St. 21, Sangkat Tonle Bassac, Phnom Penh, tel/fax 855(0)23-217-205, www.wcs.org*) have named 40 Important Bird Areas. At one of them, Kulen Promtep Wildlife Sanctuary's Tmatboey Ibis Project, locals are encouraged to take a vested interest in preserving wildlife under the auspices of renewable ecotourism revenue–as opposed to the diminishing gains of hunting.

Tonle Sap Lake is one of the last viable breeding grounds in the world for a number of threatened waterbirds. The WCS and the Cambodian government have designated the lake a biosphere reserve. At three core areas—Boeng Tonle Chhmar, Prek Toal, and Stung Sen—bird colonies are monitored by rangers. Also, environmental education encourages local people to identify and protect the nests of threatened birds.

Seima Biodiversity Conservation Area

Mondulkiri Province is one of the least populated and developed areas of Cambodia. A vast diversity of wildlife occupies the province, from orange-necked partridges to Asian elephants and pygmy lorises, but the region's population—including ethnic minority hill tribes—has historically relied on forestry, agriculture, and wildlife products to survive. The Department of Forestry and Wildlife, in conjunction with the WCS, has zoned thousands of acres for conservation purposes, called the Seima Biodiversity Conservation Area. Authorities have cracked down on illegal hunting, particularly of tigers, and helped locals manage their natural resources in a sustainable manner, but an increase in foreign forestry and mining concessions is putting a great strain on the ecosystem and the people.

The **Cardamom Mountains** are another of Cambodia's final frontiers, protected for years by impassable roads and innumerable land mines surrounding one of the last Khmer Rouge enclaves. The mountains are now one of the last refuges for the Siamese crocodile and some of the few remaining herds of wild elephants in Southeast Asia. The area also is home to nearly every amphibian, bird, insect, mammal, and reptile found in Cambodia. The Cardamom Highway, built by developers of hydroelectric power plants, is expected to be complete in 2009, and will provide greater access—and ecological threat—to the range. The Cardamom Mountain Wildlife Sanctuaries Project, initiated by Fauna & Flora International (59 St. 306, Boeung Keng Kang 1, Phnom Penh, tel 855(0)23-220-534), is striving to provide management for the two most important areas, Phnom Samkos and Phnom Aural Wildlife Sanctuaries.

The fall of the Khmer Rouge kicked off a period of widespread commercial logging, particularly in **Koh Kong** and Pailin, where Cambodians, Chinese, and Thai have been clearing land for sugarcane and oil palm plantations. Loggers have also been cutting "luxury" trees, such as

INSIDER TIP:

Birders simply cannot miss Tmatboey, breeding ground for two of the world's rarest bird species: the giant ibis and white-shouldered ibis. Visit the Wildlife Conservation Society project that's designed to help villagers in Preah Vihear earn a living through conservation.

—KAREN COATES
National Geographic writer

beng, prized for the beautiful color of its wood, used to craft furniture, doors, and carvings. Organizations such as Wildlife Alliance (109 St. 99, Phnom Penh, tel 855(0)23-211-604, www .wildlifealliance.org) are working with local villages to prevent—and reverse—the deleterious effects of logging. Reforestation programs like the one in **Chi Phat** gather seeds from the countryside, plant them in nurseries, and then relocate the seedlings to areas that have been clear-cut.

Marine Conservation

Cambodia is also is making headway in the fight against the destruction of its marine ecosystem. Dive operators such as the Dive Shop in Sihanoukville (Serendipity Beach Rd., Sihanoukville, tel 855(0)12-161-5517 or 855(0)34-933-664, www.diveshopcambodia .com), working with Reef Check (www .reefcheck.org), Marine Conservation Cambodia (www.marineconservationcambodia.org), and the Department of Fisheries, have succeeded in protecting a seahorse breeding ground—called the Corral—near Koh Rung Saloem island off the coast of Sihanoukville. Villagers, who directly benefit from crackdowns on illegal fishing, are helping preserve fish stocks. This effort benefits area fishermen and also fosters a more sustainable income source: catering to international scuba divers.

Preah Vihear Province

The province of Preah Vihear is best known for the temple of the same name that lies along the border with Thailand. The capital city of Tbeng Meanchey is gradually adopting the name Preah Vihear as well. That said, with the exception of the Angkor-era capital of Koh Ker and the ruins of Preah Khan of Kompong Svay, Prasat Preah Vihear is the only reason visitors make a journey into this remote northern border province.

Cambodian Buddhist monks at Preah Vihear temple

Prasat Preah Vihear

- 195 A4, 207
- 60 miles (97 km) N of Tbeng Meanchey
- From Cambodia $; from Thailand $$ (if border is open)

Prasat Preah Vihear

The construction of the sandstone temple of Prasat Preah Vihear was initiated by Yaso-varman I (r.889–910), possibly on the site of an earlier temple. This expansive cliffside complex was truly a work in progress, however, as other kings added to it over several ensuing centuries. Constructed on a gradual incline that starts near the border with Thailand and concludes atop the 1,800-foot (550 m) summit of Chuor Phnom Dangrek, Preah Vihear begins at a grand staircase. Nearly 260 feet long

(78 m), the staircase leads up to the first of four enclosures linked by three open avenues.

At the top of the stairs, just before the first *gopura* is the **Naga Courtyard,** so called for its seven-headed *naga* sculptures. One of the nagas is carved from a single sandstone block. Pass the first collapsed gopura and the first avenue, noting the **royal bath** just to the east. Then, stairs lead to the **second gopura,** where lintel and pediment carvings feature a reclining Vishnu and a re-creation of the Churning of the Sea of Milk (see sidebar p. 151). Toward the summit, within the final two enclosures, the temple broadens. Its subsidiary structures include two rest houses for pilgrims just before the third avenue. While the **uppermost level** is in a ruined state, its location, just inches from the precipitous edge of the cliff, makes finding an overlook equally risky and rewarding.

Prasat Preah Vihear was once almost exclusively accessible from Thailand. Visitors could leave their passports and walk across the border to explore the temple for several hours. Access from the north was often closed in 2008, however, following a border dispute related to the temple (see sidebar below). For years, horrendous road conditions and the remote location restricted travel to Prasat Preah Vihear from

the Cambodian side to all but the most hard-core explorers. Today, road improvements have made travel from Anlong Veng or Koh Ker to Tbeng Meanchey and Choam Ksant—the nearest town to the temple—manageable even in the early or late months of the rainy season, May to August. Still, an off-road dirt bike or a 4WD vehicle is strongly advised during the rainy months. Regardless of when you travel, confirm road conditions and the current state of the Thai-Cambodian hostilities before attempting to visit. It should also be noted that the area was heavily mined during the Khmer Rouge years. Though many areas have been cleared of mines, it is safest to stay on the beaten path.

(continued on p. 208)

Thai-Cambodian Conflict over Preah Vihear

In 2008 a dispute over 1.8 square miles (4.6 sq km) around the tenth-century Preah Vihear temple exploded into violence after several Thai citizens were arrested in Cambodia for evading a checkpoint at the disputed area, crossing into the frontier near the temple. Tensions had been building since UNESCO approved Cambodia's Prasat Preah Vihear as a World Heritage site. This incident may have been the straw that broke the camel's back, but the conflict has long been mired in both internal and international political and economic issues that outweigh the already complex historical and legal ones.

While there is no doubt that the temple was constructed by Angkorian kings, the territory was annexed as part of Siam (Thailand) from 1431 to 1907, although the Siamese allowed Cambodians to administer the region according to Cambodian

customs. In 1907 the Siamese ceded the territory to French-Indochina using the watershed of the Dangrek Range to delineate the northern border, though the map included Preah Vihear (north of the watershed) within Cambodian territory.

Since then, Cambodia has gradually bolstered its legal claim on the territory. In 1962 the International Court of Justice ruled that Preah Vihear was within Cambodian sovereignty—though the surrounding land continued to be under dispute. When UNESCO designated Preah Vihear a World Heritage site in 2008, the conflict flared. The ensuing military stalemate was fueled by internal politics on both sides of the border; a number of soldiers were killed and the temple was damaged by a grenade. A resolution may prove difficult, but one benefit of military occupation of the hill is that the road to the temple is now paved.

Drive: Mission to Preah Vihear

The cliffside temple of Preah Vihear is an easy day trip from Thailand. From Cambodia, however, getting there is more of an adventure along a drive requiring at least one overnight stay. Considering the distance, combine your visit to Prasat Preah Vihear with several other ruins—Beng Mealea, Koh Ker, and Sambor Prei Kuk (Isanapura).

This drive requires three or four days and the assistance of a driver/guide who knows the way (several roads are newer than most maps and are unnamed and unnumbered). The worst stretches of road get washed out in the rainy season, so the trip is only possible by car in the dry months. In the rainy season, it's a hard-core motorbike adventure.

The most convenient place to begin is **Siem Reap** (see pp. 106–113), where you can organize an off-road motorbike tour (see sidebar p. 199) or hire a car and driver through your hotel or local tour operator. Discuss your plans beforehand to get the current road conditions and determine whether the trip will be possible.

The first stop is the ruins of **Beng Mealea** ❶ *($$$$$),* an approximately two-hour, 37-mile (60 km) drive. The 12th-century temple remains

NOT TO BE MISSED:

Beng Mealea • Koh Ker • Prasat Preah Vihear • Sambor Prei Kuk

in a relatively natural state of collapsed towers and overgrown jungle, much as it was when it was "discovered" in 1913. An hour or so of exploration should suffice here. Then continue on a northeast course heading toward the next ruins, which lie roughly 30 miles (50 km) and a mere one-hour drive away.

Just before you arrive at **Koh Ker** ❷ *($$$),* the road passes through some picturesque countryside. Be aware that central Cambodia still contains numerous land mines, even around the temples of Koh Ker. Stay on established trails and walkways. As the site was the capital of the Khmer Empire for roughly 20 years early in the Angkor era, the numerous, impressive ruins here will take a few hours to explore.

After driving across open country with spectacular mountain views, spend the night in the provincial capital of **Tbeng Meanchey** (aka Preah Vihear). The next morning brings a bumpy ride north, approximately 50 miles (80 km), which takes roughly three hours. Once near the temple, unless you are on a motorbike already, you must switch to a moto-taxi for the unpaved ascent to **Prasat Preah Vihear** ❸ *($).* After exploring the temple, you may stay at the guesthouse at the base of the temple or set up camp near the temple itself (ideal for watching the sunset). Alternatively, you may return to Choam Ksant, 24 miles (39 km) southeast of the temple complex, and shave a few hours off your long journey the following day.

A Cambodian flag atop Preah Vihear, site of a recent Cambodian and Thai border dispute

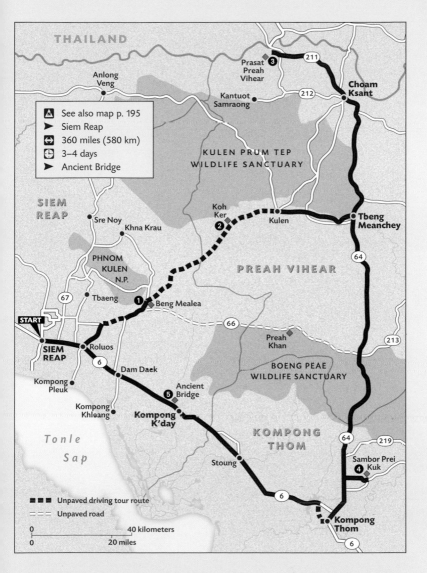

Day 3 could entail a punishing six- to eight-hour drive straight through to Kompong Thom and Sambor Prei Kuk. Those camping at Preah Vihear may wish to spend another night at Tbeng Meanchey. Yet the 100 miles (160 km) between Tbeng Meanchey and Kompong Thom must be traversed if you want to visit the ruins of Isanapura. At **Sambor Prei Kuk** ❹ ($), dozens of seventh-century temples have

been carefully reconstructed. Visit on arrival in the afternoon or in the morning after sleeping in Kompong Thom; the temples are 17 miles (27 km) from town. On your final day, the 93-mile (150 km) drive from Kompong Thom to Siem Reap is a speedy 3.5 hours on National Highway 6. Just past Kompong K'day, stop at the Angkor-era **Ancient Bridge** ❺, where the road bears left to cross the river over a newer bridge.

Koh Ker

🅰 195 A3, 207

✉ 50 miles (80 km) W of Tbeng Meanchey

💲 $$

Koh Ker

Early in the tenth century, a pair of brothers vied with their uncle over the order of ascension to the Angkorian throne. It appears that the uncle established a rival capital more than 52 miles (85 km) to the north of Angkor in a region known as Chok Gargyar (Koh Ker). Upon the death of the brothers, their uncle proclaimed himself Jayavarman IV, universal monarch of the empire, in 928. During his roughly 20-year reign, Jayavarman IV built grand temples honoring the Hindu gods, including

A road around the Rahal boasts dozens of temples to visit, though **Prasat Thom** is the prime attraction. From the most easterly structures that flank the causeway to the rear wall of the pyramid is a span of nearly 2,000 feet (600 m), with a moat-encircled complex of towers and galleries along the way. The most impressive of these subsidiary temples is **Prasat Kraham** (Red Sanctuary), whose towering, red brick spire once sheltered an eight-armed dancing Shiva image estimated to be at least 13 feet (4 km) tall. Sadly, Koh Ker's remote location ensured that most

Driving & Road Conditions

There are only two certainties regarding Cambodian roads: A road's condition is relative to the person you ask and road improvements are proceeding at breakneck speeds. Unless someone has traveled a certain road in the past week, his or her assessment of current conditions is suspect. Even then, an experienced dirt biker is more likely to tell you a road isn't bad than a Western urbanite. New bridges and roads are facilitating logging and mining in remote areas, suddenly making nearby tourist destinations, such as Koh Ker and the hill-tribe villages of Ratanakiri, accessible via decent red-dirt roads. As about 75 percent of Cambodia's roads are unsealed, monsoons can quickly turn a "good" road into a rutted, impassible mud pit—great on a dirt bike but not in a car. Fortunately, the roads that already are paved are also being upgraded. Travel between the major tourist destinations is generally smooth sailing on fresh blacktop.

Prasat Thom (Big Sanctuary)—a seven-tiered step pyramid—and the *baray* known as Rahal. In addition to producing an impressive number of temples, the Koh Ker period is remarkable for its larger-than-life freestanding statuary. For example, the limestone statue of the fighting monkey-men from this period is now displayed at the National Museum in Phnom Penh (see p. 72).

statuary was carried off, either to museums or private collections. You will see the head of a Nandi statue on the ground on the way to the pyramid, though.

The **state temple** of Prasat Thom proper is an impressive 130 feet (40 m) high. With a base of only 592 square feet (55 sq m), it is steeper than most other temple pyramids. Although the temple was once accessible via the eastern stairway, it may no longer be ascended by visitors.

Other temples of particular note are a row of westerly facing temples commencing with **Prasat Balang,** which still contains a massive *linga* and has a conduit for draining consecrated waters through its north wall. **Prasat Damrei** (Elephant Sanctuary) is guarded by both lion and elephant statuary. The aforementioned statue of the fighting monkey-men was discovered at **Prasat Chhin** (Chinese Sanctuary), and a lintel with a *garuda* atop entwined nagas remains above the south tower. Interestingly, a number of temples, including Prasat Thom, are oriented slightly north of due east, a characteristic also apparent at the seventh-century Sambor Prei Kuk (Isanapura; see pp. 197–199) and many Hindu temples in Indonesia, particularly on the island of Bali.

A new road between Beng Mealea and Koh Ker has made it possible to visit the temporary capital of the Angkor Empire on a long day trip from Siem Reap. Still, it's quite far and ought to be included in a circular route with Anlong Veng and Prasat Preah Vihear to the north or Sambor Prei Kuk to the south.

Preah Khan of Kompong Svay

Despite Preah Khan's seclusion, its immensity—larger than Angkor Thom—makes a journey here a must for serious temple hunters. Surrounded by a huge wall, the complex covers more than 1.5 square miles (4 sq km) and consists of four enclosures around a central sanctuary. All of them are oriented slightly north of due east, suggesting an original construction perhaps as early as pre-Angkorian times. Jayavarman VII (*r. ca.* 1181–1218) ultimately built up the temple into

Cows and cars often share the road in rural parts of north-central Cambodia.

a city. He linked it to his capital with an elevated, 75-mile-long (121 km) thoroughfare of the ancient highway that passes Beng Mealea 60 miles (97 km) to the west. Jayavarman VII may have operated out of Preah Khan following the sacking of Angkor by the Cham in 1177. Preah Khan's distinguishing features include the nearly 2-mile-long (3 km) baray, half of which lies within the city's exterior enclosure. **Prasat Damrei** (Elephant Sanctuary) lies at the reservoir's eastern end and Mebon-like **Prasat Preah Thkol** is at its center. Jayavarman VII's hallmark face tower rises above **Prasat Preah Stung** at the baray's west end. ∎

Preah Kahn
195 B3, 207

Cambodia's final frontier—minority hill tribes and wild tigers and elephants amid remote, unspoiled natural beauty

Eastern Cambodia

In Ban Lung, elephant rides can take you on a scenic tour to nearby waterfalls.

Eastern Cambodia

Journeying into Cambodia's most easterly provinces, Ratanakiri and Mondulkiri, has long been a rugged adventure few visitors had the time or constitution to endure. While most of these sparsely populated regions still feature wilderness generally unspoiled and unexplored, except by tigers, elephants, and the occasional bear, things are rapidly changing. New roads and border crossings with Vietnam are likely to hasten development, and more visitors are bound to make the journey from Phnom Penh.

About 77 miles (124 km) northeast of Phnom Penh, Kompong Cham separates the well-traveled part of Cambodia from the authentic by the wide Mekong River's one bridge. Kompong Cham is a shadow of the tourist hot spot it was in the 1920s and '30s—adored for its quaint charm and Parisian feel. Ruined by the Khmer Rouge, Kompong Cham is slowly shaking off the rubble's dust, among which hides a locally famed 11th-century temple, Wat Nokor, and its decapitated Buddha.

Following the Mekong River upstream another 80 miles (129 km) brings you to Kratie, another provincial capital. The few streets are dusty, but the dust's red tinge does make the famous sunsets over the Mekong more brilliant. Kratie is best experienced as an outpost from which to take a day trip to spot the direly endangered freshwater Irrawaddy dolphins and explore several charming and unique temples.

Farther north, about 95 miles (153 km) from Kratie and 282 miles (454 km) from Phnom Penh, lies tiny Stung Treng. Its four square blocks act as a quick rest stop before the road forks to either the Laos border crossing, Dom Kralor, or toward Ratanakiri. The provincial capital, Ban Lung, is a typical mountain town with Far East flavor. Treks through the surrounding region, which can venture into the largely unexplored Virachey National Park, highlight secluded hill-tribe villages, thunderous waterfalls, stunning views, and volcanic crater lakes.

Just south of Ratanakiri, Mondulkiri hugs the eastern border with diverse terrain that quickly shifts from jungle to evergreens to weeds, due to illegal logging. The sleepy capital, Sen Monorom, is a base for exceptional conservation efforts like the Elephant Valley Project.

Reaching the far eastern provinces became considerably easier in 2009 with the completion of major roadwork, though the rainy season (June–Oct.) can still make the trip a bit challenging. The most comfortable ride is a small six-seater plane with Mission Aviation Fellowship (see p. 272). ∎

NOT TO BE MISSED:

A Mission Aviation Fellowship flight over the Mekong **212, 272**

Eating tarantulas in Skuon **216**

Seeing Irrawaddy dolphins near Kratie **220**

Swimming and tubing in Ratanakiri's Yak Laom Lake **225**

Experiencing hill-tribe life in Ratanakiri or Mondulkiri **227, 231–232**

Mahout training with the Elephant Valley Project in Mondulkiri **233**

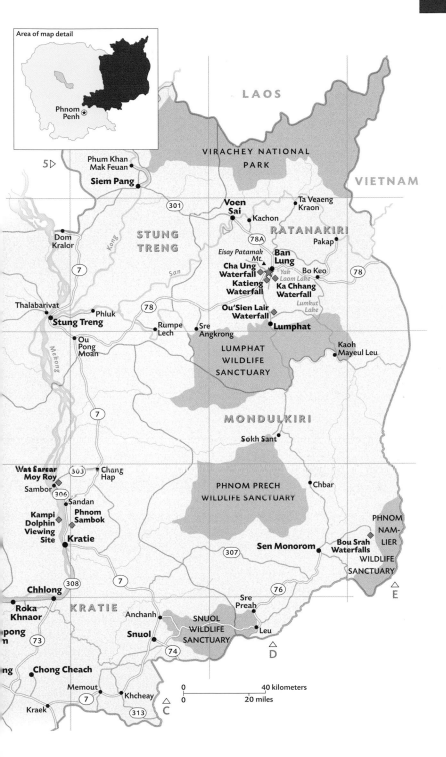

Area of map detail

Phnom
Penh ✦

5 ▷

LAOS

VIRACHEY NATIONAL
PARK

VIETNAM

Phum Khan
Mak Feuan
Siem Pang

Dom
Kralor

**Voen
Sai**

Ta Veaeng
Kraon

Kachon

RATANAKIRI

Pakap

7

**STUNG
TRENG**

(301)

(78A)

*Eisay Patamak
Mt.*

**Ban
Lung**

Bo Keo

(78)

**Cha Ung
Waterfall**
**Katieng
Waterfall**

*Yak
Laom Lake*

**Ka Chhang
Waterfall**

Thalabarivat

Phluk

(78)

Stung Treng

Rumpe
Lech

Sre
Angkrong

**Ou'Sien Lair
Waterfall**

*Lumkut
Lake*

Lumphat

Ou
Pong
Moan

**LUMPHAT
WILDLIFE
SANCTUARY**

Kaoh
Mayeul Leu

(7)

MONDULKIRI

Sokh Sant

**Wat Sarsar
Moy Roy**

(303)

Chang
Hap

Sambor

(306)

Sandan

**Kampi
Dolphin
Viewing
Site**

**Phnom
Sambok**

**PHNOM PRECH
WILDLIFE SANCTUARY**

Chbar

Kratie

**PHNOM
NAM-
LIER**

Sen Monorom

**Bou Srah
Waterfalls**

(307)

**WILDLIFE
SANCTUARY**

Chhlong

(308)

**Roka
Khnaor**

KRATIE

Anchanh

Sre
Preah

(76)

E

Leu

pong
n

(73)

Snuol

**SNUOL
WILDLIFE
SANCTUARY**

(74)

D

Chong Cheach

Memout

(7)

Khcheay

C

Kraek

(313)

0   40 kilometers
0   20 miles

Kong

San

Mekong

Kompong Cham, Kratie, & Stung Treng

The town of Kompong Cham is no longer the cosmopolitan French colonial outpost it was in its heyday. Yet the surrounding province still holds a number of interesting attractions, including temple complexes and a lighthouse on the Mekong River. Near Kratie—the busy provincial capital—and Stung Treng, you can spot endangered Irrawaddy dolphins cavorting in the river.

A woman weaves her scarf in a cashew tree orchard in tribal lands of the east-central highlands.

Kompong Cham
🔺 212 B1

Kompong Cham

Kompong Cham, or Cham Port, is so called for the Muslim Cham who have long resided there. Cambodia's largest minority ethnic group, the Cham retain their unique language, ancient history, and differing religion, despite living right in the middle of Cambodia.

Kompong Cham's difference from the rest of the country is exactly its attraction—or, more

accurately, *was* its attraction. In the 1920s and 1930s, at the height of French colonialism, the city was a cosmopolitan trendsetter boasting tree-lined boulevards, lush parks, and striking architecture. What remains standing are the sooty remains of that world, a result of the Khmer Rouge razing the city. During the regime (1975–1979), the Khmer Rouge destroyed most of Kompong Cham's charm. About 30 percent of Cambodia's

INSIDER TIP:

Cross Kompong Cham's Bamboo Bridge to Koh Paen. While the bridge looks haphazardly constructed, it's rebuilt every year and is able to carry trucks.

—LIS MEYERS
National Geographic writer

300,000 Cham people were executed during the genocide. Today, the reviving province is again becoming a populous center of sorts, this time for commercial farming of cash crops, particularly rubber and tobacco.

These days, most tourists will whiz right through Kompong Cham without really seeing it. However, the town has one important feature: It's home to the Kizuna Bridge, the only bridge in Cambodia that spans the Mekong River, completed in 2001. Just south of that span lies **Koh Paen,** one of the largest islands in the Mekong River. Despite the Kizuna Bridge's claim to fame, the attraction here is actually the seasonal, makeshift bridge. Called the **Bamboo Bridge,** this interim bridge is erected each dry season to connect Koh Paen to the mainland. The island features several modern Buddhist temples and is home to fishing and rice-farming villages that are fun to explore via bicycle, hired from a guesthouse in town. Yet crossing the unusual bridge to reach the island may be the best part of the journey.

Around Kompong Cham

The region around Kompong Cham seems to have been important during the early kingdoms era (ca A.D. 100–802). The remains of a number of temples and even a walled city have been discovered here. Consequently, kings of the Angkor era continued to build hundreds of monuments near Kompong Cham, often upon the foundations of earlier temples or cities.

During the 20th century, however, civil war and occupying Khmer Rouge forces ravaged the area, leaving the vast majority of historical temples uninteresting heaps of rubble. That said, a few sites were deemed worthy of reconstruction by contemporary Buddhists, who reestablished monasteries on these old and hallowed grounds. They built on a few sites renowned for their

Lighthouse over the Mekong

Crossing the Kizuna Bridge from Kompong Cham, one cannot help but notice the towering, redbrick lighthouse. Originally constructed during the French colonial period, the lighthouse was renovated at the turn of the 21st century. Although climbing the lighthouse is free and the views from the top are spectacular, it's a precipitous ascent. This climb is not recommended for anyone with even the slightest fear of heights.

Spiders of Skuon

The small town of Skuon, around 26 miles (42 km) west of Kompong Cham on National Highway 7, has developed a reputation as a roadside fast-food stop. Unlike any rest area in the West, however, the specialty snack in Skuon is large, furry tarantulas! Just outside the restaurant at the rest stop, vendors sell stir-fried spiders, cooked to a crisp with garlic. The tarantulas are defanged in Preah Vihear Province, where they are farmed. They have a consistency similar to soft-shell crab (or so you can try convincing yourself as you choke one down). Even if you aren't hungry at the time, have no fear, as you can buy bags of live tarantulas to go. Ten spiders will run you about 6,000 riel ($1.50). You can also try spicy stuffed frogs or grilled baby birds if spiders aren't your thing.

a nearby village had a competition to decide which gender would thereafter be responsible for proposing marriage. Whichever sex forged the taller mountain in one day could forever forgo the nerve-racking duty of proposal. During the competition, the men, duped into believing they had won, got drunk and fell asleep. Meanwhile, the women labored through the night. The victorious women's mountain stands taller to the right and features fine views from the summit. Also, several modern temples are on and around the two hills, which are approximately 3 miles (5 km) west of town on National Highway 7.

Farther from the town, on a small hilltop along the western bank of the Mekong River lies **Wat Han Chey,** the ruins of which include one mostly intact brick *prasat* (tower). These temples were long held to be the oldest in Cambodia. They are now generally dated to the Chenla period (A.D. seventh–eighth centuries), however. One may predate the others, as it is believed to be from the Funan period (ca A.D. first–seventh centuries). The ruins aren't spectacular, but the boat ride up the Mekong and the view from the temples is worthwhile if you have a half day to spare for the 13-mile (21 km) cruise upstream. Ask your guesthouse to help procure a boat for you, or to hire a boat from the riverside, simply ask longtail proprietors if they go to Han Chey.

Another good excursion from Kompong Cham is a visit to **Wat Maha Leap,** about 12 miles (20

Wat Nokor

△ 212 B1

$ $

Phnom Pros & Phnom Srei

△ 212 B1

Wat Han Chey

△ 212 B1

✉ 12 miles (20 km) N of Kompong Cham, on hill on W bank of Mekong River

$ $

🚢 Ferry or longtail boat ($$$$$) takes 15–25 min.

folklore fame. The easiest to visit is **Wat Nokor,** an 11th-century religious compound of which four original structures remain. Located just over a mile (2.2 km) west of Kompong Cham along National Highway 7, the central sanctuary of Wat Nokor still retains portions of its original sandstone and laterite construction. Most of the temple has been renovated into a brightly decorated contemporary *vihara* (monastery), though. The temple also houses a reclining Buddha, which was decapitated by the Khmer Rouge. The head was eventually unearthed and returned to the temple.

Combine a visit to Wat Nokor with a hike up **Phnom Pros and Phnom Srei** (Man and Woman Hills), a pair of hills named for a regionally popular folktale. Legend tells that the men and women of km) south of town. One of the few remaining wooden Buddhist temples in Cambodia, the *wat* was spared destruction by the Khmer Rouge because they used it as a hospital. Today, locals consider it one of the most sacred temples in the area. Its gilded wooden beams and ceiling murals depict events in the Buddha's life, which have been restored since their defacement by the Khmer Rouge. Located about 15 miles (24 km) south of Kompong Cham on a Mekong tributary called Tonle Thoit (Small River), Wat Maha Leap is in the same general vicinity as Wat Han Chey. Since the wats can be difficult to find, it may be best to travel with a guide.

Kratie

Around 80 miles (130 km) north of Kompong Cham lies the surprisingly bustling provincial capital of Kratie. Pushing up against the steep banks of the mighty Mekong River, Kratie is a fisherman's village turned up-and-coming tourist attraction. The town's growth has been spurred by both the nearby

habitat of the endangered, freshwater Irrawaddy dolphins and its convenient location along the routes to Laos via Stung Treng and to Vietnam via Ratanakiri.

Upon arrival in Kratie, stroll a few blocks west from the active central market to the riverside road, where guesthouses and eateries overlook the Mekong. While the guesthouses often are just clean enough to pass inspection, the restaurants offer slightly more hope. **Red Sun Falling Restaurant** is a great expat gossip joint that serves equally juicy fare. For a more local experience, try the street stalls lining the riverside sidewalk toward the southern end of town, which serve deer steak and baguette sandwiches at card tables. Then, grab a few beers and witness one of Cambodia's famous sunsets from the precipitous wall that parallels the river.

Beyond the food vendors to the south, cross the street to the **World Wildlife Fund** (WWF) office, where staff can explain the conservation efforts surrounding the gravely endangered Irrawaddy dolphins—a worthwhile education

Wat Maha Leap
- 212 B1
- $
- Ferry or longtail boat takes 30–45 min.

Kratie
- 213 B2

Red Sun Falling Restaurant
- Suramarit St. (by river, in front of bus station)
- $–$$$

World Wildlife Fund
- On St. Soramrith (riverside road), bet. St. 14 & St. 15
- 855(0)23-218-034
- **www.panda.org/greatermekong**

EXPERIENCE: Exploring River Life

The Mekong Discovery Trail *(tel 855-23-726-424 or 855-12-200-263, www .mekongdiscoverytrail.com)* **is a network of ecotourism experiences along the river from Cambodia's northern border with Laos to the town of Kratie. Along the way, the beauty of the river and the friendliness of the local people can be appreciated while engaging in cultural and natural activities, including mountain** biking, trekking, dolphin viewing, horse-cart riding, house boat trips, and shopping at local markets.

Broken into segments, the Mekong Discovery Trail can be explored in pieces or in its 112-mile (180 km) entirety, either alone or with a group. Visitors enjoy cultural immersion by staying in local village homestays or on the grounds of Buddhist monasteries.

Wat Roka Kandal

✉ Chhlong Rd., about a mile (1.6 km) S of Kratie

$ $

prior to a trip upstream to see these rare water beauties. Be sure to ask about the legend regarding the origin of dolphins—it's a fascinating folktale.

Kratie's other attractions lie just off the beaten track. A ferry alights from the riverside across from Red Sun Falling and carries passengers across the Mekong to what appears to be the far shore, but what is actually **Koh Trong** island. A 200-yard (183 m) stroll to the island's west bank reveals a floating Vietnamese fishing village. Since the Vietnamese cannot own land in Cambodia, the immigrant community has built a moderately interesting floating village. More of an attraction here is the **Vietnamese Pagoda,** which the residents attend on the shore beside their village. It has a viewing deck where you can relax and observe everyday life afloat.

INSIDER TIP:

Some of the world's last remaining snub-nosed Irrawaddy dolphins swim in the waters near Kratie. Hire a boat, sit quietly on the Mekong, and listen for their wonderful swoosh as they leap out of the river.

—KAREN COATES
National Geographic writer

Back on Kratie's mainland, if you have a spare sightseeing hour, hire a moto-taxi to visit **Wat Roka Kandal.** The wat occupies both sides of Chhlong Road, about a mile (1.6 km) south of town. To the east is an ornate,

A rice field and sugar palm plantation off National Highway 6 in eastern Cambodia

Cham

The Cham are a scattered people and their isolated villages are found throughout Southeast Asia. Yet these widely dispersed settlements were largely built by fleeing refugees, a reflection of the Cham's persecuted history.

This was not always the case. The Cham once dominated a powerful empire, the Champa Kingdom, which reached around the coastlines of present-day Vietnam and into Cambodia. The kingdom thrived as a wealthy maritime nation, even controlling the surrounding seas by piracy. Records as far back as the second century A.D. detail the Cham's influence over the region. Of particular note are the stealthy war strategies that allowed them to ransack the mighty Angkorian capital in 1177.

The Champa Kingdom lay along the lucrative trade routes around the Malay Peninsula to China. The Cham's frequent contact with tradesmen greatly influenced their developing culture, from their distinct language to their religion, Islam. As early as the 11th century, the Cham embraced Islamic beliefs learned from visiting Arab tradesmen. Today, over 90 percent of Cham remain Muslim.

The Champa Kingdom fell in 1471, following waves of Vietnamese invasions. Suddenly without a homeland, the Cham people scattered. Many of them congregated in small villages along the riverbanks in modern-day Cambodia.

Today, around 70 Cham villages exist along the Mekong River and Tonle Sap River. These communities make up the largest religious and ethnic minority in Cambodia, with numbers around 300,000. Sadly, this number is much smaller than it was prior to the Khmer Rouge regime, which killed nearly 90,000 Cham.

---

modern Buddhist temple that's still in use. To the west stands a retired, relatively small, and comparatively simple pagoda from the late 18th or early 19th century (one of the only ones still in existence from this era). The temple exudes charm, particularly since its 2002 renovation by the Cambodian Craft Cooperation (www.cambodian-craft.com), which converted the old pagoda into a handicraft, cultural, and tourism center. The pagoda is generally locked, but a shout "hello" usually brings out the caretaker to show you the interior crafts shop or the neighboring pair of traditional riverside houses that are available for rent. (Note: It is appropriate to tip the caretaker a couple thousand riel).

Around Kratie

Kratie's prime attraction is the Irrawaddy dolphins (see sidebar p. 220). A typical trip from a guesthouse via moto-taxi travels 9 miles (14 km) north of town to the **Kampi Dolphin Viewing Site.** Then, you take a leisurely 60- or 90-minute boat trip up the Mekong to admire the dolphins. Though it's possible to see the freshwater mammals any time of day, mornings are the best as temperatures are bearable and waters are calmer. While on the river, there also are opportunities to spy great egrets—graceful, white birds with long legs and equally long necks that frequent the river's edge.

Overlooking the river stands **Phnom Sambok,** a rare hill amid

Kampi Dolphin Viewing Site
- 213 B2
- 9 miles (15 km) N of Kratie on road to Sambor (look for sign on L)
- $$

Phnom Sambok
- 213 C2

Wat Sarsar Moy Roy & Sambor

▲ 213 B2

✉ From Kratie, take National Highway 7 N 14 miles (23 km) past Kampi to Sandan; then veer L on Rte. 306 toward Sambor for 6 miles (10 km)

$ $

the surrounding rice fields. The hill's embracing forest exudes an established peacefulness, with the mountaintop monastery adding a lingering sense of spirituality. From the base, follow the *naga* balustrades up to the monastery's initial clearing. To your left, a small enclave is painted with shocking murals illustrating the Buddhist idea of hell. From this clearing, two other staircases in either direction ascend different hilltops, a phenomenon explained by a popular folktale. These hilltops, like those in Kompong Cham (see pp. 215–216), address the duty of proposal. The legend concerns a contest between men and women to build the taller hill and thus be freed of the responsibility for proposing marriage. Again, the women dupe the men

and build the taller hill. As the nationwide dispersal of this tale seems to suggest an oral tradition, ask a friendly local to provide a recounting of the story—it's likely to be entertaining.

Farther north, approximately 21 miles (34 km) from Kratie, rests the remains of Sambhupura, a seventh-century metropolis ruled by a powerful matriarchy. The area, renamed **Sambor,** once exhibited precious pre-Angkorian artifacts, particularly sculpture dating from the era of these queens of Sambhupura. Nothing of interest from this era remains. Modern Sambor has made a name for itself by restoring Cambodia's largest temple, the 16th-century **Wat Sarsar Moy Roy,** or the 100-Pillar Pagoda. The temple actually features more

EXPERIENCE: See Irrawaddy Dolphins

The Irrawaddy dolphin is a critically endangered freshwater dolphin found in only five habitats worldwide; one is the 118-mile (190 km) stretch of the Mekong River between Kratie and the border with Laos. The dark gray dolphins have rounded dorsal fins and blunt, round heads and they grow up to 9 feet (2.75 m) long.

Sadly, efforts to protect the dolphin's habitat, including police patrol boats that have all but ceased deadly gillnet fishing, are doing little to save the species. Although the number of adult dolphin deaths has diminished slightly in recent years, the percentage of calves dying has skyrocketed. Between 2004 and 2008, an average of 75 percent of newborn calves mysteriously died each year and an average of 16 adults perished from

various causes. The Mekong population was estimated at 66 to 86 dolphins (the largest group in the world) in 2007. These dwindling numbers make it unlikely that the species will survive long, since experts believe the river's waters are polluted.

Kratie is the best place to arrange a boat trip on the Mekong and catch a glimpse of these magical creatures. During the driest months (March–May), the dolphins are forced into five pockets of river that make them visible up close, even from shore. In the wet season, when the dolphins swim freely in the Mekong, they are not difficult to locate via boat. You can hire one from a tourist center, such as the **Kampi Dolphin Viewing Site** (see p. 219), about 9 miles (15 km) north of Kratie. Trips can be arranged from any guesthouse there.

One of the few remaining Irrawaddy dolphins in the Mekong River outside of Kratie town

than a hundred columns, depending on who's counting, but the noteworthy ones are the original wooden four at the back. The Buddhist temple was rebuilt in 1997 after it was ransacked during the Pol Pot regime. Overnight stays and cultural performances at the refurbished wat can be arranged by contacting the **Kratie Wat Committee.**

Stung Treng

At the lonely crossroads where National Highway 7 intersects with Route 78, a few vendors soliciting customers wait for the predominately local passengers getting off the bus. A handful of foreigners may disembark here, to venture into Stung Treng, located 93 miles (150 km) north of Kratie and just a few miles

from the "bus station." Stung Treng is basically a smaller, quieter, and less touristy version of Kratie, roughly four square blocks of hotels, restaurants, and shop houses near the confluence of the Tonle San and Mekong Rivers. While there are some opportunities for Irrawaddy dolphin sightings near Stung Treng *(contact your hotel for information)*, most passengers simply stop over in town along the way to the nearby border of Laos at Dom Kralor. Those planning such a journey should be aware that visas to Laos are not available at the border and must be procured in Phnom Penh (or Bangkok) before venturing to this remote, yet somewhat popular, border crossing. ■

Kratie Wat Committee
- ✉ 91 St. 10, Kratie
- ☎ 855(0)11-786-847 or 855(0)11-716-311
- 💲 $$$$

Stung Treng
 213 B4

Ecotourism

After years of unrestrained development, Cambodia is at a crossroads. Some of the country's most pristine ecosystems, many of which contain endangered and threatened species, are succumbing to logging, slash-and-burn farming, and poaching. If development continues in such a way, the wildlife will be gone, the forests will be decimated, and the local villagers will have no means of supporting themselves.

Traditional farming techniques in the moat around Prasat Ta Prohm, Oddar Meanchey Province

Fortunately, communities around Cambodia have realized the value of preserving their ecosystems. In doing so, they hope to earn a living from the growth of tourism. They also seek to educate the next generation of Cambodians about the importance of their environment and heritage. The model for such projects is community-based ecotourism (CBET), which gives communities the capability to design their own cultural- and environmental-friendly activities.

The Cambodia Community-Based Ecotourism Network (www.ccben.org), comprising more than 30 conservation and development agencies, provides villages with services including training, marketing, information exchange, and lobbying. Villagers who wish to participate in CBET specialize in particular activities and take turns providing them. A certain percentage of the revenue generated goes to a community fund to help propagate the system. Visitors benefit from staying in rural villages,

EXPERIENCE: Ecotourism Opportunities

In addition to the projects mentioned at the bottom of this page, these successful community-based ecotourism (CBET) projects serve as models for the future:

Banteay Chhmar Community-Based Ecotourism

In 2007, the village beside the massive 12th-century Angkorian temple complex, Banteay Chhmar (see pp. 186–187, 190), established a tourism program *(tel 855(0)92-599-115)*. Villagers wanted to develop their community in a socially, culturally, economically, and environmentally sound way. Many of the homestay cooks and proprietors were trained by the Siem Reap–based Sala Bai school of hospitality. In addition to visiting the spectacular ruins of nearby temples, visitors can discover rural life on a bicycle or in an oxcart and visit the Enfants du Mékong silk center.

Chambok Community-Based Ecotourism

One of the first CBET projects in Cambodia, the Chambok ecotourism site *(National Highway 4 near Kirirom NP, tel 855(0)23-214-409, www.geocities.com/chambokcbet)* was initiated in 2001 in conjunction with the Ministry of Environment to conserve the community's forests. Since then, local guides have been trained to lead historical, natural, and cultural tours of the area. Visitors can go trekking, swimming, bird-watching, animal tracking, and riding in oxcarts. Adjacent Kirirom National Park (see pp. 255–256) boasts some spectacular waterfalls. Guests staying in the village's homestays can dine on traditional meals and watch traditional dance performances.

Chi Phat Community-Based Ecotourism

Single-day or multiday activities are based in the Chi Phat Commune, which consists of four villages actively involved in developing a CBET project in conjunction with the Wildlife Alliance *(109 St. 99, Phnom Penh, tel 855(0)23-211-604, www.wildlifealliance. org)*. The villagers have coordinated committees to provide the different services, from guesthouses and homestays to handicrafts development and park ranger duties. Activities include mountain biking to overnight shelters constructed of local materials, riding in an oxcart to a nearby waterfall, and taking a traditional rowboat journey for bird-watching on the river.

Prek Tnout Community-based Ecotourism

Part of this CBET site *(Prek Tnout Commune, 19 miles/30 km W of Kampot on National Highway 3, www.cambodianwildlife.org)* is in Bokor National Park, so the wildlife here is varied and includes endangered species. Take guided walks to streams, waterfalls, and mangrove forests to see birds, dolphins, dugongs, and monkeys. Villagers demonstrate sustainable traditional livelihoods, including producing non-timber forest products (rattan, bamboo, and fruit). You can stay overnight in a guesthouse.

where they can experience authentic Cambodian communities that are geared toward maintaining sustainable lifestyles and preserving the natural environment in which they live.

Current community-based ecotourism projects around Cambodia include Virachey National Park (see p. 225), Yak Laom Lake (see pp. 225, 226, 229), the Kampi Dolphin Viewing Site (see pp. 219–221), Kompong Pleuk floating village (see pp. 120–121), Prek Toal (see p. 123), Ang Trapaeng Thmor (see pp. 185–186), and Tmatboey (see p. 121).

Ratanakiri

Those turning east from the intersection of National Highway 7 to Stung Treng and Route 78 toward the Vietnamese border are sent jiggling along a relatively flat, straight, red dirt road. Depending on the season, this road features either a leafy canopy or a dusty fog.

A reclining Buddha in Ban Lung town in Rattankiri Province

The trip to Ratanakiri (Mountain of Precious Stones) Province is on a gradually ascending, curving road that underwent major improvements in 2008 and 2009. Route 78 eventually passes through Ban Lung, a town rapidly swelling under both increasing tourist arrivals and Cambodian migrants looking to benefit from the province's economic boom.

Still, Ratanakiri is a tricky place to visit. Since Ban Lung is 365 miles (588 km) from Phnom Penh, making the trip requires a significant time commitment. Once there, however, you'll realize that there are far more than a day or two's worth of sights, including a pair of volcanic lakes, numerous waterfalls, hundreds of diverse tribal villages, and Virachey National Park.

The main attraction, Yak Laom Lake, easily takes a full day (perhaps two) to enjoy. The casual visitor to Ban Lung can also see nearby waterfalls, a hilltop reclining Buddha, and the town's sole market on a hired motorbike (see pp. 228–229) or with a local guide, arranged through a guesthouse or the tourism office. Trips to tribal villages are full-day adventures generally requiring the services of a tour operator. Overnight stays in the park *(three-day minimum)* are only recommended for those willing to seriously rough it (see sidebar opposite).

Ban Lung

The wide, dusty boulevards and predominantly low-rise, yellow, ministerial buildings of Ban Lung exude a middle-of-nowhere vibe. Yet the town lies at the center of a province filled with natural and cultural wonders. Its downtown features a traffic circle with a decrepit *naga* tower, a landmark for finding the **Ban Lung Market,** which is visible to the south of the intersection. Completed in 2009, the new Ban Lung Market is an extension of the 1997 updates that enclosed the shops and stalls under a corrugated roof above a concrete floor. Vendors sell everything from fresh meats and vegetables to clothing, gemstones, handicrafts, and traditional medicines—including dried pelts of one of the world's smallest primates, the slow loris.

A few blocks east of the traffic circle is the local **tourism office,** one of very few in Cambodia that is regularly open and staffed by English-speaking locals. The office has a few maps and brochures about the surrounding attractions. The staff can give you advice for exploring on your own or procuring a guide. North of the intersection by the post office, look for the office for **Virachey National Park,** where friendly, helpful park officials offer information about and bookings for multiday tours.

Around Ban Lung

Hands down, the primary attraction around Ban Lung is **Yak Laom Lake.** The crater of an extinct volcano, it's filled with warm aquamarine water and is a half mile (0.8 km) in diameter and 165 feet (50 m) deep. At the main entrance, you can rent inner tubes and buy food, fresh fruit, and local rice wine from a picnic area. Along the shady, bamboo-fringed trail encircling the lake, several wooden platforms are great for sunbathing and swimming. On the trail you'll also see the **Cultural & Environmental Center** *($)*, and a small hill-tribe handicrafts shop. Since the lake is 3 miles (5 km)

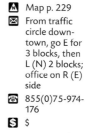

Ban Lung

🅰 213 D4

Visitor Information

✉ Ban Lung Tourism Office, on Rte. 78, 1.5 blocks W from traffic circle downtown

💲 $

Virachey National Park Office

🅰 Map p. 229

✉ From traffic circle downtown, go E for 3 blocks, then L (N) 2 blocks; office on R (E) side

☎ 855(0)75-974-176

💲 $

Virachey National Park

🅰 213 C5–E5

Yak Laom Lake

🅰 213 D4, 229

💲 $

Virachey National Park

Those looking for adventure should consider an expedition into Virachey National Park, Cambodia's largest, covering nearly 1,300 square miles (3,333 sq km) of pristine forests, expansive grasslands, towering mountains, and lush valleys. Much of it remains unexplored by anyone other than hill tribes who live off the land as they have for centuries. The park is one of the last sanctuaries for endangered primates and birds, as well as tigers and elephants.

During the Vietnam War, the Ho Chi Minh Trail passed through the area, resulting in American bombing. The park office in Ban Lung can arrange trekking and kayaking trips that include a number of hill-tribe villages and sections of the Ho Chi Minh Trail. A minimum of three days are required to visit and camping is rudimentary (visitors sleep in hammocks and bathrooms are nonexistent). For serious outdoor enthusiasts, though, this is as wild as it gets in Cambodia.

**Cha Ung
Waterfall**
▲ 213 D4, 229

**Katieng
Waterfall**
▲ 213 D4, 229

**Ka Chhang
Waterfall**
▲ 213 D4, 229

**Ou'Sien Lair
Waterfall**
▲ 213 D4

Bo Keo
▲ 213 D4

from Ban Lung, you can reach it on foot, but a rental motorbike or moto-taxi is preferable.

A number of waterfalls can be easily visited on a motorbike with a map from the tourism office. You can even visit via elephant, an adventure that can be combined with other sights through a day trip organized at your guesthouse.

The largest of the five is the 65-foot (20 m) **Cha Ung Waterfall,** a spectacle of loud, gushing sprays, which visitors can approach for a refreshing shower. The falls, which lie 6 miles (10 km) northwest of Ban Lung, are easier to reach in the dry season, when the road is far smoother. The falls are less powerful then, however.

INSIDER TIP:

Cha Ung Waterfall is a great place to hang out on a hot day. Head down to the base for a refreshing cold-water shower, or soak in one of the pools.

—KRIS LEBOUTILLIER
National Geographic photographer

Katieng Waterfall is the local favorite, thanks to its serene beauty and year-round access. Situated 6 miles (10 km) southwest of the city, it features a small **handicrafts hut,** selling wood carvings, scarves, baskets, and crossbows. The nearby falls pour over a crescent-shaped cliff into a large, circular pool accessible by wooden stairs. You may ease your way into

the water from there or scamper around the overhanging cliffs, pass behind the waterfall, and then swing from vines into the pool. Just upstream is the equally accessible **Ka Chhang Waterfall,** where reproductions of **tribal wedding huts** sit beside the stairs down to the falls. The falls are similar to Katieng, but smaller and hidden amid the overhanging jungle. Ka Chhang is 4.5 miles (7 km) from town on a well-marked road along the way to Katieng.

Either before or after a trip to the waterfalls, stop at **Eisay Patamak Mountain,** which offers panoramic views of the surrounding mountains and town. From Ban Lung's downtown traffic circle, travel about a mile (1.6 km) east along Route 78 to a small, well-marked, turnoff. The dusty road leads to a brightly painted pagoda, then continues along a steep, bumpy trail to the **reclining Buddha** for some spiritual solace.

Farther Afield

The **Ou'Sien Lair Waterfall** is farther from Ban Lung and requires a hired guide to visit. The impressive seven-tiered falls are near Ratanakiri's few remaining diamond deposits. A knowledgeable guide should be able to find areas where people still dig for the precious stones using traditional methods.

More extensive mining is under way around the town of **Bo Keo,** 25 miles (40 km) east of Ban Lung on Route 78. The mines are still dug using traditional means: A man is lowered down a small, square pit from which dirt and rock is excavated using a pick and a simple rope pulley. Around 3.5 miles (5 km) beyond Bo Keo, a well-marked turnoff leads 14 miles (23 km) south to **Lumkut Lake.** This body of water fills another volcanic crater, but is nearly twice the size of Yak Laom Lake with only a fraction of the visitors.

Most guesthouses also offer day trips and multiday treks to nearby **tribal villages,** whose 12 different ethnicities include Khmer, Chinese, Laotian, Vietnamese, and eight groups variously known as *chunchiet*—or indigenous—people, each of which has its own unique culture and language. Tribal villages make up 75 percent of Ratanakiri's population, but the villages closer to Ban Lung and Route 78 have already adopted a lot of Khmer culture. A number of day trips combine trekking, boating, and visiting some fascinating villages.

One popular trek from Ban Lung explores **Voen Sai,** a small district dotted with diverse villages amid dense jungle 25 miles (40 km) northwest of town. The typical morning starts with a scenic drive, alternatively muddy or dusty, that can take anywhere from 45 minutes to 2 hours depending on seasonal road conditions. Trading a car for a canoe, your dugout, longtail boat navigates the wide Tonle San River north to Kachon. This small village built on stilts sits atop the river's steep embankment. Here resides a Tampuon (aka Tampuan) community, a cultural minority that comprises about 24 percent of Ratanakiri's population. The

villagers have maintained their traditional customs, most prominently exemplified by their exotic cemetery. Ornately decorated, roofed graves are honored with gifts to the spirits, such as statues and a sacrificed buffalo—a testament to their rooted animist beliefs.

Lumkut Lake
△ 213 D4

Voen Sai
△ 213 D4

Cha Ung is the largest of several waterfalls in the countryside around Ban Lung town.

Back in the boat, the journey backtracks downstream to other, vastly different villages. The first is a Chinese community that feels like a city planner designed a single block around a tribal village theme. Three generations old, this community of about 200 people immigrated here in the early 1940s to escape the "Japanese Invasion," as World War II is locally known. Down the neighborhood footpath is the adjacent Laotian village, ironically appearing the most typically Cambodian of the three. Wooden houses on tall stilts create shade for the people, who are often found weaving baskets. Pigs and chickens roam free, and rice fields thrive in back. ∎

Ratanakiri Motorbike Drive

Many visitors make the trek to Ban Lung to do just that, trek. Most use the provincial capital as a quick stop, skip the town's supposed attractions, shrug off the settling dust, and head straight for the mountains. Yet some beautiful sights lie just beyond Ban Lung's desolate first impression. For a relaxing day trip, grab your swimsuit and hire a moto-taxi or your own motorbike (and a map), both available at many guesthouses.

A sunset from the hills above Ban Lung

Start by exploring the **Ban Lung Market** ❶, just two blocks south of the downtown traffic circle. In the labyrinth of stalls and tents, you will find bargains if you haggle, especially on gems—amethysts and zircons are mined nearby. To prepare for the rest of the day, stock up on fresh fruit from vendors toward the market entrance.

Starting from the traffic circle, travel about a mile (1.6 km) west on Route 78 to the turn-off for Eisay Patamak Mountain. The small, dusty road leads to a pagoda supported by candy-cane-striped columns. Continue up the beaten track's quick ascent to reach the large **reclining Buddha** ❷ (*$*). His restful posture represents the Buddha's final acceptance, eternal escape from rebirth. The summit also offers a stunning view of the countryside and distant mountains.

NOT TO BE MISSED:

Ban Lung Market • reclining
Buddha • Katieng & Ka Chhang
Waterfalls • Yak Laom Lake

Back on the main road, continue west (away from Ban Lung) and follow the signs south to **Katieng Waterfall** ❸ (*6 miles/9 km S of Rte. 78 from Ka Chhang Commune Office, $*). Tucked in a cavernous grove, Katieng is the locals' favorite swimming hole, though it is rarely frequented on weekdays. Before leaving, go 20 yards (18 m) beyond the falls to the right, where you will find a small **handicraft hut** that sells a range of crafts produced by local hill tribes.

Backtrack to the first major intersection,

near the rubber tree plantations, and follow the signs southeast to secluded **Ka Chhang Waterfall ➍** *(4.5 miles/7 km S of Rte. 78 from Ka Chhang Commune Office, $).* Before taking the stairs down to the falls, note the two reduced-scale reproductions of the Poy hill tribe's **traditional bride and groom huts** on stilts. The taller hut belongs to the groom, who proves his worthiness by shimmying up its stilts in the days before the wedding.

Undoubtedly, the jewel of Ban Lung is **Yak Laom Lake ➎** *(take Rte. 78 E from Ban Lung, turn at hill-tribe monument in traffic circle and follow side road S 1 mile/1.6 km, $).* This stunningly clear, warm body of water is nestled in a volcanic crater. Find your favorite swimming spot by hiking around the lake through evergreens and bamboo thickets. Along the way, look for

the **Cultural & Environmental Center ➏** *($),* a small museum with educational exhibits about the surrounding hill tribes.

Lumphat

Those interested in history might enjoy a trip to Lumphat, the former capital of Ratanakiri, located 15.5 miles (25 km) south of Ban Lung along the rudimentary road that eventually leads to Mondulkiri. Carpet bombing by the U.S. drove the Khmer Rouge from Lumphat, but it also nearly wiped the city off the map. Today, it's practically a ghost town, with fewer than a thousand residents. Former official structures are left to the encroaching wilderness.

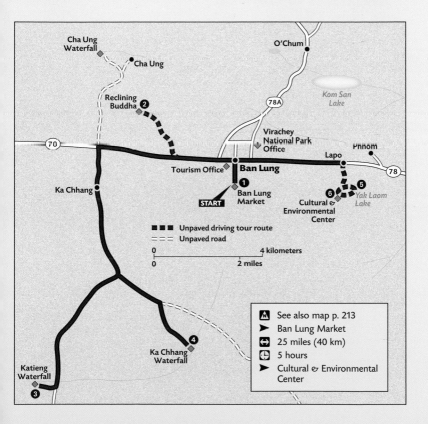

Unpaved driving tour route
Unpaved road

0   4 kilometers
0   2 miles

See also map p. 213
Ban Lung Market
25 miles (40 km)
5 hours
Cultural & Environmental Center

Mondulkiri

In 1992, when a foreign visitor arrived in Sen Monorom, the capital of Mondulkiri (Meeting of the Hills) Province, a welcoming party was arranged for the first Westerner to set foot in the town in 18 years. Today, as the Cambodian tourism industry grows, more Western travelers are finding their way to Sen Monorom. This still quiet mountain town serves as a launching point for journeys into a wilderness of hill-tribe villages, elephant rides, and quiet solitude.

Villagers work the well in a small hamlet in Modulkiri.

Sen Monorom
213 D2

While the rolling hills of Mondulkiri may be the final frontier for tourists visiting Cambodia, the province has long been on the map of speculators. Those engaged in logging and mining, in particular, have steadily increased their operations here since the Vietnamese occupation began in the late 1970s. Prior to that, during the Vietnam War, the region was heavily carpet bombed by the United States, targeting communist insurgents operating in the mountainous border province. For thousands of years before that, the Bunong (aka Pnong), a generally peaceful hill-tribe society, enjoyed an isolation that was even beyond the reach (or interest) of Angkor. Sadly, the 30,000 remaining Bunong are losing their land to encroaching development and their culture to the increasing Khmer influence in the region.

In Sen Monorom, most guesthouses and hotels can arrange tours of varying quality. Unfortunately, the tourism office that could provide some useful information is often closed.

Temperatures in Mondulkiri drop into the 40s (4°–9°C) in wintertime, so be sure to pack appropriate clothing. Furthermore, dry season in Mondulkiri features whirling dust storms. Those particularly sensitive to being covered head to toe in red dirt particles may wish to visit toward the end of the rainy season (Oct.–early Nov.) when conditions are less adverse.

Sen Monorom & Around

Sen Monorom has a distinctive mountain frontier town vibe. Unlike most other remote provincial capitals, though, a growing tourist economy is benefiting from infrastructure development spurred by the region's natural resources, including timber, gold, and other valuable minerals. The roads around town are mostly paved and there is widespread cell phone coverage. A variety of accommodation and dining options has sprung up, including the fantastic **Bananas** restaurant (S from Gaur traffic circle, L at fork, then L at bottom of hill, tel 855(0)92-412-680). That said, the primary tourist attractions are the wilderness and the ethnic minorities, both of which are under grave threat from greedy developers. Still, a few enclaves of magical Mondulkiri survive just outside of town, presuming you know where to look.

Along Sen Monorom's main road, find the **Middle of Somewhere** (S from Gaur traffic circle, across from Holiday Guesthouse, tel 855(0)16-389-750). Despite its humble exterior, the Middle of Somewhere seems to be just that,

the epicenter of all that is interesting about this remote province. The successful handicrafts center allows Bunong villagers to produce skirts, handbags, and decorative objects with traditional flair, the proceeds from which fund a beneficial community center at the local high school.

In addition to the small crafts' workshop and store here, Middle of Somewhere promotes cultural awareness and preservation through half-day and full-day tours. The village visit showcases traditional Bunong homes, built from bamboo and grassy thatch,

---

The New Road to Sen Monorom

Reaching Mondulkiri's capital, Sen Monorom, about 261 miles (420 km) northeast of Phnom Penh, used to be impossible in the wet season because the road was a morass of mud pits. However, in 2009 Route 76 from Snuol to Sen Monorom was sealed and large concrete bridges were built, allowing all vehicles access to Mondulkiri in the wet season and shaving an hour off the trip in the dry months (now only 2.5–3 hours). The improved roads, along with the recent opening of the border at Dak Dam allowing foreigners access to Vietnam's Dak Lac Province (Ban Ma Tout), should help increase tourism.

Elephant Valley Project

✉ Middle of Somewhere handicraft center; go S from Gaur traffic circle, on R before fork in road

☎ 855(0)16-389-750

💲 $$$$$+

www.elie-cambodia.org

creating a round hut resembling a tan turtle shell. But the cultural excursion is less a fascinating attraction than a sobering introduction to the subsistence living conditions of a culture slowly losing its land and its identity. However, it's gratifying to know that the fee for hiring a young Bunong guide may help preserve the Bunong way of life.

INSIDER TIP:

Few experiences rival that of an elephant ride into the jungle. The Elephant Valley Project's one-day waterfall excursion is a great option.

—NINA-NOELLE HALL
National Geographic contributor

Middle of Somewhere is also the meeting point for the internationally renowned conservation effort, the **Elephant Valley Project**—a highlight of any trip to Mondulkiri. This active project works hard to protect the vibrant jungle that blankets the valley, reserving its zigzagging depths for an elephant sanctuary. As denoted in the project's name, the staff's principal ambition is caring for these endangered animals. The cause is actually threefold, though. They also are working to preserve the area's disappearing forests—a sad result of widespread illegal logging—and to offer otherwise nonexistent job opportunities to the Bunong.

The Elephant Valley Project allows tourists to learn about and care for elephants, most of which were brought to the sanctuary to remove them from abusive situations. On a one-day trip to the serene sanctuary, visitors can ride elephants bareback through the dense jungle to unmapped waterfalls. For a lengthier, more involved stay, the nonprofit invites guests to stay a week at a time in its newly opened guesthouses, which are all built in traditional Bunong style. During your stay, you will help protect these elephants via education and hands-on work, while also relaxing amid untouched nature—the ultimate altruistic holiday. Finally, long-term volunteer opportunities, which can last months, are available to select animal lovers (see sidebar opposite). Be aware that the sanctuary is located a bumpy 45-minute ride outside Sen Monorom. Even the one-day trek is a rustic experience wading through muddy creeks and hiking sometimes slippery slopes.

Sen Monorom's other attractions center on the area's natural beauty. Nearly every road leading out of town has a waterfall, but several are more accessible or worthwhile to visit than others. The waterfall locations are generally remote, so it's best to hire a tour operator or moto-taxi to visit them. For a swim, seek out **Roma-near Waterfall,** located just off Route 76, which features several bamboo picnic platforms and a pool. Nearby, both **Sen Monorom Waterfall** and **Sihanouk Waterfall** are beautiful places to enjoy a late afternoon splash and a sunset.

EXPERIENCE: Riding Elephants

From the protected South West Elephant Corridor connecting the Cardamom Mountains to the Elephant Mountains, to the most remote forests of Virachey National Park, where there are no roads, few trails, and fewer humans, Cambodia is home to one of the world's largest populations of wild Asian elephants. While most of them survive in pockets of jungle far from sightseers, visitors can find opportunities for a Cambodian elephant experience, including those below. Elephants also can transport you to nearby waterfalls on a few short rides around Ban Lung.

Elephant Valley Project

Amid the hazy mountains of northeastern Mondulkiri Province, the Elephant Valley Project (see p. 232) offers various, adventurous experiences with its personable, endangered elephants. A one-day excursion features bareback elephant rides to otherwise inaccessible waterfalls for an afternoon picnic (*$$$$$*). A more interactive stay offers all-inclusive, weeklong educational and hands-on instruction, during which guests learn to care for an elephant like a *mahout*, or caretaker (*$$$$$*). The project also extends select opportunities to long-term volunteers, who may be brought on for a couple months to make an active difference in these animals' protection.

Compagnie des Éléphants d'Angkor

When the first foreign tourists began arriving at Siem Reap in the late 19th century, an elephant was standard transport for navigating the lush jungle surrounding the temples. You can relive this magical experience with Compagnie des Éléphants d'Angkor (*tel 855(0)63-963-561, $$$$, south gate to Bayon, $$$*) by riding one to the summit of Phnom Bakheng to catch the sunset, ambling through the gates of Angkor Thom, or taking a 20- to 25-minute stroll around Angkor Thom. Yet the recommended trip is from Bayon temple back to the south gate of Angkor Thom at around 10:30 a.m., when the 8 a.m. rush of tour buses has dissipated.

Farther afield is the most impressive set of falls, **Bou Srah Waterfalls,** located 27 miles (43 km) from Sen Monorom, just before the border of **Phnom Namlier Wildlife Sanctuary,** one of three in Mondulkiri Province. Phnom Namlier, **Phnom Prech Wildlife Sanctuary,** and **Snuol Wildlife Sanctuary** are each home to some of Cambodia's most exotic wildlife, including a few of the country's last remaining elephant and tiger populations. While a visit to Bou Srah Waterfall is possible by tour, the wildlife sanctuaries may soon be more accessible through Cambodian Community-Based Ecotourism Network projects, in association with the World Wildlife Fund. For updated information, see *www.ccben.org.*

Road to Ratanakiri

The road from Mondulkiri to Ratanakiri can only be negotiated by motorbike, oxcart, or on foot. With a sturdy motorbike, the ride takes nine hours during the dry season, when the road is passable. Only then, when one river is dry and two can be safely crossed on wooden ferries, can you take on this adventure. During the wet season, forget it. ∎

Bou Srah Waterfall
▲ 213 E2

Miles of unspoiled coastline, dozens of islands, French colonial ruins, and undiscovered dive sites with exotic marine life

Sihanoukville & Southern Coastal Provinces

"Full Moon" fire shows can be seen twice a week at Ochheuteal Beach in Sihanoukville.

Sihanoukville & Southern Coastal Provinces

Created in the mid-20th century to take advantage of its access to the Gulf of Thailand, the port city of Sihanoukville has since become a popular jumping-off point for visitors to the beautiful beaches and islands nearby. The southern coastal provinces that surround the city offer an impressive array of untouched nature preserves, dramatic wildlife, colonial and seaside towns, and pristine beaches.

In recent years, with tourism flourishing in Cambodia, the islands and beaches around Sihanoukville have been called the next Koh Samui or Phuket, alluding to their similarity to neighboring Thai islands. Some even whisper that the islands off the coast are tropical Shangri-las, where undiscovered beaches are waiting to be explored...or developed.

Both are somewhat true. Otres Beach is a

NOT TO BE MISSED:

A day trip to or overnight stay in Ream National Park 244–247

Island-hopping around Sihanoukville, particularly aboard a sailboat 248

Experiencing ecotourism in Koh Kong, Kirirom National Park, or the Cardamom Mountains 250–256

A live-aboard dive trip to Condor Reef or Poulo Wai 253

Night swimming in bioluminescence in the Kompong Bay River 256

Sampling authentic Kampot pepper, the local claim to fame 259

Joyriding on Kep's scenic coastline and viewing a spectacular sunset 264

Visiting the tiny paradise of Rabbit Island 265

Trying fresh crab from Kep's local crab market 265

long stretch of unspoiled natural beauty and peaceful solitude. Ochheuteal-Serendipity Beach is an increasingly popular hangout. Sokha Beach is already an enormous luxury resort. Beaches and islands are being eyed by international investors. The Sihanoukville coast is a little slice of tropical heaven, but one that is undergoing massive changes. The far-off islands, some hours from the mainland, are home to sleepy fishing villages. A few, notably Koh Russay and Koh Rong Saloem, feature basic beach bungalows on their sandy shores. Entire islands have been sold to developers for five-star resorts. Still there is much to be explored, including undiscovered dive sites, where rare nudibranchs and schools of seahorses are among the wealth of undersea life.

In the southern coastal provinces, pristine beaches and mountainous parks protect a range of wildlife, including elephants. You can explore waterfalls and caves here, and perhaps visit a few temples. ■

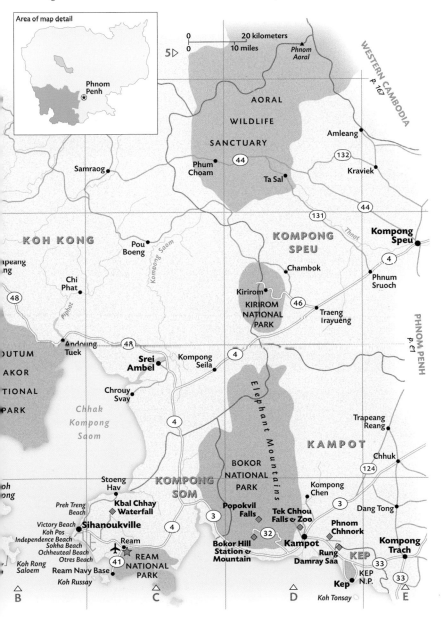

Area of map detail

Phnom Penh

0 ———— 20 kilometers
0 ———— 10 miles

5 ▷

Phnom Aoral

WESTERN CAMBODIA   p. 167

AORAL WILDLIFE SANCTUARY

Samraog

Phum Choam

44

Ta Sal

Amleang

132

Kraviek

44

131

Thnot

KOMPONG SPEU

Kompong Speu

4

KOH KONG

Pou Boeng

Kompong Saom

Chambok

Phnum Sruoch

Chi Phat

Piphot

Kirirom

KIRIROM NATIONAL PARK

46

Traeng Irayueng

48

PHNOM PENH   p. 51

Andoung Tuek

48

Srei Ambel

Kompong Seila

4

UTUM AKOR TIONAL PARK

Chrouy Svay

Chhak Kompong Saom

Elephant Mountains

Trapeang Reang

KAMPOT

Chhuk

124

Stoeng Hav

KOMPONG SOM

BOKOR NATIONAL PARK

Kompong Chen

Popokvil Falls

Tek Chhou Falls & Zoo

3

Dang Tong

oh ong

Prek Treng Beach

Kbal Chhay Waterfall

Koh Pos

Victory Beach   Sihanoukville
Independence Beach
Sokha Beach
Ochheuteal Beach
Otres Beach

Ream

4

REAM NATIONAL PARK

Koh Rong Saloem   Ream Navy Base

Koh Russay

41

Bokor Hill Station & Mountain

32

Phnom Chhnork

Kompong Trach

Kampot

Rung Damray Saa

KEP

33

KEP N.P.

Kep

33

Koh Tonsay

B   C   D   E

Sihanoukville Town & Beaches

The port town of Sihanoukville's somewhat modest charms do not in and of themselves inspire extended stays. The beaches around the town, however, are fast becoming recognized for being as stunningly beautiful as their renowned Thai counterparts nearby . . . but with only a fraction of the visitors.

Ochheuteal Beach is a magnet for sunbathers, vendors, and the occasional washed-up boat.

Sihanoukville
🔺 237 B1

The town of **Sihanoukville,** 140 miles (230 km) southwest of Phnom Penh, was born in 1955, when the dissolution of French Indochina led to Cambodia's only seaport becoming part of Vietnam. The most viable deepwater port location, then known as Kompong Som, was renamed Sihanoukville in the king's honor. Between 1955 and 1960, the French and American governments funded the development of the port and National Highway 4 to link it to Phnom Penh.

Development stalled by the late 1960s as the area became mired in the hostilities developing in Vietnam. On May 13, 1975, the Khmer Rouge commandeered a U.S. container ship, the S.S. *Mayaguez.* After a battle at Koh Tang, the port and nearby Ream Naval Base were bombarded.

With the UN-brokered peace in the early 1990s, the

area around Sihanoukville again became a major point of interest. The first investors and foreign tourists soon started to trickle back in. Today, Sihanoukville has several blocks of shop houses, plus some restaurants, bars, and guesthouses. The new town market, **Psar Leu,** was completed in 2008, making formerly muddy alleyways of sea eels and urchins more accessible. It offers an amazing variety of fish, fresh from the morning catch. Most visitors skip over the town, heading directly from the bus station to the beach of their choice.

Ochheuteal Beach is perhaps the most promising area for the average visitor. Ochheuteal Beach and its northern tip, known as **Serendipity,** have a number of budget and mid-range accommodations both on and off the beach, as well as lively restaurants and bars. Serendipity contains the majority of the development, located predominately atop the hill above the northern end of the beach. Restaurants, guesthouses, and bars cater to backpackers, offering everything from free dorm rooms and 75-cent beers to a cozy movie house and a Japanese teppanyaki restaurant. Down on the beach, the shorter northern shore features the area's best accommodations—beach bungalows ranging from basic to plush—and a few intimate beach bars and restaurants.

Ochheuteal Beach proper is a narrow stretch of sand that runs for a few miles south. It's paralleled by a beach road with rows of more makeshift beach bars and restaurants catering to a mixed clientele of locals and tourists. Many beachside businesses were torn down along the southern end of the beach to make way for a new resort. A golf course was unsuccessfully developed here before, and those businesses still standing may not last (see p. 242).

INSIDER TIP:

The game room and theater opposite the Monkey Republic Hotel on Serendipity Beach is a fun place to spend a rainy day.

—TREVOR RANGES
National Geographic author

The remainder of Ochheuteal Beach's accommodation and dining options lie along the roads running parallel to the beach off spokes leading away from the Golden Lion traffic circle just north of Serendipity Beach. These well-developed roads, two and three blocks north of the beach have comfortable, if generic, three-star lodging, ATM machines, and even a small casino. These amenities contribute to the sense of a beach boomtown in the making.

North of Ochheuteal on the beach road, the main stretch of **Sokha Beach** is dominated by the expansive Sokha Beach Resort (see p. 297), which restricts access to the sand in front of its property. Both the northern and southern ends of the beach are open to

Psar Leu
✉ Jct. of 7 Makara St. & Omui St.

Ochheuteal Beach
◭ 237 C1

Sokha Beach
◭ 237 B1

Monkey Republic Hotel
See p. 298

Independence Beach
▲ 237 B1

Koh Pos
▲ 237 B1

the public, however. The southern beach borders the road, with a narrow, grassy park and brick sidewalk. Though this section of the beach is smaller and less relaxing than its northern counterpart, it is popular with locals and visitors alike. The beach's northern end is accessible only through the resort entrance; beachgoers can rent chairs for a dollar. The sand is fine and clean, and a volleyball net stands beside the guests-only beach club. Some showers and toilets here are public. The public area is also beside one of the resort's restaurants, Lemongrass, which specializes in seafood and has outdoor dining with a view of the nearby fishing villages.

The next beach to the north of Sokha is **Independence Beach** (7-Chann Beach), which has public access directly across from the Seaview Resort. While the beach here is quite narrow, it's one of the quietest beaches along the coast. Long walks to the Independence Resort, which owns the last and nicest 500 yards (457 m) of the beach, are sublime. Next to Sokha Beach, Independence Beach is arguably the best place to find a peaceful spot away from pesky vendors, though there are still some of them around.

The next section of coast is separated into two sections by a small stream. The first, **Koh Pos Beach,** named for the island of the same name just offshore, isn't much of a beach anymore. On a break wall along the water's edge, food and drink stalls are interspersed with wooden beach chairs and tables covered by thatched roofs. Consequently, the

EXPERIENCE: Diving & Snorkeling

Scuba diving is in its infancy in Cambodia—only a handful of operators offer PADI certification and fun dives. Over 25 dive sites have been established around the 61 islands off the coasts of Sihanoukville, Kep, and Koh Kong, but many are only just being explored.

A majority of the dives are relatively shallow; be aware that visibility isn't quite as good as in neighboring Thailand. The fishing ban during the Khmer Rouge years was a boon for marine life. Yet in recent years, fishermen's use of dynamite, cyanide, and dredging have seriously impacted the ecosystem.

Coral reefs are relatively healthy and the waters around Cambodia boast an impressive diversity of marine species, particularly intriguing macrolife. Observant divers will discover octopuses, snake eels, seahorses, and many species of nudibranch, including the *Ceratosa*—the holy grail of nudibranch enthusiasts.

Most dive operators offer live-aboards to far-flung islands such as Koh Tang, Koh Prins, and Poulo Wai. At the fishing village on Koh Rong Saloem, easier overnight trips are available from **EcoSea Dive** (see p. 310) and the **Dive Shop Cambodia** (see p. 310), whose efforts have prohibited fishing around the island.

Snorkelers will benefit from the relative shallows of many dive sites and the proximity of most islands to the tourist centers. Snorkeling trips to Bamboo Island near Sihanoukville (see p. 248), Rabbit Island off Kep (see p. 265), and Koh Kong Island (see p. 253) are enjoyable day trips that usually include lunch and a few hours of relaxing on the beach.

Enjoying an Ochheuteal Beach sunset

firm, brown beach is basically just the area upon which the stalls and chairs have been set up. Yet it's still quite a popular weekend destination, particularly for locals, who enjoy the outstanding seafood, the shade, and the ability to easily pop in and out of the water. Boats are available here for day trips to the nearby islands. Just south of the beach, visitors will be able to reach Koh Pos Island via a bridge slated for completion sometime in 2010.

Hawaii Beach lies just beyond. Named for the small Hawaiian Restaurant there, the beach is small and unimpressive. A stream that feeds into the sea makes the water murky when it rains. Although it's a fine place for a picnic (if you purchase your food from the restaurant), Hawaii Beach is a far cry from the state from which it draws its name. The restaurant was built on a site that once housed the original base of operations for

the development of Sihanoukville Port, launched in 1955.

Just north of Hawaii Beach is a unique attraction, the **Snake House Resort and Restaurant.** In addition to a hotel, a restaurant, and a go-go style nightclub, the Snake House contains a small zoo that houses monkeys, a few lizards, and lots of birds, snakes, and crocodiles. Dozens of species of snake, including spitting vipers and Burmese pythons, are housed in glass aquariums along the path leading to the crocodile pits. Surrounding the pits, which are filled with crocodiles of various sizes, cages contain exotic birds from around the world. Just north of the Snake House is a massive hotel complex initiated by Japanese developers who later abandoned the project. Russian developers took over the project, which now appears to be the next five-star resort that will open along the coast.

Snake House Resort & Restaurant

  Soviet St., Victory Monument

☎ 855(0)12- 673-805

Beach Development

Nowadays coastal Cambodia, from Koh Kong to Sihanoukville and Kep, is hot property. Some of the scenic area's potential for tourism began to be developed in the 1960s, but the area was practically devoid of inhabitants during the Khmer Rouge years.

Following the war, displaced Cambodians settled along the coast. They repopulated areas such as Kep and Sihanoukville, and established new communities on beaches and islands.

The United Nations Transitional Authority in Cambodia (UNTAC), some of whom were based in Sihanoukville, arrived in 1992. For about the next decade, coastal residents built homes and established businesses, many of which

Independence Hotel beach bar overlooking the islands of the Cambodian coast

enjoyed prosperity from growth in tourism. This period coincided with a wider tourism and development boom. Particularly in Siem Reap and Phnom Penh, property values skyrocketed. International investors and speculators now focused on the country's beaches and islands.

Some coastal residents had papers from the provincial government indicating land ownership guaranteed by the 2001 Cambodian Land Law. Yet many others did not, as the Khmer Rouge systematically destroyed private land ownership and proof thereof. The national government was eager to profit from international investment,

whether it be for actual development, real estate speculation, or even money laundering. Deals struck often included initial investments in the hundreds of millions of dollars. Typical beneficiaries were members of the government and their political allies and business associates, all of whom had laid claim to prime real estate following the ascension of the Cambodian Peoples Party in 1985. Though the government had designated the entire coast as public land that could not be sold or developed, this edict was retracted in 2007, just as the frenzy began.

Today, over 20 islands off Sihanoukville and major tracts of land along the coast have been purchased or leased—for up to 99 years—by American, Chinese, European, Korean, and Russian investors. Aside from hearing whispered rumors, residents usually learn of such deals when uniformed guards and bulldozers arrive to forcibly evict them and raze their property.

A number of projects have, indeed, been initiated or completed, notably the Russian-owned Mirax resort on Koh Dek Koule and a Chinese-owned casino and golf course on Kep's Rabbit Island. Yet foreigners seem to have purchased vast areas of land in Cambodia purely for speculation, as land values have been growing far faster than the economy in general.

Cambodians evicted from their land, whether the land is developed or simply left fallow, have little hope for reparation or justice. Foreign investors unabashedly discuss the legal strength of their claim on land "owned" by locals who lack titles from the national government, which tends to support the foreign interests over its own citizens. In the meantime, those still fortunate enough to live along the coast or own businesses there, including smaller, foreign-owned guesthouses, bars, and restaurants, are left holding their breath and hoping for the best.

EXPERIENCE: Paragliding & Microlight Flying

ParaCambodia

All you need to paraglide with ParaCambodia *(tel 855(0)12-709-096, www.paracambodia.com, $650 for 3–5-day training course; rental $50/half day, $75/full day)* is a couple days of practice and clear skies. A wooden propeller attached to a two-stroke engine (for powered paragliding/paramotoring) is strapped to your body and a rectangular parachute unfurls behind you as you run down the beach and take flight. The lightness of the device allows you to fly as high as 3,000 feet (0.9 km) like a human butterfly or buzz the ocean's surface as you hop from beach to beach.

Dragonfly Cambodia

Looking to get some serious air? With Dragonfly Cambodia *(tel 855(0)92-533-269)*, you can take a microlight flight with one of the most experienced pilots in Cambodia. Eddie Smith has flown over all but two of Cambodia's provinces, shooting film and assisting with surveying and research projects. With a few weeks to spare and a serious commitment, he can even train you to fly an ultralight on your own, although there is no licensing procedure in the country to certify your accomplishment. Day trips are available at $200 per hour.

Closer to the Sihanoukville Port, just beyond the Vietnam-Cambodia Monument (Victory Monument), **Victory Beach** is a beautiful beach particularly popular with the backpackers who stay on the hillside above it. The powdery beach begins at a small pier where children frequently jump into the sea and lovers take sunset strolls. The beach isn't particularly long—perhaps 50 yards (46 m)—but it's fairly wide compared to Sihanoukville's other beaches and features a row of slanted coconut trees arching over the gently sloping shore. Hip beach bars at the far northern end of the beach offer beach chairs, music, and lively socializing in the dry season months. The newest addition is a restaurant/bar inside a converted propeller plane perched just above the beginning of the beach.

Victory Beach's guesthouses are situated on Victory Hill, better known as **Weather Station Hill**, which overlooks both Victory Beach and the port of Sihanoukville to the north. Most of the accommodations here are budget. The range of establishments catering to their guests is quite diverse. Bars and restaurants with names like the Indian Curry Pot, Sushi Square, Khmer Gourmet, and Little Sweden testify to the international clientele. However, it's a bit of a walk from most guesthouses down to the beach. After a day in the sun, the 15- to 30-minute hike back up the steep hill may be off-putting for less athletic visitors.

Beyond Victory Beach lies the **Port of Sihanoukville,** where massive shipping containers are loaded and unloaded—as are passengers from the occasional cruise ship. Turn into the port at Hun Sen Drive and pass the dock for the ferries heading to Koh Kong. Continue through miles of roadside villages until you arrive at **Prek Treng Beach** (aka Hun Sen Beach), which is surprisingly pleasant and quiet.

Victory Beach

🅰 237 B1

Prek Treng Beach

🅰 237 C1

Otres Beach

🏕 237 C1

Other than the islands off the coast, the most spectacular sights around Sihanoukville lie south of Serendipity Beach and Sihanoukville town. As of 2008, **Otres Beach** was a long stretch of almost completely undeveloped beachfront. A red dirt road ran parallel to a narrow strip of powdery sand that housed a dozen or so makeshift beach bars and bungalows, the majority of which featured

trend eventually restricts access to all of the prime beachfront land.

Preah Sihanouk "Ream" National Park

Eleven miles (18 km) southeast of Sihanoukville—just opposite the airport after Route 41 branches off National Highway 4—is the entrance to Preah Sihanouk National Park, generally known as **Ream**

Independence Beach in Sihanoukville

Ream National Park

🏕 237 C1

✉ 11 miles (18 km) SE of Sihanoukville on National Highway 4

☎ 855(0)12-875-096 or 855(0)12-215-759

💲 $

thatched roofs and no-frills accommodation. Access to the beach was via rugged dirt roads and the vibe was more Robinson Crusoe than Fantasy Island. By publication, this is likely to have changed, however, as a new development toward the southern end of the beach is rumored. Nonetheless, the beach is long enough to cede a bit of it to a private resort, unless that

National Park. The park covers more than 50,000 acres (20,235 ha) of rolling hills and coastline, including two islands. Near the entrance, at the park's headquarters, friendly rangers provide information about the diverse flora and fauna—including reptiles, dragonflies, birds, and primates—that live among the mangrove forests, along the coast, and within the inland jungle. The headquarters is also the launching point for boat trips within the park (see Day Trip Around Ream National Park, pp. 246–247), which may even include an overnight stay at the Thmor Thom Dolphin Station.

For a do-it-yourself visit to the park, start at the park headquarters and drive down Route 41 until you reach the coast. Turn left onto the coastal road, where you will see simple restaurants serving fresh coconuts and seafood that can be eaten from a hammock swinging beside the sea.

Nearby, a turnoff leads up to **Wat Ream,** where a reclining Buddha is surrounded by carved elephants, crocodiles, cobras, dolphins, and many other animals.

The coastal road eventually leads to the PTT petrochemical compound, beside which sits a small, decent beach, known as **San Soek** (Happiness Beach). Yet true happiness is located another 2.5 miles (4 km) down the bumpy sand-and-dirt road beyond PTT. The spectacular **Prek Chak Beach** is a roughly 2-mile (3 km) crescent of sand that few visitors discover. Stop by the ranger station prior to driving out to the beach—a ranger can lead you on a two-hour side trip ($$) through the jungle to **Andoung Tuek Waterfall.**

Kbal Chhay Waterfall

Halfway between Sihanoukville and Ream National Park along National Highway 4 is the turn-off to Kbal Chhay Waterfall. The volume of water passing over the falls varies greatly depending on the season. You can either shower beneath the lighter dry season flow or enjoy the spray off the raging curtain of water during the rainy season. The falls are particularly popular with locals, who often make a day of it on the weekends. A fading, but legible, sign beside National Highway 4 indicates the turnoff to the waterfall—it's hard to miss.

(continued on p. 248)

Prek Chak Beach
map p. 247

Kbal Chhay Waterfall
237 C1
Off National Highway 4 SE of Sihanoukville; watch for sign
$

EXPERIENCE: Offshore Fishing

Fishing trips in Cambodia present a bit of a moral dilemma, as the coast is notorious for the use of dynamite, cyanide, and dredging techniques to catch fish on a commercial level. Fishermen from Cambodia, Vietnam, and Thailand have depleted stocks of all varieties of marine life—a conservationist's complete nightmare. Only a few foreign operators engage in sportfishing, though. Snapper, Spanish mackerel, barracuda, and cobia aren't uncommon catches, and there even are a few black marlin out there.

Fishing is best in the calmer waters of the dry season months (late Nov.–May). With **Tradewinds Charters/ Sihanoukville Fishing** (*Munddul 1, Sangkat 2, Khan Mittapheap, Sihanoukville, tel 855(0)34-933-997 or 855(0)12-702-478*), you can fish aboard a 54-foot (16 m) boat, with gear, bait, snorkels, and lunch provided. Catching a fish isn't guaranteed, but the communal, post-outing feast always includes the catch of the day. Typical trips go about 15 miles (24 km) offshore with pre-lunch snorkeling in sheltered bays.

Day Trip Around Ream National Park

Tours of the park are fairly standardized, whether they're offered by agents around the beaches or from the park headquarters. Yet the numerous sights throughout the 50,000-acre (20,235 ha) park give visitors some ability to customize their trips.

Begin your tour opposite the Sihanoukville Airport at the **Ream National Park Headquarters ❶** *(11 miles/18 km SE of Sihanoukville on National Highway 4, tel 855(0)12-875-096 or 855(0)12-215-759).* Maps of the park here highlight the different attractions and charts of the flora and fauna provide names and pictures of the species inhabiting the area, including butterflies, birds, frogs, and primates.

A short distance from the ranger station, your guide will lead you on a ride down the **Prek Toeuk Sap River ❷** in a covered wooden

NOT TO BE MISSED:

Thmor Thom fishing village • Koh Sompoch Beach • Thmor Thom Dolphin Station • mangrove forests

boat. You'll pass through **mangrove forests ❸** where you may spot indigenous birds, including egrets, kingfishers, sea eagles, and storks. About 1.5 hours downstream, as the river mouth

Part of southern Cambodia's beautiful coastline

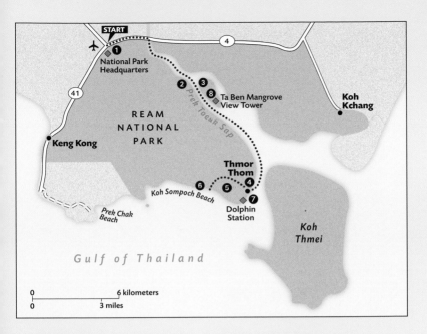

START

opens to the sea, the boat pulls up to **Thmor Thom (Big Rock) fishing village** ❹. You can spend some time observing life in a traditional fishing community.

West of Thmor Thom, you will pass through a **lowland evergreen forest** ❺. Walk slowly so as not to disturb the wildlife. During the 30-minute walk, if you are lucky, you may spot some monkeys—macaque to be exact. The rainy season turns creeks into flowing streams with waterfalls and wading pools, though it's better to wait to swim until you arrive at the beach.

On the far side of the forest, the trail opens up onto **Koh Sompoch Beach** ❻, a 5-mile (9 km) stretch of pristine powdery sand. Several hours of strolling along the shore, swimming in the crystalline waters, and relaxing in the shade of a coniferous *sngao* tree seems hardly enough time to spend at such an idyllic destination.

You can linger at the beach a bit longer if you are fortunate enough to reserve one of the two rooms in the park's **Thmor Thom Dolphin Station** ❼, back in the village. The rooms are completely rudimentary, with "air-conditioning" provided by the crisp ocean breeze blowing

⏴	See also map p. 237
▶	Ream National Park
↔	19 miles (30 km)
⏲	5–6 hours
▶	Park headquarters

through the door of the wooden structure built at the end of a pier. Wake early when the seas are calm and you are likely to spot several dolphins swimming in the bay. In addition to common dolphins, pink dolphins are also frequently sighted. The following day you may hire a kayak (with or without a guide) and explore the area around the village. If you can't reserve a room, you may still see some dolphins in the drier months *(Nov.–May)* if you visit the Dolphin Station later in the afternoon.

Returning back up the Prek Toeuk Sap River, if you aren't running out of daylight, the boat will stop at **Ta Ben Mangrove View Tower** ❽. This 40-foot (12 m) lookout tower high in the canopy of the forest overlooks much of the terrain you have explored throughout the day. Your journey concludes at park headquarters.

Koh Russay (Bamboo Island)
🅰 237 C1
☎ 855(0)17- 777- 505
🚢 Ferry from Coasters, Serendipity Beach

Koh Rong Saloem
🅰 237 B1

Lazy Beach
🅰 237 B1

Islands off Sihanoukville

Dozens of islands dot the waters off the coast of Sihanoukville. Some are close, like Koh Pos, and others are accessible only via an overnight stay aboard a boat. The islands can be visited a number of ways: aboard a longtail boat hired from the beach; by arranging for accommodations on one of the few beaches where bungalows and resorts have been developed; and through the scuba-diving and fishing-trip operators who frequent the islands.

INSIDER TIP:

The islands off the coast are the best places to visit on a trip to Cambodia's southwest beaches. In low season, many of them are absolutely deserted and pristine.

—KRIS LEBOUTILLIER
National Geographic photographer

The most popular island for day-trippers is **Koh Russay** (Bamboo Island), situated a mere hour off the coast. There are two lovely beaches on opposite shores, whose charm lies in their isolation from the far more crowded mainland. Three resorts on the island offer beach-bum basics. Start your day on the east beach, then follow the sun across the island for the spectacular sunset. Once again, however, island development is a

fickle thing and the accommodation options may change often.

While many operators advertise a three-island boat tour to Koh Russay, these tours simply skirt Koh Kteah and Koh Chraloh—two smaller islands that have no beaches—before delivering you to Koh Russay. A better option is the boat service at Coasters Restaurant on Serendipity Beach, as the real attraction is Koh Russay. It provides direct round-trips to the island, leaving in the morning and coming back in the afternoon.

The other primary island destination is **Koh Rong Saloem,** reached via a 2.5-hour boat ride from Sihanoukville. **Mai Pai Bay,** a fishing village on the island's northern coast, is of moderate interest. The waters around the village are a marine conservation area, much to the delight of divers, who have overnight options there. However, most visitors head straight to **Lazy Beach,** where the Lazy Beach Bungalows currently command the prime real estate on this gorgeous, sandy beach. There are rumors of an upscale resort scheduled to be developed there soon, however.

Dive operators have identified over 25 sites around the islands off Sihanoukville. Two dive sites have established accommodations at Mai Pai Bay on Koh Rong Saloem. Charter dive trips to the remote **Koh Tang** and **Koh Prins,** which have some of the best visibility, require guests to sleep on mattresses aboard the ships. Yet these ships stop at remote beaches that few tourists get the opportunity to explore (see sidebar p. 240). ∎

Southern Coastal Provinces

Even if your primary reason for visiting southwest Cambodia is to take in the beach scene around Sihanoukville, you should try to build in time to visit the surrounding southern coastal provinces. The untouched coast and exotic wildlife of Koh Kong Province, Kampot's quiet beaches and pepper plantations, and the unique seaside town of Kep are just some of the intriguing destinations worth exploring

Simple wooden fishing boats on the river in Krong Koh Kong

Just northwest of Sihanoukville, Koh Kong Province (see pp. 250–253) has a rapidly growing ecotourism sector that allows visitors to experience the still relatively unspoiled Cardamom Mountains and spectacular coast. Much of the area is protected as either national parks or wildlife refuges. The Cardamoms are home to crocodiles, elephants, tigers, hornbills, and dozens of other exotic and threatened animal species. On the coastline, fringing mangrove forests feature indigenous and migratory birds, dolphins, and some of the most isolated and pristine beaches in Southeast Asia.

The Kampot region (see pp. 256–261) has long served as a much needed alternative to the Sihanoukville beach scene. It provides a more peaceful and quaint option for those who want to visit Cambodia's southern region. Kampot is somewhat sleepy, more natural, and not yet touched by large-scale development—a slice of authentic Cambodia in a stunning setting. Upon visiting the region, you can't help but feel you have discovered a diamond in the rough; the province features sprawling green fields, limestone mountains riddled with enchanting caves, and sparkling seas. One can visit pepper plantations, swim in bioluminescence, enjoy the country's best seafood, and explore some beautiful nature, including Bokor National Park.

Spice of Life

Cardamom has been a valuable Asian commodity for millennia. In the eponymous mountain range bordering Thailand, a unique variety of the spice grows, providing a livelihood for the ethnic Pohls who live in the foothills. Pohls, descendants of freed royal slaves, have cultivated the shrub for generations and have centered their culture and religion on cardamom's growth, harvest, and export.

Just 15 miles (24 km) from Kampot City, the seaside town of Kep is truly unlike any other coastal area in Asia, reminiscent of a tiny New England fishing town with beautiful weather year-round. Surrounding seas are a deep cerulean blue with green, rolling hills as a backdrop. A number of small islands can be found just a short ways from the coast.

Koh Kong Province

For many years, Koh Kong Province was a remote area of southwestern Cambodia, once part of Kampot Province. It lies tucked along the Gulf of Thailand in the foothills of the Cardamom Mountains. Following the demise of the Khmer Rouge regime, the area was exploited for its unspoiled forests and waters, which held bountiful supplies of timber and fish.

In the years thereafter, the town of Koh Kong was more accessible from Thailand than from Cambodia. Thai fisherman and developers gradually exerted greater influence over the region than their Cambodian counterparts. Koh Kong was a relatively quiet frontier town. The few foreigners in residence—a number of whom established businesses there—were likely to be Western expats from Pattaya, Thailand. The turn of the millennium brought the construction of the first road to Koh Kong on the Cambodian side, but its variable conditions and few bridges did little to encourage tourists to venture this way.

Since 2007, when a new road and a number of bridges funded and constructed by Thailand were completed, Koh Kong has been well connected to Srei Ambel and the rest of Cambodia. The area is undergoing considerable changes. On one hand, foreign business interests, particularly Thai and Chinese, are developing more roads throughout the region to facilitate the construction of hydroelectric dams. Ports are expanding to import construction materials and export sugarcane and palm oil from plantations throughout the region. The area also is at the forefront of the country's burgeoning ecotourism sector. International NGOs are working with the Cambodian Community-Based Ecotourism Network (CCBEN) to balance environmental and economic concerns of increased tourism (see Ecotourism, pp. 222–223).

Koh Kong Town: Considering its reputation as a "Wild West" town, you would be forgiven for arriving in Koh Kong and exclaiming, "Where?" Granted, it is on Cambodia's southwestern border with Thailand and its relatively isolated location includes some true wilderness. Yet it is a far cry from other border towns like seedy Poipet or the still remote Pailin. Although Koh Kong also has a reputation as an infamous border-run destination for sex tourists living in Pattaya, Thailand, today it is more of a sleepy provincial capital. It boasts a wide main boulevard, a beautiful riverfront, a small market, and little else within the city limits.

For those passing through the town, a number of attractions nearby are accessible via moto-taxi or through an arranged day trip. The most convenient of these is **Kor Yor Beach** on the west side of the Koh Kong Bridge. Koh Kong Divers is planning to build a beach resort there that should allow for an activity-filled day at a relatively pleasant beach where swimming is possible in the dry season months.

One of the most popular day trips from Koh Kong is to the **Peam Krasop Wildlife Sanctuary.** Covering almost 60,000 acres (23,800 ha), the sanctuary consists of the largest mangrove forest in Cambodia. It is located less than 5 miles (8 km) from Koh Kong, just beyond the Cham village. The village of **Boeng Kayak** has an ecotourism project that includes roughly 1 mile (1.6 km) of elevated walkways that meander through the mangrove forest and feature wooden platforms for relaxing, a tall suspension bridge, and a 50-foot (15 m) observation tower. Boats are

INSIDER TIP:

Rent a paddleboat in late afternoon at Peam Krasop Wildlife Sanctuary—just after sunset you'll be rewarded with a dazzling display of fireflies.

—GEOFFREY CAIN
National Geographic contributor

also available from the sanctuary's headquarters for dolphin spotting *(Nov.–March),* fishing, bird-watching (via rowboat), and nightly firefly outings. The park, part of the East Asia/Australasian Shorebird Network, contains kingfishers, egrets, herons, ospreys, and more than 25 other native and migratory birds.

A number of rivers flow down from the Cardamom Mountains into Koh Kong Province and there

Koh Kong
⚠ 236 A4
Visitor Information
✉ Koh Kong Tourism Department, 1 Village, Smach Meanchey Commune, Koh Kong

Kor Yor Beach
⚠ 236 A4

Peam Krasop Wildlife Sanctuary
⚠ 236 A3–A4
💲 $

EXPERIENCE: Sailing the Cambodian Coast

With 61 islands dotting the coast from Kep to Koh Kong, Cambodia is a sailor's dream. Many islands see remarkably few visitors due to a lack of transportation to reach them. Your sailing options around the coast are mostly limited to small sailboats, catamarans, and the like, which are primarily suitable for fun sails near the beach. Yet several larger boats are available for those would-be skippers looking to get farther out to sea. Keep in mind, however, that the few operators offering sailing opportunities are seasonal—they run only in the drier months of October through June.

Day trips and overnight sailing charters aboard a 45-foot (14 m) boat with **Sail Cambodia** (tel 855(0)16-450-964 or 855(0)11-390-083, www.sailcambodia.info) are ideal ways to explore the islands off Sihanoukville's coast. While trip activities can be tailored to your liking, the typical voyage consists of sailing past fishing villages, snorkeling, and exploring remote beaches and inland waterfalls. Two double cabins accommodate live-aboard passengers, and prices include food and beverages.

Located on Sihanoukville's quiet, natural Otres Beach, **Otres Nautica** (tel 855(0)92-230-065; e-mail: otres.nautica@yahoo.com) is an ideal place to rent a catamaran or small sailboat and zip along the pellucid water fringing the sandy shore. Larger boats are also available via charter, as are kayaks for those who prefer paddling to sailing.

Tatai Waterfall

🏕 236 A4

💲 $

Rainbow Lodge

✉ Tatai Village, near Koh Kong

☎ 855(0)99-744-321 or 855(0)12-160-2585

www.rainbowlodge cambodia.com

are several waterfalls worth visiting. The closest of these is the **Tatai Waterfall.** It can be accessed on foot from the nearby **Rainbow Lodge,** which also offers kayaking, trekking, camping, and boat trips along the river. Those not staying at the resort will need to hire a boat to get up the river, either from the town of Koh Kong or the river crossing at Route 48, approximately 12 miles (19 km) from town. The waterfall lies within a massive gorge, and you can take a refreshing dip in a number of pools. Other waterfalls in the area include **Kbal Chhay Kah Bow Waterfall** and **Koh Por Waterfall,** both of which are accessible via speedboat (1 hour, $$) or longtail boat (2–3 hours, $) from the town of Koh Kong.

Koh Kong's local sights include a market typical of Cambodian bazaars, except that it includes a large variety of fresh fish; a safari world of questionable quality; and a casino near the Thai border. Yet all of these are less impressive than the natural attractions surrounding the town. Those coming and going from Thailand may cross the border in either direction seven days a week between 7 a.m. and 8 p.m. Americans who are coming into Thailand from Cambodia may enter the country and stay for up to 15 days without a visa. When crossing into Cambodia from Thailand, Americans must apply at the border for a tourist visa ($$$$$), which requires a passport-size photo and is good for 30 days.

Beaches & Islands Near Koh Kong:

There are 23 islands off Koh Kong and numerous beaches along the isolated coast leading south toward

Sihanoukville, many of which are quite inaccessible. However, the dedicated explorer with some free time will discover some of the nicest diving and the most pristine beaches in all of Cambodia. Since **Koh Kong Island** is the closest one to the mainland, it's the most accessible. While exploring the island's interior is prohibited, its seven beaches offer plenty of choices for relaxing on the sand and in the surf. Boats can be hired (*$$*) from Koh Kong town for a day of snorkeling along the shore.

The peninsula farther south has been protected as **Botum Sakor National Park,** which covers more than 700 square miles (1,834 sq km) of coastline and inland forest. The peninsula is only accessible by boat or dirt bike, so very few visitors have likely set foot on the lengthy stretches of pristine, sandy shoreline here. That said, the boat between Koh Kong and Sihanoukville (*Oct.–June*) does stop on **Koh Sdach,** an island roughly halfway between the two larger ports and just off the coast of the national park.

Koh Sdach is home to a large Khmer and Vietnamese fishing community that occupies most of the eastern shore. There is accommodation here for travelers who are interested in experiencing life in a fishing village. For those with passable Khmer or Thai language skills, it may be possible to hire a boat to explore some of the nearby islands that have quality snorkeling (provided you bring your own gear). You could also check out the deserted beaches

of Botum Sakor National Park, though the best of these would be a several-hour boat ride from Koh Sdach.

Scuba dive operators have only have just begun operations out of Koh Kong. Yet they've already discovered exceptional dive sites, including **Shark Island,** so called for the prevalence of blacktip reef sharks in the waters surrounding

A Khmer-Loeu tribesman sits on a kneeling elephant and awaits a passenger.

the island. Another great dive spot is **Condor Reef,** which requires overnight camping because of its remote location, and where you may see sharks, dolphins, turtles, groupers, and barracudas. At the farthest site from shore, **Poulo Wai,** you may get to dive with manta rays. It's accessible by dive boat from Koh Kong or Sihanoukville. Snorkeling is also possible on day trips or overnight adventures to islands near Koh Kong (see sidebar p. 240).

Koh Kong Island
 236 A3

Botum Sakor National Park
236–237 B2–B3
✉ 2 miles (3 km) E of Andoung Tuek Village on Rte. 48
$ $

Koh Sdach
236 A2
 Ferry from Koh Kong or Sihanoukville, $$$$$

South West Elephant Corridor

Encompassing a wide swath of land from the Cardamom Mountains to the north and east of Koh Kong to the Damrei Mountains (Elephant Mountains) just to the east of Sihanoukville, the South West Elephant Corridor (SWEC) was established to protect one of the few remaining elephant migratory channels in Southeast Asia. The corridor includes the towering and remote mountains of Phnom Sankos and Phnom Aoral, as well as Kirirom National Park and Phnom Bokor National Park.

The SWEC encompasses over a dozen different ecosystems and is populated by no fewer than 14 endangered and threatened species. Among the wildlife living within and around the protected areas are Siamese crocodiles, pileated gibbons, Asiatic black bears, Indochinese tigers, Malaysian sun bears, marbled cats, and slow lorises. SWEC also contains half of Cambodia's bird species, and herds of the largest population of wild elephants in Southeast Asia. From Koh Kong, Route 48 cuts just below the corridor before passing through it near the intersection with National Highway 4. The road here is lined with trees. It's the only stretch of road in Cambodia that hasn't been clear-cut—a direct result of conservation efforts in the area, including four ranger stations positioned along Route 48. The road crosses four rivers along the way, where boats dock to ferry locals upstream to riverside villages.

Inside the White Elephant Cave near Kampot

Until recently, the villages along the rivers flowing out of the foothills of the southern Cardamoms were engaged in logging, poaching, and slash-and-burn farming that decimated the forests and wildlife populations. Today, efforts to promote ecotourism in the region are providing villagers with more sustainable livelihoods. Upriver from Trapeang Rung and Andoung Tuek, villages situated at river crossings along Route 48 have several community-based ecotourism projects that allow visitors to live among rural villagers who are modifying their way of life to promote and preserve their surrounding ecosystems. The village of **Chi Phat** is leading such efforts. Guests can engage in a variety of cultural and outdoor activities that will eventually link with nearby villages as part of a network of like-minded rural communes (see Ecotourism, pp. 222–223).

Although conservationists may cringe, a handful of motorbike touring companies explore the most remote areas of the region. While the noise may certainly frighten wildlife, for the time being motorbikes are the only viable way to visit the farthest reaches of the Cardamom Mountains. This "problem" will soon be remedied, as major road construction is under way to facilitate the development of 12 hydroelectric power plants on rivers throughout the region. Conservationists are likely to long for the good old days when only the occasional motorbike tour passed through these tenuously protected lands.

Kirirom National Park

Preah Suramarith Kossmak, better known as Kirirom National Park (Mountain of Joy) covers around 80,000 acres (32,375 ha) atop a 2,200-foot (670 m) hill. Originally established by King Sihanouk in 1945 as a personal getaway from Phnom Penh, it was opened to the public in 1997. Although technically within the South West Elephant Corridor, the park is unlikely to contain any elephants. A variety of bird species inhabit the area, however, plus pileated gibbons and a few sun bears.

INSIDER TIP:

While a visit to Chi Phat is an outstanding experience no matter the time of year, mountain biking is near impossible in the rainy season.

—TREVOR RANGES
National Geographic author

The picturesque pine forests and waterfalls, including a 130-foot (40 m) cascade, reward adventurous travelers with great opportunities for hiking and cooling off. The **Chambok Community-Based Ecotourism** site is just outside the park and allows guests to stay within a local village and experience the wilderness and rural life for very reasonable rates (see Ecotourism, pp. 222–223) The park is situated in Kompong Speu Province,

Chi Phat
🗺 237 B3

Chi Phat Community-Based Ecotourism
☎ 855(0)12 318-445
🚤 Boat from bridge across Chi Phat River & Andoung Tuek
💲 $–$$$

Kirirom National Park
🗺 237 D3
🚤 Boat from bridge across Chi Phat River & Andoung Tuek
💲 $–$$$

Chambok Community-Based Ecotourism
✉ National Highway 4 near Kirirom National Park
☎ 855(0)23-214-409
💲 $$
www.geocities.com/chambokcbet

Kampot Town

[M] 237 D1

76 miles (122 km) southwest of Phnom Penh on National Highway 4.

Kampot Province

Kampot Town: The calm, pleasant, provincial capital of Kampot retains a charm from Cambodia's French colonial years. Kampot has a cozy, small-town feel where everyone knows each other. Although it's sleepy for the moment, there is increasing talk of future investment projects throughout the region, including commercial diving, an industrial port, and oil field development. Walking along the banks of the sprawling silver river is a must, as is wandering the wide avenues to admire the city's colonial architecture. While some buildings with chipped paint have not been touched in years, others have been painstakingly restored—an interesting juxtaposition between past and present. The town is also a great place to spend long hours in a café simply enjoying the atmosphere.

The **Kompong Bay River** is one of Kampot's main attractions. The river is clean and safe for swimming. Many guesthouses are located on the river, making it easy to jump right in. For those who like swimming after sundown, bioluminescence can often be viewed here at night. The river also offers a number of boating activities. One- and two-person kayaks are available at many guesthouses and a number of tour operators offer sunset cruises to the Tek Chhou rapids.

For those who hope to really experience the natural, untouched beauty of the region, an eccentric expatriate known as the Boatman (*Bart the Boatman, tel 855(0)92-174-280*) runs full-day, half-day, and nighttime cruises. River voyagers aboard the Boatman's slim fishing boat navigate the river's estuaries and mangroves. Itineraries are flexible and often include barbecues at the Boatman's riverside home.

Around Kampot: Aside from Bokor Mountain, Kampot's other claim to fame is its world-renowned pepper (see sidebar p. 259). Rather than simply purchasing the finished product, many find it interesting to visit nearby pepper farms. Spires of green pepper plants grow over 10 feet (3 m) tall in orderly rows.

EXPERIENCE: Swimming Among the Stars

While the Kompong Bay River offers kayaking and sunset cruises during the day, its greatest beauty can be enjoyed during a swim at night. Many Kampot guesthouses are located along the river, allowing easy access to moonlit night swims.

As you enter the water, millions of bioluminescent organisms flicker and flash, lighting up tiny blue-green sparks all around you. The river glitters and glistens with each and every movement, as if countless fireflies inhabited the water. In marine biology terms, this bioluminescence is a biochemical reaction during which chemical energy is converted to light energy as dinoflagellate plankton emit tiny bursts of phosphorescence upon contact. As the night sky shines above, it is as if you are surrounded from head to toe in stars.

Two farms to visit are **Ta Li** and **Ta Ly.** Kampot is one of the country's biggest producers of agriculture. It also features tours of fruit and vegetable farms, including one growing pungent durian fruit. *(See Sok Lim Tours, p. 311, or contact FarmLink Ltd, tel 855(0)12-365-321.)*

If you ask local Khmers what to do in Kampot, they will suggest a visit to the **Tek Chhou Falls and Zoo** *($),* just 5 miles (8 km) northwest of town on the Prek Chha River. Although these "falls"

be quite difficult to get to. Because of the lack of signage, it is best to hire a local guide who is familiar with the area and also to hire a moto-taxi or *tuk-tuk ($$).* Those with a penchant for exploration should visit the area caves. The entrance fee is generally around a dollar and local kids will happily guide you or rent you flashlights. While there are a number of caves to choose from, **Phnom Chhnork** is undoubtedly the best, with a pre-Angkorian seventh-century brick temple in its main chamber

Tek Chhou Falls and Zoo
 237 D1

Phnom Chhnork
🅰 237 D1
✉ 6 miles (10 km) from Kampot on road to Kep
💲 $

The view from Kampot overlooks Prek Kampong Bay and distant Bokor Mountain.

are really just small rapids, the site is frequently packed with locals, especially on weekends. Local children show off by diving from a high bridge and vendors rent inner tubes and sell food and drinks to picnickers. The nearby zoo displays a small variety of local fauna.

As many of the sites around Kampot are on unnamed roads or quite a ways out of town, they can

and limestone formations near the entrance in the shape of elephants. Local children can also point out the forms of dragons, snakes, eagles, and fish in the cave's stalagmites and stalactites. Phnom Chhnork is about 6 miles (10 km) from Kampot. If you are using your own transportation instead of a driver, follow the main road to Kep, but veer left once the road

Kompong Trach

 237 E1

✉ About 23 miles (37 km) from Kampot. Take the Kep road; bear left at White Horse Monument & go straight.

💲 $

Wat Kirisan

✉ 23 miles (37 km) from Kampot. Take dirt road opposite Acleda bank to foot of Phnom Sor; follow sign to right.

💲 $

becomes one-way. Stay on this road for several miles until you see signs for the temple.

Rung Damray Saa, the largest cave in the region, is called White Elephant Cave because of a stalactite formation that resembles the head of a white elephant. Another rock formation looks like a crocodile. Climbing up to the cave, there are some breathtaking views. Farther along in the same complex, the less accessible **100 Rice Fields Cave** is known for its bats. Both caves *($)* are accessible from the main road in Kampot; turn left after about 8 miles (13 km) and look for signs.

A Kampot pepper plantation, known for growing peppers served in the world's top gourmet kitchens

For those willing to travel farther, the district of **Kompong Trach,** near Vietnam, has limestone caves and passageways that have been carved into the mountain. This mountain was one of the last Khmer Rouge holdouts and is also where the victims of the 1994 Khmer Rouge kidnappings were taken. The caves include a small enclosed jungle, formed when the roof of one of the cave's main chambers collapsed. Numerous *wats* and shrines have been built within the mountain. **Wat Kirisan** is a modern temple built at the base of Phnom Sor (White Mountain) and serves as the gateway to the underground passageways. Visiting the caves at Kompong Trach will take the greater part of the day.

Finally, while Kampot Province has bucolic beauty and exciting caves to visit, one must keep in mind the violence that occurred here during the Khmer Rouge era. To pay your respects to those who suffered under the brutal regime, visit a small, poignant memorial at **Kompong Troi Lach Pagoda.** A tiny temple holds bones of several hundred victims. The memorial is free, but a donation is suggested. The pagoda is located near the Phnom Chhnork caves.

Bokor Hill Station & National Park: One of the largest protected areas in Cambodia is **Bokor Mountain,** officially named Preah Monivong National Park. The 3,543-foot (1,079 m) mountain is home to the eerie former French hill station, a two-tiered waterfall,

World-renowned Kampot Pepper

The lush countryside of Kampot Province is known for its unique variety of pepper, largely viewed by epicureans as one of the best in the world. Kampot pepper has a distinct aroma and multifaceted flavor. Normal pepper usually produces an intense taste at the tip of the tongue that then disappears. Kampot pepper, however, has highly advanced, lingering flavors that first register on the tip of the tongue and then expand to the back of the palate. It also has lingering hints of eucalyptus and fresh herbs.

The Chinese explorer Zhou Daguan described Cambodian pepper production as early as the 13th century. During the French colonial era, 99 percent of all

pepper found in France was from Kampot. After Khmer Rouge policies led to the destruction of pepper plantations, cultivation was virtually nonexistent for decades. In the late 1990s, old pepper-producing families began to revive the trade. In 2006, Tot Min Kalim and two expatriates—Jerome Benezech and Angela Vestergaard—formed a cooperative (*FarmLink Ltd, P.O. 0728, Kampot, tel 855(0)12-365-321*) for local Kampot pepper farmers. The group began building up a worldwide distribution network and Kampot pepper is now shipped to France, Denmark, Australia, and the United States. It can be found in some of the finest gourmet restaurants and kitchens throughout the world.

and an abundance of rare flora and fauna—including elephants, gibbons, leopards, and tigers. The mountain boasts spectacular views, although during rainy season the mountain is wrapped in such thick fog that it is often difficult to see even just a few yards in front of you. The hill station can get quite cold at night, making warm clothes a necessity for those staying over.

Bokor Mountain once could be experienced on a self-guided day trip from Kep or Kampot and visitors could spend the night on the peak. Visitors stayed in dormitories at the ranger station, though a new luxury resort (see below) could make visits an altogether different experience. If you want to stay on the mountaintop now, your only option is an organized tour (see p. 261).

In January 2008, the road to Bokor Mountain was closed so

that Sokha Hotels could complete its new development project on the hilltop. The lengthy project, slated for completion in 2011, involves refurbishing the old casino and hotel, as well as building a new luxury resort.

Assuming this new development hasn't completely renovated the remnants of the former colonial retreat by the time you visit, the most memorable site atop the mountain is the **Bokor Palace Hotel and Casino.** As this massive structure emerges from the fog, it is easy to imagine it as it once was—a magnificent, glittering emblem of French colonial wealth and extravagance. Yet, years of neglect have left it with crumbling stairways leading nowhere and dimly lit corridors that contribute to the haunted-house atmosphere. On a clear day, the rooftop terrace features sweeping views of the jungle below.

Kompong Troi Lach Pagoda

✉ 23 miles (37 km) from Kampot, near Kompong Trach

💲 $

Bokor Hill Station & National Park

🔺 237 D1–D2

✉ Off National Highway 3; 25 miles (40 km) from Kampot

💲 $$

Bokor's Last Stand

The Bokor Hill Station is surrounded by a dark and eerie history of battles and warfare, which greatly contributes to the haunted feeling that dominates the misty retreat. The mountain was long viewed as a strategic site due to its altitude and surrounding views.

Vietnamese and Khmer Issarak (Free Khmer) forces battling for independence took control of the mountain in the late 1940s, forcing out the French elite. Decades later, the Lon Nol regime had to surrender the site to Khmer Rouge forces, who established a base of operations on it.

Bokor was the site of yet another battle during the Vietnamese invasion in 1979, when fierce fighting between Khmer Rouge and Vietnamese forces lasted several months. Khmer Rouge forces fortified themselves in the Catholic Church as the Vietnamese attacked from the nearby Royal Palace. Thereafter, the scars of warfare—including shattered windows, graffiti, and walls riddled with bullet holes—were readily apparent on the surviving structures at the Bokor Hill Station. A lone Vietnamese gun mount serves as a reminder of the mountain's final battle.

Popokvil Falls

⚐ 237 D1

Those hoping to catch a glimpse of the past by exploring the old Bokor Mountain structures may be out of luck once the Sokha project reaches completion. The development project will replace the notoriously bumpy road to the summit, however, and many welcome this improvement.

Just a short distance from the old hotel is a small, run-down **Catholic Church** ($). While the inside of the church is empty, the altar remains intact. Due to its role in the Vietnamese invasion in the late 1970s, the walls of the church are now covered in graffiti and drawings (see sidebar above).

Additional remnants of the hill station's former glory years dot the foggy landscape, including a post office, water tower, school, and hospital. For an alternative, religious site, one can visit the ruins of **Wat Sampeau Moy Roy,** known as the Five Boats Wat due to five large boulders at the entrance that locals say resemble boats. About a 30-minute drive from the top of

the hill station, one can also find the **Black Palace,** a former weekend retreat for King Sihanouk.

While the haunted past of the former Bokor Hill Station is certainly the mountain's biggest draw, **Bokor National Park** also features some great opportunities. Established in 1993, the protected park stretches over 610 square miles (1,581 sq km). If you visit during the wet season on a sunny day, the two-tiered **Popokvil Falls** (Swirling Clouds) is great for swimming. The upper falls is the best spot for a dip, and the lower falls can be reached by a path from there. The falls are just a 15-minute drive from the hill station and 23 miles (37 km) from Kampot. There's only enough water to make them worth visiting during the rainy season (June–Oct.). The 7-mile (11 km) trail from Wat Sampeau Moy Roy to the falls is a good trek.

The ranger station, located atop the hill station, has a wealth of information about the wildlife in

INSIDER TIP:

At the top of Bokor Hill, among the landscape of stone and shrubs, you can see lasting images of Cambodia's wars, including a damaged house and the remains of an old church.

—NGUYEN VAN DU
National Geographic field researcher

the park. It also offers information on an outreach program to educate locals about protecting natural resources and preventing illegal mining. In addition to the mountain's larger mammals, the park is also home to more than 300 bird species. Note that when exploring Bokor National Park, it is best to be accompanied by a ranger ($$$$$). A former Khmer Rouge

stronghold, the hill station and park may still contain land mines; always stick to well-worn paths. Females traveling alone should know that there have been complaints about verbal harassment of women at the ranger station.

As this book went to press, it was unclear when the road to Bokor Mountain would reopen. If you just can't wait to see Bokor, the mountain is not off-limits, particularly for those with a little determination. At the time of writing, **Sok Lim Tours** (see p. 311) offers a two-day hike up and down the mountain. Trekkers spend about five hours hiking up the mountain and then spend the night atop the hill station. A seven-hour trek the following day culminates in a visit to Bokor's rapids and a sunset river cruise back to the town of Kampot. Meals, water, accommodation, guides, and an armed ranger are included.

(continued on p. 264)

Fishermen prepare to cast their net on a beach in Kep.

The Art of Silk

Silk was introduced to Cambodia in the 13th century, with the establishment of the Southeast Asian silk road. A rich silk tradition flourished for centuries, with weavers passing down techniques from one generation to the next. During the Khmer Rouge regime, the silk industry was critically damaged and knowledge of the craft was almost lost. Cambodia's silk industry has recently entered a second renaissance, however.

Mekong Blue, a silk production facility in Stung Treng

Silk is made from the cocoons of mulberry silkworms, which the worms take three days to spin. Weavers place live cocoons in boiling water and then unwind the delicate threads. This silk thread is then colored with either natural or synthetic dyes. It's woven together on massive hand- and foot-operated looms. The entire process is long and painstaking, requiring weeks to produce a final product.

Types of Cambodian Silk

Cambodian silk comes in a rich variety of motifs and textures—*phamuong* (silk fabric in plain color), *chorebap* (silk brocade), *hôl* (silk with colorful patterns) and *hôl lboeuk* (hôl combined with a brocade fabric). Takeo is the most famous province for silk, known for its ikat technique. In this traditional practice, silk is tied and then dyed to create a reversible fabric. It is estimated that 7,000 weavers live in this small province alone.

Recent Renaissance

Cambodia is currently in the midst of a great revitalization of the silkmaking process and the industry is truly blossoming. Nongovernmental organizations (NGOs) have provided a great deal of support and assistance to local communities, seeking to raise the skill level of silk weavers. These NGOs provide economic opportunities for disabled and marginalized individuals in the process. They have also encouraged the use of traditional, natural, and environmentally friendly dyes.

The Cambodian Craft Corporation encour ages young and novice weavers in its two training centers (see sidebar p. 80). Weaves of Cambodia employs women in Tbeng Meanchey who are land-mine survivors. The organization was founded by internationally acclaimed weaver Carol Cassidy (see sidebar p. 80). The Siem Reap–based Artisans d'Angkor runs a school for weavers, seeking to transport silk traditions of the past into the future (see. pp. 116-117). Even global fashion designer Eric Raisina has a long-established silk workshop in Siem Reap. He sends his wearable-art silk creations to the likes of Yves St. Laurent, Christian Lacroix, Christian Dior, and Barneys NY.

Finding Quality Silks

Despite the fine offerings of silk products available, buyers must be wary when it comes to purchasing authentic silks. The products hawked at the famous Russian Market in Phnom Penh (see p. 87) are of notoriously poor quality. Many fibers being sold as silk are actually synthetic fibers wrapped in silk. In the past, potential buyers

Spools of colorfully dyed silk, ready to be hand-woven

were advised to test the textiles by setting fire to a thread; if they detected a smell similar to burning hair, the thread was silk. Yet as silk counterfeiters become more advanced, the match test often fails to accurately differentiate the authentic from the fake. If you're in search of genuine silk, it is advisable to shop in boutiques or visit the villages where the silks are originally produced.

Fashion, textile, and art lovers, will delight in the silk textiles produced in Cambodia. Silks can be found as scarves, wall-hangings, cushions, bedspreads, clothes, and curtains. They come in every color, size, and price range, from $3 market stall steals to exquisite $80 works of art.

EXPERIENCE: Where to Buy Silk

Local NGOs have led a revival in traditional silk weaving. Support their work at the following locations.

Institute for Khmer Traditional Textiles (No. 472, Viheachen Village, Svaydongkum Commune, Siem Reap, tel 855(0)63-964437, iktt.esprit-libre.org) teaches and inspires a young generation of Cambodians to continue the traditional art of silk weaving. Their workshop and gallery is located just outside Siem Reap town (see p. 114).

Mekong Blue (tel 855(0)12-609-730, www.mekongblue.com) teaches marginalized women to produce high-quality silk. Visit their workshop and browse items in their gallery (St. 1, Sre Po Village, Stung Treng) or visit their Phnom Penh showroom (9Eo 130 St.).

For additional information on shopping for silk, see Travelwise pp. 299–304.

Kep
🔺 237 D1

Kep

The name "Kep" is derived from the French *le cap*—cape in English. The name is also attributed to a Khmer legend about Prince Sakor Reach, who put a spell on his commander and stole his horse. Surprised by soldiers while resting on the beach, the prince leapt onto the horse's back, leaving behind the saddle, or *kep seh*. Founded in 1908 as a seaside resort for the colonial elite, Kep retained its popularity for decades, becoming "the Hamptons" of Cambodia after the nation's independence in 1953. The who's who of Cambodia's wealthy elite built stunning villas along the coastline and the district became home of the country's most acclaimed zoo.

However, this little piece of paradise was destroyed during the bloody Khmer Rouge years. Properties were dismantled and looted by Khmer Rouge cadres, Vietnamese troops, and Cambodians desperate for items to sell to survive famine. Today, the glamorous villas of yesteryear lie in ruins—blackened skeletons of the country's former glory days.

It has only been in the last few years that Kep has begun to stir from its years of decaying slumber. Elegant boutique properties and shabby-chic budget bungalows can now be found along the beaches and hills. Despite this recent development, the picturesque seaside town has retained its quaint charm, serving as a much needed alternative to Sihanoukville. Yet large-scale investors are being drawn to Kep, and it is likely to become a very different place in years to come.

While weekdays in Kep remain quiet, Cambodians and expatriates from Phnom Penh flock to the town on weekends. Even King Sihanouk has a hilltop palace in Kep. The locale has long been one of the retired king's favorite retreats, where he previously entertained foreign dignitaries on a nearby island known as Île des Ambassadeurs.

More of a destination for R&R than sightseeing, Kep is the perfect

Touring the Ruins of Kep

Abandoned and blackened shells of once glamorous seaside villas still dot the landscape around Kep. The years and elements have taken their toll on these structures, but they remain interesting to sightseers. Many homes were designed in the modern style of the 1960s, while others have a marked colonial feel. In general, little is known about the houses' original owners, as the Khmer Rouge destroyed records of property ownership. However, the large house facing the sea with the well-maintained garden was the Royal Residence of former King Sihanouk.

The best way to tour these sites is by bicycle or motorbike, both of which can be rented from Kep and Kampot guesthouses. Then, simply drive around the two main roads in Kep—one along the coast and the other more inland. Be warned, however, that many seemingly abandoned houses are occupied by Khmer squatters who may not take warmly to foreign visitors poking around.

place to relax. As all beaches look westward, Kep is well known for its vibrant orange sunsets. A nearly 4-mile (6 km) road winds along the coastline and is perfect for tuk-tuk or motorbike joyriding. The tiny town is also adorned with many large statues, each associated with a different myth or legend.

For those hoping to splash in the sea, Kep's beaches may be disappointing. The bay is not naturally sandy; sand was imported from Sihanoukville during the first half of the 20th century. The beaches are now a bit dirty, but that certainly does not stop local children from enjoying the cool water with inner tubes.

Koh Tonsay: For those searching for a true beach getaway, Koh Tonsay (Rabbit Island) is a short boat ride from Kep. The island's delightful main beach is a long stretch of yellow sand dotted with palm trees amid clear, sparkling seas. Just 30 minutes from the mainland, the island is perfect for day trips or overnight stays. Boats ($$$$$) can be hired at the Koh Tonsay Boat Dock, located at the southeastern part of the district, next to the Long Villa Restaurant. Trips to the island can also be arranged by tour agencies and by guesthouses in Kep and Kampot.

Hammocks and large wooden platforms line Rabbit Island's beach. Vendors here will provide you with thin mats to stretch out on, as long as you order food and drinks from them. Fresh seafood and meat are cooked up and served on demand. Inner tubes and snorkeling equipment are also available.

EXPERIENCE:
Crab in Kep

While Kampot has pepper as its claim to fame, Kep has crab. Not to be missed, fresh and affordable crabs are fished right out of the ocean and onto your plate (with some cooking in between).

The best place to eat is the crab market along the westernmost strip of beach, where rows of bamboo shacks serve up tasty seafood prepared in a variety of ways. Extremely popular during lunchtime, these stalls also make prime sunset-viewing spots.

Crab is also served on the wooden picnic platforms opposite Kep beach. Pick an empty platform and the seafood vendors will quickly bring you an English-language menu. Most vendors at both venues also offer fish, squid, and shrimp. Crab can be ordered grilled, boiled, curried, or in soup, but highly recommend is the succulent Kampot pepper crab—fried crabs doused with flavorful green Kampot pepper.

You can spend the night on Rabbit Island in tiny, inexpensive bungalows lining the main beach. The huts are extremely basic, equipped with a thin mattress on the floor, a few blankets, and a mosquito net. Be aware that the walls are thin, making for very little privacy, and the communal bathrooms are not very appealing.

While not for those who require creature comforts, a night on Rabbit Island is highly recommended. Spending the night is the best way to get the most of the island in the hours before and after the day-trippers arrive and depart. Bungalows can be booked upon arrival or through guesthouses in Kep, who can call to reserve one for you. ∎

Koh Tonsay
⬛ 237 D1

TRAVELWISE

Boat teams gather on the Tonle Sap to prepare for a race during the Bonn Om Touk water festival.

PLANNING YOUR TRIP

When to Go

Generally speaking, Cambodia has two seasons: wet and dry. The wet season tends to be cooler than the dry one. Most visitors come to Cambodia early in the dry season, in December and January, when the weather is cool and mostly rain free. As these months draw the most visitors, hotel prices are their highest, rooms are difficult to book on short notice, and temples and beaches are crowded.

By April, temperatures begin to soar and the once lush landscape becomes lifeless and dry. Dust blankets the country and temperatures hover around 100°F (38°C). The temples of Angkor are much quieter in spring, but it isn't a particularly comfortable time to visit or capture the best photos, as many waterways evaporate and the surrounding greenery is gone. The provinces of Ratanakiri and Mondulkiri are particularly dusty in these punishingly hot, dry months. The only respite comes from the refreshing beaches and islands of Cambodia's coast.

The monsoons typically begin in June; the humidity skyrockets as the seasonal rains blanket Cambodia. Monsoon rain comes hard and fast, most typically in the late afternoon. The rainy season can be a refreshing time to visit, however. There are far fewer visitors, the countryside turns verdant and full of life, and most days are sunny and clear. That said, it could rain throughout your entire visit. Travel to more remote destinations is impossible during much of the monsoon season as dirt roads turn into muddy morasses and bridges wash out.

Schedule your visit based on the aspects of Cambodia you wish to experience. The temples are more beautiful when surrounded by full moats and lush vegetation. The hills of the east and northeast are best early in the dry season, before the dust becomes too predominant. The beaches are nice even in the most scorching, dry months, when dive conditions are their best.

Some travelers visit for festivals, such as the Bon Om Tuk Water festival in Phnom Penh, when millions flock to the capital for the annual boat races in October or November. Around mid-April, Khmer New Year draws droves of local worshippers to the temples of Cambodia, particularly Angkor.

Climate

Cambodia is a tropical country with a tropical climate. The average annual temperature is around 81°F (27–28°C). The wet season *(late May–Oct.)* typically features temperatures between 68° and 80°F (20 27°C) and the dry season *(Nov.–mid-May)* has a temperature range between 82° and 95°F (28–35°C). Consequently, there are sort of four seasons: dry and cool *(Dec.–Feb.)*, dry and hot *(March–May)*, wet and hot *(June–Sept.)*, and wet and mild *(Oct.–Nov.)*. Temperatures in the mountains, particularly in the eastern province of Mondulkiri, get quite cold in the winter months *(Nov.–Feb.)*. Visitors should be prepared for a few frigid nights without the benefit of heated hotel rooms.

What to Take

What to bring to Cambodia depends on your vacation plans. Those on a bird-watching expedition or camping in one of Cambodia's spectacular and remote national parks will need to pack differently from those heading on a honeymoon to a five-star beach resort. Seasonal differences also require different gear. Visiting in the rainy season? Bring a sturdy poncho and some waterproof shoes. Coming in the winter months? Don't forget to pack a sweater or even a light jacket. Yet many items are easily purchased at the central market in any provincial town. Since Cambodia has a massive garment industry, good clothing is cheap (though the quality of footwear here is considerably less impressive).

Sandals are convenient for slipping on and off when entering Buddhist monasteries. However, the temples of Angkor require sturdier footwear for clambering about. Active Buddhist temples require modest clothing; devotees frown on those who enter in short shorts and tank tops. Cambodians generally tend to show greater deference to those dressed more smartly. Even if you are planning a beach holiday, some respectable clothes for a quick visit to Phnom Penh may prove useful for temples, fine dining establishments, the casino, and a police office or embassy (in the event of a problem).

Consider getting a few items at home simply because they are easier to procure prior to your visit. These include a lightweight flashlight, a compass or GPS, a power adapter for hair dryers, a three-prong to two-prong adapter for computers, hand sanitizer, quality bug spray and sunblock, eye drops (for dust), extra passport photos, and copies of your passport and insurance information. You may also wish to bring a small pair of binoculars.

Though perhaps 90 percent of pharmaceutical drugs in Cambodia are counterfeit, many authentic prescription drugs are available over the counter at U-Care pharmacies in Phnom Penh and Siem Reap. Bring a prescription for medication that you need to refill while here.

Insurance

While carrying valid heath insurance that covers travel overseas or obtaining additional travel insurance for health considerations abroad are good ideas, the real issue regarding insurance in Cambodia is emergency medical evacuation. No matter how comprehensive your insurance is, there simply aren't adequate medical facilities here to treat serious injuries. Even insurance with emergency evacuation often requires a telephone call overseas to be approved. This requirement is fine if you are in the major tourist destinations, decidedly less so if you are in more remote provinces. Check with your insurance provider, or get supplemental emergency evacuation insurance from SOS *(www.sosinternational. com)* in Phnom Penh before heading out into the wilderness. Some insurance policies do not cover motorbike accidents or high-risk sports such as scuba diving. Be aware of your policy limitations before engaging in potentially dangerous activities in Cambodia.

Travel insurance that covers theft is also worthwhile, as petty crimes such as purse snatchings are not uncommon. While obtaining a police report in Cambodia feels like insult added to injury, it's better than losing your valuables without a chance for recompense.

HOW TO GET TO CAMBODIA

Entry Formalities

Passports & Visas

Visitors entering Cambodia must have a passport that is valid for at least six months after their arrival. Entering the country also requires a visa. For nationals of the United States, Canada, European Union, and Australia, tourist and business visas can be obtained upon arrival; both are a single-entry permit for 30 days. All applications require a passport-size photo. Tourist visas cost $20 and business visas cost $25, both paid in cash.

Tourist e-visas also are offered online through Cambodia's Ministry of Foreign Affairs & International Cooperation: *evisa.mfaic.gov.kh*. E-visas take three days to validate; the website charges an additional $5 processing fee.

It's easiest and cheapest to plan how long you wish to stay and obtain a visa ahead of time. However, it is possible to get visa extensions in Cambodia. Though it can be done yourself at the Department for Foreigners in Phnom Penh *(tel 855(0)12-854-874 or 855(0)12-581-558, closed*

Sat.–Sun.), the extension process is time-consuming and frustrating. It's better to pay a small commission to one of the numerous travel agencies specializing in visa services. Such agencies are easily found in Siem Reap, Sihanoukville, and particularly Phnom Penh—ask your guesthouse or hotel for guidance.

Business visas are much easier to extend, particularly for those hoping to pop in and out of the country with a multiple-entry permit. Extensions vary from a 30-day single-entry extension to 6- and 12-month multiple-entry extensions. Costs range from $50 to $180. No documentation of business activities is required. If you overstay your tourist or business visa, the charge is $5 per day.

Airport Visa Process
If arriving by air to either Phnom Penh or Siem Reap, you will be ushered into the airport's visa-processing area for a somewhat convoluted entry process with few signs and little order. The first line requires your passport, a small passport photo, and an entry form, which you will have received in flight. Here you will also pay the visa fee in cash: $20 for a tourist visa; $25 for a business visa. In the second line, you wait for an officer to hold up your passport. After claiming your passport, proceed to the immigration checkpoint and baggage claim.

If you already have a visa, you can proceed directly to the immigration windows without waiting in either of the above lines.

Customs
Cambodia's Custom & Excise Department recently increased security through a new Strategic Work Plan. (Historically, Cambodia's customs process has been vague at best.) The new rules probably won't greatly affect the time spent at airport customs, but they may slow down land border crossings, which the UN identified in 2007 as insecure and "porous."

The plan was implemented to crack down on smugglers, sadly notorious in Cambodia for drugs, weapons, and human trafficking. Offenders will be prosecuted to the fullest extent of the law, which could result in life imprisonment.

Immigration officers enforce a Green and Red Channel process to expedite the declaration process. Passengers who have nothing to declare use the Green Channel and passengers with goods to declare use the Red Channel.

Duty-free regulations allow passengers to enter Cambodia with pharmaceuticals (with valid prescriptions), 350 ml of perfume, and imported products not exceeding $100 in value (i.e., newly purchased items, not your trusty laptop). Passengers 18 years and older are eligible to possess 200 cigarettes, 100 cigars, or 40 grams of tobacco, and one bottle of liquor or two bottles of wine. Since duty-free concessions do not need declaration, use the Green Channel with them.

Anything in excess of the above requires a customs tax and must be declared in the Red Channel. For example, goods worth $100 or more are subject to customs duties and taxes. If you are bringing with you goods valued at greater than $100 but less than $300, you must declare them in a Noncommercial Customs Declaration Form. If importing merchandise worth more than $300, complete a Customs Declaration Form. All forms are received at the point of entry.

Finally, there are no currency restrictions on foreign currency imports. However, any sum over $10,000 (or the foreign equivalent) needs declaration.

Airplane Arrivals & Departures
Airports
Cambodia has two international airports: Phnom Penh International Airport (PNH; *www .cambodia-airports.com/phnompenh*) and the more modern Siem Reap International Airport (REP; *www .cambodia-airports.com/siemreap*). Both airports are small and easily navigated, with signs translated in English and French.

International Flights
Cambodia's airline industry is growing quickly, charged by the pace of development. However, as of 2008, there were no direct flights to Cambodia from outside Asia. Travel from North America, Europe, or Australia entails a layover in Thailand, Vietnam, Malaysia, Singapore, China, or Korea. Additional connecting routes will likely be incorporated soon.

International flights are scheduled most regularly from Bangkok, Thailand. The Bangkok–Phnom Penh flight, made several times daily, costs upward of $100 during tourist season *(Nov.–Feb.)*. These flights can be enjoyed most comfortably on Bangkok Airways, known as Asia's "boutique airline," Thai Airways International, an internationally top-rated airline, or budget carrier Air Asia.

Daily flights from Bangkok to Siem Reap are considerably more expensive—averaging $400 roundtrip—as the route is serviced only by Bangkok Airways. However, rumors are swirling that Air Asia will soon (perhaps in early 2010) offer some competition, resulting in lower fares. Bangkok Airways also has cornered the market on direct flights between Siem Reap and Koh Samui or Phuket, arguably worth the price to conveniently bypass Bangkok.

A growing number of international cities also offer flights

into Cambodia: Kuala Lumpur, Singapore, Taipei, Seoul, Hong Kong, Shanghai, Vientiane, Hanoi, and Ho Chi Minh City. Be aware that Lao Aviation is still struggling to maintain regular safety checks.

Airline Information

Below is information for major airlines servicing Cambodia. For a full list, try www.SkyScanner.net.

Air Asia
Tel 855(0)23-356-011 (to -015)
www.airasia.com

Bangkok Airways
Tel 855(0)23-722-545 (to 547)
www.bangkokair.com

Dragon Air
Tel 855(0)23-424-300
www.dragonair.com

Thai Airways International
Tel 855(0)23-214-359
www.thaiairways.com

Airport Transportation

At either international airport, ground transportation is found readily. Ideally, arrange for pickup through your hotel. Otherwise, taxi drivers will take you where you need to go for a fixed price. Fees from Phnom Penh airport are $9 for taxi, $7 for tuk-tuk. The airport technically is located 6 miles (10 km) outside city limits, but a taxi ride to the downtown hotels takes 30 to 45 minutes. From the Siem Reap airport, taxi fees are $7 and tuk-tuks are $4. Siem Reap's airport is about 5 miles (8 km) from central hotels, and the drive generally takes 10 to 20 minutes.

Be aware that tuk-tuks to or from the airports are highly inadvisable, as the long journey with baggage is uncomfortably crowded and the air is dusty and polluted. In Phnom Penh, drive-by snatchings from passing motorbikes are not uncommon. Instead opt for hotel transportation or taxis.

When heading to the airport for departure, factor in horrendous Phnom Penh traffic.

Taxes

Leaving Cambodia by air entails a departure tax in cash. At both the Phnom Penh and Siem Reap airports, the payment station is after the airline check-in, but before security. The charge for adult foreigners traveling internationally is $25; it's $13 for children under 12 and free for those under 2. Foreigners traveling domestically must pay $6 for departure tax.

Boat Arrivals

By boat, Cambodia is only somewhat accessible. The country can be reached via the Gulf of Thailand at Sihanoukville International Seaport, which welcomes ships, boats, and cruises. Cruise lines, such as Royal Caribbean International, stop here en route to other destinations (like Singapore or Hong Kong) to briefly enjoy Cambodia's beaches. Find the best packages to suit your tastes at www.cruiseweb.com.

The Mekong River provides access to Cambodia from Vietnam by way of the Kaam Samnor-Vinh Xuong border crossing. Ferry services navigate the route from Chau Doc, Vietnam, toward Phnom Penh. The better of these ferry services is **Blue Cruiser** (tel 855(0)16-824-343), which departs Chau Doc at 8:30 a.m. and docks in Phnom Penh around 1:30 p.m. Ferry tickets can be reserved through travel agents or usually bought right at the major docks in Phnom Penh or Chau Doc.

If going the other direction, consider a **Victoria Hotel** (www.victoriahotels-asia.com) ferryboat, which runs several times weekly from Phnom Penh to its sister luxury hotels in Chau Doc.

Multinational sea and river luxury cruises are up-and-coming industries; some offer unparalleled views and tours that merge luxury with authentic culture. One such company, **Compagnie Fluviale du Mekong** (www.cfmekong.com), explores Vietnam and Cambodia through a multiday cruise on the Mekong River.

Bus Arrivals
Border Crossings

Busing into Cambodia is a common, economical mode of entry. Bus transport from Bangkok to Phnom Penh will total about $25. However, traversing Cambodia's boundaries by land requires navigating a border crossing. Cambodia has numerous crossings along the frontiers of its neighboring countries: nine from Vietnam (one of which requires a boat ride across the Mekong), six from Thailand, and one from Laos. From wherever you hail, pack light, keep your wits about you, and bring a sense of adventure. These crossings have international reputations to maintain—some as sleepy nowhere towns, others as hotbeds of riotous con artists.

Before embarking on your bus adventure know that most Cambodian border crossings offer on-site visa services from 7 a.m. to 8 p.m. This means there's usually no need to apply for your visa in advance; rather, just remember to bring cash and passport photos to apply. These border visa services offer standard 30-day Cambodian tourist or business visas upon arrival. However, be aware that this stands true for visitors entering Cambodia, but not necessarily for those leaving. While Thailand permits qualifying nationalities a 15-day visa waiver at its borders, both Laos and Vietnam require visas before arrival. These can be arranged in advance through your hotel or travel agencies in Siem

Reap or Phnom Penh. For either the Laos or Vietnam visa, there are same-day rush services for an additional fee, but, even so, it's best to allot a few days for the process.

Finally, also realize that bus schedules in Cambodia change whimsically (as may border regulations). For fairly regularly updated information on bus schedules and border crossings, check *www .canbypublications.com*.

The six border crossings from Thailand require changing transportation at the border, as no buses or taxis are allowed through to Cambodian destinations. Generally, your options are simply to change buses, switch taxis, or try a combination of the two. Both buses and taxis crowd either side of the border, leaving as regularly as every 30 minutes between around 7 a.m. and 8 p.m. As you navigate these sometimes confusing crossings, stick with official bus and taxi companies (see Bus Services, p. 271) to avoid scam artists.

Of the six border crossings, the most traversed is Poipet (called Aranyaprathet on the Thai side). Open from 8 a.m. to 8 p.m., Poipet serves as the crossing point on the well-traveled Bangkok to Siem Reap route. It's a constant whirl of chaos among backpackers, immigration officers, con artists, and people soliciting business. Be very alert here, as scams have become a particular problem (see Border Scams, opposite).

Due to its tourist influx, though, Poipet is one of two checkpoints along the Thai border with an international ATM and money exchange counters. Be extra vigilant using either, or plan ahead by bringing U.S. dollars or Thai baht in smaller denominations to cover your visa fees and other expenses.

After reaching the checkpoint from the Thailand side, ignore hustlers and search for a bus company such as Mekong Express or Capitol

Transport. These will sell legitimate bus tickets at the normal fee: $15 to Phnom Penh (7–8 hours); $10 to Siem Reap (4–6 hours); and $8 to Battambang (2–3 hours).

Your other, more comfortable, option is to continue by taxi instead of bus. This option requires negotiating with the aggressive, persistent taxi drivers who, at first, will offer some outrageous fees, like $100 to Siem Reap. Counter by starting very low (perhaps $15) and try to settle near around $40 to Siem Reap, $25 to Battambang, and $80 to Phnom Penh, though often these taxis don't offer transportation to a destination as far away as Phnom Penh.

Leaving Cambodia by bus through Poipet is fairly straightforward as nearly all tourist agencies (and guesthouses) offer a bus package from Siem Reap, Battambang, and even Phnom Penh. Once you've passed through immigration in Poipet, take a tuk-tuk (about $3 or THB100) to the bus station on the Thailand side (Aranyaprathet), from which you can catch buses that leave about every 30 minutes. There is no departure tax to leave Cambodia at the land border crossings.

The other beaten border track between Thailand and Cambodia is the Cham Yeam (called Trat or Hat Lek in Thailand) checkpoint. It connects southeast Thailand (Trat Province) to western Cambodia, near the beach town of Koh Kong. Commonly, travelers on the island and beach tour cross here, coming from the Thailand beaches such as Pattaya or Koh Chang to reach the beaches of Sihanoukville, Cambodia (about an 8-hour ride). This popular crossing processes tourists and their visas from 7 a.m. to 8 p.m.

A bus from Bangkok to the Cham Yeam border crossing will take five to six hours; from Pattaya, the drive will take three to four hours. Buses to Cham Yeam depart daily; tickets can be booked at

Pattaya's bus station and Bangkok's East Bus Terminal (Ekkami) for around THB200.

As with the crossing at Poipet, beware of scams and stick to official transport companies. If you're being asked to pay for anything more than a visa, ask for a receipt. This demand generally will filter the scammers from legitimate business.

The other border crossings from Thailand include: O Smach (Chong Jom on the Thai side) that connects Si Saket Province in Thailand to Oddar Meanchey; Choam (Choam Srawngam) linking Sangkha, Thailand, to Anlong Veng; Psar Prom (Ban Pakard) from Thailand's Chantaburi to Pailin; and Kamrieng District's Daung Lem (Dong) joins Chantaburi Province, Thailand, to Battambang Province. For all the above, bring U.S. dollars in small denominations for your fees because banks are hard to find.

The nine border crossings from Vietnam are generally open between 7 a.m. and 6 p.m. The most traversed by far is Bavet (Moc Bai in Vietnam), which connects tourists from Ho Chi Minh City with Phnom Penh via a direct five- to seven-hour bus ride (no bus change at the border). These tickets are most easily booked through a travel agency or your hotel, who can also arrange taxi transportation to both cities' remote bus stations. Several bus services offer this route for between $9 and $15, including Mailinh Open Tour and Mekong Express (see Bus Services, p. 271).

The other border crossings between Vietnam and Cambodia have traditionally been less traveled because they linked outlying provinces that were difficult to reach. However, in 2009 the roads from Phnom Penh to both Ratanakiri and Mondulkiri were finally sealed all the way to the Vietnam borders, so these rarely explored and sparsely populated mountainous provinces should see greatly increased traffic.

From Ratanakiri's capital, Ban Lung, the journey to the border, which once took five hours, now takes just one. The newest border crossings are O'Yadaw (Le Tanh on the Vietnamese side), which bridges Cambodia's Ratanakiri Province to its neighboring Vietnamese province, Pleiku, and a crossing just beyond Sen Monorom, Mondulkiri, between the Cambodian town of Dak Dam and Vietnam's Dak Lac Province (Ban Ma Tout).

The Lao border at Dom Kralor can be crossed by road or river; this crossing is popular with intrepid adventurers looking to explore the stunning wilderness of southern Laos and northern Cambodia. Getting to these checkpoints is a rustic journey, though. The primary crossing is by land at Dom Kralor (or Voen Kham in Laos). Open from 7 a.m. to 5 p.m., the border offers Cambodian visas on-site. Note that Laos does not offer visa services at the border.

Navigating the Dom Kralor checkpoint from Laos to Cambodia requires a tour package from your guesthouse or travel agency in Laos—the only way to ensure transportation after crossing into Cambodia's Stung Treng Province. No buses or minivans wait at the border and cons seek to transport you to a village homestay here.

Another Laos-Cambodia crossing is by river at Koh Chheuteal Thom. However, there have been numerous reports of price gouging by boats here, and some visitors have reported not being granted Cambodian visas here. The boat from Don Khone or Don Khong to Voen Kham should cost between $2 and $6. The next leg, entailing a boat trip from Voen Kham to Stung Treng, should cost about $10.

Border Scams
In a country like Cambodia where poverty prevails, tourism is a sort of catch-22. On one hand,

tourism boosts a needy economy. On the other hand, the industry is a disconcerting parade of what many locals will never have: affluence, advantage, and privilege. This latter reason is often behind scams, as desperate and unfair as it feels to those on the receiving end. Border crossings often are a concentration of charlatans.

The Poipet checkpoint has earned a particularly nasty reputation. Travelers here have reported being hassled into changing dollars or baht into riel at outrageous rates—as much as $100 converted into the riel equivalent of $40. Other visitors have been asked to produce a SARS or health card or pay significant "bribes" for immigration to "sneak" them across the border. These health cards are not required legally. If you find yourself in this situation, attempt to keep your cool, but also stand firm, and you should get through just fine.

Poipet checkpoint also offers a free tourist shuttle bus. Seek out the official bus company stands instead, as this tourist shuttle herds tourists to the Tourist Lounge, which overcharges for bus tickets.

Poipet's scam artists even start their wiles before the border crossing from time to time. Unscrupulous bus drivers have faked breakdowns, which take place conveniently in front of a guesthouse that then charges exorbitant room rates. Such occurrences have been reported predominantly en route from Bangkok (especially the Khao San Road area) to Poipet. More commonly, however, buses stop for dinner breaks at outrageous hours, such as 1 a.m., at a food stand from which the drivers receive commission. While these food stops aren't necessarily all bad—they also provide a bathroom break and fresh air—double-check your change if you buy anything.

The most frequent scam, however, is from the immigration

officers who often overcharge a few dollars for visas (usually by about $5). Generally, however, they will reimburse the additional fee if you ask for a receipt.

Bus Services
Mai Linh Open Tour
Tel 855(0)23-211-666
(Phnom Penh)
Tel 855(0)63-762888 (Siem Reap)

Mekong Express
Tel 855(0)23-427-518
(Phnom Penh)
Tel 855(0)63-963-662
(Siem Reap)

Capitol Open Tours
Tel 855(0)23-724-104
(Phnom Penh)
Tel 855(0)23-217-627
(Siem Reap)

Other bus companies include Phnom Penh Sorya Transport, GST Express Bus Co., Hua Lian, Neak Krorhorm, Paramount Angkor Express, and Raksmey Angkor Corporation.

Train Travel
As of 2009, no rail service connects Cambodia to neighboring countries. However, a new rail line linking Singapore to China is in the planning stages.

GETTING AROUND
Getting around Cambodia is harder than one might expect due to the lack of infrastructure. Air travel is essentially limited to Siem Reap and Phnom Penh, there are no functional rail lines, and the distances between destinations can be quite far. Though the roads between major tourist destinations are quite good and the rest of the roads are developing rapidly, the majority remain unsealed and are subject to monsoon season washouts.

For traveling between towns, buses and hired cars (or shared taxis) are your primary means of transport. While there once were boat services to many destinations, road improvements have ended nearly all boat transportation except around the Tonle Sap and along rivers in remote provinces where roads have yet to reach.

Within towns, the standard form of transportation is the tuk-tuk, a small motorbike with a covered carriage on the back. Motorbike taxis are also available for quick rides. Motorbike rentals are available in a few locations, making travel a bit more convenient, if dangerous. Larger 250cc and 400cc dirt bikes allow more experienced adventurers to explore the most remote areas of Cambodia. Bicycles can also be rented in many towns and make travel around smaller towns quite enjoyable. A few organizations even allow you to ride bicycles between towns.

All of the following information is not only subject to change, it is almost certain to do so. Speak with a tour agent or your hotel or guesthouse about current travel times, prices, and transportation options.

By Airplane
Domestic Flights
In 2009, Cambodia Angkor Air became the new national flag carrier, connecting Siem Reap with Phnom Penh. They offer codeshare flights to and from Cambodia and Saigon on Vietnam Airlines. You also can fly between Phnom Penh and Siem Reap on Bangkok Airways. The 50-minute route is flown daily for about $30 to $70 each way. Even with the 30-minute drive to the Phnom Penh airport and predeparture check-in, the flight is far superior to the six-hour bus ride. (Perhaps consider taking the boat from Phnom Penh to Siem Reap and

then flying back.) Sadly, the flight pattern doesn't take in any spectacular views of the temples.

A small, private airline: Mission Aviation Fellowship (MAF) flies to other provinces, such as secluded Ratanakiri and Mondulkiri. Be forewarned that MAF flies a GA-8 Airvan, a small plane holding eight seats at most and very little luggage. The plane is maintained routinely, and the experience offers some of the best views over Cambodia.

Airlines
Bangkok Airways
Tel 855(0)23-722545 (to 47)
www.bangkokair.com

Cambodia Angkor Air
Tel 855(0)23-990-840
www.cambodiaangkorair.com

Mission Aviation Fellowship
Tel 855(0)23-880-060 or
855(0)12-879-426
www.mafcambodia.org

By Automobile/Taxi
By far, the easiest way to get around Cambodia is renting a car. Car rentals here come in three varieties: day trips out of a certain town or city, multiday excursions, and trips between two destinations (taxis). Rentals almost always include a driver, who can typically speak some English and knows about the places you intend to see. You can ask your driver to stop at interesting sights along the way or visit attractions off the beaten path. That said, most cars are Toyota Camrys that have some difficulty on the more rugged roads. Comfortable travel to more remote provinces may require a more expensive 4WD vehicle.

For day trips, the best way to hire a car is through your guesthouse or hotel. While prices may be slightly higher than if you shop around for your own car and driver,

the time saved is worth the added expense. Talk with a few local tour operators if you are looking for a day trip out of Phnom Penh or Siem Reap, though, where prices and trips are highly variable. Gasoline is more expensive in Cambodia than in the United States, so this expense is factored into your trip's cost. The more driving you do, the more you should expect to pay. If you are looking to save some money, some guesthouses will arrange for you to join other travelers on a day trip.

A multiday excursion in a private car is a great way to see Cambodia, since you can design your own itinerary. Prices for multiday tours need to be negotiated with a car rental company, who will factor in the cost of gas and charge you an additional fee for providing the driver with room and board (typically around $10–$20/day). If your trip terminates in a town other than where you began, you will have to pay for the driver to return home. Ask your hotel or a tour operator for a couple car companies to compare prices.

Finally, taxis in the traditional sense are quite uncommon in Cambodia. Taxis will take you from the airport to your hotel and a few meter taxis are appearing on the streets of Phnom Penh, but they are by far the exception rather than the rule. In Cambodia, a tuk-tuk, not a taxi, is how you get around town. Taxis here are cars or trucks that will take you on a one-way trip from one town to another. Taxis can either be private or shared with other passengers. A private taxi is more expensive but significantly more comfortable. If you get a share-taxi, expect to be crammed in a car or truck with as many people as can possibly fit. You can pay for "three seats" for two passengers, which will still seem like 1.5 seats. If you don't want to pay for the whole car yourself, go through your hotel or guesthouse to find another person or two to share the cost of a private taxi. If you are really thrifty, you can ride in the bed of a pickup truck with the local passengers, luggage, and cargo. It's cheaper, but not very comfortable or safe.

Car Rental

Lyna-CarRental.Com
18ABE, St. 460 Phnom Penh
Tel 855(0)12-924-517
www.lyna-carrental.com

By Boat

Travel by boat was once the best way to get around Cambodia. Waterways function as natural highways for the majority of the population who still reside on or near the Mekong River, Tonle Sap River and Lake, and numerous smaller tributaries. In recent years, major road development throughout the country has made much boat travel obsolete. Ferry services between Koh Kong and Sihanoukville, Kratie and Phnom Penh, and Kompong Chhnang and Phnom Penh, for example, no longer offer commercial routes.

Nonetheless, traveling by boat is one of the most enjoyable ways to see the country and its plentiful rivers and lakes. Operators such as Compagnie Fluviale du Mekong offer multiday voyages up the Mekong from Ho Chi Minh City in Vietnam to Phnom Penh, and then up the Tonle Sap to Siem Reap, stopping at cultural and natural attractions along the way. Speed boats between Phnom Penh and Siem Reap offer similar voyages, either with or without stops. Nonstop, the boat trip between Phnom Penh and Siem Reap takes roughly as long as the bus does (5–6 hours). You can climb on the roof and get some sun, though, and the scenery is more interesting, particularly the ride up the Tonle Sap River and the floating villages along the way.

More spectacular but uncomfortably longer is the journey

from Siem Reap to Battambang. Despite the promises of the ticket salesman that it only takes five to six hours, it can take up to ten, depending on water levels and the boat type. Nonetheless, the boat passes through floating villages and flooded forests and is a wonderful and unique voyage.

For transportation information regarding ferries between Siem Reap and Phnom Penh or Battambang, contact your hotel or guesthouse for prices and times.

Compagnie Fluviale du Mekong
?1? Sisowath Quay, Phnom Penh
Tel 855(0)12-240-859
www.cfmekong.com

By Bus

The bus is the most popular way to get around Cambodia, because it is the most affordable. A number of bus companies provide service between the major towns. The more popular the route is with foreigners, the more comfortable the journey is likely to be. The three major operators between Siem Reap and Phnom Penh offer onboard toilets, for example, while buses from Kratie to Ban Lung fill the aisle with local passengers on little plastic stools and stop occasionally for passengers to squat in the bushes. More expensive buses like Mekong Express are more likely to show American movies (as opposed to Khmer karaoke videos). All buses stop at restaurants with whom they have contracts. Many of these bus trips include lunch at the halfway point, though it's often a better idea to pack a picnic lunch—Western stomachs may have difficulty with roadside restaurant food. In most towns buses leave from a single location to which any tuk-tuk driver can easily bring you. Buses from Phnom Penh depart from all

over the city, though, with each bus company departing from a different location. Ask for a pickup from the bus company when booking your ticket at your hotel or guesthouse or ask about getting a tuk-tuk to take you to the proper departure point.

Distances and average travel times by bus:
Phnom Penh to Siem Reap:
   197 miles (317 km), 6 hours
Phnom Penh to Sihanoukville:
   143 miles (230 km), 3–4 hours
Phnom Penh to Battambang:
   182 miles (293 km), 5 hours
Phnom Penh to Kratie:
   216 miles (348 km), 7 hours
Phnom Penh to Kampot:
   92 miles (148 km), 4 hours
Phnom Penh to Sen Monorom:
   230 miles (370 km), 7–8 hours
Siem Reap to Poipet (Thai Border):
   94 miles (152 km), 4 hours
Siem Reap to Battambang:
   106 miles (171 km), 5 hours
Sihanoukville to Koh Kong:
   143 miles (230 km), 4 hours
Sihanoukville to Kampot:
   65 miles (105 km), 4 hours

Bus Companies
Angkor Express:
Phnom Penh
121 Sisowath Blvd.
Tel 855(0)23-992-788

Siem Reap
Tel 855(0)99-842-946 or
855(0)92-523-229

Sihanoukville
Tel 855(0)34-933-796 or
855(0)92-638-699

Mekong Express:
Phnom Penh
87 Sisowath Quay; corner
of St. 102
Tel 855(0)23-427-518

Siem Reap
14A Sivatha Blvd.
Tel 855(0)63-963-662

Sihanoukville
Sihanoukville Bus Station
Tel 855(0)34-934-189

Paramount Angkor Express:
Phnom Penh
24E0 St. 102, near Wat Phnom
Tel 855(0)23-427-567

Poipet
Bus Station at Poipet Market
Tel 855(0)12-366-337

Battambang
In front of LAE Gasoline Station
Tel 855(0)92-575-572

By Train

Domestically, trains make a slow voyage between Phnom Penh and Battambang only twice per week. The only other option for traveling on the rails is bamboo railway cars (see sidebar p. 173).

By Tuk-Tuk

Hands down the most popular "public" transportation in Cambodian towns and cities, the tuk-tuk is unavoidable. This can be one of the highlights or lowlights of your trip. Particularly in Phnom Penh, Siem Reap, and Sihanoukville, tuk-tuk drivers relentlessly offer their services with the sole aim of charging you as high a fare as possible. Fares should be agreed upon beforehand, a process that invariably includes the driver bemoaning how expensive gas is, how far it is to your destination, and how every passenger must pay separate fares. Gas really is expensive, but fares from one side of Phnom Penh to the other should cost no more than $2, even if your tuk-tuk is packed with ten passengers, perhaps a few pigs, and maybe even a broken-down motorbike. In Siem Reap fares across town should cost $1, or $2 if you are heading farther afield (on National Highway 6 toward

the airport) or it is particularly late at night, regardless of the number of passengers. Firmly explain what you are willing to pay; if a driver disagrees, turn to walk away. He will adjust his price or the next tuk-tuk will gladly accept your business.

Many tuk-tuk drivers are hardworking Cambodians who are simply trying to make a living. A good tuk-tuk driver offers more than a hassle-free negotiation; he may become a new friend, eager to guide you around town, teach you a few words in Khmer, and make the experience of sightseeing from an open-air chariot a memorable one.

Tuk-tuks have roll-down "walls" that are quickly deployable in the event of rain, but drivers often don't think about their ability to protect riders from dust. A *krama* or other scarf is a useful shield against inhaling dust, though many provincial tuk-tuk rides—from Siem Reap to Banteay Srei temple, for example— are likely to leave you covered in a fine layer of red dirt. Ask to put the "walls" down or take a car if you are particularly sensitive to dust.

Other Modes of Travel

By Bicycle

A leisurely bicycle ride around provincial capitals such as Pursat or Battambang is a pleasant way to pass a day; a ride around the temples of Angkor is magical. Many hotels and guesthouses rent bicycles to guests for $2 to $15 per day, depending on whether it's a decrepit Chinese one-speed, or a Western 12-speed.

A number of companies offer tours, as much of the country is flat and the major roads smooth. While none will rent you a bike and send you off on your own, so it's better to join an expedition with a leader who can show you attractions along the way. Those with their own bikes will enjoy biking here. Avoid riding

at night, as vehicles often have no lights and foreign bicyclists are occasionally run down.

Bike Companies
Grasshopper Adventures
Thailand/International: 66(0)87-929-5208
U.S.: (818)912-7101
www.grasshopperadventures.com

Pepy Ride
No. 188, Salakanseng Village, Siem Reap, off National Highway 6 toward the airport
Tel 855(0)12-474-150
www.pepyride.org

By Off-road Motorbike

If you wish to see the "real" Cambodia, the remote villages and spectacular wilderness where few tourists venture, you need to get a 250cc off-road motorbike (aka dirt bike). A number of operators provide rentals and tours on off-road bikes, either for day trips from Siem Reap, Phnom Penh, or Ban Lung to nearby temples and rural villages or for multiday adventures over challenging terrain in the most remote regions of the country. No license is required and prior experience is not necessary, but conditions vary greatly. Day trips from Phnom Penh or Siem Reap are doable by novices, provided the outfit you rent from is aware of your lack of skills. However, motorbike travel here is some of the most extreme riding in the world, so it is likely to be challenging for even the most experienced riders. Most dirt-bike companies provide gear for riders and will arrange lodging along the way (occasionally in a hammock strung between trees). Do not undertake a multiday excursion into remote areas without adequate insurance that covers motorbike injuries and emergency medical evacuation.

Dirt-Bike Companies:
Dancing Roads
66C St. 368 (W of St. 163),
Phnom Penh
Tel 855(0)12-822-803
www.dancingroads.com

Jungle Cross
Sauna Garden, main street of Koh
Kong town
Tel 855(0)15-601-633
www.junglecross.com

Norden House
Yak Laom Rd., Ban Lung, Ratanakiri
Tel 855(0)12-880-327
www.nordenhouseyaklom.com

Siem Reap Dirtbikes
Tel 855(0)99-823-216
www.siemreapdirtbikes.com

By Moto-taxi
Moto-taxis or "motos," as they
are commonly known, are small
100cc motorbikes that can whisk
you around. In Phnom Penh,
where chaotic traffic may keep
your tuk-tuk log-jammed for an
hour, a moto can weave in and out
of traffic, often on the wrong side
of the street. While this option
gets you to your destination much
more quickly, it could also end
in a bloody mess. Many expats
who ride motos bring their own
helmets. In smaller cities motos are
great for short day trips, such
as the ride to the Irrawaddy dolphin site outside of Kratie. While
motos are slightly cheaper than
tuk-tuks, they may not be worth
the additional risk.

You can rent small motorbikes
to explore on your own. Considering the four motorbike deaths per
day in Phnom Penh, it's inadvisable
to rent one there. In Siem Reap, it's
not legal to rent them. Sihanoukville
is the best place for exploring on a
motorbike. Even there, rentals are
occasionally outlawed, but often
a decent bike can be procured for
around $5 a day. You don't need a

license, but you will be expected to
turn over your passport as collateral.
If renting a motorbike, any damage,
even scratches you may not have
been involved in, will be expected to
be paid in full by you (you may be
able to negotiate, but remember to
keep your cool). If you are involved
in an accident, it will almost invariably be your fault. You may be
forced to pay for damages to the
vehicle that crashed into you and
perhaps even the policeman who
arrives to "file a report." Make sure
your insurance covers motorbike
accidents and wear closed-toe
shoes, jeans, and a helmet to mini-
mize injury. And finally, make sure
your motorbike comes with a padlock or chain and use the wheel lock
(turning the key all the way to the
left while the handlebars are turned
likewise) to prevent someone from
pushing your bike away when you
have left it unattended. There have
been rumors of bikes being "stolen"
by the rental company using a spare
key to make off with the vehicle.
Mind your motorbikes well.

Harley Tours Cambodia
If you are really into motorcycle
touring, Harley Tours offers a
fun way to make a weekend trip
from Phnom Penh to Siem Reap
or Sihanoukville.
Tel 855(0)12-948-529
www.harleycambodia.com

PRACTICAL ADVICE
Communication
Internet Access
Internet service is widely available
throughout Cambodia—even the
smallest provincial towns have
at least one Internet café. While
Internet speeds vary, from painfully slow in the smaller provinces
to surprisingly fast in Phnom
Penh, service is still affected by
weather conditions and frequent
power outages. Prices vary from
50 cents per hour to $2 per hour,

though some cafés in Phnom
Penh and Siem Reap offer free
Internet from in-house computers
and complimentary Wi-Fi. Those
traveling with netbooks should
have no trouble finding places to
log on for free to send emails or
call home using Skype.

Free Internet access is available
at the following locations:

Corner 33 Café
E1 Sothearos Blvd. (corner of
St. 178 by National Museum)
Phnom Penh

Le Tigre de Papier
Pub St., Old Market Area, Svay
Dangkum Commune, Siem Reap

The Blue Pumpkin
No. 365, opposite Pub St., Old
Market Area, Svay Dangkum
Commune, Siem Reap

The Bus Stop
149 2nd Rd., Battambang

Post Offices
Cambodia is practically the poster-
child for nations where you wonder if your package will ever arrive
at its intended destination. If simply sending a postcard, worldwide
delivery costs around 2,000 riel
(50 cents) and your postcard is
likely to arrive several weeks later.
While rural post offices are little
more than one-room affairs that
lack street addresses or even zip
codes, the office in Phnom Penh
is a proper post office with beautiful colonial architecture. Mail
sent from anywhere in Cambodia
must eventually pass through
Phnom Pehn, so all mail has a fair
chance of arriving safely. Shipping
souvenirs or surplus baggage is far
more expensive (and unreliable)
from Cambodia than from Thailand, especially if you include the
additional expense levied by some
postal agents on foreigners. If you
must send a parcel home or need

something delivered to you, consider using one of the following couriers, who deliver throughout Cambodia and provide tracking numbers for packages worldwide. If you urgently need mail delivered to you, it is best to have it sent to you care of your hotel (written in bold block letters). Inform the hotel that you are expecting a package or letter.

UPS
30E0 Sihanouk Blvd., Phnom Penh
Tel 855(0)23-219-213
www.ups.com

EMS (Express Mail Service)
Phnom Penh Post Office, corner of St. 13 & St. 102
Tel 855(0)23-725-209 or 855(0)23-723-511
www.ems.com.kh

Phnom Penh Post Office
Corner of St. 13 & St. 102
Phnom Penh

Telephones
By far the cheapest, most convenient way to call home, Skype lets you to make long-distance calls over the Internet (www.skype.com). Most Internet cafés in Cambodia have Skype headsets, though for security purposes its best to set up a Skype account from home, purchasing minutes with a major credit card. When signing on to Skype at a public computer, uncheck the "sign me in when Skype starts" box and to sign out when you leave, or the next patron may use up all your credit.

If you aren't computer savvy enough to figure out Skype, or need frequent phone communication, 3G and GSM compatible foreign phones should work in Cambodia, though roaming rates are far higher than your alternatives. Tourist SIM cards are sold at the international airports as well as selected hotels and stores. These cards are good

for 12 days and the price includes credit that can be used for local and international calls. However, once your minutes are up, the card will no longer receive calls and cannot be refilled. Most hotels also allow you to make long-distance calls, though rates vary widely.

An additional option, calling cards, are affordable and widely available at convenience stores in Phnom Penh and Siem Reap. In the outlying provinces, calling cards are harder to come by.

When calling Cambodia from overseas, it is necessary to dial the country code, 855, and then leave out the following zero. If making calls within Cambodia, it is unnecessary to dial 855, simply begin with dialing the zero.

Conversions
1 kilo = 2.2 pounds
1 liter = 0.2 U.S. gallons
1 meter = 1.1 yards (3.3 feet)
1 kilometer = 0.6 mile

Electricity
Cambodian voltage is 230, alternating at 50 cycles per second (50Hz). This means American and most European electrical devices will require a voltage converter or adapter. The standard Cambodian outlet accepts a flat blade plug shape (two vertical lines), similar to the American type.

Cambodia has frequent power outages, so save your work often. If using a laptop, keep your battery inserted even while plugged in.

Health
Cambodia's health care system lags far behind the health care systems in Western countries, but don't let this sad reality hold you back. Rather, prepare before your departure: Get the necessary vaccinations and malarial prophylactics and communicate with your doctor about what else you

need to pack and understand.

Predeparture preparations will prevent or at least ameliorate the most common discomforts inherent to this part of the world. The most prevalent trouble is the dreaded upset stomach, which seems to have become somewhat of a required initiation when roving Cambodia. If you find yourself needing medical care, the only somewhat reasonable care is found in Phnom Penh or Siem Reap. Even these clinics do not always meet Western medical standards. Medical facilities in rural areas are generally out of the question. Unless your condition is severe, you'll probably be better off self-treating until you reach Phnom Penh or Siem Reap. For severe illness or injury, use medical evacuation insurance purchased before your trip to get you to a hospital in Bangkok or Singapore.

Most important, support your immune system by maintaining good health: eat nutritious food, drink plenty of bottled water, and get plenty of sleep. This textbook advice is sometimes easily forgotten when distracted by travel.

For the latest health care information, check the Centers for Disease Control and Prevention website: www.cdc.gov/travel/destinationcambodia.aspx.

General Precautions
Make sure you're healthy before heading to Cambodia. A functional immune system is key, so maintain your wellness. Bring all your routine and precautionary medications, multivitamins, injections, inhalers—anything you might possibly need, healthwise.

It may seem elementary, but the best way to avoid disease and germs is by washing your hands often. Bring antibacterial soap from home. Keep a first aid kit handy to treat cuts immediately, as open wounds can develop infection easily in the dusty, humid environment.

Drink at least three to four liters of bottled water daily to prevent dehydration, a common malady in Cambodia. Don't allow thirst—itself an indication of dehydration—to sneak up on you. Dehydration is a particular danger if you have traveler's diarrhea. Stay hydrated, even if that means sucking on ice cubes made from bottled water until your stomach can handle more.

Finally, to cover what you can't prevent, invest in insurance, including emergency evacuation (see Insurance, p. 267). In Cambodia, clinics and hospitals expect cash payments for treatment. In a medical emergency, contact the International SOS clinic (see Emergencies, p. 281).

Infectious Diseases

The daunting list of potential infectious diseases in this part of the world includes cholera, tuberculosis, fungal infections, bilharzia (schistosomiasis), giardiasis, dysentery, typhoid fever, dengue fever, hepatitis A and B, Japanese encephalitis, intestinal worms, malaria, and sexually transmitted infections (Cambodia has the highest rate of HIV/AIDS in Asia).

Also, though the bird flu (avian influenza) hysteria has calmed, human cases were reported in Cambodia during the 2004–2005 epidemics. Though human cases are rare, travelers should avoid bird farms, markets, or other places where contact with fowl or pigs might occur.

It is imperative to talk to your doctor for up-to-date specifics regarding these diseases, especially as some, such as cholera or Japanese encephalitis, may necessitate additional vaccinations depending on the time of year you travel.

Malaria and dengue fever pose particular problems year-round:

Malaria

Cambodia is a disaster zone for malaria, but not because the entire country is at risk. The tricky inconsistencies of malaria are the problem—just when people think they're safe, they're not.

Though rare in the West, malaria remains one of the world's biggest killers. It is contracted by specific infected mosquitoes. The CDC warns that, as of 2008, there is no malarial risk in Phnom Penh or immediately around the Tonle Sap Lake. However, malaria is found just north of the Tonle Sap in Siem Reap and the Angkor Archaeological Park. As this puts most travelers at risk, you should take prophylactic drugs regularly as prescribed and protect yourself against mosquito bites.

Malarial prophylactic drugs are recommended as prescribed, generally during and after your travels. Talk to your physician about which malarial drug is right for you, as the medicines have various side effects. Also, different malarial drugs are recommended in different regions of Cambodia, depending on the dominant strain of malaria. Antimalarial medications do not prevent malaria, but rather decrease the risk of the disease developing into severe or fatal stages.

Easily mistaken for the flu, malarial symptoms include fever, chills, sweats, headaches, diarrhea, upset stomach, and achy muscles and joints. It is improbable that a the onset of a fever during the first week of travels is malaria, as the disease can take anywhere from a week to a year to manifest. If malaria is suspected, though, seek medical attention in Phnom Penh or Siem Reap. Even after returning home, be cautious about fevers, which you should report to your physician in context of your travels.

Dengue Fever

A mosquito-borne virus, dengue fever is common to Cambodia. Nicknamed "break bone fever,"

the malady can be very painful, though it is rarely fatal. Since there are no vaccinations or prophylactic drugs against dengue, be extra vigilant about protecting yourself from mosquito bites. The mosquitoes that carry dengue are daytime feeders. They are found throughout Cambodia in both rural and urban areas (including Phnom Penh), mostly during and immediately after the wet season.

Initially symptoms of dengue fever, such as sudden fever, headaches, nausea, vomiting, and joint and muscle pains, often are mistaken for influenza. Closely monitor any fevers, especially in Cambodia, where health treatment is often hit or miss. After three or four days of dengue fever, a small rash of red spots will appear. Seek immediate treatment, if you haven't already.

To ward off mosquito bites, wear long-sleeve shirts and long pants, particularly around dawn and dusk and in shady forested areas. As the heat can be fierce, bring flying-insect spray that contains pyrethroid insecticide. Use this spray to clear rooms of flying insects, including any lingering mosquitoes. The CDC recommends sleeping under nets treated with permethrin if you're not sleeping in air-conditioned or well-screened rooms. Check your net for holes and close the net securely. Finally, consider a bug repellent containing 30 to 50 percent DEET (not recommended for children, however). It may be best to bring your own mosquito net and repellent from home, as many nets in Cambodia are not maintained and repellents are sometimes ineffective knockoffs.

Pharmacies

Pharmacies are found at nearly every intersection in Cambodia's cities, towns, and even floating villages. These pharmacies sell almost all treatments imaginable—from antimalarial tablets to exceptional-looking traditional powders. Unfortunately, this convenience creates a false sense of security, because many pharmacies actually carry imitation drugs for brand prices. Up to 90 percent of these drugs are fake. U-Care Pharmacies, which double as a convenience store and carry real imported drugs from France, the United States, and Thailand are found in major cities like Phnom Penh and Siem Reap and are starting to pop up in provincial capitals like Battambang and Sihanoukville.

For self-treatable discomforts, it's worthwhile to stock up on medicines—anything from acetaminophen to antimalarial tablets—at these stores, open from 7 a.m. to 8 p.m. Note that those working behind the counter are rarely pharmacists; usually, they're salespeople with minimal, if any, English skills. U-Care is where you want to shop for medical supplies, mosquito sprays, sunblocks, etc.

Vaccinations

Though most vaccinations are not legally required to enter Cambodia, most, if not all, are highly advisable. If coming to Cambodia directly from Africa or South America, you are bound by law to get a yellow fever vaccine.

The CDC recommends vaccinations for hepatitis A, hepatitis B, typhoid, rabies, and Japanese encephalitis, as well as boosters for measles, rubella, diphtheria, and polio, all of which are still prevalent in Cambodia. Some vaccinations, such as Japanese encephalitis, are particularly important if you plan to visit rural farming areas; discuss potential side effects of this vaccination (which does not guarantee immunity) with your doctor. Plan your vaccinations well in advance, as some require multiple injections over an extended time period, such

as rabies. Others take effect four to six weeks post-injection and your doctor will need to monitor you during that time.

Water

Tap water is not potable; always drink water from a secured bottle. Do not drink from a bottle with an broken seal. If anything seems amiss, stick to some bottled familiarity, like Coca-Cola. Coconut water, straight from the coconut, is another safe alternative. Safe bottled water is readily found throughout the country, at convenience stores, markets, restaurants, and even roadside stalls (look for the large, orange coolers).

Ice is usually not served in drinks unless requested. If you're sensitive to stomach problems, avoid ice.

Be wary of fruits and vegetables rinsed in water, as well. Try to stick to peeled fruits and vegetables—mangoes, bananas, peeled cucumbers—or rinse the produce yourself with bottled water. Conveniently, most fruit from street vendors is peeled and thus safe.

Brushing your teeth with tap water is a gamble. Many travelers rinse with tap water, but some suffer mild gastrointestinal problems.

Holidays

January 1—International New Year's Day: A new celebration incorporated as a national holiday in the last decade. Cambodia celebrates its own New Year in April.

January 7—Victory Day over Genocide: Celebrates the 1979 overthrow of the Khmer Rouge.

February—Meak Bochea Day: Full moon holiday celebrating a gathering of monks who attended a lecture by the Buddha.

March 8—International Women's Day

April 13–15—Khmer New Year Celebration (Bonn Chaul Chhnam): This three-day celebration marks the harvest season's end through playing traditional games and cleaning their homes as the symbolic beginning of a New Year.

May 1—International Labor Day

May—Bonn Visaka Bochea: On the sixth full moon of the lunar calendar, Buddhists honor the birth and enlightenment of the Buddha.

Early to mid-May—Royal Plowing Ceremony (Bonn Chroat Preah Nongkoal): The date of this holiday celebrating the start of the sowing season varies based on the lunar calendar and royal astrological predictions. The King of Meakh and Queen Me Hour carry out a traditional plowing ceremony in front of the National Museum. The holiday ends with a soothsayer interpreting what the Royal Ox—an auspicious creature in Khmer culture possessing astrological powers—ate, which prophesies the success of the upcoming year's harvests.

May 13–15—King Norodom Sihamoni's Birthday Celebration: One of the most important non-public Cambodian holidays, this three-day celebration honors the king with festivities nationwide.

June 1—International Children's Day

June 18—Queen-Mother Norodom Monineath Sihanouk's Birthday

September 24—Constitution Day and Recoronation of H.M. Preah Bat Samdech Preah Norodom Sihanouk

Late September to early October—Spirit Commemoration

Festival (Bonn Pchum Ben): This important traditional festival is a three-day public holiday. It is the culmination of a 15-day period (based on the lunar calendar) in which people return to their home villages to visit seven pagodas to provide offerings to the spirits of their relatives and food to monks. Temple visits occur in the wee hours of the morning, with candlelight processions offering rice balls. If the spirits do not locate their families during the temple visits, they may curse their descendants for the year.

October 29—Royal Coronation of King Norodom Sihamoni

October 31—King-Father Norodom Sihanouk's Birthday

November—Water and Moon Festival (Bonn Om Touk): The most extravagant of Cambodia's holidays, the Water Festival features boat races down the Mekong River in Phnom Penh in late November (based on the lunar calendar). It marks the beginning of the Tonle Sap's seasonal reversal of direction and of the fishing season. It's believed that the festivities originally commemorated historic, heroic river battles. The races attract over 200 crews from the city, the provinces, and even internationally, crowding the city with parties and fireworks.

November 9—Independence Day: Celebrates Cambodia's 1953 independence from France.

December 10—International Human Rights Day

Liquor Laws

Cambodia's legal drinking age is 18. Alcohol sales sometimes are banned during election weekends and special religious holidays. Otherwise, alcohol can be purchased throughout the week at central groceries, like Lucky's, or corner stores.

Most restaurants, even street stalls, serve alcohol. In Phnom Penh and Siem Reap, bars generally stay open all night, closing only when the crowds disperse. Small-town bars, however, generally close at 10 p.m., except for the occasional karaoke bars, which stay open late into the night, generally on weekends.

Media
Magazines

Several local magazines cover Khmer lifestyle and events for tourist and expat readers. The monthly Phnom Penh *AsiaLIFE Guide* features a detailed events calendar, as well as colorful sections featuring controversies, food and drink, and shopping and fashion. For restaurant and bar addresses, but not much more, find the guide's online version at *www.asialifecambodia.com.*

Another worthwhile magazine is *Touchstone Magazine,* published quarterly in both English and Khmer by the NGO Heritage Watch. This guide offers its slant on preserving Cambodia's culture through features, event calendars, honest restaurant reviews, and information on responsible tourism. Again, find these free periodicals at city markets, restaurants, and cafés.

Newspapers

There are two major Cambodian newspapers: the *Phnom Penh Post* (*www.PhnomPenhPost.com*) and the *Cambodia Daily* (*www.Cambodia Daily.com*). Both are published daily from Monday to Friday in English with a Khmer insert. They are found readily at corner stores, supermarkets, and many restaurants and cafés. Both papers cover international and domestic issues, and include local classified sections and event advertisements. The Phnom Penh Post does not publish on weekends; the *Cambodia Daily,* however, publishes a weekend edition in periodical format, the *Cambodia Daily Weekend.*

Tourist Periodicals

Several periodicals are published specifically for tourists as small, durable guides. Canby Publications issues worthwhile city guides for Phnom Penh, Siem Reap, Sihanoukville, Koh Kong, Kampot, Kep, and Battambang, as well as a Ratanakiri/Mondulkiri Provinces edition. With localized reviews, information, maps, and features, these glossy guides prove very useful in hand or online at: *www.canbypublications.com.*

Pocket Guide also prints area-specific handbooks. These are extensive leaflets of advertisements and bar and restaurant listings. They also feature handy maps and worthwhile information, such as which restaurants accept credit cards. Pocket Guides include a drinking and dining guide (*D&D: Drinking Dining*) and an activities guide (*O&A: Out and About*).

You can find guides at your hotel's information desk or at local restaurants and bars.

Money Matters

Officially, the Cambodian currency is the riel, but the U.S. dollar is also de facto legal tender for almost all transactions in Cambodia. Since the exchange rate usually hovers just above or below 4,000 riel per U.S. dollar, this is the accepted norm for conversion. Also, Thai baht are accepted frequently along the Thai border, especially in the border crossing towns like Poipet and Koh Kong. In recent years, the baht has fluctuated somewhere between 30 and 37 baht to the dollar.

Riel bank notes are printed in

Khmer and English numerals in varying sizes, colors, and denominations, including 50, 100, 200, 500, 1,000, 2,000, 5,000, 10,000, 20,000, 50,000, and 100,000 riels. A 50-riel note is worth just over a penny, while a 100,000-riel bill is valued at $25. Only 100-, 500-, and 1,000-riel notes are used regularly and most establishments use them as small change (under a dollar). Otherwise, dollars are standard.

ATMs dispense U.S. dollars and are found throughout Cambodia's tourist destinations. Most machines accept major credit cards (Visa and MasterCard) and international ATM card networks, like Cirrus, Plus, and Maestro, which will be marked. If you're headed off the major tourist routes, do not expect many ATMs. Instead, prepare by bringing enough cash, as business in these areas won't accept credit cards either.

No matter where you are, inspect your change closely, as many establishments strictly do not accept dollar bills that have been torn or damaged even in the slightest. Also, counterfeit dollars have made their way into Cambodia's monetary circulation, so filter through bills for obvious counterfeits, as well. If you come across bills that are torn, damaged, or fake, ask for replacements.

Most banks are open Monday to Friday from 8 a.m. to 4 p.m., though some have morning business hours on Saturdays. In the major tourist destinations, there are 24-hour ATMs available and usually working. Most banks offer cash advances on credit cards—most frequently with Visa—but foreigners require passport identification. Banks also exchange currencies and cash traveler's checks, but rates can be steep. Major hotels also usually accept traveler's checks, but, again, charges may be costly, a minimum of 2 percent. Often, money changers offer a slightly better rates.

The most common international bank is Western Union,

which is linked to Cambodia Asia Bank (CAB). These CAB Western Unions (www.cab.com.kh) are in all major towns, including Phnom Penh, Siem Reap, Sihanoukville, Battambang, Kompong Cham, Svay Rieng, and Banteay Meanchey. Branch hours vary, but most are open from 7:30 a.m. to 9 p.m.

The other major international bank is ANZ Royal Bank (www.anz royal.com), which helpfully features branches in some destinations not yet covered by Western Union, including Poipet, Takeo, and Kompong Cham. ANZ also has branches in Phnom Penh, Siem Reap, Battambang, and Sihanoukville, with ATMs with international access.

Opening Times

Cambodians are pretty laid-back when it comes to regular business hours. Other than banks, visitors shouldn't expect places to be open at the hours listed. Businesses, museums, and government offices tend to open as early as 7 or 8 a.m., take 2-hour lunches (anytime between 11 a.m. and 3 p.m.), and close around 4 or 5 p.m. Many banks have weekend hours, typically in the morning. Museums are frequently closed on weekends despite signs indicating otherwise. Your guesthouse or hotel staff and competent tuk-tuk drivers should know the actual hours for local businesses. In the smaller provincial capitals everything shuts down by 10 p.m. In Phnom Penh and Siem Reap, many spots remain open during lunch and late into the evening and even accept business on the weekends. The exception is during the major festivals, such as Bonn Pchum Ben, Water and Moon Festival, and Khmer New Year when Cambodians close up shop and either travel to their home villages or to Phnom Penh.

Religion

Cambodia's predominant religion is Theravada Buddhism. In addition to Buddhist beliefs, most Cambodians are highly superstitious and they continue to believe in a variety of spirits (see pp. 47–51). Minority groups in the country practice Christianity, Islam, Hinduism, and animist spirit worship. Buddhism is highly tolerant of other religions and there are a number of places for practitioners of various religions to worship.

Anglican Church
21 St. 294, Phnom Penh
In English 10 a.m. Sun.

Baha'i Prayer
7 St. 184, Phnom Penh
www.bahai.org
9 a.m. Sun.

Baptist Church
Russian Cultural Center, near Norodom Blvd. & St. 222, Phnom Penh; In English 10 a.m. Sun.

Catholic Mass
No. 20, Street 71, Phnom Penh
In English at 5 p.m. Sat.

The Church of Jesus Christ of Latter-day Saints:
267 St. 63, Phnom Penh
Tel 855(0)23-214-081
In English 10 a.m. Sun.
757 Salakanseng Village, Siem Reap
In Khmer with English translation, 8 a.m. Sun.

Rest Rooms

Visiting a rest room can be quite an experience in southeast Asia. Westerners will find familiar toilets only in establishments like hotels, Western-style restaurants, museums, and government buildings. Otherwise, prepare yourself for the "squat toilet," a floor-level basin you squat over. Since these facilities are standard for most locals, they're encountered in culturally authentic destinations, like outdoor markets or ferryboats.

Also, toilet paper is rare, even in some nicer establishments, so bring your own. Rarer still are functional soap dispensers and paper towels or hand dryers. Consider packing gel sanitizer, such as Purell Hand Sanitizer, and a small hand towel. The bucket of water with the ladle is used to flush squat toilets. The hose next to Western-style toilets is a type of manual bidet, which is a convenient way to clean off if you have forgotten your toilet paper.

Security

With prevalent poverty, Cambodia has pickpockets and beggars, especially in Phnom Penh and Siem Reap. Use standard traveling precautions, such as fitted money belts and tightly secured bags. Belt packs and backpacks are easy targets for pickpockets. Leave valuables in hotel safes and lock luggage. Do not leave purses or bags unattended in public places or even while traveling in tuk tuks—grab-and-go drive-bys are common in the bigger cities.

Time Differences

Cambodia is +7 GMT (Greenwich mean time). Since Cambodia does not observe daylight savings time, the time difference with most of the United States changes by one hour when the United States adjusts its clocks. In the winter, Cambodia is 12 hours ahead of the East Coast and 15 hours ahead of the West Coast. In the summer, Cambodia is 13 hours and 16 hours ahead, respectively. Confused? Visit www.timeanddate.com/worldclock.

Tipping

Tipping is not standard, but it's becoming more common with the rise of tourism. Even major hotels and restaurants include only a 5 to 10 percent service charge. Tipping is not required, though a tip of $1 or so is greatly appreciated (it's often the equivalent to your server's entire day's pay).

Travelers with Disabilities

Although Cambodia has one of the highest disability rates in the world, it has very few services to accommodate disabled travelers. A few hotels have installed elevators, but only have stairs. Sidewalks are frequently cracked and uneven and are often high off the street to prevent flooding. Most temples around Angkor feature steep stairways with no handrails; even flat temples require visitors to scramble over debris or the occasional root of a massive tree. Visitors with moderate back or knee problems often struggle to get around many parts of Cambodia.

Visitor Information

While Cambodia has tourist information offices in every provincial capital, they are almost invariably closed. If one is actually open and staffed by an English-speaking representative, it often still has very little in the way of helpful information. The exception is the amazingly friendly and helpful Battambang Tourist Information Office (St. 1, Kamakor Village, tel 855(0)12-928-092). Otherwise, your best sources of information are books, magazines, and websites. Nonetheless, some provincial tourism offices are helpful, so it can't hurt to pop in if they happen to be open.

EMERGENCIES
Crime & Police

While far from the safest country in the world, Cambodia has come a long way in recent years in regards to violent crime against foreigners. It is now generally safe to travel the most remote parts of Cambodia without an armed escort. It still isn't safe to wander the streets of Phnom Penh or other urban areas late at night, as petty crime is still quite prevalent. Bag snatchings conducted on speeding motorbikes are one of the most common crimes against foreigners. Even in a tuk-tuk or a restaurant, keep your possessions securely attached to your person, but remember that no possession is worth risking injury. Never leave valuables in your room; you are just inviting theft. Avoid flaunting anything that will make you a target for crime (see sidebar p. 18).

Though muggings are less frequent than in the past, they do occur. Pickpockets (particularly children who have a height advantage for such skills) are not uncommon at crowded tourist destinations like markets. It's best not to carry more cash than you need on an outing.

Generally, Khmer culture is respectful to and protective of women, both local and foreign. As of 2008, reports of attacks on women have been infrequent. Yet women, especially those traveling alone, should take precautions to stay safe. Even though Khmer culture isn't necessarily aggressive, avoid wearing revealing clothing so as not to draw unwanted attention. Friendliness is appropriate, but overfamiliarity can sometimes be misconstrued as flirtation in this rather formal culture. If you feel threatened, cause a loud commotion, making evident that the aggressor is behaving inappropriately. Usually, the public uproar will shame the person into leaving you alone. Otherwise, call the tourist police: 855(0)23-726-158.

If you are a victim of any crime, contact the police immediately. You must file a police report in order to submit a travel insurance claim, though the police will likely charge a fee for doing so. While this practice is not policy, it can facilitate the process. Such fees can be negotiated down to perhaps $5 or $10—a small price to pay to make sure the report is processed quickly. Police in Phnom Penh and Siem Reap are far more likely to speak English than their counterparts in the provinces. It's convenient to bring along a Khmer speaker to translate.

Be aware of your own actions that could violate local laws and land you in serious trouble. While illicit drugs are commonly offered in Phnom Penh and Siem Reap, the purchase and consumption of drugs such as marijuana is illegal in Cambodia and may result in stiff penalties. You may be stopped on a rental motorbike and be informed that such rentals are illegal or that you have violated some obscure traffic violation (shocking considering that there don't seem to be any actual laws that Cambodian drivers don't violate regularly). Never argue with a police officer; just negotiate a reduced fee of several dollars for your crime rather than get yourself into greater trouble.

If you are involved in a serious crime, it may be best to contact your embassy in Phnom Penh for assistance. If you plan to be in Cambodia for longer than a week, it's advisable to register with the embassy. Provide the staff with a photocopy of your passport and your travel plans, so they are aware of your whereabouts and can assist you more easily.

Finally, while patronizing businesses engaged in prostitution is not illegal in Cambodia, be aware that many sex workers are underage. Other than the moral considerations of supporting an industry that frequently abuses women and the obvious dangers of sexually transmitted diseases, you may inadvertently violate anti–child sex laws. Sex with children is not tolerated; to paraphrase an anti–child sex advertisement: "For pedophiles, Cambodia has the best bars in the world, those of a prison cell."

Embassies & Consulates

Cambodian embassies and consulates in the United States and neighboring countries:

Washington, D.C.
4530 16th St. NW,
Washington, DC 20011
Tel (202)726-7742
Fax (202)726-8381

Seattle
1818 Westlake Ave. N., Ste. 315,
Seattle, WA 98109
Tel (206)217-0830
Fax (206)361-7888

New York
866 UN Plaza, Ste. 420,
New York, NY 10017
Tel (212)223-0676
Fax (212)223-0425

Los Angeles
422 Ord St., Ste. G,
Los Angeles, CA 90012
Tel (213)625-7777
Fax (213)625-7766

Bangkok
185 Rajddamri Rd.,
Lumpini, Patumwan
Bangkok 10330
Tel 66(0)2-254-6630

Ho Chi Minh City
41 Phung Khac Khoan
Ho Chi Min City
Tel (848)829-2751

Foreign Embassies in Cambodia (Phnom Penh)

The U.S. Embassy in Phnom Penh provides U.S. Citizen Services Monday through Thursday from 1 to 4 p.m. A 24-hour emergency hotline is routed through the embassy's regular phone number. Many foreign embassies are closed for their nations' respective holidays as well as some Cambodian holidays. For visas for foreign countries, such as Thailand or Laos, expect to wait at least one day for processing. In addition to those listed below, there are consulates for neighboring Asian countries in various provincial capitals, such as Battambang.

United States
1 St. 96 (near Wat Phnom)
Tel 855(0)23-728-000
http://cambodia.usembassy.gov

Canada
11 St. 254
Tel 855(0)23-213-470

United Kingdom
27–29 St. 75
Tel 855(0)23-427-124

Kingdom of Thailand
196 Norodom Blvd.
Tel 855(0)23-726-306

Laos
15–17 Mao Tse Toung Blvd.
Tel 855(0)23-982-632

Vietnam
436 Monivong Blvd.
Tel 855(0)23-362-741

Emergency Telephone Numbers

Ambulance: 119
Fire: 118
Police & Medical Emergency: 117
Tourist Police, Phnom Penh:
855(0)97-778-0002
Tourist Police, Siem Reap:
855(0)97-778-0013
Police, Siem Reap: 855(0)12-630-863 or 855(0)12-630-002
Tourist Police, Battambang:
855(0)97-778-0014
Tourist Police, Sihanoukville:
855(0)97-778-0008
International SOS Clinic, Phnom Penh: 855(0)23-216-911

Royal Angkor International Hospital, Siem Reap: 855(0)12-235-888

Health

Few clinics or hospitals in Cambodia provide health care that is up to Western standards. The following are your best options for medical treatment.

International SOS Medical Clinic
161 St. 51, Phnom Penh
Tel 855(0)23-216-911
Fax 855(0)23-215-811
www.internationalsos.com
/en/ourresources clinics
cambodia_35.htm

Royal Angkor International Hospital
National Highway 6 on way to airport, Phum Kasekam, Khum Sra Ngea, Siem Reap
Tel 855(0)63-761-888
www.royalangkorhospital.com

Land Mines & Unexploded Ordnance

Literally millions of unexploded land mines and undetonated rockets, bombs, and artillery shells are scattered throughout Cambodia. While most densely populated areas have been safely cleared of deadly remnants from Cambodia's decades of war, it cannot be overemphasized that these weapons are still a serious threat. When in the countryside, NEVER wander off established trails and avoid touching any metal object found.

FURTHER READING

Despite a dearth of literature by Cambodian authors published in English, more than a century's worth of insight on Cambodian art, culture, and history has been written by Westerners, particularly the French. In recent years, numerous websites have begun providing useful information and practical advice for travelers, as

well as context for the country's past (see below). For additional resources, see Media, p. 279.

Books

Ancient Angkor, by Michael Freeman and Claude Jacques (River Books, 1999). Perhaps the best Angkor temple guide with maps, photos, and highlights.

The Ancient Khmer Empire, by Lawrence Palmer Briggs (White Lotus Press, 1999). Impractically large to read on the road; a comprehensive account of every known Angkor and pre-Angkor king and high religious official, and the cities, temples, and irrigation works they built over roughly 1,300 years.

Angkor: An Introduction to the Temples, by Dawn Rooney (Airphoto International/Odyssey, 2004). This guide's simple style and efficient organization have made it one of the most popular books among Angkor visitors.

Angkor and the Khmer Civilization, by Michael D. Coe (Thames and Hudson, 2003). This intriguing account of the Angkor era emphasizes culture with some coverage of art, religion, and archaeology. Excellent illustrations and insightful discussion of theories.

Art and Architecture of Cambodia, by Helen Ibbitson Jessup (Thames and Hudson, 2004). This history of Khmer artistic development from pre-Angkor to the early 20th century incorporates other aspects of Cambodian culture.

Cambodia: Year Zero, by François Ponchaud (Holt, Rinehart and Winston, 1978). The first account of the Khmer Rouge takeover presents a worthwhile early view.

Daughter of the Killing Fields, by Theary C. Seng (Fusion Press, 2005). An autobiographical account of a young Khmer girl torn from her family. The book also covers her difficult return to Cambodia, and her fight for human rights.

A History of Cambodia, by David P. Chandler (Westview Press, 2000). A fairly concise account of Cambodian civilization from pre-history through the late 20th century.

The Pol Pot Regime, by Ben Kiernan (Yale University Press, 1996). A thorough account of the four-year Khmer Rouge revolution, persecution, and war based on hundreds of interviews with those who lived it and rare documentary evidence.

Web

Andy Brouwer's Cambodia Tales, www.andybrouwer.co.uk. Brouwer's passion for Cambodian culture and history shine through insightful essays on his travels throughout the country and photographs of temples he has explored.

Cambodia Community-Based Ecotourism Network, www.ccben .org. CCBEN assists in developing attractions that provide unique experiences but preserve Cambodia's culture and environment.

Cambodian Ministry of Tourism, www.mot.gov.kh. The MOT provides some useful information about the country, including holidays, festivals, food, and language.

Canby Publications, www .canbypublications.com. The most comprehensive online resource for visitors to Cambodia.

ChildSafe, www.childsafe-cambo dia.org. ChildSafe raises awareness about child-sex tourism and offers tips on travelers' impact on impoverished Cambodian youth.

Stay Another Day, www.stay anotherday.org. This website and booklet available throughout Cambodia provide information on various organizations promoting sustainable tourism.

Tales of Asia, www.talesofasia .com. American expat Gordon Sharpless provides insights on Cambodia and a forum for travelers to share their thoughts on Cambodia and neighboring Asian countries.

Hotels & Restaurants

Cambodia features a variety of lodging options from rudimentary homestays in local villages to international standard five-star resorts and everything in between. On the dining front, Khmer cuisine is slowly being revitalized, especially in Phnom Penh, where international chefs hailing from all corners of the world are infusing the city's eateries with a global flair. The quality and variety of both hotels and restaurants decline when you leave Phnom Penh and the other big cities.

In the major tourist areas of Phnom Penh, Siem Reap, and Sihanoukville, most hotels and guesthouses feature Western-style toilets and hot-water showers. Most rooms also include air-conditioning, or at least offer it as an option. Outside these three areas, the standard of accommodation is generally much lower. Many provincial capitals have only a handful of lodging options, which are usually located in the center of town near the market and bus stop.

Organization: The hotels and restaurants listed below have been grouped first according to their region (by chapter), then listed alphabetically by price category.

L = Lunch
D = Dinner

Credit Cards: Abbreviations used are: AE (American Express), DC (Diner's Club), MC (Master-Card), V (Visa).

■ PHNOM PENH

HOTELS

🏨 AMANJAYA
🍴 $$$$$
1 SISOWATH QUAY
TEL 855(0)23-214-747
www.amanjaya.com
Centrally located along the breezy Mekong River near the Royal Palace, the Amanjaya offers a convenient and luxurious retreat from the city's dusty heat. The hotel

is accented by dark woods and deep colors in traditional Khmer style with a flare. On the ground floor, the **K-West Café** complements the reputation with delicious contemporary fare.
ⓘ 21 🅿 🔁 🈁 🆎 All major cards

🏨 HIMAWARI HOTEL APARTMENTS
$$$$$
313 SISOWATH QUAY
TEL 855(0)23-214-555
FAX 855(0)23-217-111
www.himawarihotel.com
The Himawari prides itself on apartment-style living with the comforts and amenities of a hotel. Larger suites boast living rooms and stocked kitchens. With over 100 rooms, the hotel has lost a homey feel. Still, the grounds offer features standard to most Western hotels (pools, Jacuzzis, & gym). A short *tuk-tuk* ride from Phnom Penh's main attractions.
ⓘ 115 🍴🅿️🈁🈁➰🔽 🆎 All major cards

🏨 INTERCONTINENTAL PHNOM PENH
$$$$–$$$$$
296 BLVD. MAO TSE TOUNG
TEL 855(0)23-424-888
www.ichotelsgroup.com
A modern hotel, with full amenities, in downtown Phnom Penh. Beautiful rooms and an outdoor pool terrace invite you to relax after a day of sightseeing.
ⓘ 346 🍴🈁🈁➰🔽 🆎 All major cards

🏨 NAGAWORLD HOTEL & CASINO
$$$$–$$$$$
HUN SEN PARK
TEL 855(0)23-228-822
www.nagaworld.com
A Las Vegas–style hotel and casino in the heart of Phnom Penh.
ⓘ 508 🍴🈁🈁 🆎 All major cards

🏨 RAFFLES LE ROYAL
$$$$–$$$$$
92 RUKHAK VITHEI DAUN PENH (CORNER OF MONIVONG BLVD. & ST. 92)
TEL 855(0)23-981-888
www.phnompenh.raffles.com
Colonial grandeur at its best, Le Royal has a reputation for

elegance, luxury, and excellent service. Established in 1929, the hotel has hosted international clientele ranging from royalty to journalists. Tasteful rooms are equipped with all possible amenities. The expansive grounds include tropical gardens and a swimming pool. The hotel also features several restaurants and upscale boutiques. If you can't afford the necessary splurge to stay here, stop for happy hour cocktails at the famous **Elephant Bar.**

ⓘ 172 🍴 🅿 Ⓢ Ⓒ 🏊 📺 ☒ MC, V

🏨 THE QUAY
$$$–$$$$$
SISOWATH QUAY
TEL 855(0)23-224-894
FAX 855(0)23-224-893
www.thequayhotel.com
This metropolitan hotel stands alone in Phnom Penh for its combination of location (along the riverside), hospitality (charming and professional), and amenities (rooftop hot tub, happy hour, and stylish guest rooms). The restaurant serves pan-Asian cuisine. Free *tuk-tuk* service to various locations around town. River-facing rooms have outstanding views; the others have no windows.

ⓘ 16 Ⓢ Ⓒ 🏊 MC, V

🏨 BOUGAINVILLIER HOTEL
🍴 **$$$–$$$$**
277C SISOWATH QUAY
TEL 855(0)23-220-528
FAX 855(0)23-220-529
www.bougainvillierhotel.com
On the riverfront near the sights, the Bougainvillier is known for their spacious rooms. However, with all that space, the rooms are difficult to air-condition. The hotel and restaurant decor beautifully balances Asian simplicity with traditional Khmer intricacies.

The restaurant serves Royal Khmer and French Mediterranean dishes

ⓘ 32 Ⓢ Ⓒ 🏊 MC, V

🏨 FCC (FOREIGN CORRE-
🍴 SPONDENTS' CLUB)
$$$
363 SISOWATH QUAY
TEL 855(0)23-210-142
www.fcccambodia.com/phnom_penh
Although the club is no longer an authentic information swap for foreign journalists as the name implies, this is the place to revel in adventurous memories from days of old amid the photo galleries and colonial ambience. Today, the hotel and restaurant serve as Phnom Penh's central landmark by which tourists and *tuk-tuks* alike measure the lay of the land. Looking over the riverfront, the cozy, boutique rooms boast minimalist styles. The second-floor restaurant is the real attraction, less for the food than for the drink specials, the diverse patrons, and the always eccentric conversations.

ⓘ 10 Ⓢ Ⓒ 🏊 All major cards

SOMETHING SPECIAL

🏨 THE PAVILION
$$–$$$$
227 ST. 19
TEL 855(0)23-222-280
www.thepavilion.asia
Despite being in the heart of bustling Phnom Penh, you can't help but feel you have escaped the city entirely upon entering Pavilion's gates. Centered on a shady pool and garden and set in two stunning colonial villas, this boutique hotel is nothing less than a sanctuary. Rooms are large and airy with a colonial minimalist design and platform beds. All rooms have balconies or small gardens, and some feature private swimming pools. There's a small outdoor bar and restaurant. The hotel does not

allow children under the age of 16. Pavilion also maintains a strict policy against sex tourists. Book well in advance.

ⓘ 20 🍴 Ⓢ Ⓒ 🏊 MC, V

🏨 VILLA LANGKA
$$–$$$$
14 ST. 282
TEL 855(0)12-449-857
www.villalangka.com
Another boutique gem, Villa Langka is tucked away on a small lane next to Wat Lanka. Lovely, vibrant rooms fuse contemporary elegance with Khmer influences. The gated grounds feature a garden patio and pool area, perfect for cooling off after long, sweaty days. Designed to suit a wide range of needs, the hotel has free Wi-Fi and large desks, but is also very family friendly. The restaurant has indoor and outdoor seating, serving French and international classics.

ⓘ 27 🍴 Ⓢ Ⓒ 🏊 MC, V

🏨 BLUE LIME
$$–$$$
42 ST. 19Z, OFF ST. 19
TEL 855(0)23-222-260
www.bluelime.asia
One of the city's more modern hotels, with a distinctive urban feel. Minimalist rooms have gray concrete furniture accented by colorful silks. Daybeds surround the saltwater pool in a lush garden. At this environmentally friendly hotel, water is heated through solar power. While Blue Lime epitomizes chic to some, others find the concrete off-putting. Children under the age of 16 are not permitted to stay on premises.

ⓘ 14 Ⓢ Ⓒ 🏊 MC, V

🏨 THE KABIKI
$$–$$$
22 ST. 264
TEL 855(0)23-222-290
www.thekabiki.com

The first hotel in Cambodia designed specifically for families, Kabiki features two saltwater pools (including a kiddie pool), a playground, and an expansive garden with plenty of room to run around. This centrally located boutique hotel is in a quiet, secluded alley. Well designed, kid-friendly rooms, complete with bunk beds.

🛈 11 🍴 ⓢ ⓒ ⊿ ⓢ MC, V

🏨 HOTEL CARA
🍴 $$

NO. 18, CORNER OF ST. 47 &
ST. 84
TEL 855(0)23-430-066
FAX 855(0)23-430-077
www.hotelcara.com

Hotel Cara is centrally located near Wat Phnom and the U.S. Embassy, a quick *tuk-tuk* ride away from the tourist destinations. The few rooms featuring balconies look out over the chaos of another dusty, busy street and neighboring nightclub. Though some rooms are small and windowless, they all have a fresh modern vibe. The hotel's **Fusion Sushi** offers Japanese-Korean fusion and is known for savory soups.

🛈 51 🅿 ⓢ ⓢ ⓒ ⓢ MC, V

🏨 BRIGHT LOTUS I
$

22 ST. 178
TEL 855(0)23-990-446 OR
855(0)12-676-682

The Bright Lotus I offers the best of budget accommodation with cleanliness, security, air-conditioning, and fans. It even has a view, though it's only accessible via a series of steep staircases (so are all of the rooms, for that matter). Skip the patio restaurant, as superior restaurants are a stroll away. The front desk is a very helpful resource for tourism.

🛈 14 🍴 ⓒ ⓢ MC, V

RESTAURANTS

Recent years have seen a veritable explosion of new restaurants in Phnom Penh, placing the capital city on the map for its wealth of fine culinary offerings. A wide variety of restaurants can be found along the riverfront on Sisowath Quay or the Boeung Keng Kang area, but there are great finds throughout the city.

🍴 LA RESIDENCE
$$$–$$$$$

22–24 ST. 214
TEL 855(0)23-224-582

Undoubtedly the most elegant restaurant in town, La Residence is the perfect spot for a romantic dinner. Roasted rack of lamb in a sauce of mustard and fine herbs is incredibly tender. The passion fruit and lychee crème brûlée is a fun twist on a traditional dessert. Highly regarded for its well-prepared modern French cuisine, with prices to match.

💺 100 🕐 Mon.–Fri. 11:30 a.m.–2 p.m., 6 p.m.–10:30 p.m. ⓢ MC, V

🍴 KWEST STEAKHOUSE
$$$–$$$$

1 ST. 154 (CORNER OF SISOWATH QUAY IN LOBBY OF AMANJAYA HOTEL)
TEL 855(0)23-214-747

For those with carnivorous cravings, KWest serves up succulent steaks in a classy sophisticated setting. Sirloin steak topped with green peppercorn sauce is juicy and flavorful. The roasted rib eye topped with porto sauce and cheese is absolutely divine.

💺 100 🕐 6:30 a.m.– 11:30 p.m. ⓢ MC, V

🍴 VAN'S
$$$–$$$$

5 ST. 102 (NEXT TO POST OFFICE)
TEL 855(0)23-722-067

Set in a striking colonial mansion, dinner at Van's seeks to transport you back in time to the height of French Colonial Cambodia. Frogs' legs, snails, and soufflés are all on the extensive menu of French classics. Fried beef filet in coffee and pepper crumbs, flambéed with cognac is prepared very well. While the food is good, it's not quite up to par with the prices and romantic setting.

💺 70 🕐 11:30 a.m.–2:30 p.m., 5:30 p.m.–10:30 p.m.; closed L Sat.–Sun. ⓢ MC, V

🍴 PYONGYANG
$$–$$$$

400 MONIVONG BLVD.
TEL 855(0)12-565-311

The experience alone makes the only North Korean restaurant in town worth a visit. While the food is hardly noteworthy, the nightly 8 p.m. floor show is vastly entertaining. North Korean waitresses clad in matching dresses dance, sing, and play an array of instruments. Perfectly rehearsed dances resemble a cross between ballet and synchronized swimming, making for some great photo ops. The noodle soup isn't bad either.

💺 100 🕐 11 a.m.–9 p.m. ⓢ None

🍴 XIANG PALACE
$$–$$$$$

HOTEL INTERCONTINENTAL
296 MAO TSE TOUNG BLVD.
TEL 855(0)23-424-888

Located in the Hotel Intercontinental, this elegant, upscale Chinese restaurant is popular among businessmen and wealthy Khmers. It's widely regarded as the best Cantonese food in town. The crispy, roast Peking duck is the restaurant's claim to fame. For those with deep pockets, the menu also offers exotic Chinese dishes such as sea cucumber and bird's nest.

💺 80 🕐 11:30 a.m.–11 p.m. ⓢ MC, V

🏨 Hotel 🍴 Restaurant 🛈 No. of guest rooms 💺 No. of Seats 🅿 Parking 🕐 Open ⓢ Elevator

BAI THONG
$$–$$$
100–102 SOTHEAROS BLVD.
TEL 855(0)23-211-054
Excellent Thai food in a beautiful, sumptuous setting. The chicken satay is expertly cooked and nicely marinated, with a thick peanut sauce. The duck with tamarind sauce is truly special.
🍴 80 🕐 11:30 a.m.–2 p.m., 5:30 p.m.–10 p.m. 🚫 MC, V

MALIS
$$–$$$
136 NORODOM BLVD.
TEL 855(0)23-221-022
In a cream-colored villa, Malis serves "living Khmer cuisine," royal Khmer recipes with modern flair. Baked sea clams in tamarind sauce let diners safely taste classic Cambodian street food. The city's most lavish Khmer restaurant, but the food doesn't always live up to the setting.
🍴 200 🕐 6 a.m.–11 p.m. 🚫 MC, V

PACHARAN TAPAS & BODEGA
$$–$$$
389E1 SISOWATH QUAY
TEL 855(0)23-224-394
Pacharan is the definitive place for tapas in Phnom Penh, executing authentic Spanish small plates with gusto and flair. The succulent *conhinillo asada*, or roast suckling pig, melts in your mouth. *Calamares à la romano* are golden fried and tender. Order the sangria with fresh fruit by the pitcher. Reservations recommended.
🍴 40 🕐 11 a.m.–11 p.m. 🚫 MC, V

POP CAFÉ
$$–$$$
371 SISOWATH QUAY
TEL 855(0)12-562-892
This intimate restaurant prides itself on "Italian Food Like Momma Makes." The simple menu includes appetizers, crispy thin-crust pizza, and pastas. The homemade gnocchi is a big hit. Pop Café's owner, the very friendly Giorgio, always makes sure everyone is satisfied with their meal.
🍴 30 🕐 11:30 a.m.–2 p.m., 6 p.m.–10 p.m. 🚫 None

SCOOP BISTRO & BAR
$$–$$$
2–6A REGENCY COMPLEX
MAO TSE TOUNG BLVD.
TEL 855(0)23-424-457
A modern, stylish restaurant next to the Hotel Intercontinental, Scoop serves some of the most delectable food in town. Traditional dishes are given a fresh spin. All pasta is homemade and comes with a choice of sauce. Caesar salads have never tasted so good.
🍴 80 🕐 11:30 a.m.–12 a.m. 🚫 MC, V

CAFÉ YEJJ
$–$$
170 ST. 450 (OPPOSITE RUSSIAN MARKET)
TEL 855(0)12-543-360
This friendly cafe is a hospitality training program for at-risk youth and women. It has a cozy, charming feel, with wonderful staff who serve up appetizing sandwiches, salads, pasta, and burritos. Locally sourced and organic products are used whenever possible. All-day breakfast is always a hit and smoothies are excellent.
🍴 50 🕐 7 a.m.–9 p.m. 🚫 V

FRIENDS
$–$$
215 ST. 13
TEL 855(0)23-426-748
Dinner at Friends will leave you feeling satisfied from stomach to soul. The setting is bright and cheerful at this nonprofit training restaurant for street children, and service could not be more attentive. An extensive menu of vegetable, fish, and meat tapas makes it nearly impossible to settle on just a few dishes. Sun-dried tomato hummus on crispy wonton wrappers provides the perfect texture, taste, and crunch, while Chinese spinach and cheese ravioli with tomato and basil is packed with flavor. The city's most popular restaurant, reservations are required.
🍴 60 🕐 11 a.m.–2 p.m., 6 p.m.–9 p.m. 🚫 MC, V

KHMER THAI RESTAURANT
$–$$
26EO ST. 135
TEL 855(0)92-810-812
Popular among Khmers, this restaurant offers good Khmer and Thai food in a lovely setting. Minced pork on crisp rice patties is a specialty. Curries are packed with flavor. Chilled tea and steamed rice come with the meal and are refilled frequently. The upstairs features floor seating that is perfect for large groups.
🍴 75 🕐 8 a.m.–10 p.m. 🚫 None

ROMDENG
$–$$
74 ST. 174
TEL 855(0)92-219-565
The second nonprofit eatery of Mith Samlanh (Friends), Romdeng serves what is arguably the city's best Khmer food. Situated in a lovely villa and surrounding garden, food is authentic and service always comes with a big smile. The Khmer Muslim beef and peanut curry is intensely flavored. The truly brave can order the crispy tarantulas. All proceeds go to Mith Samlanh.
🍴 120 🕐 11 a.m.–2 p.m., 6 p.m.–9 p.m. 🚫 MC, V

TAMARIND
$–$$
31 ST. 240

🚭 Nonsmoking 🆒 Air-conditioning 🏨 Indoor Pool 🏊 Outdoor Pool 💪 Health Club 💳 Credit Cards

TEL 855(0)12-830-139
This Mediterranean and North African eatery has an extensive menu with tapas, kebobs, pizza, pastas, couscous, and tagines. Cheese lovers will delight in the spinach and feta spring rolls—the perfect combination of creamy cheese and crispy fried shell. Lunch or dinner is best enjoyed on the restaurant's picturesque rooftop terrace with twinkling fairy lights, North African—style seating, and a lovely breeze.
🪑 100 🕐 9 a.m.–12 a.m. (open later on weekends)
🚫 MC, V

🍴 CHINESE NOODLES
$
553–551 MONIVONG BLVD.
TEL 855(0)12-937-805
This beloved hole in the wall serves up thick, savory homemade la mian noodles, which are kneaded, stretched, cut, and cooked by hand at the restaurant's front. Noodles can be ordered fried or in soup, with your choice of meat. While the place lacks atmosphere, the food is fantastic and amazingly inexpensive.
🪑 80 🕐 8 a.m.–10 p.m.
🚫 None

🍴 K'NYAY
$
25 SURAMARIT BLVD. (ST 268)
TEL 855(0)23-225-225
Khmer for ginger, K'nyay serves vegan-friendly interpretations of numerous Khmer favorites. Roasted red pepper soup bears subtle flavors and a smooth texture. Smoothies are refreshing and inventive.
🪑 30 🕐 Tues.–Fri. 12 p.m.–9 p.m., Sat. 7 a.m.–9 p.m., Sun. 7 a.m.–3 p.m. 🚫 None

🍴 LE RITS
$
14 ST. 310
TEL 855(0)23-213-160
Operated by NGO Nyemo, Le Rits offers vocational training for vulnerable women, helping them to support themselves and their children. The cute café offers set breakfast and lunches for a real deal. A great opportunity to sample fresh, traditional Cambodian dishes.
🪑 30 🕐 7 a.m.–5 p.m., closed Sun. 🚫 None

🍴 THE LIVING ROOM
$
VILLA 9, ST. 306
TEL 855(0)23-726-139
This leisurely spot prides itself on its organic and fair-trade products, most of which are grown locally in Cambodia. The fusion menu features sushi rolls, vegetarian platters, and creative salads. The café experience is complete with alfresco dining on a breezy balcony, as well as Wi-Fi and a children's play area. Known for some of the friendliest service in town.
🪑 70 🕐 7 a.m.–8:30 p.m.
🚫 V

🍴 THE SHOP
$
39 ST. 240
TEL 855(0)23-986-964
A breakfast and lunch favorite, The Shop features healthy soups, salads, and sandwiches in a sweet café setting. Breads and cakes are baked fresh daily and there are weekly changing specials. Chocoholics should not miss the decadent chocolate brownies.
🪑 40 🕐 7 a.m.–8:30 p.m., Sun. 7 a.m.–3 p.m. 🚫 None

■ SIEM REAP

HOTELS

🏨 AMANSARA
$$$$$
ROAD TO ANGKOR
TEL 855(0)63-760-333
FAX 855(0)63-760-335
www.amanresorts.com
The former residence of King Father Norodom Sihanouk, this 1960s-style resort has been carefully restored with pool suites and a spa added. Lectures by historians, personalized services (including cooking classes in a village home and helicopter tours), and an open wine cellar are a few features of this exclusive retreat.
🛏 24 🅿 🚫 🚫 🚫 🚫 All major cards

🏨 FCC ANGKOR
$$$$$
POKAMBOR AVE.
TEL 855(0)63-760-280
FAX 855(0)63-760-281
www.fcccambodia.com
Small, comfortable rooms are set around a courtyard with a small swimming pool. The hotel bar and restaurant is the main attraction, with seating on the deck or lawn overlooking the Siem Reap River.
🛏 31 🍴 🚫 🚫 🚫 MC, V

🏨 HOTEL DE LA PAIX
$$$$$
SIVATHA BLVD.
TEL 855(0)63-966-000
FAX 855(0)63-966-001
www.hoteldelapaixangkor.com
This Bill Bensley–designed hotel was renovated in 2005 after having been used as a rice depot during the Khmer Rouge regime. This stylish, comfortable luxury hotel feels surprisingly intimate. The regularly changing arts lounge keeps the hotel fresh.
🛏 107 🅿 🚫 🚫 🚫 🚫
🚫 MC, V

🏨 LA RÉSIDENCE D'ANGKOR
$$$$$
RIVER ROAD, EAST BANK OF SIEM REAP RIVER
TEL 855(0)63-963-390
www.residencedangkor.com
La Résidence d'Angkor has a quiet location just across the

Siem Reap River, a five-minute walk from town. Rooms feature plush bedding and small sun decks. *Apsara* dances are performed regularly and lectures by archaeologists and historians are planned for 2009. A pool with lockers is available for those taking evening flights out of town.
[i] 54 ⬛ ⬛ ⬛ ⬛ ⬛ MC, V

RAFFLES GRAND HOTEL D'ANGKOR
$$$$$
1 CHARLES DE GAULLE ST.
TEL 855(0)63-963-888
FAX 855(0)63-964-223
www.siemreap.raffles.com
The Grand was Siem Reap's first hotel, built in the 1930s to cater to Angkor's early high-society visitors, including Jacqueline Kennedy. Rooms in the old wing honor French explorers; those in the new wing mimic the original structure's Old World charm. One of the restaurants features royal Khmer cuisine. The hotel also boasts the largest wine cellar in Cambodia.
[i] 131 ⬛ ⬛ ⬛ ⬛ ⬛ ⬛ ⬛ MC, V

SHINTA MANI
$$$$$
JCT. OF OM KHUM ST. & 14TH ST.
TEL 855(0)63-761-998
FAX 855(0)63-761-999
www.shintamani.com
This small boutique sister property of the Hotel de la Paix is a cozy retreat away from the main street's bustle, but close to the river and downtown. Rooms feature plush bedding and multidirectional showers. This hotel is set apart from other small luxury hotels by its on-site hospitality training school. Guests can visit impoverished villages and then donate to build a well for a Cambodian family.
[i] 18 ⬛ ⬛ ⬛ ⬛ ⬛ All major cards

SOKHA ANGKOR RESORT
$$$$$
JCT. OF NATIONAL HIGHWAY 6 & SIVATHA ST.
TEL 855(0)63-969-999
www.sokhahotels.com
One of the premier hotel chains in Cambodia, the Sokha Angkor is conveniently located near the Royal Gardens and downtown Siem Reap. Deluxe rooms are tastefully decorated, fairly standard rooms that are perhaps overpriced. A salt-water swimming pool where *apsara* dances are held is near the Japanese restaurant, one of the resort's three eateries.
[i] 275 ⬛ ⬛ ⬛ ⬛ ⬛ ⬛ ⬛ All major cards

VICTORIA ANGKOR RESORT & SPA
$$$$$
CENTRAL PARK
TEL 855(0)63-760-428
FAX 855(0)63-760-350
www.victoriahotels-asia.com
Alongside the Royal Park, the Victoria Angkor is a quality representation of a colonial style hotel with touches of Khmer style and design. Luxurious modern amenities include a huge swimming pool. Offers every amenity of a five-star hotel, along with outstanding service and an ideal location.
[i] 130 ⬛ ⬛ ⬛ ⬛ ⬛ ⬛ MC, V

MYSTÈRES D'ANGKOR
$$$–$$$$
BEHIND WAT PO LANKA
TEL 855(0)63-963-369
www.mysteres-angkor.com
In the shadows of Wat Po Lanka, this quaint hotel, surrounded by a tropical garden, offers a relaxing Khmer experience. Each of the three styles of rooms comes complete with private bathrooms and individual terraces. The chef, Saray, prepares delectable dishes in the French-Khmer fusion

restaurant. Free transportation from the airport or Tonle Sap pier upon arrangement.
[i] 23 ⬛ ⬛ ⬛ ⬛ ⬛ MC, V

THE RIVER GARDEN
$$$–$$$$
113 MONDUL 3, KHUM SLOKRUM
TEL 855(0)63-963-400
www.therivergarden.info
Tropical gardens surround the jungle pool and outdoor dining area of this quiet boutique resort in the shady neighborhood on the west bank of the Siem Reap River just north of downtown. The spacious, comfortable rooms are in traditional Khmer wooden houses. Regular cooking demonstrations are available and proprietress Deborah always makes her guests feel at home.
[i] 11 ⬛ ⬛ ⬛ ⬛ ⬛ MC, V

GOLDEN BANANA BOUTIQUE HOTEL & RESORT
$$–$$$
NEAR WAT DAMNAK
TEL 855(0)12-654-638
www.goldenbanana.info
Just across the river to the southeast of downtown Siem Reap, the Golden Banana is an extraordinarily stylish complex with everything from small, cozy guest rooms to boutique resort accommodations. Many rooms have a nouveau colonial theme with high ceilings and balconies overlooking the pool. It's an ideal location to relax close to town. The staff is incredibly helpful and friendly.
[i] 23 B&B, 9 hotel, 16 resort ⬛ ⬛ ⬛ ⬛ MC, V

AUBERGE MONT ROYAL D'ANGKOR
$$
497 TAPHUL RD.
TEL 855(0)63-964-044
FAX 855(0)63-964-528

www.auberge-mont-royal.com
Set in a colonial-style house
and adjoining Old World property with hardwood floors.
Many rooms have balconies
overlooking the pool. The
Auberge Mont Royal d'Angkor
is on a quiet side street in walking distance from downtown,
ideal for the nearby nightlife of
Siem Reap.

🏨 30 🅿 🕭 🎔 🏊 🅰 MC, V

🏨 THE VILLA SIEM REAP
$–$$$
153 TAPHUL RD.
TEL 855(0)63-761-036
www.thevillasiemreap.com
Rooms in the villas and
the treehouse fuse classic
Khmer and modern design
and even standard rooms
feature touches of local style.
Gorgeous wooden homes
are decorated with wooden
furnishings and colorful silks.
Many rooms have private bal-
conies or terraces. Guests can
learn Khmer cooking through
the Cooks in Tuk-Tuks program.

🏨 18 🅿 🕭 🎔 🏊 🅰 None

SOMETHING SPECIAL

🏨 SALA BAI HOTEL
SCHOOL
$–$$
1 BLOCK W OF SIVATHA BLVD.
TEL 855(0)63-963-329
www.salabai.com
This tiny hotel allows disadvantaged Cambodian youth
to learn about the hospitality
trade. Simple, immaculate
rooms are cleaned twice a day
by charming, nervously polite
staff in training. The suite is
the real steal, a spacious, bright,
and colorful room above the
training restaurant that serves
equally excellent food. Closed
mid July to mid Oct. & Khmer
New Year (April).

🏨 4 🅿 🕭 🅰 None

🏨 EI8HT ROOMS
GUESTHOUSE
$
138–139 STREOUNG THMEY
VILLAGE, NEXT TO ARTISANS
D'ANGKOR
TEL 855(0)63-969-788
www.ei8htrooms.com
Boutique-style touches make
these fairly standard rooms
feel a bit more cozy. Bright,
comfortable rooms near the
center of town make this hotel
a fine budget option.

🏨 12 🅿 🅰 None

🏨 TWO DRAGONS
GUESTHOUSE
$
NO. 110 WAT BO VILLAGE
TEL 855(0)63-965-107
http://talesofasia.com/
cambodia-twodragons.htm
This guesthouse is owned
and operated by an American
and Thai husband and wife.
They provide the best of both
cultures through helpful tour
info, good food, and meticulous attention to detail. The
location is just across the river
in a quieter part of town but
has *tuk-tuks* on call just outside.
No-frills rooms have small TVs
and clean bathrooms, making
Two Dragons one of the best
budget options in the country.

🏨 13 🅿 🕭 🎔 🅰 MC, V

RESTAURANTS

Siem Reap's Pub Street and parallel alleyways are walking streets
lined with restaurants and bars.
Given Siem Reap's rapid turnover
of guests, many of these restaurants are high on atmosphere
and low on quality. There are a
number of hidden gems, though,
including a few frequented by
the small expatriate community.
Outside the nicer hotels, a handful of quality eateries are spread
throughout Siem Reap, rather
than centered around Pub Street.

🍴 GURU MOTHER CAFÉ
$$
NO. 26 OUM KHUM ST.
TEL 855(0)92-713-519
This hole-in-the-wall eatery
just west of the Shinta Mani
hotel has an authentic Japanese
atmosphere serving food with
perfect texture, temperature,
and taste. The $5 set menu
changes daily. Other fare
includes omelettes, curries,
tonkatsu, and even pasta.

🕑 11 a.m.–2:30 p.m., 6 p.m.–10
p.m., closed Sun. 🅰 MC, V

🍴 AHA
$–$$$
ALLEYWAY BEHIND PUB ST., OLD
MARKET AREA
TEL 855(0)63-965-501
Western/Asian tapas are hit-or-
miss at this swanky downtown
fine dining establishment. One
of the few air-conditioned
restaurants near Pub Street, its
a great place for a date, though
you may be tempted to eat here
simply to escape the heat.

🎔 50 🕑 12 p.m.–11 p.m.
🅰 None

TELL RESTAURANT
$–$$$
SIVATHA RD.
TEL 855(0)63-963-289
The sole German restaurant in town, Tell's menu includes schnitzel and even Hungarian goulash, washed down with Erdinger beer. The restaurant is one of the oldest in town, perhaps a testimony to their quality and local following. The location near the night market is easy enough to find and the food is quality German fare with a few local recipes thrown in the mix.
🛏 30 🕐 10 a.m.–10:30 p.m. 🚫 None

ANGKOR PALM RESTAURANT
$–$$
OLD MARKET AREA, 1 BLOCK S OF PUB ST.
TEL 855(0)63-761-436
Alfresco and air-conditioned dining, combination platters for one or two with Khmer classics like *amok* curry, and specialty *samlor* soups. Free, tasty banana chips while you wait. People-watching from the patio is especially enjoyable on winter evenings. A great introduction to Khmer cuisine.
🛏 60 🕐 9 a.m.–11 p.m. 🚫 AE, MC, V

BASHO
$–$$
C4–C5, SIVATHA NO. 5 AT MONDUL 1
TEL 855(0)12-162-9117
Difficult-to-find Basho is arguably the best Japanese restaurant in town, serving fat sushi rolls in half and whole portions, soba noodles, and bento box sets. Their green tea shakes are outstanding and the atmosphere is stylish and comfortable. Ask some expats if they know the way, as it's worth the effort to find Basho if you need a sushi fix.

🛏 25 🕐 11 a.m.–3 p.m., 5 p.m.–10 p.m. 🚫 None

BLUE PUMPKIN
$–$$
ACROSS FROM PUB ST.
TEL 855(0)63-963-574
The Blue Pumpkin has a respectable bakery on the ground floor with pastries and coffee available for takeout or dining alfresco. Upstairs is a chic, air-conditioned lounge with Wi-Fi and ambience that slightly overshadows the quality of the cuisine. The chai tea is excellent.
🛏 40 🕐 6 a.m.–11 p.m. 🚫 V

CAFÉ DE LA PAIX
$–$$
SIVATHA BLVD.
TEL 855(0)63-966-000
Outstanding panini and great coffee are served at this air-conditioned bakery/café just north of the main downtown area. Free Wi-Fi and delectable ice cream make this an excellent place for breakfast, lunch, coffee, or a small snack.
🛏 20 🕐 8 a.m.–10 p.m., closed Mon. 🚫 MC, V

CAMBODIAN BBQ
$–$$
ALLEYWAY JUST S OF PUB ST.
TEL 855(0)63-966-052
Considering how chewy most Cambodian beef is, it's a wonderful treat to nosh on some tender meat. The cook-it-yourself menu includes kangaroo, crocodile, ostrich, and other exotic fare—no beef. Raw meat is served at your table where you grill it yourself, family-style on a charcoal-heated BBQ.
🛏 40 🕐 10 a.m.–11 p.m. 🚫 MC, V

CHILI SI-DANG WINE BAR & RESTAURANT

$–$$
EAST RIVERSIDE
TEL 855(0)12-723-488
One of the owners is Thai and locals say it's some of the best Thai food in town. This restaurant also serves great burgers and has a popular, well-stocked bar.
🛏 25 🕐 9 a.m.–11 p.m. 🚫 None

DEAD FISH TOWER RESTAURANT
$–$$
SIVATHAT BLVD., NEAR CCB BANK
TEL 855(0)63-963-060 OR 855(0)015-630-377
Thai set menus allow you to sample four or five dishes while you watch nightly *apsara* and traditional dance performances. Free Wi-Fi, pool tables, and a funky atmosphere are great reasons to visit Dead Fish, despite its odd name. Various other Asian cuisines are available on the large menu.
🕐 10 a.m.–12 a.m. 🚫 None

D'WAU
$–$$
126 WAT BO VILLAGE
TEL 855(0)012 356 030 OR 855(0)63-966-955
The first Malaysian restaurant in Siem Reap offers a casual atmosphere and incredibly reasonable prices for classic dishes, such as *nasi lemak*, fried chicken, and red chili sambal. Halal food is also available, as are catering and delivery.
🛏 30 🕐 7 a.m.–9 p.m. 🚫 None

IN TOUCH RESTAURANT & BAR
$–$$
PUB ST.
TEL 855(0)63-965-005
Standard Western and Khmer fare, such as *lok lak*, Khmer-style beef and rice. The dining room is pleasant, but the real atmosphere is upstairs. A live

band plays here nightly and guests sitting along the railing can people-watch on the bustling Pub Street corner below.
🛏 60 🕐 3 p.m.–1 a.m. 🚫 None

KHMER KITCHEN RESTAURANT
$–$$

ALLEYWAY 1 BLOCK S OF PUB ST.
TEL 855(0)63-964-154
One of the best places to sample Khmer cuisine, this reasonably priced restaurant features classics such as *lok lak* and *amok*, plus unusual treats like cashew milkshakes. The location is ideal for people-watching. Local Khmers eat here from time to time—a sign of quality Khmer cooking.
🛏 80 🕐 10 a.m.–10:30 p.m. 🚫 None

LA NORIA HOTEL
$–$$

EAST BANK OF SIEM REAP RIVER, N OF NATIONAL HIGHWAY 6
TEL 855(0)63-964-242
French and Khmer cuisine, such as pomelo salad and curries, served with a music, shadow-puppet, and dance performance by youth from Krousar Thmey. Reservations required in high season (Dec. –Feb.)
🛏 60 🕐 6 a.m.–10 p.m. 🚫 MC, V

LE JARDIN DES DELICES
$–$$

NATIONAL HIGHWAY 6
TEL 855(0)63-963-673
www.ecolepauldubrule.org
Run by the reputable Paul Dubrule School of Hotel and Tourism, this café lets students practice and refine their hospitality skills. The set lunch is excellent. All proceeds go to the NGO to finance scholarships for disadvantaged youths.
🛏 250 🕐 Tues.–Fri., 12 p.m.–2 p.m. 🚫 MC, V

LE TIGRE DE PAPIER
$–$$

PUB ST.
TEL 855(0)63-760-930
Wood-fired pizza and fresh pasta are excellent, and Khmer food is tasty enough for the foreign palate. Their signature dish, Le Tigre de Papier pasta, penne in a cream curry sauce, is outstanding. Free Wi-Fi; located on one of the most interesting people-watching streets in Cambodia.
🛏 75 🕐 24 hours 🚫 None

RED PIANO
$–$$

PUB ST., OLD MARKET AREA
TEL 855(0)63-964-750
The house in which the Red Piano is located has survived over a hundred years and the restaurant has thrived on the corner of Pub Street for about a decade. The food is fair, and rooms in their nearby guesthouse are reasonable. Ideal location to meet for a drink after a day at the temples.
🛏 30 🕐 7 a.m.–11:30 p.m. 🚫 None

SINGING TREE CAFÉ
$–$$

OFF WAT BO RD., 4 BLOCKS N OF WAT DAMNAK
TEL 855(0)92-635-500
www.singingtreecafe.com
Vegetarian restaurant with a social conscience. Outstanding smoothies and tasty sandwiches are served in the garden. Weekend monk chats, yoga and meditation classes, performances by disabled Cambodian dance troupes, and singing performances by children are the real draw. Offers volunteer opportunities and Khmer language classes.
🛏 50 🕐 8 a.m.–9 p.m., closed Mon. 🚫 None

SUGAR PALM RESTAURANT & BAR
$–$$

TAPHUL RD. (ONE BLOCK WEST OF SIVATHA BLVD)
TEL 855(0)63-964-838
Proprietress Kethana shares her mother and grandmother's Khmer recipes both at the dining table and in the kitchen of this traditional wooden house. Kethana offers cooking classes during the day.
🛏 45 🕐 11:30 a.m.–3 p.m., 5:30 p.m until late 🚫 None

TEMPLE BALCONY RESTAURANT
$–$$

PUB ST.
TEL 855(0)15-999-909
Standard Khmer and Western fare in a large second-floor dining room whose primary focus is the *apsara* and folk dances performed nightly from 7:30 to 9:30 p.m. Downstairs is a raucous bar with pool tables and dance floors.
🛏 150 🕐 Upstairs 4:30 p.m.–11 p.m.; downstairs 7 a.m.–3 a.m./4 a.m. 🚫 All major cards

VIROTH'S
$–$$

246 WAT BO ST.
TEL 855(0)12-826-346
Terrace dining in a tropical outdoor garden. Pumpkin soup, stuffed tomatoes, and Khmer grilled chicken are a few of the reasonably priced dishes offered at this popular and romantic restaurant.
🛏 94 🕐 7 a.m.–10 p.m. 🚫 MC, V

VIVA
$–$$

CORNER OF OLD MARKET
TEL 855(0)92-209-154
Not technically authentic cuisine, though miniature southern-style tortillas are featured in their occasionally $1 tacos. The burritos are considerably tastier. Margaritas are a bit watery, but the tequila selection is fair. Fine if you are craving some Mexican fare.

🏨 Hotel 🍴 Restaurant ℹ️ No. of guest rooms 🛏 No. of Seats 🅿 Parking 🕐 Open ⬍ Elevator

⚏ 40 ⏲ 10 a.m.–12 a.m.
🚫 None

🍴 BUTTERFLIES GARDEN RESTAURANT

$

EAST SIDE OF SIEM REAP RIVER,
2ND BRIDGE RD., OFF WAT
BO RD.

TEL 855(0)63-761-211

Dine in a mesh-enclosed outdoor room while butterflies flit around the floral tropical garden. Breakfasts include blueberry pancakes with organic maple syrup, and entrees include traditional Khmer recipes such as royal Khmer egg salad, and the "best burgers in Siem Reap." The chefs are from a hospitality training school, the butterflies benefit a stay-in-school program, and the gift shop supports local charities.

⚏ 30 ⏲ 8 a.m.–10 p.m.
🚫 None

■ ANGKOR

HOTELS

See Siem Reap pp. 288–290

RESTAURANTS

🍴 MOM'S RESTAURANT

$

ANGKOR THOM, ANGKOR
ARCHAEOLOGICAL PARK

Located just beside the Bayon temple in Angkor Archaeological Park are several dozen restaurants and souvenir stands. While the fare is pretty standard (various stir fry dishes served with rice) Mom's Restaurant serves food a notch above the rest. Dishes are around 3 dollars a piece and can be tailored to your liking—I suggest adding pineapple to the chicken with ginger.

⏲ 6 a.m.–6 a.m., rain or shine

See also Siem Reap pp. 290–293

■ WESTERN CAMBODIA

HOTELS

BATTAMBANG

🏨 STUNG SANGKE HOTEL

$$$–$$$$

NATIONAL HIGHWAY 5,
PREKMOHATEP VILLAGE,
SVAYPOR COMMUNE

TEL 855(0)53-953-495 (TO 7)

FAX 855(0)53-953-494

www.stungsangkehotel.com

Opened on the auspicious date of 8/08/08, this modern hotel and casino is possibly the largest building in town. Deluxe rooms have either twin or king-size beds; suites have balconies that overlook the pool. The small casino features video baccarat and roulette as well as slots. The two restaurants specialize in Khmer and international cuisine.

ℹ 130 (incl. 6 suites) 🍴 🅿
🔄 📶 🏊 📺 🚫 MC, V

SOMETHING SPECIAL

🏨 LA VILLA

$$$

185 POM ROMCHEK 5, KOM
RATTANAK, SROK BATTAMBANG
(EAST BANK OF RIVER, IN FRONT
OF CITY CENTER)

TEL (855)053-730-151

www.lavilla-battambang.com

This charming French colonial villa, which was built in 1930, once housed occupying Vietnamese soldiers. It has been restored as a wonderful boutique hotel. Each of the rooms has a different design, from the two grand suites with a connecting balcony overlooking the river to the cozy third-floor "lofts" with wooden beams that are popular with honeymooners. The glass-enclosed dining room serves Khmer cuisine and international entrees and wine. The setting, location, and hospitality make La Villa the

finest option for accommodation in Battambang.

ℹ 5 rooms, 2 suites 🍴 📶 🏊
🚫 MC, V

🏨 HOTEL SPRING PARK

$–$$

ROM CHEK 4, RATTANAK

TEL 855(0)53-730-999

The hotel's location, on the quieter eastern side of the river is slightly less convenient than some others. It's close to the park, however, which is nice in the evenings. Although their generic rooms may be nothing to write home about, they are also modern and comfortable. Prices are reasonable, for no-frills accommodation with oddly incongruous mismatching bedsheets. When the city is busy during the high season, this large hotel may be one of the few with an available room.

ℹ 90 🅿 🔄 📶 🚫 MC, V

🏨 STAR HOTEL

$–$$

LA' ER ST., PREKMOHATEP
VILLAGE, SVAY POR COMMUNE

TEL 855(0)17-545-455

The central location near the markets, banks, and riverside and the reasonable rates make Star the city's best mid-range hotel. Rooms have optional air-conditioning and hot water for reduced room rates. Each room has a different price, depending on size, which allows people to find decent lodging regardless of their budgets. The rooftop restaurant has a nice breeze, but the view is of the tops of other nearby buildings. Internet is available, as is tourist information from the friendly, helpful staff.

ℹ 26 🍴 📶 🚫 MC, V

🏨 BUS STOP BAR & GUESTHOUSE

$

149 2ND RD.

TEL 855(0)53-730-544

🚫 Nonsmoking 📶 Air-conditioning 🏊 Indoor Pool 🏊 Outdoor Pool 📺 Health Club 🚫 Credit Cards

www.busstopcambodia.com
This Australian-run guesthouse has small, basic rooms that are a fair deal. The central location is ideal, and the free Wi-Fi is the fastest in Battambang. The manager is friendly and helpful; he can help you organize day trips or simply give you advice about what to see, where to eat, and what to do in the city.
🛏 8 🆘 🚫 None

RESTAURANTS

🍴 LA VILLA
$$
185 POM ROMCHEK 5, KOM RAT-TANAK, SROK BATTAMBANG
TEL (855)053-730-151
The restaurant serves classic dishes from the East and West, including fish *amok* and beef lasagna. Mediterranean-style greenhouse dining room with open kitchen. French, Italian, South American wines.
🪑 40 🕐 12 p.m.–3 p.m., 6:30 p.m.–9 p.m., closed Tues. for nonguests 🚫 None

🍴 THE RIVERSIDE BALCONY
$–$$
JCT. OF ST. 1 & RTE. 57
TEL 855(0)12-437-421 OR 855(0)53-730-313
The Riverside, in a 1940s wooden house beside the Sanker River, has the best ambience in town. It also serves the best enchiladas and fish and chips this side of the Tonle Sap. As in a Khmer home, you remove your shoes to enter. The staff is gracious and John, the Aussie propri-etor, is an outstanding host.
🪑 50 🕐 5 p.m.–12 a.m., closed Mon. 🚫 None

🍴 PHKAY PROEK RESTAURANT
$
ST. 3, W OF BATTAMBANG COURT
TEL 855(0)53-952-870 OR

855(0)92-858-680
This open-air restaurant is popular with the expat community and locals alike. The pan-Asian menu includes Chinese, Thai, Korean, and Khmer food, indicative of Battambang's multicultural mix of residents. The lively atmosphere on the weekends can make getting a table tricky sometimes and the service is a bit slow, but the food and atmosphere are great.
🪑 50 🕐 7 a.m.–10 p.m. 🚫 None

🍴 SNOW WHITE CAFÉ
$
ROMCHECK 4 VILLAGE, RATANAK COMMUNE
This cozy, open-air restaurant is slightly out of the way, on the east side of the river near Hotel Spring Park, but it's worth the walk. Creative Khmer and international fare, such as Bat-tambang orange, fried coconut, and garlic salad, and king prawn (shrimp) flambé in wine cream sauce with garlic and coriander.
🪑 30 🕐 6:30 a.m.–9:30 p.m. 🚫 None

🍴 WHITE ROSE RESTAURANT
$
HOUSE 102/8 ST. 2
TEL 855(0)17-529-641
The generally indifferent and unfriendly staff at the White Rose can be tolerated if you have adjusted to the leisurely pace of Battambang. Standard Khmer, Thai, and international fare is reasonably priced. The corner location and outdoor seating, combined with late-night hours make the restaurant immensely popular. Local businesspeople, travelers, expats, and the neighborhood homeless people may be pres-ent here at any given hour.
🪑 40 🕐 7 a.m.–10 p.m. 🚫 None

■ CENTRAL CAMBODIA

Tourist facilities in Central Cambodia are sparse at best. Most visitors make day trips to the region from nearby cities such as Phnom Penh *(see pp. 284–288)* and Siem Reap *(see pp. 288–293)*.

■ EASTERN CAMBODIA

HOTELS

RATANAKIRI

SOMETHING SPECIAL

🏨 NORDEN HOUSE
$$
0.5 MILE (0.8 KM) S OF HILL-TRIBE MONUMENT, NEAR YAK LAOM LAKE
TEL 855(0)12-880-327
www.nordenhouseyaklom .com
The nearest accommodation to the number one attraction in Ratanakiri, Yak Laom Lake,

Norden House has seven very comfortable rooms, amazing food, gracious staff, and dirt bikes for hire. Twenty-four-hour electricity should be installed around Ban Lung by 2009, but in the meantime, Norden House has solar-powered hot-water heaters. A generator provides electricity through the night, perfect for watching a DVD in your room from their in-house library.

[I] 7 [P] [AC] [CC] None

🏨 YAKLOM HILL LODGE
$–$$

3 MILES (5 KM) EAST OF BAN LUNG, BEYOND HILL-TRIBE MONUMENT
TEL 855(0)11-790-510
www.yaklom.com

Those looking for a balance between comfort and the outdoors should try Yaklom Hill Lodge, a nature resort set amid a tropical paradise. While it's a bit of a walk to the lake, there are sunrise and sunset lookouts. You may spy the occasional snake, spider, and scorpion wandering around the expansive resort, not to mention mosquitoes. A traditional tribal house sleeps eight.

[I] 15 [P] [CC] None

■ SIHANOUKVILLE & SOUTHERN COASTAL PROVINCES

KAMPOT

HOTELS

🏨 BOKOR MOUNTAIN LODGE
$–$$

RIVERSIDE RD.
TEL 855(0)33-932-314
www.bokorlodge.com

Named after the mountain that is Kampot's claim to fame, the lodge is set in a restored French colonial building with a long history. Rooms with televisions, fridges, and attached bathrooms are spacious, but could use a few extra soft touches. The downstairs restaurant is quite popular among local expats and tourists, serving up hearty meals and a large range of spirits and cocktails. It's also a great place to stop by for information about tours and activities in Kampot.

[I] 6 bungalows, 1 house, 3 rooms in main house [AC] [CC] None

🏨 LES MANGUIERS
$–$$

1 MILE N OF KAMPOT
TEL 855(0)92-330-050
www.mangomango.awardspace.com

Undoubtedly the most charming of all Kampot lodgings, the family-run Les Manguiers (The Mango Trees) is a small resort tucked away off a narrow dirt road. Spacious wooden bungalows are scattered around the lush grounds. An entire traditional wooden house can be rented—perfect for families. A two-story main house offers slightly less expensive rooms with slightly less charm. The restaurant's menu changes daily and all food is prepared fresh. Inform the staff several hours ahead of time if you will be eating lunch or dinner at the resort. Right on the river, it's a great spot for night swims in bioluminescence and kayaks can be rented for a small fee.

[I] 4 bungalows, 1 house, 3 rooms in main house [CC] None

🏨 RIKITIKITAVI
$–$$

RIVERSIDE ROAD (NEXT TO POST OFFICE)
TEL 855(0)12-235-102
www.rikitikitavi-kampot.com

The best bet for those who want to sleep in Kampot town, this immaculate guesthouse has a distinctive feel and is a great value. Located in what was originally a rice barn, the dark wooden guesthouse has a unique, inviting feel. Rooms are decorated in a warm, modern-Asian style and come with all the trimmings, including Wi-Fi, minibars, TVs, and DVD players (with an extensive free library of DVDs). The garrulous, affable owner provides tips for exploring the region. The balcony restaurant features an eclectic menu with many appetizing options.

[I] 7 [CC] [AC] None

RESTAURANTS

🍴 BOKOR MOUNTAIN LODGE
$$

ON THE KAMPOT RIVERFRONT
TEL 855(0)33-932-314

This friendly restaurant in a colonial house overlooking the Kompong River boasts a large menu of international fare and Khmer favorites. The *hakari* burger is cooked to perfection with golden fries and coleslaw on the side. Also offers a number of vegetarian options.

[seats] 30 [clock] 7 a.m.–9 p.m. [CC] None

🍴 RIKITIKITAVI
$$

ON THE KAMPOT RIVERFRONT
TEL 855(0)12-235-102

This rooftop balcony restaurant features lovely river and mountain views in a modern Asian setting. The diverse menu offers selections from around the world, including fish *amok*, enormous sandwiches, and crepes. The grilled chicken pesto pasta is fresh and quite good. Staff are well trained and very amiable.

[seats] 30 [clock] 7 a.m.–10 p.m. [CC] None

🍴 JASMINE
$–$$

ON KAMPOT RIVERFRONT

Known for serving the best Khmer food in Kampot, this charming restaurant should not

be missed. Classics like fish *amok* and curry are brimming with flavor. Run by a friendly couple always ready to impart tips on the surrounding region.
🛏 25 🕐 5 p.m.–9 p.m.
🚫 None

🍴 EPIC ARTS CAFÉ
$
NEAR PSAR GRANATH (OLD MARKET)
TEL 855(0)11-376-968
This tiny café employs deaf and disabled staff and all profits go toward Epic Arts Cambodia, an organization that seeks to change perceptions of disabled individuals through performance art. The atmosphere is sweet and charming and the staff certainly impress. Menu features a variety of comfort foods including quiches and all day breakfast. The gooey chocolate brownies are known throughout the region. Tables have books that show you how to order in sign language to promote communication.
🛏 20 🕐 7 a.m.–6 p.m.
🚫 None

🍴 LUCKI FOOD RESTAURANT & BAR
$
ON KAMPOT RIVERFRONT
For something a bit different, head to this Indian and Sri Lankan eatery. While the decor is minimal, food is spiced to taste and quite good. The meats, vegetable, and seafood paalands are excellent. Free drink or snack with each dish.
🛏 25 🕐 7 a.m.–11 p.m.
🚫 None

KEP

HOTELS

🏨 KNAI BANG CHATT
🍴 RESORT
$$$$$

PHUM THMEY, SANGKAT PREY THOM
TEL 855(0)12-879-486
www.knaibangchatt.com
One of Cambodia's most luxurious resorts promises exclusivity, serenity, and privacy. Three renovated 1970s villas have a distinctive, modern style. Rooms have been individually decorated and boast some of the country's most heavenly beds. Set on Kep's southeastern coastline, the entire resort offers spectacular sea views. Expansive gardens and a stunning infinity pool help create the sense of a private paradise. Delicious multicourse meals are served in the dining area overlooking the ocean. The resort also features an adjacent boating club and boathouse, with small sailboats and other marine craft available to rent. Three percent of all proceeds help fund a nearby community development project.
🛏 11 🅿 🚫 ♿ 🍴 🚫 MC, V

🏨 CHAMPEY INN
🍴 $$$–$$$$
25 AVE. DE LA PLAGE
TEL 855(0)11-300-039
www.nicimex.com
A cluster of cute cottages surround a large pool and garden area. Cottages are simple, but tastefully adorned and quite comfortable. The resort also has its own section of beach with imported white sand, one of the best spots for viewing the famous Kep sunsets. The mostly French restaurant serves meals in an al fresco dining area, by the pool, or on a terrace by the sea.
🛏 8 🅿 ♿ 🚫 MC, V

SOMETHING SPECIAL

🏨 VERANDA NATURAL
🍴 RESORT
$–$$$$$
TEL 855(0)33-399-035
www.veranda-resort.com
A lush, natural hideaway

high on a hill, Veranda is truly special. Rustic wooden bungalows are connected by raised wooden walkways, creating a tropical effect. They come in all shapes, sizes, and price ranges. Vacation villas and the newly constructed Residence are quite spectacular, achieving the perfect blend of nature and luxury. Each bungalow has a balcony or veranda overlooking the sea or gardens. The restaurant offers an extensive menu and breathtaking views. Popular among expats, so it is best to book well in advance.
🛏 20 🅿 🚫 MC, V

RESTAURANTS

🍴 CRAB MARKET
$–$$
Kep Beach
Rows of tiny seafood shacks along the beach offer fresh crab, shrimp, squid, and fish. The crab market is the best place to sample the tasty Kampot pepper crab, a local classic and perhaps one of the best dishes found in Cambodia.
🛏 80 🕐 11 a.m.–10 p.m.
🚫 MC, V

🍴 JUNGLE BAR
$–$$
VERANDA NATURAL RESORT
TEL 855(0)12-888-619
Perhaps the most popular non-seafood restaurant in Kep. Rustic wooden structures perched atop a hill provide beautiful ocean views. The large wooden tables are perfect for grabbing evening drinks with friends. Kabobs are juicy, but pizzas tend to be a bit greasy. The *bong karem* gelato should not be missed.
🛏 60 🕐 6:40 a.m.–11 p.m./ 12 a.m. 🚫 None

🍴 PICNIC STANDS
$–$$
ROAD OPPOSITE KEP BEACH AT MAIN INTERSECTION

🏨 Hotel 🍴 Restaurant 🛈 No. of guest rooms 🛏 No. of Seats 🅿 Parking 🕐 Open 🛗 Elevator

As Khmers love picnicking, Kep is full of platforms and seafood vendors along the beach. Pick a platform and a vendor will come to you with a menu offering a variety of fresh seafood. Menus are in English, but since some vendors speak minimal English, be very clear when ordering.

🎏 Seats 6–8 per stand
🕐 7 a.m.–8 p.m. 🚫 None

SIHANOUKVILLE

HOTELS

🏨 INDEPENDENCE HOTEL
$$$$$

ST. 2 THNOU, SANGKAT NO. 03
TEL 855(0)34-934-300 TO 303
855(0)12-728-090 (RESERVATIONS)
FAX 855(0)34-933-660
www.independencehotel.net

Built in 1960, just as the port at Sihanoukville and the road from Phnom Penh were completed, this landmark hotel was closed in 1969 and shattered by the Khmer Rouge. Designed by renowned Cambodian architect Vann Molyvan, also responsible for the Phnom Penh Central Market and Olympic Stadium, its interior was designed by King Sihanouk himself. The hotel reopened in 2007 after a major renovation preserving its structure. It sits on the bluff at the northern, finest end of Independence Beach. Four-star accommodations with the best sea views from the fourth through seventh (and top) floors.

ℹ️ 52 🅿️ 🔄 🚫 🅰️ 🏊 🎽
🚫 MC, V

🏨 SOKHA BEACH SIHANOUKVILLE
$$$$$

SOKHA BEACH
TEL 855(0)034-935-999
www.sokhahotels.com

The Sokha Beach resort is a quintessential, tropical paradise

five-star beach hotel. Multiple bars and restaurants include a beach bar and seaside seafood eatery, a kids club and playground, and activities such as volleyball and jet-skiing, and lavish accommodations and gracious staff. The beach is beautiful and the location is isolated but only a five-minute ride from Serendipity Beach's bars and restaurants.

ℹ️ 210 🍴 🅿️ 🔄 🚫 🅰️
🏊 🎽 🚫 All major cards

🏨 ABOVE US ONLY SKY
$$

SERENDIPITY BEACH
TEL 855(0)89-822-318

Perched on a manicured hillside, the only thing between your balcony and the water is the seaside beach bar. Air-conditioned, thatch-roof bungalows have crisp linens, mosquito nets, and hot water.

ℹ️ 4 🅰️ 🚫 None

🏨 GARDEN HILL HOTEL & RESORT
$$

WEATHER STATION HILL
(VICTORY HILL)
TEL 855(0)92-574-282
www.gardenhill-sihanouk
ville.com

This former Ramada Hotel was renovated by new owners in 2008. They've turned the hotel with the best view on the island—overlooking all of Sihanoukville port and the islands beyond—into an affordable, quality property. The standard three-star rooms have tile floors and work desks, while amenities include tennis courts and a gym. The distance from everything in the area requires that you have your own transportation, however.

ℹ️ 90 🅿️ 🚫 🅰️ 🏊 🎽 🅰️ 🚫 V

🏨 HOUSE OF ANGEL
$$

SERENDIPITY BEACH
TEL 855(0)92-502-140

Cutesy names such as Sweet Heart and Orchid suit boutiquey rooms with lots of beachy decoration and flowery landscaping. The peaceful location at the northern end of Serendipity is great for swimming, but near all the action.

ℹ️ 18 🅿️ 🚫 None

🏨 SEABREEZE
$–$$

BEACH RD., INDEPENDENCE BEACH
TEL 855(0)34-934-205
www.seabreezesite.com

A bit like an Australian roadhouse in both function and form, Seabreeze is one of the best places to relax around Sihanoukville. The hotel is the only one along the main stretch of Independence Beach. The quiet beach is a narrow strip of sand with shade trees. The rooms are spacious, if characterless, ideal for those willing to share. The common area has lots of charm with a few computers, a fairly large bookshelf, and the restaurant/bar **Steakhouse**. Offers free Wi-Fi.

ℹ️ 16 🍴 🅿️ 🚫 🅰️ MC, V

🏨 LAZY BEACH
$

TEL 855(0)16-214-211 OR
85(0)017-456-536
www.lazybeachcambodia.com

Lazy Beach is situated on the western side of Koh Rung Saloem, a 2.5-hour boat ride from the mainland. It doesn't get more remote or more idyllic. The wide sandy beach may draw a few day-trippers, but the sunsets from a hammock are sublime. The owners charge guests for transportation to and from the island, but once you are relaxing at the beach bar or exploring the waterfall behind the resort, you'll likely forgive them.

ℹ️ 10 🚫 None

🚭 Nonsmoking 🔄 Air-conditioning 🏊 Indoor Pool 🏊 Outdoor Pool 🎽 Health Club 🚫 Credit Cards

🏨 🍴 LE VIVIER DE LA PAILLOTE

$

WEATHER STATION HILL
(VICTORY HILL)
TEL 855(0)12-227-001

This restaurant/bar/guesthouse sits atop Victory Hill, just off the main drag where all the other restaurants and bars are located, yet it's the apex of the budget accommodation options there. The restaurant serves such French delicacies as foie gras, but also sautéed shrimp with tomato coulis and feta cheese, rice, and cumin, and eggplant caviar. Dine beside the only swimming pool in the area and chill out in your fan-cooled room with colorful stuffed geckos on the walls.

ⓘ 10 🅿️ 🏊 🚫None

RESTAURANTS

🍴 CHEZ CLAUDE

$–$$$

BET. INDEPENDENCE BEACH &
SOHKA BEACH

The eclectic menu features sashimi, fondue, couscous (ordered one day in advance), and fresh seafood. The dining room on the hill above Sokha Beach has, by far, the best view of any restaurant on the coast.

🪑 75 🕐 8 a.m.–10 p.m
🚫MC, V

🍴 THE MEXICAN

$–$$$

REEF RESORT, SERENDIPITY RD.
TEL 855(0)12-315-338

With adobe-colored floor tiles, a selection of hot sauces (including Cholula and Tapatio), 100 percent agave tequila, and Latin beats, The Mexican is as authentic a Mexican restaurant as you are likely to find in this part of the world. After a burrito or the barracuda tacos and a few Pacificos, you will be

ready to limbo at the pool bar.
🪑 75 🕐 7 a.m.–late 🚫MC, V

🍴 HAPPA

$–$$

SERENDIPITY BEACH RD.
TEL 855(0)12-728-901 OR
855(0)92-202-451

Happa serves Japanese teppanyaki cooked at a grill in the center of the narrow, open-air dining room. Fish, prawns, beef, etc. are cooked in garlic ginger, miso sesame, or *kroeung* sauce, a Khmer mixture of lemongrass, tumeric, chilli, coconut milk and other local spices. Happa and its sister Khmer restaurant are hands down the best eats in Serendipity Beach.

🪑 50 🕐 5 p.m.–11 p.m.
🚫None

🍴 HOLY COW

$–$$

EKAREACH ST.
TEL 855(0)12-478-510

This colorful, funky, restaurant has a two-story dining room and second-floor bar serving a variety of international and Khmer food, including chicken in Kampot pepper sauce. The name derives from a contemporary Sihanoukville tale of a miraculous cow whose licks had restorative powers.

🪑 25 🕐 9:30 a.m.–11 p.m
🚫MC, V

🍴 MONKEY REPUBLIC

$–$$

BET. GOLDEN LION CIRCLE AND
SERENDIPITY BEACH
TEL 855(0)12-490-290

Arguably the liveliest bar/restaurant in Serendipity Beach, Monkey Republic is where both expats and young tourists begin their party nights and rendezvous with old friends and new. They serve inexpensive and tasty Khmer and international cuisine and provide tourist information.

🪑 50 🕐 8:30 a.m.–10 p.m.
🚫None

🍴 PACO'S SPANISH TAPAS BAR & RESTAURANT

$–$$

198 EKAREACH ST., VICTORY HILL
(MAIN ROAD)
TEL 855(0)92-673-911

The location along the main drag is hardly ideal, but Paco's serves sangria, mini *bocatas* (small sandwiches with sausages, peppers, and the like), tapas, and main courses, such as paella and *flamenquines.* Throw in some Thai or Vietnamese appetizers and you'll have a decent meal on your way back from Ream National Park.

🪑 40 🕐 7 a.m.–11 p.m.
🚫None

🍴 STARFISH BAKERY & CAFE

$–$$

1 BLOCK E OF SOKIMEX GAS
STATION ON EKAREACH RD
www.starfishcambodia.org

Offers freshly made baked goods and fresh fruit juices and smoothies, plus healthful salads and sandwiches. The staff of the restaurant, arts-and-crafts project, and massage parlor—all of which occupy the same grounds—are disadvantaged Cambodians. Beautiful atmosphere, great food, and worthy cause.

🪑 25 🕐 8 a.m.–8 p.m. 🚫None

🍴 Q & A BOOK CAFÉ

$

95 EKAREACH ST.
TEL 855(0)12-598-225

This friendly café is worth driving into town for and a must if driving by. Over 3,000 books are for sale in this friendly bookstore. Amazing banana pancakes, freshly brewed coffee, and fairly priced tourist info from very helpful staff.

🪑 15 🕐 8 a.m.–8 a.m

🏨 Hotel 🍴 Restaurant ⓘ No. of guest rooms 🪑 No. of Seats 🅿️ Parking 🕐 Open 🚪 Elevator

Shopping

Cambodia can be a shopper's paradise. Handicrafts range from wood and stone carvings to silk and silverwork (including jewelry). Clothing and handbags—both knockoffs and authentic items—offer bargains on brand-name products, though quality and prices vary greatly. Even gemstones are available in remote provincial markets, though buyers with no experience should be wary. Most products are available at open-air, local markets; those in tourist centers typically offer a greater variety of tourist-oriented products. More remote, provincial markets cater to a predominately local clientele.

Bargaining

The cost of products at open-air markets is negotiable. When haggling, realize that you are often dickering over small amounts. Though Cambodians are shrewd salespeople, they also are good-natured people; maintain an air of cordiality. Begin bidding at half the asking price and aim to settle around 70 to 80 percent of the original price. If they don't come down to an acceptable figure, politely decline and walk away; they will often offer a lower number.

Purchasing items early is significantly advantageous, as superstitious vendors often believe that early sales portend a prosperous day. You are likely to hand over fewer dollars during this time.

Cautions

Shoppers in Cambodia should exercise a degree of caution when shopping for products either in open-air markets or in proper shops and stores. Generally speaking, no matter where a product is purchased, it is unlikely to carry a guarantee. Even if a receipt is given, you are unlikely to get a refund or return on a defective product. In Cambodia all sales are typically final. Examine all products carefully to be sure all parts are included and functional prior to handing over your cash.

Cambodia also features a variety of knockoff Western products, including counterfeit designer clothing and bootleg DVDs. Be aware that many of these products are of inferior quality. Examine the stitching of a bag and test zippers to determine the durability of a product. Furthermore, purchasing some products, like copied DVDs, is a violation of international antipiracy laws. You may be subject to fines if customs in the United States comes across your new movie collection as you return home.

Finally, although Cambodia is renowned for inexpensive gems, such as emeralds, the quality varies greatly. Some vendors may take advantage of naive foreigners. Unless you have experience purchasing stones, you are unlikely to get the bargain you are looking for.

Shopping Centers

The massive shopping complexes so ubiquitous in neighboring Thailand have yet to make a widespread appearance in impoverished Cambodia. The entire shopping mall concept is so foreign that when the **Sorya Shopping Center** (St. 63, S of New Market) in Phnom Penh opened and debuted the nation's first escalator, Cambodians flocked to the mall to ride the amazing moving stairs. The mall had to hire attendants to help shoppers on and off the escalators. The multistory Sorya remains the country's premier mall, though travelers won't find much to shop for there except computer or camera accessories, such as flash drives and compact memory cards. **Paragon Cambodia** (12 St. 214, behind Royal Palace) is the newest of Phnom Penh's shopping centers, catering to the small but growing middle and upper classes. It features international brand-name cosmetics and electronics.

Along the western bank of the Siem Reap River, about a block north of the Old Market, lies Siem Reap's air-conditioned, three-story, escalator-endowed **Angkor Trade Center** (Pokambor Ave.). With a Swensens and a Pizza Company (franchises from Bangkok), it's one of the places to be seen if you are a teenage Khmer in Siem Reap. For tourists...not so much. The **Museum Mall,** a Thai-owned and -managed shopping center next to the Angkor Museum, plans to revolutionize the Siem Reap shopping scene when it opens mid-2009.

Markets

Nearly every town of moderate size, including all provincial capitals, has at least one market, called a *psar* (a variant of "bazaar"). A town's sole market is typically called the Central Market, though the Khmer name varies from town to town. If a town has more than one market, they are typically referred to as Psar Leu and Psar Chas, New Market and Old Market respectively. These markets offer everything from household supplies; clothing; jewelry; and electronic appliances to fresh produce; seafood; and even traditional herbal remedies, like dried loris: a small primate that is ground up and drunk with rice wine to alleviate postpartum maladies. These markets are fascinating places to explore, though the old markets and rural central markets are often muddy and foul (particularly in the butcher's "department"). Nonetheless, they are fine places to shop for T-shirts, sunglasses, batteries, and other sundries, typically at incredibly low prices. The markets begin buzzing with shoppers in the wee hours of the morning and stay open until the early afternoon.

In major tourist centers, vendors have abandoned their fruit stands to peddle souvenirs to tourists. While much of these markets is still devoted to, say, motorbike parts, dozens of stalls sell wood carvings and silk scarves. These markets are equally enjoyable to explore as they are to shop in. Haggle and guard your wallet from pickpockets.

Finally, Phnom Penh and Siem Reap have caught on to the night market craze that is standard fare for any shopping scene in neighboring Thai cities and towns. In addition to handicrafts, clothing, and luggage, these markets feature food, drinks, and often cultural performances, such as music by bands of disabled musicians.

Specialties
Cambodia produces a number of unique handicrafts, from stone and wood carvings to handwoven fabrics, including silk cloth and clothing. While shopping for such items is more rewarding when purchased directly from the village (or family) where they were produced, handicrafts from all over Cambodia (as well as Vietnam, China, Thailand, and Myanmar) eventually make their way to the markets of Phnom Penh and Siem Reap. While traveling, it's not uncommon to see locally produced wares exhibited on the side of the road. A village approximately halfway between Sisophon and Kralanh, for example, showcases sandstone carvings just beside its workshops along National Route No. 6 between Poipet and Siem Reap. If you have a hired car ask your driver to stop, so you can not only see how such handicrafts are produced, but also purchase them for a fraction of the price asked in Siem Reap.

A number of craft shops train and employ disadvantaged Cambodians in various handicrafts. These organizations support impoverished Cambodians by teaching them a trade, and they are often staffed by elderly masters of various mediums. Therefore, they often produce some of the finest goods in the country.

What to Buy
Cambodian silk is renowned for its quality and patterns and is available in villages where silk is produced as well as markets and boutiques in Phnom Penh and Siem Reap. Kampot pepper is one of the finest spices in the world, and can be purchased at various shops around the province. Souvenir handicrafts come in all materials, shapes, and sizes, from paperweight sandstone carvings of Jayavarman VII's head to life-size bronze images of Vishnu. Carved wooden elephants or marble likenesses of the Buddha are inexpensive, portable gifts or keepsakes from your travels.

However, products for sale at markets here are not necessarily produced in Cambodia. Uniquely Cambodian items, such as silver (alloy) betel nut containers or carvings of *apsara* dancers are more likely to be produced in Cambodia than chopstick sets or opium pipes, which are often imported from Vietnam. Buying from upscale boutiques or organizations that train disadvantaged Cambodians and sell their products ensures higher quality and the proceeds directly aid those who need it most.

Payment
Credit cards are not widely accepted in Cambodia yet. If you shop at upscale boutiques you are likely to be able to pay with a Visa or MasterCard (less so American Express). Some stores charge a commission for using a credit card, particularly AmEx. Virtually everywhere else,

you will be required to pay cash, either U.S. dollars or Cambodian riel at the commonly accepted exchange rate—4,000 riel per dollar.

VAT
Value Added Tax (VAT) ought to be charged more widely than it is, but Cambodia's tax collection system is still too rudimentary to attempt to gather taxes from most businesses. Consequently VAT is generally only passed on to consumers who patronize establishments generating enough revenue to make it worthwhile for the government to collect such taxes. VAT of 10 percent is thus only charged at larger retail stores, big hotels and restaurants, and any other highly popular business. There is no VAT refund for tourists as part of the duty-free program.

■ PHNOM PENH

Shopping Centers
Paragon Cambodia
12 St. 214, behind Royal Palace
A modern shopping center that is slightly more upscale than its counterparts. Many shops carry international labels and brands. Contains a very large supermarket with some foods that cannot be found elsewhere in Cambodia.

Sorya Shopping Center
South of New Market
A good place to shop for outrageous 1980s-style Khmer fashions or budget electronics.

Markets
Central Market
St. 130, N of St. 63
The Central Market is packed to the brim with just about anything and everything you can imagine. However, it does not have much in terms of souvenirs for tourists, other than a great selection of

cheap Cambodia T-shirts.

Olympic Market
Corner of St. 286 & St. 193
If you're having clothes made, this
market offers the widest selection
of fabrics in town. Cottons, synthet-
ics, and traditional Khmer fabrics
can be found on the second floor.

Orrusei Market
Corner of St. 182 & St. 141
Has a wide selection of costume
jewelry, Khmer fashions, and toiletries, but few souvenirs

Russian Market
Corner of St. 450 & St. 163
A veritable souvenir treasure trove,
this market has an incredible selection of silks, carvings, handicrafts,
Western-label clothing, and other
curios. Goods vary in quality.

Antiques
Lotus Pond
245 St. 51
Tel 855(0)12-348-865
Closed Sun.
This large shop has a wide range
of antiques and home furnishings.
Antique gilded statues depicting
Buddhas or fierce Chinese warriors
are quite magnificent, as are deli-
cately carved wooden panels.

Pavillon d'Asie
24-26 Sihanouk Blvd.
Tel 855(0)12-497-217
Goods include Chinese-made or
inspired statues, wood carvings,
lacquerware, lamps, and ceramics. Antique lovers will delight
in restored decor and furniture,
including French colonial pieces.

Art
Asasax Art Gallery
192 St. 178
Tel 855(0)12-363-030
Paintings, sculpture, and home
decor incorporating bold splashes
of color with traditional designs,
fusing ancient and modern art.

Le Lizard Bleu
61 St. 240

Tel 855(0)23-986-978
Le Lizard Bleu features framed
artwork of Khmer inspirations,
including striking statues, photographs, etchings, shadowboxes,
and watercolors and also frames
artwork purchased elsewhere.

Reyum Gallery
47 St. 178
Tel 855(0)23-217-149
Works range from traditional *apsara*
dancers and scenes from the court
at Angkor, to more modern and
abstract pieces. The gallery also
features books on Khmer art and
art history for aspiring aficionados.

Books
D's Books
79 St. 240
Tel 855(0)23-221-280
Over 20,000 new and secondhand
books for sale or exchange. Great
collection of literature on Cambodia and travel guides.

Monument Books
111 Norodom Blvd.
Tel 855(0)23-217-617
Modern, English-language bookstore with a fabulous children's
section and a very relaxing café.

Computer Equipment
Integrated Computer Enhancement
No. 246 E0–E1, Monivong Blvd.
Tel 855(0)23-222-924
Not exactly your one-stop computer shop, but if you are looking
for a decent selection of hardware
and computer accessories sold by
English-speaking, knowledgeable
staff, this is a good place to start.

Fashion/Accessories
Ambre
High-end fashions for women and
men are created by international
Khmer designer Romyda Keth.
Designs range from sophisticated
business attire to elegant ball
gowns and wedding dresses.

Beautiful Shoes
138 St. 143
Tel 855(0)12-848-438
This family-run business specializes
in custom-made shoes for men and
women, according to your design
and color preferences. Allow at
least a week to have shoes made.

Bliss
29 St. 240
Tel 855(0)23 215 754
The charming Bliss Boutique sells
colorful, light dresses, bags, and
other apparel, predominately made
of airy cotton instead of silk.

Friends 'n' Stuff
215 St. 13
Tel 855(0)12-426-748
Unique items designed by former
street children and their parents.
Bags, wallets, and accessories are
made from recycled materials.

Keo
92 St. 222
Tel 855(0)12-941-643
Exquisite Cambodian haute couture
by the fashion house of Sylvain
and Keopiserh Lim. This boutique
also carries a sampling of the duo's
ready-to-wear fashions.

Smateria
8 St. 57
Tel 855(0)12-647-061
The bags, wallets, hats, and table
linens found here have been produced from recycled plastic bags,
mosquito netting, and juice cartons.

SONG
75 St. 240
www.songresort.com
Men and women's apparel made
mostly from linen and other lightweight, breathable materials. These
airy clothes are perfect for resort
wear or trekking through hot and
humid Asia.

Tooit Tooit
Stall 312, Russian Market
www.friends-international.org
This funky stall stands out among
the stalls of the Russian Market.
Run by Friends-International,
home-based products are made by

parents of former street children to help send their children to school.

Water Lily
37E0 St. 240, behind Royal Palace
Tel 855(0)12-812-469
Unique and extravagant jewelry creations by designer Christine Gauthier. Browse through drawer after drawer of necklaces, earrings, and bracelets. Pieces can be custom-made according to your color preferences.

Food
Camory-Premium Cookie Boutique
167 Sisowath Quay
Tel 855(0)23-224-937
Recipes use ingredients from the provinces, like Mondulkiri honey and nuts from Kompong Cham.

Chocolate by the Shop
35 St. 240
Tel 855(0)23-998-639
This charming café sells quality Belgian chocolate and other sweets, many of which feature local ingredients such as Mondulkiri honey, Kampot pepper, and coconut.

Open Wine
219 St. 19
Tel 855(0)23-223-527
Housing the Wine Restaurant, Butcher & Co., and Fanny's Ice Cream under one roof, Open Wine is truly the total package for your fine-food needs.

Handicrafts
Nyemo
14 St. 310
Tel 855(0)23-213-160
Previously unskilled and unemployed women receive training and produce a wide range of products through a program to integrate them into the workforce. A great place for handicrafts, funky bags, and children's toys.

Rajana Association
170 St. 450, near Russian Market
Tel 855(0)23-993-642

This spacious, nonprofit boutique has beautiful handicrafts, most of which are far superior to what can be found at the nearby Russian Market. Also has some nice silks and unique jewelry.

Home Furnishings
Couleurs d'Asie
33 St. 240
Tel 855(0)23-221-075
It is all about colors at this charming boutique bearing French-designed silkware and other soft furnishings and home accents.

I Ching Décor
85 Sothearos Blvd.
Tel 855(0)23-220-873
This interior-design boutique carries an incredible selection of modern Asian furniture, plus home accessories, lighting, and kitchenware.

Silk
Cambodian Craft Cooperation
1 Norodom Blvd.
Tel 855(0)11-984-879
A must-stop shop for silks, this nonprofit training organization produces some stunning textiles in a wide range of vibrant hues, as well as silks colored by natural dyes.

Jasmine Boutique
73 St. 240
Tel 855(0)23-223-103
www.jasmineboutique.net
Dresses, blouses, skirts, and accessories are all made of hand-woven silk. Many designs incorporate unique weaving techniques.

Subtyl/Kashaya Silk
39 E0 St. 240 & 55 E0 St. 240
Tel 855(0)12-900-014 &
855(0)12-800-110
Specializes in wall hangings, purses, and custom-made shoes.

Village Focus
12 C St. 308
Tel 855(0)23-221-748
This NGO is an outpost for world-renowned silk creations by Weaves

of Cambodia, an organization that produces the best quality silks in the country.

Pharmacy
U-Care
128 Sothearos St. &
14 Sihanouk Blvd.
Tel 855(0)23-222-499 &
855(0)23-224-099
The best Western pharmacy in town sells authentic pharmaceuticals and over-the-counter drugs, plus a wide range of Western bath and beauty products.

■ SIEM REAP

Siem Reap is arguably the best place for souvenir shopping in Cambodia. The Old Market, Central Market, and two night markets specialize in an array of products oriented toward the town's booming tourist population. Dozens of boutiques focus on a variety of handicraft products, particularly around the "downtown" triangle between the Old and Central Markets.

Shopping Centers
Angkor Shopping Center
Opposite Royal Gardens, SW corner
Tel 855(0)63-963-522
This two-story, air-conditioned boutique shopping complex sells a wide range of quality handicrafts, from wood and stone carvings to silver and gold jewelry.

Lucky Mall
Sivatha Blvd., across from Hotel de la Paix
Grocery store, U-Care pharmacy, and various stores with all the supplies you need for everyday life.

Museum Mall
Charles de Gaulle St., next to Angkor National Museum
Attached to the Angkor National Museum, this Thai-owned and

-operated shopping mall has introduced a little bit of Bangkok-style shopping to Siem Reap. It has air-conditioning, fast food, and a wide variety of shops and stores.

Markets
Angkor Night Market
Khum Svay Dangkum, off Sivatha Blvd., downtown
Tel 855(0)92-654-315
www.angkornightmarket.com
The open-air night market sells handicrafts, clothes, jewelry, luggage and every other type of souvenir. It also features a crafts workshop, movie theater (of sorts), a bar, and the Dr. Fish foot "massage" parlor.

Noon-Night Market
Phnum Steung Thmei, next to Night Market, off Sivatha Blvd., downtown
www.noonnightmarket.com
The Noon-Night Market is a smaller, less atmospheric version of the Night Market, except that it opens at noon. It's a great place to shop for any type of souvenir or unwind over dinner or drinks.

Psar Chas (Old Market)
Along the Siem Reap River, downtown
The old market features everything from Cambodian and imported handicrafts to clothing and household supplies. Visit to explore the market, even if you choose to do your shopping elsewhere.

Psar Leu Thom Thmei (Big New Market)
National Highway 6, E of Siem Reap
The current one-stop shop for local residents. The expansive market features hundreds of vendors selling everything imaginable, from tobacco by the pound to whole eviscerated pigs. Not good for souvenir shopping, but a great sightseeing attraction.

Books
D's Books
Pub St.
www.ds-books.com
The Siem Reap branch of this franchise bookstore allows visitors to buy, sell, and trade new and used books. The large selection and prime location makes D's an excellent place to buy the books the kids at the temples don't want you to buy at retail prices, or simply the ones the kids don't have in stock.

Clothing
Boom Boom Room
Old Market Area, 1 block S of Pub St.
Tel 855(0)12-709-096
Potentially authentic brand-name clothing, their own line of T-shirts, and stylish gear that is reasonably priced compared to home and yet arguably too expensive for Cambodia. The music and café draw a youthful clientele.

Computer Equipment
iOne
1776 Sivatha St., opposite Hotel de la Paix
Tel 855(0)63-761-019
The iOne Apple Store sells Apple computers, iPhones, and iPods, as well as Apple accessories. Prices are exorbitantly higher than back home, but if you need Apple products in Cambodia this is your best bet.

Handicrafts
Artisans d'Angkor, Angkor Crafts Center
Stung Thmey St.
Tel 855(0)63-963-330
www.artisansdangkor.com
Cambodian fine arts and crafts, including wood and stone carvings, as well as silk products from their nearby silk farm. All products are created by disadvantaged Cambodians who have graduated from their training school. While prices are the highest in town, their products are arguably the highest quality.

Carving Association & Orphan Career Center
No. 0152 Group 2, Nondol 3, Slorkram Commune, East Bank of Siem Reap River, due E of Sofitel Royal Angkor Hotel
Tel 855(0)12-473-647
This local sandstone-carving workshop produces remarkable statuary, some far too large to fit in your house. Custom orders are available and overseas shipping can be arranged.

House of Peace
Salarean Kok Patri, Krous Village, National Highway 6 toward the airport
Tel 855(0)12-913-398
www.house-of-peace.de.ms
Produces *sbek* shadow puppets in the likenesses of Hindu figures and the shapes of animals from tanned, perforated cowhides. Proceeds benefit disadvantaged children.

National Center for Khmer Ceramics Revival
Phum Thnorl, Khum Sror Ngea, National Highway 6 toward airport
Tel 855(0)63-761-519
www.khmerceramics.com
In addition to single-handedly attempting to re-create the ancient art of Angkor-era ceramics, this project features a small shop selling historically re-created examples from the ancient Khmer Kingdom as well as contemporary ceramics.

Saron Sculpture Workshop
Kor Koh Jrum Village, along Rte. 67 to Banteay Srei
Tel 855(0)92-991-002
This tiny workshop produces handcrafted wood carvings of Hindu, Buddhist, and Christian inspirational design. Their on-site display is small, but you can see the works in progress and the disabled workers who craft them.

Senteurs d'Angkor
Opposite Old Market
Tel 855(0)63-964-801
www.senteursdangkor.com
Another project to benefit impoverished Cambodians, the downtown shop of the nearby crafts factory specializes in handmade soaps, but also sells silk products and other handicrafts from Khmer artisans around Cambodia.

Photography
Lhor Pehn Chet Digital Center & Studio
22–23 Sivatha Blvd.
This shop sells cameras and camera supplies, such as battery chargers. They also process prints and burn photo CDs.

McDermott Gallery
FCC Complex & Pokambor Ave.
Tel 855(0)12-274-274
www.mcdermottgallery.com
The McDermott Gallery sells gorgeous photos and prints of various sizes taken at the temples of Angkor and around the Cambodian countryside. Rotating exhibitions by featured artists also showcase and sell their works. Two galleries are located in town, one by the FCC hotel, and one in the alleyway behind Pub Street.

Silk
Artisans d'Angkor– National Silk Center
Puok Village, 10 miles (16 km) from Siem Reap off National Highway 6, beyond airport
Tel 855(0)63-963-330
This collection of some of the kingdom's finest silk products is made on-site at the factory where disadvantaged Cambodians are trained in the craft. Free tours are available between 8 a.m. and 5:30 p.m.

Cambodian Handicraft Association for Landmine and Polio Disabled (CHA)
1 mile (1.6 km) N of intersection of Route 67 & Route 204
Tel 855(0)23-881-720
www.online.com.kh/users/wthanchashop
Located along the road to Banteay Srei temple, this small workshop and showroom of the Phnom Penh–based organization sells silk scarves, bags, and other items produced by disabled Cambodians.

Institute for Khmer Traditional Textiles
House No. 472, road to Tonle Sap Lake
Tel 855(0)63-964-437
This project helped revive traditional silk production and weaving in Cambodia. It has a shophouse, workshop, and museum in one building, just outside town, on the road to the lake. Watch silk being woven downstairs, and then enter the old wooden house to shop for traditional silk cloth and clothing, as well as modern interpretations of traditional products.

Khmer Attitude
1 Vithei Charles de Gaulle, in Raffles Grand Hotel d'Angkor
Tel 855(0)63-963-888
A collection of some of the finest designed handicrafts in Siem Reap, from elaborate silver bowls to small wooden elephant key chains and elaborate silk clothing.

Rajana Association
153 Sivatha St., in front of street leading to Night Market
www.rajanacrafts.org
Their workshops in Phnom Penh and Siem Reap produce a variety of handicrafts for sale at their centrally located Siem Reap store. This nonprofit organization uses proceeds to provide Cambodians with an income-generating trade.

Samatoa
98 Provincial Hospital Rd., Old Market area, 1 block NE of Pub St.
Tel 855(0)63-965-310
www.samatoa.com
Samatoa sells tailored made-to-measure silk clothes, ready in a day, inspired by French fashions. The silk is manufactured by disadvantaged Cambodian women, and the selection of clothing is one of the finest in Siem Reap.

Pharmacy
U-Care
Locations include: Old Market area (across from Pub St.); Lucky Department Store; Siem Reap International Airport; and the Museum Mall
U-Care sells authentic pharmaceuticals and Western bath and beauty products.

■ WESTERN CAMBODIA

BATTAMBANG

Handicrafts
Rachana Handicrafts Battambang
No. 97 Group 5, Preak Preasdach Village, near Bat Dambang Kranhoung monument
Tel 855(0)12-940-358
This workshop sells a small selection of their handicrafts manufactured on-site by disadvantaged Cambodian women. The rest of their products are sent to Siem Reap and Phnom Penh boutiques.

■ SIHANOUKVILLE

Books
Q&A Book Café
95 Ekareach St., downtown
Tel 855(0)12-598-225
Great selection of new and used books in this cute little café that also specializes in tours and providing tourist information.

Entertainment

During Cambodia's turbulent recent past, a number of the nation's performing arts were nearly destroyed by the Khmer Rouge regime, which targeted many artists. There has been a 21st-century revival of a number of forms of traditional entertainment, however, both to preserve classic art forms and to serve the growing tourism market.

Circus Performances

Circus performances have been held since the Angkor era, as evidenced by bas-relief carvings on the Terrace of the Elephants and Bayon temple. You may get lucky and witness a performance of *pahi* by an itinerant "medicine man." If not, circus performances are semiregularly held in both Phnom Penh and Battambang, which showcase modern variations on traditional Khmer circus routines, the exact art of which has been lost to the ages.

Phare Ponleu Selpak

Anh Chanh Village, Ochar Commune, Battambang
Tel 855(0)12-890-360
www.phareps.org
Seak samai (modern circus) is performed beneath a genuine big-top tent by disadvantaged Khmer children who are trained as in professional circus routines that fuse circus with traditional and modern dance. Their grown-up performers have gone on to travel the world as a renowned circus troupe.

Dance Performances

Dancing is an important aspect of Cambodian culture. *Apsara* dancers, the human representations of the celestial beings renowned for their dancing ability, performed for the kings of Angkor and the gods whom they worshipped. *Robam borane,* Khmer classical or court dance entails female performers reenacting stories from the *Reamker* (the Cambodian version of the Hindu epic *Ramayana*). *Robam propehni,*

Khmer folk dance, varies from village to village and employs natural props such as coconut shells to tell tales of everyday life that incorporate spiritual themes. Today, there are many dance performances of varying quality regularly scheduled in tourist destinations such as Phnom Penh. They are particularly common in Siem Reap.

Amrita Performing Arts

128G9, Sothearos Blvd., Phnom Penh
Tel 855(0)23-220-424
www.amritaperformingarts.org
This performance art company puts on classical and contemporary music, theater, and dance performances. While the company does not offer daily or weekly events in Cambodia, it holds several touring festivals throughout the year, even traveling as far as New York and Florida for performances.

Apsara Theatre

Front of Angkor Village Hotel, off Wat Bo Rd., Siem Reap
Tel 855(0)63-963-561
In a gorgeous wooden theater, dancers conduct *apsara* dance performances while diners feast on a set menu of Khmer food. Nightly from 7 p.m. to 9 p.m. Reservations recommended.

Classic Café

42 St. 19, behind Royal Palace, Phnom Penh
Tel 855(0)12-857-525
Not your typical *apsara*-based dance performance, Classic features PG-13–type shows with

outrageous acts such as impressive break dancing, runway routines, and melodramatic karaoke/dance numbers by glittering drag queens. There are two shows each night of the week, at 10 p.m. and 11:30 p.m. The club doubles as a school for drag queens.

Dead Fish Tower

Sivatha Blvd., Siem Reap
Tel 855(0)12-630-377
Both *apsara* and traditional folk dances are performed nightly from 7:30 p.m. to 10 p.m. on an elevated stage in the middle of this massive, multitiered restaurant that specializes in Thai set menus and other Asian fare.

Epic Arts Cambodia

Angus Lawson Arts Centre, Kampot
Tel 855 (0)33-932-247
www.epicarts.org.uk/cambodia
This unique dance troupe integrates disabled and able-bodied individuals in original and rather stunning performance art that incorporates modern and ancient dance styles and techniques. Performances are presented by both professional and youth groups. The Accessible Arts Center in Kampot, which will host shows and workshops, is scheduled to open in 2010.

La Noria Hotel

East side of Siem Reap River, 1 block N of National Highway 6, Siem Reap
Tel 855(0)63-964-242
Following a traditional shadow puppet performance, disadvantaged children sponsored by the

NGO Krousar Thmey put on a variety of traditional dances for diners each Wednesday from 7:30 to 8:30 p.m. Reservations recommended.

La Résidence d'Angkor
East side of Siem Reap River, 1 block N of Wat Bo Bridge, Siem Reap
One of the finer venues for dining and watching traditional dance performances, La Résidence has outdoor performances Tuesday, Thursday, and Saturday evenings from 6 to 10:30 p.m.

Raffles Grand Hotel d'Angkor
1 Charles de Gaulle St., Siem Reap
Tel 855(0)63-963-888
Each Monday, Wednesday, and Friday, the Raffles puts on an elegant dance performance in the gardens across from the hotel. Show includes an Asian barbecue buffet, beginning at 7 p.m.

Sovanna Phum
111 St. 360, Phnom Penh
Tel 855(0)23-221-932
Classical and folk dances performed by an art association which began in 1994 to revive Khmer arts and give Khmer artists an opportunity to perform and make a living. Performances, including dance, shadow puppetry, and music are held every Friday and Saturday at 7:30 p.m.

Temple Balcony
Pub St., Siem Reap
Tel 855(0)15-999-909
While the downstairs of the Temple is a raucous late-night club, the upstairs features a large stage where nightly *apsara* and traditional dance performances are performed. Passable Western and Asian fare is served during the 7:30 p.m. to 9:30 p.m. shows.

Tiny Toones Cambodia
4 St. 460, Phnom Penh, next to Russian Market
Tel 855(0)12-968-815
www.tinytoonescambodia.com
A less traditional dance troupe, this social organization teaches break dancing to disadvantaged youth, providing a positive after-school activity and building self-esteem. Participants also receive English lessons and mentoring to encourage them to value their educations. Break dancing practices are open to the public from 6 p.m. to 9 p.m. daily.

Khmer Boxing
While Khmer boxing is less well known than Muay Thai (Thai boxing), the roots of that sport lie in Cambodian history. The armies of Angkor employed both weapons and hand-to-hand combat techniques to subjugate wide expanses of land. Today, Khmer boxing generally follows the rules of Muay Thai. Cambodian boxers are not yet as skilled as those in neighboring Thailand, but watching a Khmer boxing match is an exciting exhibition to behold. Live matches are most easily seen at one of Phnom Penh's two venues, though open-air bar/restaurants throughout Cambodia serve as frenzied hives of wagering by local television spectators. (Watch your wallet when attending a local boxing match, as child pickpockets are taught to target foreigners.) The two venues for watching boxing in Phnom Penh feature matches on alternating days. Ask your hotel concierge or a *tuk-tuk* driver for information and venue locations.

Shadow Puppet Shows
La Noria Restaurant
East side of Siem Reap River, one block N of National Highway 6, Siem Reap

Tel 855(0)63-964-242
Performed to live music before a dining audience, disadvantaged children sponsored by the NGO Krousar Thmey put on a traditional shadow-puppet performance followed by a variety of traditional dances each Wednesday from 7:30 p.m. to 8:30 p.m. Reservations recommended.

Sovanna Phum
Next to House No. 159A, St. 99 Phnom Penh
Tel 855(0)23-987-564 or 855(0)23-221-932
This organization of artists was one of the first to revive the art of shadow-puppet theater in Cambodia in the wake of decades of war. In addition to providing visitors the opportunity to create their own shadow puppets, Sovanna Phum gives performances, including dance, shadow puppetry, and music every Friday and Saturday at 7:30 p.m.

Activities

While Cambodia's primary tourist activity is visiting its magnificent temples, as the number of expatriates has swelled in recent years, many have imported Western activities to cater to tourists. Some seem perfectly natural, such as cooking classes, elephant experiences, trekking and mountain biking, and scuba diving. Others, like golfing, horseback riding, and paragliding, are new. In addition, organizations reviving traditional cultural activities are offering visitors hands-on cultural experiences.

Most activities are centered around the main tourist destinations: Phnom Penh, Siem Reap, and Sihanoukville. Specialized activities such as bird-watching and elephant trekking are available in the more far-flung provinces. Opportunities to do volunteer work or experience traditional Cambodian life through a Community-Based Ecotourism (CBET) project are found in even the most remote provincial towns.

Bird-watching

Home to some of the world's most exotic and endangered bird life, Cambodia is a bird-watching paradise.

Sam Veasna Center for Wildlife Conservation

No. 0552, Group 12,
Wat Bo Rd., Siem Reap
Tel 855(0)63-963-710
www.samveasna.org
Leads organized day trips around Siem Reap and overnight visits to more remote regions of Cambodia to search for some of the country's most renowned bird species, including the sarus crane, bengal forican, greater adjutant, milky stork, spot-billed pelican, white-rumped vulture, slender-billed vultures, white-shouldered ibis and giant ibis—Cambodia's national bird (see sidebar p. 121).

Boat Tours

Since so much of Cambodia is occupied by rivers and lakes, boat tours make a great way to experience its gorgeous scenery and natural beauty.

The Boatman

Kampot
Tel 855(0)92-174-280
For those who hope to really experience the natural, untouched beauty of Kampot, the friendly, eccentric Bart the Boatman offers a variety of river voyages in a small fishing craft. Itineraries can be catered to individual preference and often include barbecues at the Boatman's riverside home.

Chenla Luxury Boat

Sisowath Quay, passenger port near St. 104, Phnom Penh
Tel 855(0)12-758-992
Deluxe two-level riverboat with lunch and dinner cruises. Very lovely for private parties. Service is a little shaky.

Kanika Catamaran

Sisowath Quay, docked opposite St. 136, Phnom Penh
Tel 855(0)12-848-802
Nonprofit boat tours offering high tea and dinner cruises. Can be rented for private parties and charter cruises.

Commuity-Based Ecotourism

The Cambodia Community-Based Ecotourism Network (CCBEN) supports projects throughout the country in which villages develop sustainable tourism programs that allow tourists to experience the culture and environment of Cambodia. Such projects typically let visitors spend the night in a village through a homestay program, ride oxcarts around the countryside, go on wildlife-watching expeditions, ride mountain bikes, and learn about the lives of Cambodian villagers, including their farming, fishing, or handicrafts activities.

Current CCBEN (www.ccben .org) projects around Cambodia include Chi Phat and Chambok ecotourism villages, Virachey National Park, Yak Laom Lake, the Mekong Irrawaddy Dolphin Pool, Kompong Phluk floating village, Prek Toal, Ang Trapaeng Thmar and Tmatboey (see Ecotourism, pp. 222–223).

Cooking

A number of opportunities let you learn about Khmer cuisine through cooking schools and restaurants, which typically include a market tour, discussion of ingredients, demonstrations followed by hands-on experiences, and finally, a feast of multiple courses (see sidebar p. 58).

Cambodian Cooking Class

67 St. 240, Phnom Penh
Tel 855(0)12-524-801
www.cambodia-cooking-class.com
Run by the nearby Frizz Restaurant, hands-on classes are held on a rooftop terrace, with three courses to choose from, including a vegetarian option.

Cooks in Tuk-Tuks

River Garden, Siem Reap
Tel 855(0)63-963-400
www.therivergarden.info
High on style, Cooks in Tuk-Tuks features tuk-tuk drivers dressed as chefs who lead market tours followed by cooking demonstrations. Participatory cooking classes available upon request.

Shinta Mani Hotel
1 block SE of post office,
Siem Reap
Tel 855(0)63-761-998
www.shintamani.com
Years of experience as a hospitality training school ensures that Shinta Mani provides professional instruction in a friendly, fun environment.

Cycling/Mountain-Biking Tours
Self-guided cycling tours of small towns and cities are possible through daily bike rentals at your guesthouse or hotel ($2–$15 per day, depending on quality of bike). Multiday excursions around Cambodia are available through a select few organizations (see sidebar p. 91).

Biking Cambodia
668 Hup Guan St., Siem Reap
Tel 855(0)12-843-401
www.bikingcambodia.com
They have the best bicycles available to rent in Siem Reap for exploring the temples of Angkor either on your own or with a guided tour.

Chi Phat Community-Based Ecotourism
Tel 855(0)12-318-445
This relatively remote ecotourism village up the Chi Phat River in the southern foothills of the Cardamom Mountains offers outstanding mountain-biking day trips and overnight stays in shelters built of local materials.

Grasshopper Adventures
Tel/U.S. (818)912-7101;
Thailand/International:
66(0)87-929-5208
www.grasshopperadventures.com
Leads specialized tours around multiple Asian nations, including Cambodia, which can be joined as an individual leg of their larger southeast Asian adventures.

Pepy Ride
No. 188, Salakanseng Village,
National Highway 6 to airport,
Siem Reap
Tel 855(0)12-474-150
www.pepyride.org
Pepy Ride combines community development with bicycle tours of Cambodia; riders' fees are used to fund the educational development and environmental projects that you visit while exploring the countryside.

Off-road Motorbiking
Guided dirt-bike tours allow visitors to literally get off the beaten path and explore parts of rural Cambodia infrequently visited by other tourists.

Dancing Roads
66C St. 368, Phnom Penh
Tel 855(0)12-822-803
www.dancingroads.com
Conveniently located for day trips from Phnom Penh. Dancing Roads' staff are knowledgeable and experienced on all Cambodia's bumpy (dancing) back roads.

Jungle Cross
Main street in Koh Kong town
Tel 855(0)15-601-633
www.junglecross.com
Bike rentals or guided tours of the southern Cardamom Mountains, terrain which is not for the inexperienced rider.

Norden House
Road to Yak Laom, Ban Lung,
Ratanakiri
Tel 855(0)12-880-327
www.nordenhouseyaklom.com
The ultimate base of operations for exploring the remote hill-tribe province of Ratanakiri.

Siem Reap Dirtbikes
Tel 855(0)99-823-216
www.siemreapdirtbikes.com
Great bikes, friendly guides, and spectacular terrain. Safe but adventurous day trips around Siem Reap for novices

and hard-core adventures throughout Cambodia for the more experienced.

Quad Adventure Cambodia
0.3 miles (0.5 km) from Old Market, Siem Reap
Tel 855(0)92-787-216
www.quad-adventure-cambodia.com
Select either an hour-long joyride or a day trip around the villages near Siem Reap. Both are conducted on four-wheel all-terrain vehicles (ATVs), a great way to see some rural life just outside Cambodia's least authentic town, touristy Siem Reap.

Elephant Experiences
Only a few domesticated elephants remain in Cambodia, but there are some opportunities to get hands-on experiences riding elephants or learning to work with them (see sidebar p. 233).
    You can ride elephants to waterfalls just outside Ban Lung, the provincial capital of Ratanakiri. Contact your guesthouse in Ban Lung for information on half-day and full-day combined elephant ride–waterfall visits.

Film
Le Cinema
French Cultural Center,
218 St. 184,
Phnom Penh
Tel 855(0)23-213-124
www.ccf-cambodge.com
Phnom Penh's best bet for a cinema, this hundred-seat theater shows international art-house films, documentaries, and mainstream movies in a wide variety of languages (usually with French or English subtitles). Also hosts numerous film festivals.

Meta House
6 St. 264
Phnom Penh
Tel 855(0)12-607-465
www.meta-house.com

This arts center hosts a full schedule of screenings, mostly showing films and documentaries from or about Cambodia and Asia. All showings start at 7 p.m.

Movie Mall
Angkor Night Market, Siem Reap
Tel 855(0)23-991-150
Documentary films on land mines and the Khmer Rouge, as well as a 3-D film on snakes.

Fishing
Serious fishermen with their own gear are likely to fall in love with Cambodia, whose plentiful rivers, streams, and lakes are rife with fish. However, fish is a staple of the Cambodian diet and some coveted fishing areas are protected by armed guards. Casting a rod into a river is unlikely to get you into trouble, however. One outfit caters to visiting fishermen (see sidebar p. 245).

Tradewinds Charters/Sihanoukville Fishing
Munddul 1, Sangkat 2, Sihanoukville
Tel 855(0)34-933-997 or 855(0)12-702-478

Golf
Golf is relatively new to Cambodia, but golf courses are starting to spring up. There are currently four golf courses in Cambodia, two located near the temples of Angkor, just outside the town of Siem Reap, and two on the outskirts of Phnom Penh.

Angkor Golf Resort
Kasekam Village, Siem Reap
Tel 855(0)63-392-288
www.angkor-golf.com
This Nick Faldo–designed course is considered by some to be one of the finest courses in Southeast Asia. The par 72 course totals 7,230 yards (6,611 m) of perfectly manicured fairways and greens

designed to challenge golfers with some bold bunkering and some tricky greens.

Cambodia Golf & Country Club
56A St. 222, Phnom Penh
Tel 855(0)23-366-689
Located 22 miles (35 km) from Phnom Penh. Though slightly more challenging than the capital's other course, it consists of relatively flat terrain with just a handful of tricky bunkers.

Royal Cambodia Golf Club
National Highway 4, Kop Srov District
Tel 855(0)23-366-689 or 855(0)11-290-552
Just 6 miles (10 km) from Phnom Penh, this was the first 18-hole golf course to break ground in Cambodia. While the course is not as challenging as those in Siem Reap, its proximity to the capital provides easy access for visitors and a who's who of Phnom Penh's elite.

Sofitel Phokeethra Country Club
Charles de Gaulle St., Siem Reap
Tel 855(0)63-964-600
www.sofitel.com
This par 72, 7,145-yard (6,540 m) course starts near an Angkor-era bridge discovered on the grounds. The course is home to the Cambodian Open golf tournament, which was inaugurated in December 2007.

Horseback Riding
The Happy Ranch Horse Farm
Off National Highway 6 toward airport, Siem Reap
Tel 855(0)12-920-002
Trail rides, riding lessons, and cart rides cover all the options for equestrian enthusiasts at Cambodia's sole horse farm. The countryside just outside the town of Siem Reap is spectacular and yet still conveniently

located for half-day or full-day adventures.

Karaoke
Le West Club Karaoke
504 St. 230, across from the Mondiale Center, Phnom Penh
Tel 855(0)23-997-800
Private karaoke rooms at this club offer a large selections of English, Khmer, Chinese, Korean, and French hits. Great for all sizes of groups (see sidebar p. 43). Sing your heart out.

Meditation
While Buddhism is Cambodia's national religion, there are few opportunities for foreigners to learn about Buddhism and meditation in Cambodia. The following are places do have services for foreigners, though. (See sidebar p. 51)

Battambang Vipassana Centre
Chhoan Phieu (Phnom Penh Office)
126 E. St. Vihea Cham Sangkat Chroy Chongva, Khan Russei Keo
Tel 855(0)92-931-647 (Battambang)
Tel 855(0)12-870-766 (Phnom Penh)
www.dhamma.org
Ten-day meditation courses for both beginners and experienced students include vegetarian meals and simple accommodations at an isolated retreat near Phnom Sampeau, Battambang.

Dhammaduta Association–Wat Lanka
Sihanouk (St. 274), Wat Lanka, Phnom Penh
Main temple, upper floor
Tel 855(0)12-482-215 or 855(0)23-721-001
Informal classes on meditation and Buddhism are offered (6 p.m. Mon.–Tues., Thurs., Sat.–Sun.) at

this revered Buddhist monastery located near the Independence Monument in Phnom Penh.

Singing Tree Café
Wat Bo Rd. area, Siem Reap
Tel 855(0)92-635-500
www.singingtreecafe.com
Closed Mon.
Weekly chats with English-speaking monks from nearby temples on Saturday evenings, and Buddhist meditation study on Sundays.

Paragliding
ParaCambodia
Tel 855(0)12-709-096
www.paracambodia.com
While the course takes up to a week and your life is literally in your own hands, learning to fly a motor-driven parachute around the beaches and islands of Cambodia is sure to be a once-in-a-lifetime experience (see sidebar p. 243).

Photography Tours
See sidebar p. 94.

Sailing
During the dry season months (Nov.–May), visitors to Cambodia's beaches can try a variety of sailing options, from small catamarans to live-aboard luxury vessels (see sidebar p. 252).

Knai Bang Chatt Sailing Club
Phum Thmey Sangkat Pret, Kep
Tel 855(0)-92-882-750
www.knaibangchatt.com/
#sailingclub
Open to the public, with catamarans, kayaks, surfboards, windsurfers, and a motorboat available to rent. Kep has especially strong winds that make for perfect sailing conditions.

Otres Nautica
Otres Beach, Sihanoukville
Tel 855(0)92-230-065

On quiet Otres Beach, Otres Nautica offers rental catamarans, small sailboats, and even kayaks.

Sail Cambodia
Tel 855(0)16-450-964 or 855(0)11-390-083
www.sailcambodia.info
Offers day trips and overnight sailing charters aboard a 45-foot (14 m) boat around the islands off Sihanoukville's coast.

Running
Hash House Harriers
Phnom Penh
Tel 855(0)12-832-509
www.p2h3.com
Hash House Harrier running clubs can be found throughout the world and provide a unique opportunity to keep fit, meet new people, see the countryside, and enjoy some post-run drinks. The Phnom Penh Hash meets at the railway station every Sunday at 2:45 p.m.

Scuba Diving
Scuba diving is still relatively new in Cambodia and many dive sites are only just being discovered, primarily off the coasts of Sihanoukville and Koh Kong. Diving is a seasonal activity, generally restricted to the dry months of November to May, when the seas are calm and the visibility is better. Although the diving in Cambodia is not yet as renowned as in neighboring Thailand, some of the dive sites located on islands farther from the coast—which require overnight stays either on board or in an a tent on the beach—have superior visibility. There are a number of reasons divers enjoy Cambodia's waters, particularly the prevalence of macrolife species, such as nudibranchs and seahorses. Manta rays and the occasional whale shark are even possible to spot (see sidebar p. 240).

The Dive Shop Cambodia
Serendipity Beach Rd., Sihanoukville
Tel 855(0)12-161-5517 or 855(0)34-933-664
www.diveshopcambodia.com
One of the few National Geographic Dive Centers in Cambodia, the Dive Shop has a major emphasis on environmental protection and one of the most energetic, personable, and passionate staffs in the business, providing a truly memorable dive experience.

EcoSea Dive Shop
Serendipity Beach Rd., Sihanoukville
Tel 855(0)12-606-646
www.ecoseadive.com
Quality gear and multilingual staff provide excellent dive trips including overnight stays in a fishing village or beneath the stars on board the boat.

Scuba Nation
18 E0, Sothearos Blvd., Phnom Penh
Tel 855(0)12-715-785
Mohachai Guesthouse, Serendipity Rd., Sihanoukville
Tel 855(0)34-933-700
www.divecambodia.com
Another National Geographic Dive Center in Cambodia, Scuba Nation has an office in Phnom Penh and a dive shop in Sihanoukville. While only open in the dry season months, their environmental and educational focus sets them apart from many other dive operators.

Spas
Massages are a must while in Asia. These spas are clean and professional and offer high-end services and packages.

Amara Spa
Corner of Sisowath Quay &
St. 110, Phnom Penh
Tel 855(0)23-998-730

www.amaraspa.hotelcara.com
One of the most upscale day spas in Phnom Penh, Amara boasts a striking modern Asian, Zen ambience and interior, in which no detail has been overlooked. Try the spa's signature East-West fusion massage.

Bliss
29 St. 240, Phnom Penh
Tel 855(0)23-215-754
A tranquil spa in a beautiful colonial building, Bliss offers massages, facials, exfoliations, wraps, nail treatments, and packages that will melt your troubles away.

Dermal Spa
4C St. 57, Phnom Penh
Tel 855(0)12-222-898
Tucked away in NGO-land, this tiny, friendly spa offers quality services at very affordable prices. The best place in town for facials, Dermal uses specialty dermalogica products and provides free skin consultation with services.

Nata Spa
31D Sihanouk Blvd., Phnom Penh
Tel 855(0)23-223-938
www.nataspa.com.kh
A popular choice among wealthy Khmers, Nata aims to provide a VIP experience for all customers. The hot-stone massage is highly recommended. The spa also has its own high-end beauty salon. A branch in Siem Reap is in the planning stages.

Tennis

Narmada Sports Center
Imperial Garden Villa & Hotel
315 Sisowath Quay, Phnom Penh
Tel 855(0)23-219-991
The quality tennis court is available to rent both on weekdays and weekends.

VIP Sport Club
Norodom Blvd., Phnom Penh
Tel 855(0)23-993-535
Popular sports club among many of the city's expats, VIP has a

number of tennis courts that can be rented out by the hour.

Trekking
There are few solely trekking-oriented businesses in Cambodia. Most day trips and overnight hiking and camping trips are organized out of guesthouses and hotels, who will procure the services of a guide and get passes from a nearby national park or wildlife sanctuary if necessary. Bird-watching tours are one way to get out into the wilderness. Ecotourism projects coordinated through CCBEN (www.ccben.org) are your other best opportunity for hiking in the wilderness. The Cardamom Mountains and Elephant Mountains of southwest Cambodia and the northeastern province of Ratanakiri offer the most spectacular trekking. Be advised that there aren't Western-style facilities for overnight trekking trips; accommodation typically consists of a hammock with built-in mosquito nets or rudimentary lodging in a village home. Toilets, if available at all, are extremely basic as well. That said, the countryside through which you trek is likely to be unspoiled by human development of any kind.

Chambok Community-Based Ecotourism
National Highway 4 near
Kirirom National Park
Tel 855(0)23-214-409
www.geocities.com/chambokcet
One of the first CBET projects in Cambodia, the Chambok eco-tourism project has local guides, trained to lead historical, natural, and cultural tours of the area, where visitors have the opportunity to engage in

trekking, bird-watching, animal tracking, swimming, and riding in oxcarts.

Nature Lodge
Several miles outside of Sen Monorom town, Mondulkiri
Tel 855(0)11-494-449
www.naturelodgecambodia.com
Two-day and three-day trekking trips usually include hiking, swimming, and climbing through the spectacular Mondulkiri countryside. These treks help provide a positive source of income, training, and experience for Khmer and Bunong guides

Sok Lim Tours
Opposite Blissful Guesthouse, downtown Kampot
Tel 855(0)12-719-872
www.soklimtours.com
Two-day, one-night treks into Bokor National Park, beyond the remaining ruins of Bokor Hill Station, into the wilderness. Guests can opt to sleep in the jungle or back at the ranger station. Other nearby adventures are available either as standard trips or customized adventures.

Virachey National Park
Park office: 3 blocks E &
1 block N of Ban Lung traffic circle, Ban Lung, Ratanakiri
Tel 855(0)75-974-176
www.ccben.org
The largest and most remote park in Cambodia, bordering both Vietnam and Laos, Virachey features unspoiled mountains, forests, grasslands and valleys where endangered wildlife, and perhaps a few undiscovered species, still roam. Activities include three- to eight-day trekking and camping adventures that may also include bicycling, kayaking, wildlife viewing, and cultural immersion.

Language Guide

While not a tonal language like Thai or Chinese, Khmer can be tricky to learn as there are more letters in the Khmer than English alphabet. Many of these letters produce sounds that are difficult for foreigners to pronounce. Furthermore, as Khmer uses a script that is rather difficult to learn quickly, foreigners must rely on transliterations of Khmer words, for which there is no agreed-upon system.

To further complicate matters, many Khmer words written with roman characters are transliterations based on French pronunciations. Consequently, maps, books, road signs, and other written text is likely to vary from one source to the next. To make matters worse, many books that attempt to translate Khmer words insist on using confusing transliterations such as the addition of the silent h. This problem is best illustrated in an example from neighboring Thailand, where most visitors invariably look forward to their holiday on Foo-ket Island (Phuket), which has a confusing silent h.

With these things in mind, and taking into account that no transliteration can reproduce Khmer sounds exactly, try to read the transliterations as you would with an American accent. When letters or sounds cannot be perfectly reproduced, the word has been broken down into the most simple pronunciation, regardless of proper syllabization.

Ultimately, however, it will be much easier for you to learn to pronounce the following words if you read them to a native Khmer speaker (a tuk-tuk driver or staff at your guesthouse) and have them help you fine-tune your pronunciation of Khmer words.

The following letters are difficult for Westerners to pronounce:

pb, dt, and *gk:* Khmer has individual *p, b, d, t, g,* and *k* sounds, but also combinations of both. Try saying both at the same time to accurately pronounce words employing these letters.

ng: Pronounced just like the *ng* in sing, but often at the beginning or middle of words

eu: You need to hear this one spoken by a native speaker and practice saying it.

ny: As used in words like K'nyom, the first person pronoun I, ny also takes some practice listening and saying.

rr: R's are often rolled.

Some words end in barely pronounced silent k's or t's.

A note on English: Many foreigners speak English to Cambodians as if they were talking to another native English speaker, which is to say very rapidly. Sometimes foreigners speak to Cambodians very slowly and loudly, as if they were stupid. Consider how poorly you can speak and understand Khmer and you ought to have an appreciation of how difficult it is for the people here to speak English. If you speak somewhat slowly and carefully enunciate your English words, then Cambodian people will be able to understand you and help you better. Many speak English quite well and most are eager to practice their English with you and teach you some Khmer in exchange.

Casual Conversation

Hello	Soo-ah s'day
Goodbye	Juhm ree-uhp lee-ah/ Leah hi (informal)
How are you?	Nee-ak soak sa-buy chia day
I'm fine	K'nyom soak sa-buy

Please	Som
Thank you	Awe coon
Excuse me/ I'm sorry	sohm dtoe
No problem	Ot ben-ya-haa
Yes	Baat (men)
	Jaa (women)
No	Dtay

What's your name?
Nee-ak cha-mua away

My name is...
K'nyom cha-mua...

Where are you from?
Nee-ak mao beh pro-tey nar?

I'm from... K'nyom mao bpee...

Eating & Drinking

I'm a vegetarian
K'nyom pboo-ah

Not sweet	Ot pbah-aim
Not spicy	Ot hahl

May I have some...
Nee-ak mee-un...

I don't want... Ot...

Chili	mut-dtay
Ice	dtuck caulk
Peanuts	sundike die
Water	dtuck

Emergencies

Help Jew-ee! / Jew-ee k'nyom pong!

Does anyone here speak English?
Tee-nee meean neeak jeh pee-assa on-glay dtay?

I don't understand.
K'nyom, mun yule dtay.

Call the police!
Jew-ee hav po-lee mao!

I have been robbed.
K'nyom trrow jao plawn.

Call a doctor.
Jew-ee hav crrew pbai mao!

Please take me to a hospital.
Som june k'nyom dtoe montee pbait.

I am ill K'nyom chheu

I have...	*K'nyom mee-un...*
Diarrhea	*rowke jo ree-ak*
Fever	*gkrune*

Where is the toilet?
Mee-un bong-coon nu eye-na?

Do you have... *Nee-ak mee-un...*

Toilet paper	*grow-da ah-naa-mai*
Soap	*sa-boo*
Aspirin	*para-setamol*
Sanitary napkins	
	sahm-loy ah-naa-mai
I am lost	*k'nyom vungvee-ung pleu*

Getting Around

Where is the... *Now eye nar?*

I'm looking for the...
K'nyom roke

Please take me to...
Som june k'nyom dtao

Airport	*prrro-lian yune-ha*
Bank	*t'nee-a-gear*
Bus Station	*setanee laan kerong*
Embassy	*sa-tarn-toot...(Ah-mer-ee-kaa)*
Hospital	*mon-tree pbuil*
Market	*p'sar*
Pharmacy	*farm-a-see*
Police Station	*pos polee*
Post Office	*pbrai-sa-nee*
Toilet	*toy-let*

Go straight	*Dtoe drong*
Turn left	*Bot cha-wayne*
Turn right	*Bot sa-dam*
At the corner	*New gite jaroong*
Next to...	*New jobe...*
Slow down	*Some yeuht yeuht*
Watch out!	*Praw-yat*
Stop here	*Chop tee-nee*

I want to get off
K'nyom jong joe

Shopping

Shopping is one occasion where it will be quite useful to speak some Khmer. The logic is that if you can speak some Khmer then you aren't clueless about how much things in Cambodia should cost. However, if you ask questions in Khmer you should expect to be answered in Khmer. Make sure you are familiar with Khmer numbers or your pretense of being a local will quickly disappear.

How much is this?
Neek talay bone-maan?

That's too much.
Talay bpake

I'll pay you... *K'nyome ohwee...*

Numbers

1	*moy*
2	*pbee*
3	*buy*
4	*pboon*
5	*pbram*
6	*pbram–moy*
7	*pbram–pbee*
8	*pbram–buy*
9	*pbram–pboon*
10	*dawp*
11	*dawp-moy*
12	*dawp-pbee*
13	*dawp-buy*
14	*dawp-pboon*
15	*dawp-pbram*
16	*dawp-pbram–moy*
17	*dawp-pbram–pbee*
18	*dawp-pbram–buy*
19	*dawp-pbram–pboon*
20	*ma-pai*
21	*ma-pai-moy*
30	*saam sep*
40	*sai sep*
50	*haa sep*
60	*hoke sep*
70	*jet-sep*
80	*pbatsep*
90	*gkowsep*
100	*moy roy*
200	*pbee roy*
1,000	*moy pboan*
10,000	*moy muh-un*

INDEX

Bold page numbers indicate
illustrations
CAPS indicates thematic categories.

ILLUSTRATIONS CREDITS

Cover, Luciano Mortula/Alamy Ltd.

All interior images by Kris LeBoutillier unless otherwise noted:

27, Tang Chhin Sothy/AFP/Getty Images; 31, Leonard de Selva/CORBIS; 32, AFP/Getty Images; 34-35, Paula Bronstein/Liaison/Getty Images; 44-45, W.E. Garrett/NationalGeographicStock.com; 54, Barbara Walton/epa/CORBIS; 88, Peter Treanor/Alamy; 92, F1online digitale Bildagentur GmbH/Alamy; 96, Heng Sinith/epa/CORBIS; 100, Tang Chhin Sothy/AFP/Getty Images; 102, Robert Harding Picture Library Ltd /Alamy; 111, Bruno Morandi/Robert Harding World Imagery/CORBIS; 120, Keren Su/CORBIS; 128, Martin Gray/National Geographic Stock; 133, Paul Chesley/National Geographic Stock; 140, David Alan Harvey/National Geographic Stock; 153, Trevor Ranges; 158, Steve McCurry; 163, Vladimir Korostyshevskiy/Shutterstock; 165, Vladimir Korostyshevskiy/Shutterstock; 178, Andrea Pistolesi/Reportage/Getty Images; 184, Reza/Webistan/CORBIS; 191, Tang Chhin Sothy/AFP/Getty Images; 196, Mak Remissa/epa/CORBIS; 200, Michael Parton/Alamy; 204, Tang Chhin Sothy/AFP/Getty Images; 206, Whitehead Images/Alamy; 221, Tang Chhin Sothy/AFP/Getty Images; 246, Atmotu Images/Alamy; 249, David Myers Photography/Alamy; 253, Thomas J. Abercrombie/National Geographic Stock.

National Geographic
TRAVELER
Cambodia

Published by the National Geographic Society
John M. Fahey, Jr., *President
and Chief Executive Officer*
Gilbert M. Grosvenor, *Chairman of the Board*
Tim T. Kelly, *President, Global Media Group*
John Q. Griffin, *Executive Vice President;
President, Publishing*
Nina D. Hoffman, *Executive Vice President;
President, Book Publishing Group*

Prepared by the Book Division
Barbara Brownell Grogan, *Vice President and Editor in Chief*
Marianne R. Koszorus, *Director of Design*
Barbara A. Noe, *Senior Editor*
Carl Mehler, *Director of Maps*
R. Gary Colbert, *Production Director*
Jennifer A. Thornton, *Managing Editor*
Meredith C. Wilcox, *Administrative Director, Illustrations*
Cinda Rose, *Series Art Director*

Staff for This Book
Lawrence M. Porges, *Project Editor*
Kay Kobor Hankins, *Art Director*
Kevin Eans, *Illustrations Editor*
Paula J. Kelly, *Text Editor*
Lise Sajewski, Jane Sunderland, *Editorial Consultants*
Lyn Yip, *Researcher*
Steven D. Gardner, Michael McNey, Nicholas P.
Rosenbach, and Mapping Specialists, *Map Research
and Production*
Rob Waymouth, *Illustrations Specialist*
Bridget A. English, *Editorial Assistant*
Al Morrow, *Design Assistant*
Connie D. Binder, *Indexer*
Caroline Hickey, Elliana Spiegel, *Contributors*

Manufacturing and Quality Management
Christopher A. Liedel, *Chief Financial Officer*
Phillip L. Schlosser, *Vice President*
Chris Brown, *Technical Director*
Nicole Elliott, *Manager*
Rachel Faulise, *Manager*

National Geographic Traveler: Cambodia
ISBN: 978-1-4262-0520-0

The National Geographic Society is one of the
world's largest nonprofit scientific and educational
organizations. Founded in 1888 to "increase and
diffuse geographic knowledge," the Society works
to inspire people to care about the planet. It reaches
more than 325 million people worldwide each month
through its official journal, *National Geographic,* and
other magazines; National Geographic Channel;
television documentaries; music; radio; films; books;
DVDs; maps; exhibitions; school publishing programs;
interactive media; and merchandise. National
Geographic has funded more than 9,000 scientific
research, conservation and exploration projects
and supports an education program combating
geographic illiteracy. For more information, visit
nationalgeographic.com.

For more information, please call 1-800-NGS LINE
(647-5463) or write to the following address:

National Geographic Society
1145 17th Street N.W.
Washington, D.C. 20036-4688 U.S.A.

Visit us online at www.nationalgeographic.com

For information about special discounts for bulk
purchases, please contact National Geographic
Books Special Sales: ngspecsales@ngs.org

For rights or permissions inquiries, please contact
National Geographic Books Subsidiary Rights:
ngbookrights@ngs.org

The information in this book has been carefully
checked and to the best of our knowledge is accurate.
However, details are subject to change, and the
National Geographic Society cannot be responsible for
such changes, or for errors or omissions. Assessments
of sites, hotels, and restaurants are based on the
author's subjective opinions, which do not necessarily
reflect the publisher's opinion.

Printed in China

09/RRDS/1

ACKNOWLEDGMENTS

Special thanks to H. E. Son Soubert, H. E. Sisowath Tesso, Julien Colomer, Terry Wooltorton, Oran Shapira,
Simon Herbert, Brett Matthews, Ray Zepp, Miriam Stark, Derek Phatry Pan, Andy Brouwer, Sharee Bauld,
Supote Prasertsri, Sheery Dancona, Olivier Cunin, Jediah Byrom, Siddharth Mehra, Nick Butler, Gordon Sharp-
less, Lak Puon, Nisse Almroth, Luu Meng, Tim Denny, Beni Chhun, Sor Sokny, Tom Evans, Paul Baines, Laurent
Holdener & Compagnie Fluviale du Mékong, Richard & Siem Reap Dirt Bikes, Sonia & Paeng @ Dancing
Roads, Hotel de la Paix, La Residence D'Angkor, Sala Bai, Middle of Somewhere, Bananas Restaurant, Un
"Mekong" Vichea, Mr. Bontim, and Sean Brett.

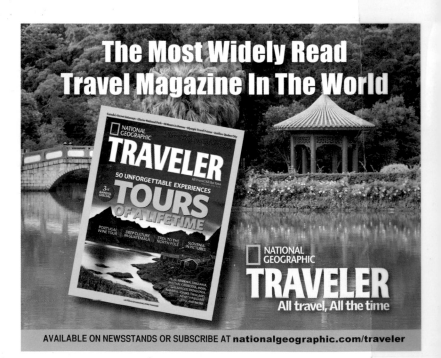